Globalization and the Semi-Periphery: Impacts, Opposition, Alternatives

Series editor Gordon Laxer, Director, Parkland Institute, University of Alberta, Edmonton, Canada.

About this series Starting from the unique vantage point of resource-rich countries located in what may be called the semi-periphery, this series presents the empirical investigations and theoretical reflections of an international network of researchers working together and based in four middle-ranking powers – Canada, Mexico, Norway and Australia. They are studying neo-liberal globalization with a view to understanding the social forces at work which may have the potential to transform it. These scholars reject the ideologically loaded idea of the historical inevitability of globalization. They argue instead that globalization is in reality a political project whose proponents are seeking a form of economic and ecological recolonization of the world under the auspices of the American model of capitalism. In analysing the social, economic, political and environmental impacts of globalization in middle-ranking countries, as well as the potential effectiveness of sources of opposition to it, they hope to contribute to the development of a post-neoliberal paradigm which explores how to re-embed countries' economies under democratic control and in greater harmony with natural processes. Their working assumption is that the condition of semi- peripherality, whether defined in social, cultural, economic or spatial terms, provides the citizens of these countries with both the consciousness of subordination and the means of resistance and transformation. This is in contra-distinction to the countries of the core (like the United States) which may lack the consciousness, and the countries of the periphery (in particular, the countries of the periphery) which may lack the required means. The longer-term outcome of this ongoing inter-disciplinary research effort will be the identification of social forces and ideas that hold out the hope to humanity of political choice, and of alternative social paths not totally constrained within the current parameters of globalization.

Now available

Marjorie Griffin Cohen and Stephen Clarkson (eds): *Governing under Stress: Middle Powers and the Challenge of Globalization* (2004)

Gerardo Otero (ed.): *Mexico in Transition: Neoliberal Globalism, the State and Civil Society* (2004)

GERARDO OTERO | editor

Mexico in transition

Neoliberal globalism, the state and civil society

Fernwood Publishing
NOVA SCOTIA

Zed Books
LONDON · NEW YORK

Mexico in transition: neoliberal globalism, the state and civil society was first published by Zed Books Ltd, 7 Cynthia Street, London N1 9JF, UK and Room 400, 175 Fifth Avenue, New York, NY 10010, USA in 2004.

www.zedbooks.co.uk

First published in Canada by Fernwood Publishing Ltd, 8422 St Margaret's Bay Road (Hwy 3) Site 2A, Box 5, Black Point, Nova Scotia B0J 1B0, in 2004.

Research for this book was supported by the Social Sciences and Humanities Research Council of Canada

Cover designed by Andrew Corbett
Set in Monotype Dante and Gill Sans Heavy by Ewan Smith, London
Printed and bound in the United Kingdom by Biddles Ltd,
www.biddles.co.uk

Distributed in the USA exclusively by Palgrave Macmillan, a division of St Martin's Press, LLC, 175 Fifth Avenue, New York, NY 10010

A catalogue record for this book is available from the British Library
Library of Congress cataloging-in-publication data: available
Canadian CIP data available from the National Library of Canada

ISBN 1 84277 358 5 hb
ISBN 1 84277 359 3 pb
Canada
ISBN 1 55266 153 9 pb

Contents

Figures and tables | viii
Acknowledgements | ix

**1 Mexico's double movement: neoliberal globalism, the
state and civil society | Gerardo Otero** **1**
Neoliberal globalism, the state and civil society | 2 Mexico's two
cycles of double movements | 6 Conclusions and organization of
this book | 11

**2 Rebellious cornfields: towards foods and labour self-
sufficiency | Armando Bartra** **18**
Mexico's countryside can endure no more | 20 A brief history of
the collapse | 22 Dealing with Mexico's lower half: Plan Puebla-
Panamá | 29 Beyond neoliberal globalism | 31 Conclusion | 33

**3 Fruits of injustice: women in the post-NAFTA food
system | Deborah Barndt** **37**
Precious human cargo | 37 The Tomasita project | 37
Interlocking analysis of power | 39 Mexican women workers –
in Mexico | 41 Factories in the fields: hi-tech greenhouse
production | 43 Into the fields | 45 Mexican women workers –
in Canada | 47 Fruits of injustice and seeds of hope | 50

**4 Conservation or privatization? Biodiversity, the
global market and the Mesoamerican Biological
Corridor | Laura Carlsen** **52**
Conservationist thought and the birth of corporate con-
servation | 53 The Mesoamerican Biological Corridor | 59
An alternative model of indigenous/peasant stewardship | 67

**5 State corporatism and peasant organizations: towards
new institutional arrangements | Horacio Mackinlay and
Gerardo Otero** **72**
Corporatist theory and Mexican authoritarianism | 73
The Mexican *ejido* system and corporatist authoritarianism | 78

Leadership–constituency relations | 81   Towards new institutional
arrangements | 86   Conclusions | 88

**6   Institutional democratization: changing political
     practices and the sugarcane growers' unions of the
     PRI | Peter Singelmann** **89**

The post-revolutionary regime and the cane growers'
unions | 89   Industrial crisis and new challenges | 92
The changing political parameters of the growers' unions | 95
Conclusions | 101

**7   Manufacturing neoliberalism: industrial relations, trade
     union corporatism and politics | Enrique de la Garza
     Toledo** **104**

The macroeconomy in the 1990s: the neoliberal transition | 106
Changes in the industrial relations system | 110   Conclusions | 119

**8   Who reaps the productivity growth in Mexico?
     Convergence or polarization in manufacturing real
     wages, 1988–99 | Enrique Dussel Peters** **121**

Concepts and overall tendencies in Mexico's labour market and
productivity | 121   Real wages, productivity and employment:
international comparisons and national performance | 125
Performance of branches with highest labour productivity | 130
Conclusions | 136

**9   Labour and migration policies under Vicente Fox:
     subordination to US economic and geopolitical
     interests | Raúl Delgado Wise** **138**

The true face of trade between Mexico and the USA | 140
Dialectic between export growth and international
migration | 143   Mexico's migration policy: from 'no policy'
to open subordination | 147   The migrant community and
the challenges of neoliberal globalism | 152

**10 | Community, economy and social change in Oaxaca,
     Mexico: rural life and cooperative logic in the global
     economy | Jeffrey H. Cohen** **154**

The community | 154   *Usos y costumbres*: some ways to co-
operate in Santa Ana | 155   Approaching identity | 159
Santañero past and present | 160   Economy and identity | 162

Cooperative traditions and change | 165 Cooperation and
solidarity in contemporary Santa Ana | 166 Conclusions | 167

**11 Survival strategies in neoliberal markets: peasant
organizations and organic coffee in Chiapas | María
Elena Martínez Torres** **169**

Coffee, neoliberalism and international markets | 170
Responding to market and state reconfiguration | 172
Case studies | 179 Conclusions | 184

**12 The binational integration of the US–Mexican
avocado industries: examining responses to economic
globalism | Lois Stanford** **186**

Establishment, growth and economics of the avocado industry
in California and Mexico | 188 Mexican entry into the US market,
1997–2002: impacts of globalism | 192 Market integration | 192
Company operations at the local level | 195 Challenges and
alternatives to neoliberal globalism: state alliance with elite
producers | 198 Conclusion | 202

**13 Convergence: social movements in Mexico in the era of
neoliberal globalism | Humberto González** **204**

New social movements: convergence, participation and
equality | 204 Neoliberal policy in Mexico | 206 Bank debtors
opposed to state policy: the civil arena | 208 The struggle in the
juridical and political arena | 214 Political action and political
parties | 217 Conclusions | 218

**14 Contesting neoliberal globalism from below: the EZLN,
Indian rights and citizenship | Gerardo Otero** **221**

Political-class formation (PCF) and civil society | 222 Regional
cultures, collective identity construction and indigenous
demands | 224 Expanding national borders within: Indian rights
and citizenship | 227 Conclusions | 233

About the contributors | 236 Abbreviations | 238
Bibliography | 242 Index | 265

Figures and tables

Figures

8.1 Manufacturing: wages per hour in US$, 1993–2002   126
8.2 Open unemployment rate in selected countries, 1987–2002   127
8.3 Labour market conditions, 1980–2001   129
8.4 Real wages and labour productivity, 1988–99   129
8.5 Typology of manufacturing branches: real wages and productivity, 1988–99   134
11.1 Price of Mexican Santos 4 coffee in New York Exchange Market, 1982–2000   173

Tables

8.1 Productivity in selected countries, 1993–2002   125
8.2 Mexico: general information on population and employment, 1990–2000   128
8.3 Typology of Mexico's manufacturing branches by growth rate of labour productivity, 1994–99   131
8.4 Results of typology of Mexico's manufacturing branches selected by productivity growth, 1994–99   132
9.1 Importance of remittances in foreign exchange earnings   145
9.2 Contribution of remittances to the net external trade balance   146
11.1 Coffee producers in Mexico and Chiapas by amount of land planted to coffee   171
12.1 Volume marketed during winter season by California, Michoacán and Chile in the US avocado market, 1998–2002   193
12.2 Number of weeks in the winter season market for California, Michoacán and Chile in the US avocado market, 1998–2002   193
12.3 Average price in US$ received for size 40 box during winter season by California, Michoacán and Chile in the US avocado market, 1998–2002   193

Acknowledgements

I am grateful to Gordon Laxer for talking me into editing this book as part of the research project he directs, 'Globalization and the Semi-Periphery', and in which I am a co-investigator. This project is funded by a Major Collaborative Research Initiative grant from the Social Sciences and the Humanities Research Council of Canada. After some initial hesitancy I became increasingly excited as the project progressed, particularly as I began to receive excellent chapter proposals, following a call for papers specifically framed for this book. I considered twenty-five chapter proposals, apart from my introductory and concluding chapters. The present chapters were selected following an external review of the semi-finalist papers, which assessed each paper's fit within the overall project. Although they will remain anonymous, I sincerely thank all of those colleagues who were kind enough to send their proposals for consideration; their papers were worthy of publication but not necessarily in this particular book.

My greatest debt is to the final contributors, for their great intellects, their contribution to the project, and their commitment to detailing the effects of neoliberal globalism on the state and civil society of Mexico. In addition I appreciate the time that each of them took to revise his or her paper following reviewers' and my own comments, often under a tight schedule. The beauty of this project is that it gathers the collective effort of various people who had been working on their own, but with very similar substantive concerns about the impacts, challenges and alternatives to neoliberal globalism.

Thanks are due to those colleagues who served as external reviewers of one or more semi-finalist papers. They are: Paul Bowles, William Friedland, Marilyn Gates, Martha Rees, Jonathan Fox, Yolanda Massieu, Thomas Legler, Anil Hira and Sara Lara. Although Peter Singelmann ended up as a contributor, he also reviewed several chapters, including both of my single-authored ones. My debt to Peter for his timely critiques and suggestions is greater than I can express here. While these colleagues certainly share in the merits of this book, they are excused from any remaining limitations.

Two chapters were translated from Spanish by people other than their authors. I thank the highly professional work of Laura Carlsen for translating Armando Bartra's chapter, and Haydn Rawlinson who translated Raúl Delgado Wise's chapter.

I thank the logistical support from the Globalism Project's office at the University of Alberta, particularly from Kate Nunn and Richard Horne. At Simon Fraser University in Vancouver, I had the able and efficient editorial assistance of Susan Grove, who helped put the manuscript in shape for final submission. Robert Molteno at Zed Books has been supportive and patient all along.

Finally, I thank my wife, Paty Ordóñez, for giving up so many hours of shared enjoyment so that I could finish this project on time. As always, her love and support have been crucial for my intellectual endeavours.

Gerardo Otero

Para Paty Ordóñez, el amor de mi vida, y para
Alex Otero-Ordóñez, mi esperanza

1 | Mexico's double movement: neoliberal globalism, the state and civil society

GERARDO OTERO

§ THE purpose of this book is to address the impacts, challengers and alternatives to neoliberal globalism in Mexico. Because the main impacts of neoliberal globalism have negatively affected the peasantry, the working class and middle classes in rural and urban Mexico, we pay most attention to them. Given that the ruling classes and the Mexican state have been the main architects of neoliberal globalism, along with suprastate organizations such as the International Monetary Fund and the World Bank, we focus our attention on challengers and alternatives coming from below, particularly from the subordinate groups, classes and communities that are becoming increasingly organized in civil society.

In this chapter I provide a broad conceptual and historical outline of what neoliberal globalism has involved for Mexico during the past two decades in economic and political terms, and how organizations in civil society have responded to its challenges. I will first draw on Karl Polanyi's classic work, *The Great Transformation* (1944), to outline conceptually the most salient impacts of the process of economic liberalization in Mexico. Polanyi is arguably the classical social theorist who, after Karl Marx, has mounted the most forceful critique of market society (Block and Somers 1984). If Marx focused on the alienating and exploitative nature of capitalist production, Polanyi focused on the market's ravaging effects on the fabric of society itself. Among many other ideologues, he targeted Hayek and von Mises, two of the idols of today's free-marketers. I also draw on the work of Antonio Gramsci and my own past work to outline briefly a conceptual framework for understanding the rise of civil society organizations that are contesting neoliberal globalism and the limited character of the electoral democratic transition from below.

The second section provides a brief historical outline of the two cycles of 'double movements' in Mexico, in which a strong drive to economic liberalization has been followed by society's protective responses. This will set the context for the third section on Mexico's economic integration with its northern neighbours, which has taken place silently or openly since the onset of the debt crisis of 1982, i.e. before and after the establishment of the North American Free Trade Agreement (NAFTA), in place since 1994. Throughout these sections, I draw parallels between concepts and history and make reference to the chapters that follow which offer in-depth coverage of the various central issues brought about by neoliberal globalism and the rise of civil society.

Neoliberal globalism, the state and civil society

> The true criticism of market society is not that it was based on economics – in a sense, every and any society must be based on it – but that its economy was based on self-interest. Such an organization of economic life is entirely unnatural, in the strictly empirical sense of *exceptional*. (Polanyi 1944: 249)

The purpose of this section is to present a conceptual discussion of neoliberal globalism, by drawing on Polanyi's work. Given his focus on the transformation of economic relations, I will supplement this with a discussion of civil society as the sphere in which society's protective movement has been located against the state and the privatized economy today. My main argument is that a merely liberal democracy is insufficient to address the societal threats posed by neoliberal globalism. A variety of social movements must consolidate civil society to accomplish a reform of the state and its economic programme, so that human development can be taken care of and the natural environment sustained.

Polanyi and society's double movement

Polanyi's main argument is that the movement to create a 'self-regulating market' was the result of a utopia that can never be fully realized without at the same time destroying society. The uniqueness of nineteenth-century society lies in its motive and justification for action, which has once again been placed centre-stage by neoliberal globalism: gain. If all human history is ultimately conditioned by economic factors, says Polanyi, never before had these been placed at the centre of human action: 'The mechanism which the motive of gain set in motion was comparable in effectiveness only to the most violent outburst of religious fervour in history' (Polanyi 1944: 30). Therefore, when catastrophe hits society as a result of attempting to impose the self-regulating market, society in turn launches a counter-movement to protect itself. Such a counter-movement can emerge either from the top down or from the bottom up, from the state itself or from one or more of the subordinate groups or classes in society. Protection initiated from the top tends to result in paternalistic or statist and authoritarian solutions that are ultimately degrading for subordinate groups and classes (ibid.: 99). In contrast, protective movements coming from the bottom up invigorate society and are therefore more sustainable in the long run.

A prevalent myth that Polanyi debunks is that, far from minimizing or reducing state intervention in the economy, the self-regulating market requires intervention to create markets and sustain them (de la Garza Toledo, this volume). This is a critical point; for one of the main ideological claims of neoliberal globalism is that the state should stay out of the economy to save taxpayers' money and spur private initiative. But Polanyi thinks that interventionism hardly diminishes (Polanyi 1944: 66, 140). Furthermore, the emergence of national markets was in no way the result of the gradual and spontaneous emancipation of the economic sphere from governmental control. On the contrary, says Polanyi, 'the market has been the outcome of a conscious and often violent intervention on the part of government which imposed the market organization on society for non-economic ends' (ibid.: 250).

The basic characteristic of the Industrial Revolution, then, is the establishment of the capitalist market economy. All other factors are incidental: the rise of factory towns, the emergence of slums, long hours of child labour, the low wages of some categories of workers, the increase in population rate; and the concentration of industries. In agricultural society, the transformation involves a change in the motive of action: 'For the motive of subsistence that of gain must be substituted' (ibid.: 41). This is a central drive that the Fox administration wants to promote in Mexico's countryside, with dreadful consequences: 25 million people live in the countryside and most are being negatively affected (Bartra, this volume; Cohen, this volume).

Polanyi tells us how, against the Physiocrats, Adam Smith asserted from the start of classical political economy that not geography or nature but the skill of labour and the proportion between the useful and the idle members in society are what explain the wealth of nations. More importantly, 'wealth was to him merely an aspect of the life of the community, to the purposes of which it remained subordinate' (Polanyi 1944: 111). From this humanist perspective of Adam Smith's, however, the utilitarian philosophers such as J. Bentham would adopt a 'naturalist' approach to forcing workers to sell their labour-power by the sheer force or compulsion of hunger: 'Poverty was Nature surviving in society; its physical sanction was hunger' (ibid.: 117).

For Bentham, there was no contradiction between the simultaneous existence of prosperity and poverty: 'In the highest stage of social prosperity,' he said, 'the great mass of the citizens will most probably possess few other resources than their daily labor, and consequently will always be near indigence' (cited in ibid.: 117). Later on, Polanyi criticizes classical political economists for focusing just on the penalty of starvation as the only way to create a labour market. He wonders about the inexplicable omission of discussing the possibility of the allurement of high wages to achieve the same goal of a functioning labour market (ibid.: 164).

Of local, external and internal (or domestic) trade, only internal trade tends to be based on the principle of competition, says Polanyi. Local and external trade may be based primarily on complementarities (ibid.: 60). This was the case in the national phase of capitalism. But now that it has moved to the global stage, one of the main things that neoliberal globalism is trying to achieve is, precisely, to extend the principle of competition to the global sphere, regardless of the fact that many diverse standards prevail in the different societies that are being integrated.

Now, why is the self-regulating market so destructive of society's foundation? Let us start with a definition of the central concept: a *self-regulating market* is said to exist when an economic system is controlled, regulated and directed by markets alone. The neoliberal expectation is that 'human beings behave in such a way as to achieve maximum money gains'. Furthermore: 'Order in the production and distribution of goods is ensured by prices alone.' State policy is not to interfere with prices, supply or demand; policies exist only to help insure the self-regulation of the market (ibid.: 68–9). The self-regulating market requires *institutional* separation of society into an economic and a political sphere. Hence, 'a market economy can exist only in a market society' (ibid.: 71). Here's why: launching labour, land and money into the market implies that the substance of society itself (i.e. humans, nature and the organization of production) will become subordinated to the main dynamic mechanism of the market: profit-seeking.

This is the crux in Polanyi's theory: that the establishment of a self-regulating market involves creating *fictitious* commodities out of labour, land and money. The problem for him is as follows: while *genuine* commodities are empirically defined as objects produced for sale on the market, in the sale of labour-power humans must go with it, suffering all the consequences. A similar thing occurs with land, another term for nature: when it becomes commodified, the conditions are ripe for environmental destruction (see Carlsen, this volume). Thus, while labour, land and money markets are essential for a market economy, no society could stand the effects of such a system of crude fictions, says Polanyi, 'unless its human and natural substance as well as its business organization was protected against the ravages of this satanic mill' (Polanyi 1944: 73). Polanyi's thesis is that leaving these aspects of society (humans, nature and productive organization) to the whims of the market 'would be tantamount to annihilating them' (ibid.: 131).

The counter-movement of society consists in checking the action of the market in respect to the factors of production though intervention-ism of some sort. In the case of England, the landed aristocracy and the peasantry tried to defend the land, while the labouring people, to a smaller or greater extent, 'became the representatives of the common human interests that had become homeless' (ibid.: 133). On this aspect, Polanyi seems to agree with Marx that the proletariat represents the universal interests in human emancipation.

Society's protective movements emerge specifically in view of three points of attack: (i) when the competitive labour market hits the bearer of labour power, namely the worker; (ii) when international free trade becomes a threat to the largest industry dependent upon nature, namely agriculture; and (iii) when the movement of prices and exchange rates imperil the productive organizations that may have become heavily indebted to keep functioning. Remarkably, these three points all seem to be present in Mexico today: a significant portion of workers is unified around the recently organized National Union of Workers (Unión Nacional de Trabajadores, UNT), which is rallying side by side with teachers and peasants in protest of NAFTA (see chapters by Bartra, de la Garza Toledo and González below). Thus, both labour and land concerns are fighting in unison. If we take into account the constituency of El Barzón, which includes small and middle-sized agricultural entrepreneurs and small- to medium-sized creditors in the cities, then we might see that indebtedness (money, prices and so on) is also wreaking havoc in the realm of productive organization. This leaves only the large corporations in Mexico, both domestic and transnational, which are among the few beneficiaries of the neoliberal model of economic globalization.

Gramsci and the theory of political class formation (PCF)

If Polanyi gives us a good grounding for conceptually understanding the changes in the economy, we need a political theory to understand how subordinate groups, classes and communities in society become organized to mount a protective counter-movement to the onslaught of neoliberal globalism. In the context of an emerging liberal democracy, such mobilization is located in the realm of civil society. Now, when it comes to the strengthening of civil society *vis-à-vis* the state, Antonio Gramsci is one of the classic theorists of the twentieth century that provides the very best insights for a theoretical understanding of the process. Based on some of his concepts and my own previous work, in this section I offer a synthesis of the theory of political class formation (PCF). This is a process by which civil society becomes strengthened within semi-authoritarian or weak liberal-democratic regimes (Otero 1999; Otero and Jugenitz 2003; Otero, this volume). Although this theory is phrased in terms of the political formation of social classes, it is equally applicable to groups and communities (Cohen, this volume; Martínez-Torres, this volume).

Let us begin with Gramsci's expanded definition of the democratic state. Rather than restricting his definition to juridical and political structures, Gramsci usually refers to the state as the sum of 'political society', or the realm of domination, plus 'civil society', or the realm of hegemony. The less democratic a state, the more it relies on domination or force. Conversely, the more democratic a state, the more it relies on hegemony, or the consent of its people: democracy, says Gramsci, 'must mean that every "citizen" can "govern" and that society places him, even if only abstractly, in a general condition to achieve this. Political democracy tends towards a coincidence of rulers and the ruled' (Gramsci 1971: 40).

Within this conception of radical democracy and the state, a further central question becomes: how can subordinate groups or classes become hegemonic or dominant, or at least gain the ability to push for state interventions in their favour? For Gramsci, answering this question regarding subaltern classes requires the identification of two phases, which are part of what I call political class formation: first, 'autonomy *vis-à-vis* the enemies they had to defeat'; and second, 'support from the groups which actively or passively assisted them' in their struggles (ibid.: 53). A third point posited elsewhere by Gramsci deals with the nature of leadership: lest it be democratic and accountable to its social constituency, demoralization and cooptation may be the result. Too often, the character of leadership does not depend on the leaders themselves, but on the state's action. As Gramsci puts it: '[b]etween consent and force stands corruption/fraud ... This consists in procuring the demoralization and paralysis of the antagonist (or antagonists) by buying its leaders ... in order to sow disarray and confusion in its ranks' (ibid.: 80 fn).

Political formation, then, is the process through which direct producers and other social groups shape demands, form organizations to pursue them, and generate a leadership to represent them before the state and other organizations with which alliances are built. PCF theory is clearly located in a post-Cold War era, one in which the struggle for socialism through violent revolutionary means is essentially over. The struggle for democratic socialism must be waged by expanding liberal-democratic structures and building a new hegemonic project around human needs and environmental sustainability (Angus 2001). In the context of neoliberal globalism, the question becomes: how can subordinate groups and classes organize to advance their demands without becoming coopted into bourgeois-hegemonic discourse?

Mexico's two cycles of double movements

Mexico has experienced two cycles of economic liberalization and societal protection since independence from Spain in 1821. The first happened during the last two decades of the nineteenth century and the first decade of the twentieth. This cycle involved a movement of economic liberalization that included the expropriation and privatization of the Catholic Church and Indian lands, and ended with a cataclysmic protective movement from society against the devastation of market liberalism. In fact, Mexico experienced one of the world's first major revolutions of the twentieth century between 1910 and 1920. Among the triggering factors of the revolution, historians include Mexico's increasing dependence on the US economy, which experienced a deep slump in 1907, and the unbearable consequences for indigenous communities of having lost 90 per cent of their lands to the advancement of market capitalism during the *Porfiriato* (Katz 1982; Womack 1969; Gilly 1974).

The regime emerging from the revolution laid the foundations for a top-down resolution of peasants' and workers' demands in a largely agrarian society, and for building an inward-looking, state-led capitalist development model with a semi-authoritarian, one-party-dominant political regime (Cornelius 1996; Hellman 1983). The 1917 Constitution was the main political accomplishment of the revolution. It contained some of the most socially advanced pieces of legislation in the world, including Article 123, which granted workers the right to organize and strike; and Article 27, which contained the basis for a major agrarian reform and land redistribution among the peasantry. Through Article 27, the agrarian reform process redistributed about 50 per cent of agricultural, forestry and livestock grazing land to peasants by 1992. The state thus refounded itself based on an alliance with workers and peasants, whose interests it set out to protect.

It was not until the 1930s, however, that the thrust of the reformist content of the constitution was implemented. During the administration of Lázaro Cárdenas (1934–40), the state implemented a sweeping agrarian reform, nationalized the oil industry affecting US and European interests, introduced 'socialist education', and organized workers and peasants as 'sectors' of the new ruling party to promote a 'mass politics' (Medin 1972; Córdova 1972, 1974). The bases were laid for developing a mixed economy intent on achieving economic growth with social justice, 'neither capitalist nor socialist', said Cárdenas.

But the administrations that followed Cárdenas would soon diminish the popular character of the revolution. Many generals and high-level politicians became industrial-capitalist tycoons who used the state to develop their private empires, at the same time as a bureaucratic elite surfaced to command the working-class and peasant organizations and share in the spoils of the new political system (Mackinlay and Otero, this volume). Economic development was pursued with a focus on the internal market, based on a policy of import-substitution industrialization, heavy state intervention in the economy, protectionism and subsidies. Despite the increasingly authoritarian nature of the state, Mexico managed to experience high economic growth rates until the late 1960s, and the workers and peasants who were organized under the 'corporatist' unions (i.e. dependent on the ruling party and the state) affiliated to the ruling party made some economic gains for at least three decades (de la Garza, this volume). Despite its authoritarian character, state-led development and corporatist politics conferred considerable legitimacy upon the regime of the 'Mexican Revolution'.

From the late 1950s, however, the authoritarian nature of the state was becoming increasingly evident and troubling for significant sectors of the working class and the peasantry, some of whose organizations were being severely repressed when they dared to express their discontent outside of 'official' channels, i.e. the corporatist organizations. This situation burst into the open with the 1968 student and popular movement, which started a few months before the Olympic Games were to be held in Mexico City. Just before the Games began, on 2 October 1968, the state massacred hundreds of students engaged in a peaceful protest in the capital's Plaza of Tlaltelolco. For most political observers, the 1968 movement marks the end of society's acquiescence with the authoritarian state regime that emerged from the revolution. From then on, some groups of activists would pursue guerrilla tactics seeking to overthrow the state (most of them were crushed militarily during the 1970s); others engaged in popular mass movements in the cities and the countryside, building neighbourhood or peasant organizations; while still others enlarged the ranks of existing Left political parties, even though most of them were illegal from the 1940s until 1977 (Bruhn 1997; R. Bartra 2002).

Mexico would have to wait until the 1970s for some political openings to take place, in the aftermath of the political crisis and student movement of 1968. Until then, the political system relied almost exclusively on its corporatist strand (de la Garza Toledo, this volume; Mackinlay and Otero, this volume; Samstad 2002). In 1977, after a deepening legitimacy crisis, the government began to introduce a series of reforms in the electoral system. These included the legalization of some leftist parties and the increased participation of non-PRI minorities in Congress through expanding the system of proportional representation. Yet, the PRI-state continuously maintained control of the electoral system and resorted to electoral fraud as needed, in order to stay in power. There were a few gubernatorial and local-level elections in which the PRI's defeat was recognized, with the first state-gubernatorial level defeat taking place only in 1989. Most of the opposition triumphs that were recognized, however, took place when the winning party was the right-of-centre National Action Party (Partido de Acción Nacional, PAN). The left-of-centre opposition most often faced electoral fraud and repression. In the 1988 presidential elections, for instance, Cuauhtémoc Cárdenas, the candidate of a broad left-of-centre coalition, is widely believed to have won. Yet, the PRI's candidate was imposed (Chand 2001).

For its part, by the 1970s the now expanded bourgeoisie itself grew increasingly disenchanted with the state-led model and wanted to move into a liberalized and privatized economy, one in which profits not populist politics would provide the main logic of development. By 1974, the Mexican bourgeoisie formed the first class organization that was independent of the corporatist networks of the state: the Entrepreneurial Coordinating Centre (Consejo Coordinador Empresarial, CCE). From then on, organizations that represented the top business leaders became active in promoting economic liberalism (Valdéz Ugalde 1996; Bizberg and Meyer 2002). The major impetus for this second movement for economic liberalism and free markets came after 1982, when Mexico had to declare a moratorium on the servicing of its foreign debt, one of the largest in the developing world at the time. There was thus a confluence of bourgeois internal forces and the conditions imposed by the International Monetary Fund and the World Bank to restructure Mexico's foreign debt: the country had to introduce major economic restructuring if it was to continue being part of the circuits of international finance (foreign loans and investment), along the lines of neoliberal globalism.

Neoliberal globalism is variously known as Structural Adjustment Programmes, the Washington Consensus, the Wall Street–Treasury Complex, Liberal Productivism and the New World Order. Mexico's debt crisis of 1982 fundamentally challenged the protectionist, inward-looking and statist development model that had been in place since the 1930s. By the mid-1980s, a series of neoliberal reforms were introduced to cut substantially the government deficit by eliminating most subsidies, dismantling or privatizing state-run firms, allowing the entry of foreign products, promoting foreign capital investment and deregulating most sectors of the economy, not least the agricultural sector, which may have been the most protected since the revolution, although not supported for self-sustaining growth (Bartra, this volume). One of the key goals of neoliberal reform was to integrate Mexico more closely with the North American economy (Delgado Wise, this volume).

Politically, the right-of-centre PAN had been considered a 'loyal opposition' to the revolutionary regime until the 1980s. In 1986, however, electoral fraud in the gubernatorial elections of the northern state of Chihuahua spurred tremendous mobilization for democratizing Mexico's political system. To that point, the ruling Institutional Revolutionary Party (Partido Revolucionario Institucional, PRI), whose forerunner had been in power since 1929, had either won most elections comfortably or resorted to fraudulent electoral tactics to impose its own candidates (Cornelius 1996; Chand 2001; Loaeza 1999).

The second great cycle of economic liberalization thus started in the mid-1980s, with legislation and policy geared to open up and privatize Mexico's economy. Some observers have touted this process as putting Mexico on the road to graduating into developed-country status since joining its northern neighbours in NAFTA in 1994 (Giugale et al. 2001). With the political triumph in the 2000 presidential elections by opposition candidate Vicente Fox (coming from PAN), ousting the Institutional Revolutionary Party (PRI) after seventy-one years of uninterrupted rule, Mexico is even said to have completed its transition to democracy (Chand 2001; Levy et al. 2001). While both of these events no doubt represent significant watersheds in Mexican history, the country is still far from being developed or democratic in any meaningful sense of these terms. Officially-defined poverty still afflicts about 50 per cent of the population, and many institutions are still authoritarian, not to mention the elitist character of Mexico's liberal democracy. Furthermore, with the dismal economic and political performance of the Fox administration during its first three years, we cannot rule out the possibility of an electoral restoration of PRI rule in 2006 (Bizberg 2003). Hence the importance of a detailed study of corporatist organizations of peasants and workers, the extent to which they have changed, and the ways in which they could be converted into new forms of corporatism or transcended into new institutional arrangements (Mackinlay and Otero, this volume; Singelmann, this volume; and de la Garza Toledo, this volume).

When I explored Mexico's political futures in 1995, I proposed nine theoretical scenarios for the near and mid-term future, but argued that only six of them were more or less historically feasible, depending on which economic model and political regime were combined. I predicted a 2000 presidential election triumph by a PAN candidate as the historically 'most likely' outcome, based on the combination of continued neoliberalism and liberal democratization from below. I argued that this would be the most desirable result for transnational corporations and transnational finance capitalists, as well as for large and medium-sized domestic entrepreneurs. One reason I gave was that a PAN triumph would be allowed by the regime because it 'might ensure greater political stability while keeping neoliberal economic polices intact' (Otero 1996a: 242). But I also suggested that there would be growing political discontent, especially in the south and south-eastern states, as a result of the socioeconomic polarization brought about by neoliberalism (Dussel Peters 2000).

To be sure, the PAN is a more wholehearted advocate of neoliberal globalism than the PRI was. In fact, some of the internal divisions that debilitated the PRI in the past two decades can be attributed to its abandonment of 'revolutionary nationalism'. This led to the major split in 1988 by which Cuauhtémoc Cárdenas (son of 1930s reformist President Lázaro Cárdenas) and others left the party. Eventually they joined other forces of the traditional and nationalist Left to form the Party of the Democratic Revolution (PRD) in 1989 (Bruhn 1997). On cultural policy, however, the PAN tends to be much more conservative than the PRI. For instance, in early 2001, the vast majority of PAN members of the Lower Chamber of Congress (all but one who abstained) voted against allowing representatives of the Zapatista National Liberation Army (EZLN) to be heard by a plenary session of Congress. Instead, they wanted to have only a committee of ten members from each of the two chambers hear the Zapatistas, despite the fact that Vicente Fox had (in)famously promised during his presidential campaign that he would resolve the Chiapas conflict in fifteen minutes.

With regard to the United States, the PAN also advocates much closer ties than the PRI or PRD would like. This may be related not only to ideological preferences, but also to Mexico's deep trade dependence on its northern neighbour. Mexican exports to the United States were about 70 per cent in the 1980s, and they are now about 90 per cent. Mexico has dramatically increased its food imports from the United States, even if the agricultural trade balance is in favour of Mexico due to its increased exports of fruits and vegetables. But there is now a question as to whether Mexico can achieve food sovereignty (Bartra, this volume). Given the devastation of rural Mexico that this dependency has created, masses of workers cannot find employment in their own country and thus have to migrate to the United States. This calls into question Mexico's capacity to have labour sovereignty (Bartra, this volume; Delgado Wise, this volume).

Conclusions and organization of this book

The 1980s was called the lost decade for Latin America by the UN Economic Commission for Latin America and the Caribbean. For Mexico, despite – or because of? – increasing integration with North America and neoliberal globalism, the 1990s continued to be a lost decade. The exception was 1997–98, when real wages increased and the percentage of the officially poor declined (Giugale et al. 2001). In contrast, the 1990s embodied a considerable gain for US consumers in general and workers in particular (Mandel 2002). US workers, however, were merely recovering some of the purchasing power lost during the previous decade. The gains in purchasing power for US workers during the 1990s came in the midst of historically very low unemployment;

hence real wages were on the rise. Mexican workers, peasants and even the middle classes, in contrast, have yet to see any sustained benefits from North American economic integration. Their wages and incomes have deteriorated dramatically since the debt crisis of 1982. Significantly, there has been a growing gap between productivity and manufacturing wages, particularly in the most dynamic sectors (Dussel Peters, this volume). This empirical observation is completely counter to neoclassical economics' theoretical expectations.

Given that Mexico experienced economic liberalization in the midst of an authoritarian political regime, workers confronted an inflexible wage policy that tended to keep wages down in order to lure foreign investment. Furthermore, sheer 'market forces' were created by the state in order to swell the contingent of unemployed workers. A series of state policies were geared to dismantle the formerly protected agricultural sector, in which 30 per cent of the population lived in 1992.

The central piece for agricultural neoliberal restructuring was thus the new Agrarian Law of 1992, created to end the process of land redistribution, and to open up the *ejido* lands (the land-reform sector) to the market. *Ejidos* concentrate about 50 per cent of Mexico's agricultural land, much of which is exploited communally (DeWalt et al. 1998). The new agrarian policy of the state was also designed to remove most subsidies and protection from agriculture, while almost ending agricultural loans (Myhre 1998) and most other support programmes (Bartra, this volume). Even the London-based conservative weekly, *The Economist* (2002), an enthusiastic supporter of free-market policies, as well as *BusinessWeek's* correspondent in Mexico City (G. Smith 2002), expressed their dismay about the Mexican government's lack of support for its agricultural sector. For the international context is one of widespread agricultural subsidies throughout the advanced capitalist countries, most prominently in the United States, the European Union and Japan.

Organization of this book

The contributors to this book were asked to address the impacts, challengers and/or alternatives to neoliberal globalism within their areas of expertise. Hence each chapter treats some aspect of these three phenomena to varying degrees, generally with an emphasis on one or the other. Chapters 2 to 4 offer an account of the most salient impacts of neoliberal globalism in Mexico's countryside, clearly the sector most affected by the swiftness and extent of reform. Armando Bartra begins in Chapter 2 with a balance sheet of state policies and their impacts for the past two decades and then outlines some alternatives. He describes how Mexico's development model went from anti-agricultural policies that exploited peasants during the import-substitution decades, to the exclusionary policies of the neoliberal era. The new situation has rendered Mexico dependent on food imports from the United States, and it has even compromised its labour sovereignty to the extent that increasing masses of workers must seek employment in the northern country. A re-appreciation and support of peasant economy in terms of its social, cultural and environmental virtues might lead to the recovery of food and labour sovereignty.

Putting a human face on the impacts of restructuring, Deborah Barndt addresses in Chapter 3 the feminization of labour in Mexican fruit production and the varying positions that women occupy in the labour process. Neoliberal trade policies have made fruit and vegetable exports a key source of foreign exchange in Mexico. The production of these 'fruits of injustice' builds not only on north/south asymmetries but also on deeply entrenched structural inequalities based on gender, race/ethnicity, class, rural/urban context, and age and family status. Barndt applies an interlocking analysis of power to women workers in the fields, packing plants and greenhouses of a leading Mexican tomato exporter.

Laura Carlsen addresses in Chapter 4 the issue of privatization of nature, and how corporations are linking up with conservation organizations in an effort geared to guarantee future profits. This global partnership of would-be adversaries with seemingly contradictory agendas threatens local and national control over the most biologically rich regions of the planet. Carlsen's chapter offers an analysis of the objectives and activities of corporate conservation, the Mesoamerican Biological Corridor, as a case study in the integration of biodiversity in the world market. But she also offers an alternative model of long-term biodiversity management: the peasant/indigenous stewardship model.

The next three chapters address one of the key features of Mexico's authoritarian political system, one which has not gone away with the achievement of electoral democratization: state corporatism. This is the system by which the Mexican state has virtually confiscated civil society throughout most of the twentieth century, and kept a tight political control of peasants, workers and the so-called popular sectors under the ruling PRI. Liberation of citizens from the grip of corporatism is an essential condition for the political formation of subordinate groups, classes and communities, and for creating a vigorous civil society that may successfully contest neoliberal globalism.

Horacio Mackinlay and Gerardo Otero's Chapter 5 provides an overview of corporatist relations between peasants and the state during the PRI era, and how this system became both an instrument of control and subordination of popular groups and classes, and one of the main modes of political participation that existed in Mexico. The chapter ends with a profile of the emerging institutional arrangements in substitution or modification of traditional corporatism. Some of the new arrangements represent a restoration of traditional corporatism, but others contain the promise of building organizations of direct producers that are independent of the state and autonomous. Peter Singelmann's Chapter 6 moves closer to the inner workings of rural corporatism by describing the changes taking place in the two sugarcane growers' unions affiliated to the ruling PRI. It explores the conflicting forces within these unions over feasible directions they might take in response to the breakdown of their party's hegemony. Also explored is the increasing inability of that party and its union confederations to access the traditional resources for ensuring loyalty or accommodation of their rank-and-file.

In Chapter 7, Enrique de la Garza Toledo discusses corporatism in the manufacturing industry, the other pillar of Mexico's corporate authoritarianism. He addresses the process of industrial restructuring and changes in the economic model related to the new production models that insist on work flexibility in Mexico's industrial sector and the recomposition of trade union corporatism. Corporatist trade unionism nevertheless continues to prevail in Mexico in its mutual support of the new state regime under the new Fox administration. The concluding section explains why trade union corporatism persists in spite of the consolidation of the neoliberal model and the supposed transition to democracy.

With perhaps a direct causal relation to the corporatist authoritarian structure, Enrique Dussel Peters's Chapter 8 describes who reaps the benefits of neoliberal globalism in Mexico's manufacturing industry. He shows that, between 1988 and 1999, rather than a wage convergence among workers in Mexico, Canada and the United States, there has actually been a further polarization. This in-depth analysis of Mexico's labour market conditions shows that productivity growth has not spread into real-wage growth. Paradoxically, the industrial branches that have achieved the highest productivity growth have also resulted in the highest gap between productivity and real-wage growth. They have been far away from achieving positive effects on employment and real-wage growth. In fact, these branches have deepened the socioeconomic polarization in Mexico between rich and poor.

It is not surprising, then, that Raúl Delgado Wise argues in Chapter 9 that the Mexican government, particularly that of President Vicente Fox (2000–06), has subordinated its labour and migration policies to the economic and geopolitical interests of the United States. Because Mexico's economy cannot provide gainful employment to a very large contingent of its citizens, as argued in Armando Bartra's Chapter 2, they have become dependent on selling their labour power in the United

States, often illegally, and this has become a key feature of the lack of labour sovereignty for the country.

In different ways, each of the last five chapters addresses manners in which people have responded to the ravages of neoliberal globalism and tried to create alternatives. Whether as communities, as class organizations or social movements, or as broad coalitions of diverse groups whose interests have converged in social mobilization, masses of Mexicans have organized to contest neoliberal globalism. Chapters 10 and 11 discuss responses from the bottom up, from a community or regional level. Jeffrey H. Cohen describes in Chapter 10 the life of people who do not migrate in a rural community in the state of Oaxaca. He explains how they maintain their solidarity ties and cooperative logic in the midst of a globalizing economy that tends to marginalize peasant economy. Chapter 10 thus defines how rural Oaxacans adapt local traditional practices to global processes and markets, the outcomes of these patterns, and the possibilities that such patterns hold for the future.

In Chapter 11, María Elena Martínez-Torres describes how small peasant farmers in Chiapas have coped with neoliberal globalism and the collapse of the international regime that protected coffee producers by creating new, independent organizational capacities and new market niches. The most important growers of organic coffee in the global economy are generally indigenous Mayan peasants, ensconced in rugged mountain ranges and ravines across the poor southern Mexican states of Chiapas and Oaxaca. This chapter analyses the critical elements involved in this small-farmer organic coffee boom in Chiapas, including their ability to (re)create organizational capacities through describing three case studies.

If Chapter 11 addresses the challenges posed by a deregulated international market for small-farmer coffee producers, Lois Stanford's Chapter 12 discusses the challenges for large avocado producers who have had to cope with a series of political obstacles to gain access to the US market. Focusing on the economic and political process of market integration as Mexican avocados enter the US winter market, Stanford examines the case of the avocado industry in the state of Michoacán, the world's largest avocado-producing region. Employing the methodological model of a binational commodity chain, the case examines the political and economic strategies adopted by Californian and Michoacán avocado growers prior to the lifting of the 1914 phytosanitary ban against Mexican avocados in the US market, as well as the subsequent impacts of market integration from 1998 to 2002. Stanford contrasts political actions by growers in both countries with strategies adopted by large avocado-buying companies, contextualizing an analysis of binational market integration within a political arena.

Intimately connected with the movement to liberalize the country-side, a broader social mobilization was on the rise during the 1990s. The two most important movements to emerge during this decade were no doubt El Barzón and the one that formed around the Zapatista National Liberation Army (EZLN), which launched an armed insurrection in 1994. As Humberto González argues in Chapter 13, a broad-based coalition of small and medium-sized farmers and city-based debtors converged in El Barzón after 1993. The trigger for this movement was the deep indebtedness of its constituents that was threatening to destroy their livelihoods and the very organization of production in many regions of Mexico's countryside. Pluralism appears to be a fundamental feature of emerging social movements, yet pluralism is also the collective purpose of aligned individuals and groups who define common objectives and interests and carry out actions to try to achieve them.

Using the theory of political-class formation outlined above, Gerardo Otero's Chapter 14 discusses how the EZLN has been contesting neoliberal globalism from below. The EZLN started out as a typical guerrilla organization struggling over state power and class issues. But it was soon converted into the leading organization in the struggle for Indian rights and culture, as well as for land reform, a reform of the state and for women's rights. Never before the emergence of the EZLN had the Indian question become such a prominent issue in Mexican national debate. In particular, Chapter 14 offers a conceptual and normative framework for the discussion of civil society, Indian rights and citizenship.

One central argument that runs through this book, implicitly or explicitly, concerns the relation between globalization and the nation-state. Our position is that the nation-state continues to be the ultimate terrain of struggle for subordinate groups, classes and communities, even if transnational or international solidarity is welcome and can help in some dramatic instances. This is an argument against those who claim that the forces of globalization have fundamentally debilitated nation-states, and that the fate of social movements now depends on the degree and extent of international solidarity from the 'global village' or a transnationalized civil society (e.g. Brysk 2000). While some aspects of the nation-state have in fact been debilitated by new commitments with suprastate organizations such as the International Monetary Fund, the World Bank or the World Trade Organization, others have actually been strengthened (Snyder 2001). But the nation-state continues to be the critical sphere for the imposition of ruling capitalist interests. Any substantial modifications in the economic, political and cultural conditions of subordinate groups, classes and communities will have to be fought and won at this level, even if international solidarity will always be a welcome, but not *the* determinant, ingredient.

Specifically, the articles presented here demonstrate that globalization as an economic process can hardly be contested. But the prevalence of its guidance by neoliberal ideology and policies has been subject to contestation from the very beginning by an increasing multiplicity of citizens and groups such as environmentalists, indigenous communities or political parties with different programmatic agendas. Such movements have always represented countervailing forces against those who promote a social order that is purely guided by economic principles, be they liberal or not. Indeed, the purity of these principles themselves has been questioned in the long-standing theoretical tradition outlined at the beginning of this chapter. Today the sought-after hegemony of these principles is the subject of contestation by a multiplicity of organizations around the world. Such groups face new challenges in the context of the social and environmental implications of globalization in its current course. They seek programmatic and institutional alternatives through bottom-up mobilizations. A key challenge for popular democratic, politically formed groups is that they must articulate concrete alternatives to neoliberal globalism that are also environmentally sustainable. The chapters below outline some such proposals for this contestation.

2 | Rebellious cornfields: towards food and labour self-sufficiency

ARMANDO BARTRA

> Their flesh was formed of yellow corn and of white corn; of corn-meal the arms and legs of man were formed. Only cornmeal formed the flesh of our fathers, the four men who were created. (*Popol Vuh, Mayan Book of Counsel*)

> My country: your surface is corn. (Ramón López Velarde, *Suave Patria*)

§ THE *Popol Vuh* and *Suave Patria*, texts emblematic of indigenous Mexico and mestizo Mexico, emphatically suggest that the Mexican countryside is much more than a giant food factory and source of raw materials for industry. Peasants not only harvest corn, beans, chilli and coffee; they also harvest clean air, pure water and fertile land; biological, social and cultural diversity; a myriad of landscapes, smells, textures and flavours; a variety of stews, headdresses and traditional garments; a plethora of prayers, songs, *sones* and dances. Peasants harvest the inexhaustible medley of practices and customs that make us Mexicans.

Despite the all-out free-traders, the rural world does not end with the production of commodities; it is also – and above all – nature, community, culture. As Europe begins to recognize the non-conventional values of its hoed fields, all the more should Mexico – a nation where a quarter of the population lives and works in the rural environment, a nation with a powerful indigenous heritage conserved mainly in the agrarian community, a mega-diverse territory populated by innumerable and largely native plants, animals and microorganisms.

During the so-called Uruguay Millennium Round of agricultural negotiations for the European Union (EU) in March of 2000, the agriculture ministers defined an agenda based on the recognition that agriculture has many functions in addition to food production, among them: preservation of the landscape, environmental protection, food quality and security, the well-being of animals and others. They felt it was urgent to balance the commercial and non-commercial aspects of agriculture and they designed a series of 'complementary measures' to the 1992 reform that allow subsidies to farmworkers in underprivileged zones to guarantee the sustainability of their agricultural activities, conservation of habitat and compliance with environmental norms. These measures also include training for agricultural workers in ecological technologies, support for youth planning to begin agricultural production, early retirement for workers over fifty-five years old and compensation for those who seek to convert their fields to forests or biological reserves.

True, the powerful European economy can afford to subsidize a relatively modest sector of its production and society. And, as a major food exporter, the EU also seeks to expand markets by reducing tariff barriers and subsidies in other countries, so it is to its advantage to introduce a system of agricultural support that presumably does not distort prices since it is oriented towards redistributing social and environmental values. Even so, the European focus is far more creative and indicative than the crude food imperialism of the United States, which wages a silent and global war against small farmers by using subsidies to drive down prices and dumping products at below-cost prices. Franz Fischer, European Commissioner for Agriculture and Fisheries, has pointed out that precisely when all the industrialized countries have agreed to orient their support for agriculture so that it does not translate into discretionary measures for trade and production, the United States is moving in the opposite direction.

Recognition of and compensation for environmental and social goods and services is important for Europe and for the 'first world', but it is indispensable in 'fringe' countries like Mexico. Here the decline of agricultural production relative to total production has *not* led to a corresponding reduction in the economically active rural population. As a result, the productivity and income of rural labour have plummeted. In our countries the farmlands are characterized by neglect and environmental crisis; they have become disaster zones where the young flee not to jobs in industry and services – sectors that have scarcely grown over the past decades – but towards urban jeopardy or the uncertain fate of undocumented migration.

We need a new pact between the urban world and the rural world. The point is not to hasten the dissolution of the agrarian past and the advent of a purely industrial future, but to guarantee a habitable future where social history prolongs and transcends natural history instead of catastrophically interrupting it.

The rest of this chapter is divided into five sections. It starts with an account of the peasant mobilization of 2002–03, which has gathered rural and urban social movement organizations under the name 'El campo no aguanta más' (The countryside can endure no more). Section two offers a brief history of the rural collapse and the loss of food and labour sovereignty, followed by a third section on how the neoliberal regime is approaching Mexico's poorest half. The fourth section discusses Mexico's loss of labour sovereignty and suggests ways of moving beyond neoliberal globalism. These suggestions are further elaborated in the concluding section, which outlines the social, cultural and environmental services provided by the peasant economy.

Mexico's countryside can endure no more

On 31 January 2003, 100,000 peasants and supporters from every state of the nation took over Mexico City to the cry of 'The countryside can endure no more'. The massive demonstration was neither the first nor the last. Throughout 2002 producers of corn, sorghum, beans, coffee, sugarcane, pineapple and livestock, along with rural debtors, carried out numerous actions. On 3 December, the demonstrations reached the doors of the San Lázaro Legislative Palace where the Mexican House of Deputies convenes. There, 2,500 peasants described the problem to deputies of the Party of the Democratic Revolution (PRD) and the Institutional Revolutionary Party (PRI), then marched on to the US Embassy. There they protested that US agricultural policies and imperial arrogance lay at the root of the current rural crisis.

The peasant mobilizations of late 2002 and early 2003 were called by the National Network 'Plan de Ayala' (Coordinadora Nacional Plan de Ayala, CNPA), the Independent Peasant and Agricultural Workers' Central (Central Independiente de Obreros Agrícolas y Campesinos, CIOAC), the National Union of Autonomous Regional Peasant Organizations (Unión Nacional de Organizaciones Regionales Campesinas Autónomas, UNORCA), the National Network of Coffee-growers' Organizations (Coordinadora Nacional de Organizaciones Cafetaleras, CNOC), the National Association of Marketing Agencies of Rural Products (Asociación Nacional de Empresas Comercializadoras de Productos Rurales, ANEC), the Mexican Association of Social Sector Credit Unions (Asociación Mexicana de Uniones de Crédito del Sector Social, AMUCSS), the National Front in Defence of the Mexican Countryside (Frente Nacional de Defensa del Campo Mexicano, FNDCM), the Mexican Network of Peasant Forestry Organizations (Red Mocaf), the National Union of Community Forestry Organizations (Unión Nacional de Organizaciones Forestales Comunitarias, UNOFC), the Democratic Peasants' Front of Chihuahua (Frente Democrático Campesino de Chihuahua, FDC) and the State Network of Coffee Producers of Oaxaca (Coordinadora Estatal de Productores de Café de Oaxaca, CEPCO), as well as the national El Barzón organization (see González, this volume). Later the Permanent Agrarian Congress (Congreso Agrario Permanente, CAP) and the National Peasant Confederation (Confederación Nacional Campesina, CNC) also joined, although separately to preserve their deteriorating images as major players (Mackinlay and Otero, this volume; Singelmann, this volume).

The demands of the rural workers are summed up in a common platform called 'Six proposals for the salvation and revaluation of the Mexican countryside'. It calls for:

1. A moratorium on the agricultural chapter of the North American Free Trade Agreement (NAFTA).
2. An emergency programme immediately to reactivate the countryside and another long-term programme to restructure the agriculture and livestock sectors.
3. A real rural financial reform.
4. A budget for 2003 that assigns at least 1.4 per cent of GDP to productive development in the countryside and another portion to rural social development.
5. Food policies that guarantee consumers safe and high-quality agricultural goods.
6. Recognition of the rights and cultures of Indian peoples.

The peasant demonstration drew support from the National Coalition of Education Workers (Coordinadora Nacional de Trabajadors de la Educación, CNTE), the Mexico Electricians' Union (Sindicato Mexicano de Electricistas, SME), the Union of Workers of the National Autonomous University of Mexico (Sindicato de Trabajadores de la Universidad Nacional Autónoma de México, STUNAM) and the National Union of Workers (Unión Nacional de Trabajadores, UNT). The programme – signed by over twelve grassroots organizations – also has the explicit endorsement of the Party of the Democratic Revolution (Partido de la Revolución Democrática, PRD) and its legislative groups. Many deputies and senators have expressed support for the peasants' demands, particularly for increased spending on agriculture and livestock in the Budget Law of 2003, for a change in the Energy Law to provide subsidies on diesel fuel and electricity for agricultural use, and for a reform of the Foreign Trade Law that legally protects national producers faced with northern imports. Some legislators also expressed a willingness to renegotiate the agriculture chapter of NAFTA. Even some cabinet members reluctantly conceded a willingness to open up NAFTA for renegotiation. Within the Senate, however, all parties voted against renegotiation of NAFTA.

Today, as never before, Mexican peasants are battling for their lives. At the outset of the new millennium, rural workers from all regions and sectors struggle to ensure their future; for a country that includes and defends its agrarian communities; for a model of development with food sovereignty and labour sovereignty. It is not just any cause; it is a battle for their very existence. If they are defeated, in the upcoming months the situation that afflicts producers of grain, vegetable and seed oils, coffee, sugarcane, pineapple, tobacco and so on will spread to producers of chicken, pork and forestry goods. It will extend, in short, to all rural sectors. If the crisis continues, in just a few years the Mexican countryside – already a disaster zone – will become a wasteland for agriculture, livestock and humans alike.

And the fate of peasants is the fate of all Mexicans; not only because the rural devastation extends dramatically to the cities through migration, but also because a country incapable of producing its own food and generating decent and stable jobs for its citizens is a nation crippled and on its knees before the empire. A people without a future.

A brief history of the collapse

This disaster has a history. In the 1960s, Mexico had 35 million inhabitants, half urban and half rural. Four decades later, the 17 million rural dwellers had grown to 24 million, but the city population had skyrocketed to over 75 million. Thus, in the last forty years, the rural population grew in absolute terms but decreased in relative terms and the country urbanized.

At the beginning of the third millennium, one of every four Mexicans lives in the countryside in towns of fewer than 2,500 inhabitants. In productive terms, only one of every five of the economically active population is involved in agricultural/livestock activities. However, this significant rural population and employment of about 25 million people does not translate into economic weight. The agricultural sector provides only about 5 per cent of the Gross Domestic Product (GDP) and this proportion has steadily declined under NAFTA from 7.3 per cent in 1992.

In part, the problem arises from the anti-agriculture bias in prices and the extremely low relative productivity of rural labour. But it also stems from the lack of options in industry and services for an agricultural workforce that, in spite of its low economic yields, few and poor jobs and minuscule incomes, remains rooted in the countryside.

According to the last agricultural census, nine out of every ten farmers produce for self-consumption to a greater or lesser degree, and only four of these sell their surplus on the market or market complementary production of cash crops (coffee, sugarcane, cocoa, tobacco, copra, and so on). Our agriculture, then, produces more subsistence than commercial crops; instead of performing a major economic function, it fulfils a vital social need.

At the outset of the third millennium, Mexican agriculture is made up of some 4.5 million units of production with 3 million corresponding to the social sector (ejidos and communal lands, created by agrarian reform after 1917) and the rest to private property. Of the latter, barely 15,000 proprietors possess large businesses and in this tiny group is concentrated nearly half the value of rural production. Some 150,000 have small private operations and the rest – including *ejido* members and communal farmers – are subsistence smallholders who produce purely for family consumption or combine family consumption with commercial production. Less than a third of social sector farmers generate agricultural income sufficient to live on and over half earn most of their income from off-farm sources (Otero 1999).

Mexican agriculture has certainly performed poorly by macroeconomic standards, but it has also made a poor showing in social terms. Levels of subsistence and well-being in the countryside are the lowest they have been in years. Eight out of every ten persons are poor and of these six or seven are extremely poor. Although only a quarter of the Mexican population lives in the countryside, two-thirds of people in extreme poverty live there.

Peasants have always been poor, but in the last fifteen years market-promoting public policies have deliberately forced the ruin of rural Mexico. Arguing that most small farmers are redundant due to their inability to compete, farm policy in the 1980s explicitly sought to drain off the rural population. A demographic purge was launched to remove some 3 million 'unnecessary' workers from the congested Mexican countryside, freeing agriculture of more than 15 million 'extra' people. Where would all these superfluous farmers go? For the neoliberal planners set on administering a streamlined rural sector, the ultimate fate of these people mattered little. When pressed, they alleged that ex-peasants would find work in industry, commerce and other services, for which they predicted an annual growth of between 6 and 7 per cent in the 1980s and 1990s. As we now know, during the tunnel years (and there's still no light) the Mexican economy did not grow and the expelled country people wound up in urban marginality, swelling the parasitic informal sector, or risked undocumented migration. The fortunate found work in offshore sweatshops which, despite being products of the third millennium, are reminiscent of the infamous factories of nineteenth-century England.

This genocidal restructuring, via savage economic conversion, operated through legal changes and constitutional reforms, such as the reform to Article 27 of the constitution that ended the interminable agrarian reform and opened the door to the privatization of *ejido* land and, indirectly, communal farms. But it also operated through a hasty and unilateral deregulation of agriculture and livestock trade that was supposed to orient production towards Mexico's comparative advantages on the global market. The production of fruits, vegetables and other exportable crops did, in fact, gain ground over staple crops (Barndt, this volume). But the negative result was greater since, in the same period, food imports grew exponentially. The agriculture balance of trade sunk into the red and farmer incomes took a nosedive.

The cross that farmworkers have been nailed to was built in the 1980s, but the nails were hammered in place in 1994 when NAFTA became law. In less than a decade, Mexico went from exporting an already high 70 per cent of exports to the United States to an overwhelming 90 per cent. This ties Mexico completely to the vicissitudes of the US economy. For agriculture, and particularly in the case of grain, it is the impetuous growth in imports that causes grave concern. In the period 1987–93 Mexico imported 52 million tons of grains, and for 1994–99 the total came to 90 million. The proportional increase of 73 per cent for grain was still greater in the case of corn because in 1987–93, Mexico imported 17 million tons and in 1994–99 nearly 30 million tons – an increase of over 76 per cent. The result was that, by the end of the century, we depended on the United States for 60 per cent of rice consumption, half of wheat, 43 per cent of sorghum, 23 per cent of corn and nearly all soybeans.

Mexico has clearly joined the world tendency towards the growing food dependency of peripheral countries on developed nations. In the last half-century, planetary production of cereals practically tripled, but growth was concentrated in developed nations that currently produce approximately 0.7 tons of grains per capita compared to the 0.25 harvested in underdeveloped countries.

These asymmetries will deepen with the new US Farm Bill. The United States Agricultural Security and Rural Investment Act, approved by the US Congress in 2002 for six years, increases agricultural subsidies between 70 and 80 per cent, to the stratospheric quantity of $183 billion. The new bill includes new products, such as soybeans and some food oils, added to the list of crops receiving fixed subsidies; it adds new crops to the list of those receiving compensation payments when the market price is below that fixed by the government, increasing this subsidy by nearly 5 per cent; and it establishes additional anti-cyclical compensations to be paid when a farmer's income, including other subsidies, does not reach a predetermined level. Even so, the subsidies do not assure equity for US farmers since only 8 per cent of farmers receive half the support payments. But in a country that exports 25 per cent of its harvests – 40 per cent in the case of wheat – these transfers ensure that US agricultural exports have artificially low prices on the global market, prices that force less subsidized farmers out of the competition.

The politics of pricing is being used as a new colonial weapon to ruin farmers in poor countries, where naïve or complicit governments take seriously the injunction to eliminate their own agricultural support programmes so as not to distort the market. With respect to Mexico, the new US Farm Bill serves only to deepen the asymmetries of our agricultural systems and drive in another nail, since subsidies represent on average 23 per cent of US farmer incomes and only 13.2 per cent for Mexican farmers. The damage extends to all walks of life: the predictable consequence for our trade balance in agriculture and livestock will be a reduction in exports and an increase in imports. In the social terrain, the result will be the general ruin of the remaining peasants. And in terms of national security, direct effects include the complete loss of labour sovereignty and food sovereignty.

As if that were not enough, on 1 January 2003 an event took place that was as important as the Zapatista uprising of 1 January 1994, but in the opposite sense. Since that day, nearly all agricultural products from the United States and Canada enter Mexico tariff-free. The list includes poultry, pork, sheep and lamb, beef, wheat, rice, barley, coffee, potatoes, warm-weather fruits and tobacco, among others, plus all their derived products such as sausages, fats and food oils. Three exceptions remain: corn, beans and powdered milk, which are scheduled for full liberation in 2008. Corn is only nominally controlled – the Ministry of the Economy recently established an additional importation quota of 2,667,000 tons of corn over and above the NAFTA level, thus maintaining the policy established since 1994 of permitting virtually unrestricted, tariff-free corn imports.

No wonder corn growers in the country are going down the drain. The current crisis affects not only low- and medium-yield, seasonal farmers in southern and central states, but also those who produce on irrigated land with high technology (but also high costs) in Sinaloa and other northern states. In the past years corn production in Mexico has not grown. Instead, it has held steady at around 18 million tons – an amount totally inadequate for satisfying internal demand when taking into account industrial and livestock needs.

'It's comparative advantages, stupid,' some would say. In agro-ecological terms, Mexico is simply not competitive in grains. Maybe. But then how to explain the fact that farmers of products for which Mexican territory is obviously well suited are also suffering? Why does the main crop of the south and south-east – coffee – stumble out of one price crisis only to fall into the next? Coffee growers are well organized and technologically innovative farmers who have made Mexico the world leader in organic production; they are experienced in marketing and, since the 1980s, well entrenched in the construction of Fair Trade markets. But even so they are on the edge of ruin. Anyone who has not found a commercial niche that offers a price premium, or developed value-added on their product definitely cannot make it. Coffee-growing zones which in the past offered an economic respite from the general rural poverty now contribute amply to the population exodus. The new migrants no longer come only from the arid Mixteco region or the mountains of Guerrero, they also pour out of the formerly proud coffee region of Soconusco, Chiapas and the coffee emporium of central Veracruz.

The catastrophe of the countryside is a national emergency. Imports of wheat and yellow corn, which have fluctuated between 5 and 6 million tons a year over the past NAFTA decade, are ruining commercial farmers in the north-east and driving down prices for the marketable production of more modest corn growers. They also discourage production for self-consumption, resulting in nearly 3 million producers being left without a lifeline. The sugarcane agroindustry is in crisis, since the USA does not accept the import levels originally negotiated in NAFTA and imports of high fructose sweetener have displaced sugarcane in soft drinks (Singelmann, this volume). Massive rice imports at dumping prices have bankrupted rice growers. The influx of canned pineapple has hurt national growers in Oaxaca and Veracruz. And the same can be said of milk and meat production, buffeted by powdered milk and imported cuts, and with poultry displaced by the entry of chicken parts considered throwaway in the United States, not to mention the problems in wheat, rice, sorghum and beans. The general agriculture and livestock débâcle is further exacerbated by the breakdown of peasant coffee production that directly sustains nearly 400,000 growers and – through day labour and related industry – feeds some 3 million people.

All in all, we are facing a major emergency, an issue of national security. A problem worsened by the huge increase in subsidies to US agriculture under the new Farm Bill and the tariff elimination of January 2003 under NAFTA. Elimination of tariffs means, among other things, the possible loss of hundreds of thousands of jobs in the pork and honey industries.

In the face of this crisis, the administration of Vicente Fox has indicated it has no serious proposals. Among its latest responses to peasant demands was the importunate recommendation of Agriculture Secretary Javier Usabiaga: 'Pay attention to the market signs, guys.' As if organized producers had not already been doing that for years. Worse yet, governmental response to the recent conflicts shows all the signs of becoming some kind of bank-rescue programme, a rural Fobaproa. Fobaproa was a fund made up of public resources in the late 1990s and used to subsidize corrupt bankers and businessmen under the pretext of protecting small savers. Today, fiscal resources are being channelled to moneyed rural sectors, which are part of the problem rather than the solution, alleging that this helps peasants. The most obvious case is the detour of 1.2 billion pesos that Acerca (the state agricultural insurance company) should have used to support sugar mills – a historically parasitic sector – so they could pay sugarcane producers what they were owed for the harvest. Another case of unwarranted subsidies was when Acerca channelled resources tagged for transportation and storage to huge international traders like Cargill, which moves nearly half the grain in Mexico and has its sights set on monopolizing the trade by buying up Silos Miguel Alemán, run by SAGARPA (the Secretariat of Agriculture), and the Grain Terminal of Veracruz. If Cargill takes over these strategic installations, Mexico's already eroded food security and sovereignty would fall into the hands of a transnational corporation that has over 1,000 storage facilities in sixty-seven countries all over the world. Corn subsidies resulting from the recent mobilizations in Sinaloa followed a similar course and to a large degree wound up in the pockets of traders and a small capitalized corn sector that works irrigated fields. Meanwhile, the 2.5 million peasant corn growers nationwide who contribute three-quarters of national production are not only left in the cold; they are also attacked for being uncompetitive and for devoting part of their crop to family consumption or local markets. A final example is the coffee sector, which received emergency government funds to confront the worst and most prolonged crisis in its contemporary history. But while a quarter of the subsidy goes to some 23,000 large growers with fields of over five hectares, 95 per cent of growers – over 300,000 peasant and indigenous families – receive only 75 per cent of the funds. This rural version of Fobaproa channels subsidies to the major traders, mill owners and wealthy farmers who often bear some responsibility for the emergency they now decry. The major problem is that these are emergency subsidies, stop-gap measures to put out fires or twist arms, without real projects behind them for recovery in agriculture or livestock.

In this context, to talk about a national emergency is neither empty rhetoric nor an exaggeration. The crisis has jeopardized the lives of the 25 million Mexicans who live and work in the countryside, among them the poorest part of the country's population and almost all its Indian population. It presents us with an economic, social and environmental disaster of colossal dimensions: a crisis in food sovereignty, a terminal crisis in labour sovereignty, an ecological crisis and, eventually, a socio-political crisis because calamities in agriculture have historically been associated with the emergence of guerrilla forces.

Due to the perversity of neoliberal conversion, food sovereignty has been lost. But we have also lost *labour sovereignty* – the capacity to provide decent jobs and sufficient income for all Mexicans. A poor country that does not produce enough food for its population is at a disadvantage in the game of globalization, since it is forced to buy basic consumer goods under global market conditions. In the same way, a nation marked by a massive and structural exodus, incapable of putting the labour power of its inhabitants to productive and remunerative use, places its sovereignty in the hands of the nation that receives its emigrants (Delgado Wise, this volume). Mexico is not a European country that consciously cedes sovereignty to intensify mutually beneficial and complementary ties; its food and labour dependency make Mexico a diminished and subordinated nation.

Faced with the agrarian débâcle, a national emergency that deepened with the 2002 US Farm Bill and the NAFTA tariff elimination of 2003, the government 'of change' that followed the PRI in 2000 has offered only sonorous phrases; plans and programmes with resounding names and little substance. At the end of 2002 the Secretariats of the Economy and Agriculture (Agriculture, Livestock, Rural Development and Fisheries, SAGARPA) announced an *agricultural shield*. The phrase is meaningless since the proposal fails to question the trade opening and lacks resources to create subsidies of a magnitude anywhere near comparable to those of our unfair trading partners in the north. What does 'shield' mean if it rejects any possibility of revising the agricultural chapter of NAFTA, while offering a severely reduced public budget with an infinitesimal allotment for rural development. The President of the Republic extolled the virtues of the agricultural shield, and announced that in 2003 the government would spend US$10 billion in the countryside. Once again the words rang hollow. The amount actually represents the sum of all budget categories that include rural expenditures, while SAGARPA – the only ministry that funds rural development and promotion – received around US$3.4 billion, a decrease of nearly 4 per cent with respect to the previous year. Although the Chamber of Deputies increased the rural budget by about 10 per cent, the resources are still insufficient. For any farmer who had not understood the government's message, the Secretary of Agriculture translated it into colloquial terms: 'Farmers will have a period of five years to become efficient and competitive,' he said. And if they do not, they can forget about subsidies and 'they better find another line of work ... We are offering a choice to producers of grain and other crops: they can become efficient according to international standards or go find something else.'

Just like that. Two years after assuming the presidency, the 'government of change' endorsed the crudest market plans of former president Carlos Salinas (1988–94), insisting that the Mexican countryside needed a population laxative consisting of strong doses of free market. And like the PRI neoliberals, Javier Usabiaga, who recently proposed reviving 'social liberalism' – the market-led ideology proposed by Salinas as a substitute for worn-out 'revolutionary nationalism' – is not concerned with defining 'international standards' that in reality derive from artificially low prices, depressed by developed-country subsidies. And he seemed even less concerned with identifying the 'something else' that presumably 'non-competitive' peasants could do in a country with a stagnant economy and contracting industrial employment (de la Garza Toledo, this volume; Dussel Peters, this volume).

For export crops, the secretary's prescription was much the same:

> In the case of coffee, we find producers that have a quarter of a hectare, another three hectares of corn and beans, and a little of this and that. They don't live off coffee. We have to give these producers a way out … And if you still want to keep producing (on small plots of coffee) go ahead, but the government doesn't have to share with you. We'll give you one or two years, so you can see that the income is marginal. But don't affect the interests of the country.

This means abandoning ('offering a way out') some 300,000 smallholder coffee growers with a diversified economy, nearly 2 million Mexican peasants who no doubt do not only live off coffee and who over the past years have maintained their plantations at a loss.

The Secretary of Agriculture was seemingly unimpressed by the fact that peasant coffee production on small mountain plots benefits the environment by retaining rainfall, preventing soil erosion, conserving fertility, fixing carbon and reproducing biodiversity. Nor was he concerned that for several decades coffee has provided a monetary income for thousands of peasant and indigenous communities throughout the country (Martínez-Torres, this volume). It did not seem to matter that the geography of coffee production overlays regions of the most acute social conflicts and high guerrilla activity. Mr Usabiaga knows only about growing and selling garlic and has shown little interest in anything but the market. That would have its merits – were it not for the fact that he is in charge of the fate of the entire Mexican countryside.

While European governments insist on recognizing the many roles agriculture plays in addition to producing food, the government of Mexico – a country where a quarter of the population depends on the rural economy – chooses to ignore them. Usabiaga recently stated: 'an agrarian society in need of fiscal resources, unaware and closed to markets, focuses on raising incomes through budgets and not through productivity' (interview by Lourdes Edith Rudiño, *El Financiero*, 21 November 2002). This is the government's basic offer for agriculture and livestock: compete or retreat.

Dealing with Mexico's lower half: Plan Puebla-Panamá

The other policy refers specifically to the Mexico that lies below the beltline and was euphonically dubbed Plan Puebla-Panamá (PPP). The programme promotes renewed colonization for the south and south-east, aided by deregulation, fiscal incentives and public works. It constitutes a marketing ploy whereby social programmes serve to mask a garage sale of the 'ugly' half of the country that still has not been bought by transnationals (Carlsen, this volume). Santiago Levy, current director of the Mexican Social Security Institute and wunderkind of the Salinas technocrats, argues that the task consists of seducing foreign funds by exploiting the region's comparative advantages. This will bring investment and, with it, badly needed economic growth. According to Levy, whose fathering of the programme has never been denied, the problem of the south-east is not really social. Southern poverty and marginality, he asserts, will be resolved by exiling the excess population so they can go cause shame somewhere else. The answer is to forget about poverty – or leave it to charity – and promote investment at all costs without inconvenient social concerns. If this growth model increases poverty, the newly minted poor can go somewhere else too.

Levy states this explicitly in the introduction to 'The South Also Exists: An Essay on Regional Development in Mexico', co-written with Enrique Dávila and Georgina Kessel:

> If those who do not find income opportunities in the area emigrate, the area can have low development without facing severe poverty problems. In this way, extreme rural poverty in backward regions is converted into moderate urban poverty … Inversely, the creation of a development pole in a backward region does not necessarily resolve its poverty problems … For these reasons, public policy design for the southeast should separate the objectives of combating poverty from those of regional development. (Dávila et al. 2000)

Intensive private plantations of monocrops, commercial and service corridors that facilitate the flow of merchandise between the east coast of the United States and the Pacific, offshore assembly plants, high-rent tourism, bioprospecting – these are some of the development lines that, according to Levy, will not necessarily improve the standard of living and could indeed do the opposite.

But the PPP has been ailing lately. Over two years into the programme, little has been done besides talk, because the global recession has discouraged new investment and even caused some investors – including *maquiladoras* and tourism projects – to back out of the region. Also because the government did not funnel public finances into infrastructure and the nation's debt has inhibited new loans to the ad hoc fund negotiated by the Interamerican Development Bank.

Beyond neoliberal globalism

So, has the recession stalled the danger? Not at all. With or without the Plan Puebla-Panamá, savage globalization continues its course running roughshod over nature and humanity. For years, the south/south-east of the country has lived under an unjust and exclusive order where growing poverty is the inevitable counterpart to new wealth. Mesoamericans still live under this order and suffer its chronic inequities. But the form of suffering and its intensity depend on short-term tendencies and events. During periods of expansion, capital takes over new spaces, resources and capacities, upsetting fragile equilibriums and in general increasing and extending destruction and poverty. During periods of retraction, investment stagnates or pulls out, leaving workers jobless and forcing local inhabitants to join the ranks of the super-exploited or excluded. So within an oppressive and unfair order, such as that of the south-east, both expansion and retraction are harmful. But it is still relevant to recognize that in the past years the latter has predominated.

Temporary retraction or stagnation within the new process of colonization does not bring benefits but only a different kind of costs – for example, unemployment in construction, *maquiladoras*, plantations and tourism; and a reduction in the demand for certain agricultural raw materials. This just goes to show that the transnationalization of Mesoamerica and globalization itself cannot be avoided. It is not that it cannot be avoided because globalization is a natural force but simply because it already arrived a long time ago. We live in it, and as long as it lasts we depend on it for subsistence. What is needed is therefore not an effort to stop, slow down or prevent the arrival of an order that already surrounds us; what is urgently needed is to change the course of development and reorganize priorities. This means modifying the neoliberal nature of globalization.

The mass exodus of Mexicans looking for a future in the north that their own country has denied them is the most ignominious result of the kind of development adopted in the 1980s. That model took us from exploitation to exclusion; from an unfair system whereby peasants produced cheap food and raw materials that subsidized industrial development, to a system that pushes farmers out of basic crops through imports and ruins agroexporters through falling international prices. The Mexican diaspora is not a form of migration that can be stopped through repression, or remedied by recolonizing the south. Its negative impacts cannot be significantly alleviated by capitalizing on remittances or even turning back NAFTA or the proposed Free Trade Area of the Americas (FTAA).

In the beginning of a new millennium, an important part of the national peasantry and a significant part of the indigenous population live and work on the other side of the border. And a no less relevant part of the peasant and indigenous communities that stayed behind live suspended by a thread, dependent on the remittances sent by migrants (Cohen, this volume; Delgado Wise, this volume).

Mexico is a pluriethnic and also an eminently binational country. If its 10 million Indians make it multicultural, then the 23 million compatriots living in the United States more than qualifies it as multinational. One out of every five Mexicans lives in the United States and half have family members there. Of every three Mexicans, one works on the other side of the border. If we add in the one million *maquiladora* workers who get paid in pesos but produce in dollars, most of whom work in thirty cities along the northern border with one eye on the other side, we have a portrait of a profound demographic and labour overlap between the two nations – a medley of cultures, an inextricable intermix of visions.

Half of the Mexico that exists north of the border is made up of men and women born in the countryside. Half of them are undocumented workers, because the owners of the nation next door do not want to share it. But the human transit, legal or illegal, cannot be controlled. This population shift, this unchecked and growing diaspora, is unprecedented. In times of great sociopolitical convulsions, such as the ten years of armed struggle and the first decade after the Mexican Revolution, many Mexicans took refuge over the border; by 1930, 3.73 per cent of those born in Mexico resided in the United States. But the exodus diminished between 1940 and 1970, the longed-for years of 'stabilizing development'. The recurring crises of the last quarter century again heightened the migratory phenomenon, and since the mid-1980s adjustment policies have been more effective than the war and hunger of the revolution in converting patriots to pilgrims – albeit reluctant ones. In 1997, 7.75 per cent of Mexico-born citizens lived in the United States and by the beginning of the third millennium the uprooted make up 10 per cent. And the stampede continues (Delgado Wise, this volume).

Today more than ever it is necessary to demand the right of Mexicans to food and 'decent' (a term used by the International Labour Organization) jobs. That means to demand food security and labour security in the country. And this will not be possible if we do not rescue our mortgaged sovereignty. The Mexican state must recover and exercise the right to orient the course of the economy towards the well-being of its citizens and not to sacrifice those citizens to the requirements of the global marketplace.

But even this is not exactly true since neoliberal policies have been and are at the service of the giant corporations and not some abstract market (Otero, Chapter 1, this volume). As corn growers face ruin, Roberto González Barrera of Maseca (the main producer of cornflour) gets rich buying cheap North American corn above the import quota negotiated in NAFTA. Wheat farmers are going under while the Bimbo Group (a major bread producer) of Lorenzo Servitje hikes profits thanks to subsidized imports at rock-bottom prices. The same is true of the Bachoco Group (major poultry producers), and of the Robinson Bours family, which imports corn and sorghum for feed without paying tariffs. And the list goes on. In addition to the Mexican companies, the world's most powerful transnationals have also profited. Cargill currently controls our grains production; Purina monopolizes livestock inputs, Nestlé controls entire dairy regions, PepsiCo owns sugar mills, Becafisa-Volcafé buys huge volumes of coffee. And while a handful of corporations get rich, the small farmers face economic ruin and whole towns are abandoned.

The uprooted in the United States send home $10 billion a year, nearly the same amount as the value of food imports from that country; the same food that the farmer-migrants could have grown here. But for that to happen we would need industrial and farm policies designed to defend and broaden the productive plant and promote crops of national interest. We must re-establish food security, supporting small and medium-sized peasant production and strengthening the domestic markets – national, regional and local. We need to restore labour security, defending and broadening the factory plant, strengthening agricultural and livestock activities, and increasing the integration of productive chains that make full use of productive complementarities.

Conclusion

To correct the course that has led Mexican agriculture into bankruptcy presupposes a series of fundamental changes. The most important is to correct the perception that the last few administrations have had of small and medium rural producers.

Peasants are polyphonic. That means that their efficiency and ability to compete cannot be judged only on the basis of the products they sell on the market directly and visibly. It must also be judged on the many goods and services they generate. Polyphonic means that if we limit ourselves to a cost/benefit analysis of the productive system, they would be considered externalities. These services – practically invisible from a mercantile perspective but very real – can be classified as social, cultural and environmental.

Social services

In a country with severe problems of labour self-sufficiency, security and sovereignty, the peasant economy generates employment and income at significantly lower costs than industry or services. In the context of the loss of food self-sufficiency, security and sovereignty, peasant production of basic foods, for national or local markets, or for family consumption, reduces the risk of food crisis and famine.

Our rural society has disintegrated due to the lack of options and mass emigration; the urban world is saturated with people living on the edge, often tied to a parasitic informal economy. The rural domestic economy roots the population and strengthens community. Confronted with economic activity that pulverizes human society, peasant production based on a broadened domestic model that combines family labour and associative activities generates economies of scale and reinforces organic ties as part of social solidarity and community.

Cultural services

The diversity of Indian, migrant and mestizo cultures is one of Mexico's greatest assets and the original root of this plurality is almost always rural and community-based. Therefore we must credit the peasant economy for its role as the main economic and social sustenance of our identity as a nation. The peasant economy is the principal and incontrovertible productive base from which to exercise the cultural rights and the right to autonomy of indigenous peoples. Indigenous cultures include the proverbial crafts but also a wide range of linguistic, political, religious, musical and culinary customs, as well as ancestral productive knowledge and agricultural techniques. The restoration, preservation and development of these cultures will be sustainable only if they have a secure economic base in a peasant production that renovates tradition and fortifies change (Otero, Chapter 14, this volume).

Environmental services

In these global times, the fragile ecosystems that life depends on confront production and consumption models that destroy the precarious balance between nature and society. In this context, the virtues of a community-based society and economy – capable of maintaining and developing a more harmonious relationship with the environment – become obvious. Some domestic productive practices that were sustainable have been lost or have ceased being sustainable due to population growth and the impact of aggressive technological packages. But there is no doubt that the new environmental paradigms are leading to the rediscovery of the value of diversified uses, of low or no agrochemical use and of small- and medium-scale production that adjusts to the different requirements of the environment. Both 'grey' paradigms, that embrace clean technologies, and 'green' paradigms, that call for respecting the capacity of ecosystems, have given new value to a changing but obstinate and long-lasting peasant model of production. Now that drinking water, a clean atmosphere and fertile soil have become scarce and ever-more valuable natural resources, the peasant production model that places diversity and well-being above earnings offers an imperative alternative to homogeneous technological patterns and profit motives.

If the twentieth century was the era of petrochemicals, the twenty-first is the century of 'life science industries'. Genetic engineering is now the decisive activity in the production of foods, medicines, cosmetics and other products and within this scheme biodiversity – seen as natural germplasm banks – becomes the strategic resource of the future. Transnational corporations and bioprospectors seek to extract and patent biological materials that agrarian communities and peasants have preserved for years. In many cases, the materials in question are not really natural resources but the result of ancestral domestication (Carlsen, this volume).

For the most part, the market does not recognize or credit the multiple functions of the peasant economy. A few environmental services, such as carbon fixing or watershed protection have become visible, but efforts to estimate the value and apply a price to these have just begun. In some cases, those who generate negative environmental externalities (polluting companies) would pay for these services. In others, the consumer seeking out products that are organic, green, clean, sustainable and so on pays a special price for these attributes, in part to recompense the intrinsic virtues of the product and in part to reward the environmentally friendly nature of production. Finally, through public spending, governments fund some environmental objectives, including support for farmers who develop sustainable practices. However, neither the incipient environmental services market, nor the limited market for ecological products, or the scanty public spending devoted to supporting sustainable smallholder production significantly compensate for the many socioenvironmental functions of the peasant economy.

To identify these multiple services and establish mechanisms to quantify and price them is the first step. Achieving compensation will not be easy, since although it seems to be a market issue, recognizing the social, cultural and ecological functions of peasant production violates the fundamental principles of absolute mercantilism. The system does not concede exchange value to social, cultural and environmental goods and services that cannot be privatized and used for profit. To propose that society be recompensed for strengthening values such as equity, harmony and cultural diversity, or that one should pay for preservation and restoration of natural resources and biodiversity even when these goods are claimed as collective and not up for privatization, is very difficult for free-trade integrationists to accept. However, it is a struggle that has begun and cannot be abandoned since what is at stake is not only the survival of peasants but also the future of humanity. Fortunately, evidence that a general ecological catastrophe is approaching and signs indicating that rural poverty and urban poverty with rural origins are about to explode have focused attention on the virtues of small and medium sustainable production. It is now necessary to deepen this incipient recognition and initiate just compensation.

For several decades, peasants justified their right to exist by alleging that they could be 'efficient' in business. This proved to be a losing battle, since, in terms of technical direct yields and strictly defined economic profitability, the gap between small- to medium-sized domestic agriculture and private farming has been growing. With these criteria, some policy-makers insist that peasants are already an unnecessary and disposable group whose exclusion is as inevitable as it is necessary. The lines of battle must be changed; perhaps peasant producers are not as efficient as rural entrepreneurs when measured by the standards of private business, but without a doubt they are infinitely more efficient if we consider social, cultural and environmental impacts, categories where agribusiness clearly flunks the test of sustainability.

3 | Fruits of injustice: women in the post-NAFTA food system

DEBORAH BARNDT

Precious human cargo

As we approached the Toronto airport in the still-dark dawn, I asked Irena which terminal her plane was leaving from. I expected her to say Terminal 3, which is the main departure point for international flights, and by far the most elegant, with skylit bodegas and chic restaurants. When she said 'Terminal 1', I questioned her, especially as the sign for Terminal 1 said 'Cargo'. 'But I'm going as cargo!' she jokingly explained.

I was well aware of the Foreign Agricultural Resource Management Services, established in 1974, known as the FARMS programme, which brings Jamaican and Mexican farmworkers such as Irena to Canada every summer to pick our fruit and vegetables. I knew it was considered the '*crème de la crème*' of migrant worker schemes, selecting the heartiest who tolerate a few months of backbreaking work in our fields, twelve hours a day, six and a half days a week, because they can make as much in an hour here as they made in Mexico in a day. And while I knew that they are brought *en masse* by plane in the spring and sent home *en masse* in the autumn, no reading or interviews prepared me for the sight I faced as we entered Terminal 1 that day: a sea of brown and black bodies, primarily men, in massive line-ups, pushing carts bursting with boxes of appliances they were taking home. Security guards surrounded them, this precious human cargo, moving less freely than goods now move across borders in the post-NAFTA context. I imagined lighter-skinned Mexican professionals boarding planes in Terminal 3, briefcases in hand, having just completed a new trade deal with Canadian-based companies, or even middle-class and upper-class students now availing themselves of increased exchanges among North American universities. Irena's story is a little-known part of the complex puzzle of food production and consumption in the increasingly integrated continental economy, a puzzle which involves many women workers who have been invisible to those of us who eat the food they plant, pick, pack, process, prepare, sell and serve.

The Tomasita project

Between 1994 and 2001 I coordinated a unique cross-border research project with collaboration from feminist academics and activists in Mexico, the United States and Canada, that took advantage of this deepening economic and cultural integration of the continent, and the privilege of university research monies to move academics and graduate students across borders much more easily than Irena can move. Calling it the Tomasita Project,[1] we mapped the journey of a corporate tomato from a Mexican agribusiness to a Canadian supermarket and US-based fast-food restaurant as a device for examining globalization from above (the corporate agendas) and globalization from below (the stories of the lowest-waged women workers in these sectors).

The neoliberal context was revealed through profiles of three different kinds of multinational corporations in the globalizing economy. Empaque Santa Rosa, the second largest tomato producer in Mexico, represented domestic agribusinesses in the south that are pushed into increasing agroexport by neoliberal trade policies. Canadian-based Loblaws supermarket, one of eighteen retail chains owned by George Weston Ltd which controls over 30 per cent of Canada's food retail market, epitomized the 'bigger is better' phenomenon reflected in increasing corporate concentration and the growing dominance of retailers over food production. Finally, US-based McDonald's fast-food restaurants served as both the quintessential symbol of global cultural homogenization as well as a model for the reorganization of work (or McDonaldization) that is replicated in many other sectors of the global economy.

While there are differences between these three companies, they share a common corporate labour strategy, pushed by just-in-time production towards the increasing flexibilization of labour. In all three cases, the predominant flexible labour force is female. Since the 1970s, many feminist scholars have pointed to the dependence of mobile corporate capital on women workers, initially in the export processing zones and *maquiladoras* region of Mexico. With the trade liberalization of the 1990s, exemplified by agreements such as North American Free Trade Agreement (NAFTA), free-trade zones and geographically defined *maquiladoras* lose their uniqueness. In fact, *maquiladoraization*, which referred originally to the northern border region in Mexico which allowed US industries to operate freely, now refers to a more generalized work process characterized by (i) the feminization of the labour force, (ii) extreme segmentation of skill categories, (iii) the lowering of real wages, and (iv) a non-union orientation (Kopinak 1997: 13). With the dropping of trade barriers, not only all of Mexico but even northern countries such as Canada have virtually become giant *maquiladoras*.

The women workers that we interviewed in the three corporate sectors reflect this flexibility in different ways. The Mexican workers, who will be the focus of this chapter, reflect what Lara calls a 'primitive flexibility' (Lara 1994: 41) which depends on labour-intensive processes of production, sorting and packing. In the agroexport economy, there is a growth of such unstable and temporary employment, relegated primarily to the most 'flexible' workers in the rural labour market: women, children and indigenous peoples. The fact that most agricultural work is also seasonal contributes to the instability.

Workers in the consumption end of the tomato chain, however, are managed through a 'negotiated flexibility', with higher-skilled and relatively stable employment. Nevertheless, the cashiers at Loblaws supermarkets and the women workers at McDonald's fast-food restaurants both represent a precarious workforce, as part-time work proliferates and two-tiered wage structures are introduced. In some ways, the technologization of their work, while making company labour practices and inventory more flexible, has also bound these retail and service workers within rigid definitions of work, highly engineered, speeded up and even scripted.

In this chapter, I will focus exclusively on the Mexican women workers in the tomato food chain,[2] those who like Irena are part of a mobile transnational labour force and those who would never dream of boarding a plane for Canada, but move in and out of seasonal production processes, key actors in the deepening agroexport economy of post-NAFTA Mexico.

Interlocking analysis of power

The increasingly globalizing food system builds on and perpetuates deeply rooted inequalities of race and ethnicity, class, gender, age, urban–rural and marital status. As we followed the tangled routes of women workers along the tomato trail, we evolved an interlocking analysis of power that took into account five key dimensions of power which emerged as the most salient to understanding hierarchies within this food chain.

Our gender analysis is located, first, within a context of *north/south* asymmetries, and, in the case of the food system, in the dynamic that the south (ever more dependent on agroexports for foreign exchange) increasingly produces for consumption in the north. I don't want to perpetuate a simplistic north/south analysis, however, and thus recognize its limitations by revealing the dynamics within Mexico of southern impoverished regions feeding cheap migrant labour to the richer industrial north of that country, disintegrating rural communities sucked into the demands of an increasingly urban Mexico, poor indigenous peasants now salaried labour serving the food needs of a wealthier mestizo population as well as consumers in the north. In the continental food system, this north–south axis has allowed us to compare the similarities and differences between women who plant, pick and pack tomatoes in Mexico and those who scan and bag, or slice and serve, tomatoes in Canadian retail and fast-food industries.

Class

There are clearly different socioeconomic statuses among women in the food system, even among the lower-waged workers in each sector that we studied. Each company constructs its own hierarchy of workers, sometimes though not always related to educational level, but usually defined by skill levels, disparate wage levels and working conditions. The greatest differences are between those working in the north and the south, of course, and between mestizo and indigenous workers in Mexico.

Race/ethnicity

Also interacting with class and gender are race and ethnicity, shifting in meaning from one place and time to another. Ethnic differences are perhaps most pronounced in the Mexican context, between the indigenous workers that the agribusiness brings by truck to pick tomatoes under the hot sun and the more skilled and privileged mestizo women they bring in buses to pack tomatoes in the more protected packing plant.

Age and family status

The interrelated factors of age, marital status and generational family roles are clearly significant in the Mexican agricultural context, where the workforce is predominantly young and female, particularly in the packing plants. The family becomes critical, too, as family members often work together in the tomato fields and combine wages to survive a deepening economic crisis.

Rural/urban

In the context of food and agriculture, the rural–urban dynamic is central. Development strategies in both Mexico and Canada have favoured urban dwellers, but still depend on rural workers to feed the populations of the burgeoning cities. Mexican peasants are migrating to both rural and urban areas in Mexico, and the survival of most families depends on the migration of some family member(s) to the USA or Canada, even if temporarily as in the case of Irena.

It is almost impossible to describe the above dimensions of power in isolation. The stories of women in the tomato chain reveal the complex interaction between these categories of identity, and thus enrich our understanding of gender and women's experience as plural, diverse and constantly changing.

The Tomasita Project was by definition a feminist and an ecological project. First, it is a feminist act to make visible the women workers in the food system, redressing their invisibility in other studies of global agriculture and trade regimes as well as in the public consciousness. Beyond filling in the gaps left by male-dominated perspectives, this study benefited from the rich development of diverse feminist theories over the past decade. I drew from a wide array of fields, ranging from political economic labour studies to feminist ecological economics, from socialist feminism to feminist environmentalism, from gender and sustainable development to social ecofeminism.[3] My own positions have also been shaped by three decades of research and activism in the USA and Canada, as well as in Peru, Nicaragua and Mexico.

In the Mexican context, I have consulted the research of Lucila Rooner (1981) and Gilda Salazar (1986) in the 1980s. I have also drawn heavily from Sara Lara's work in the 1990s on both the history of tomato work and gender, as well as her work on the flexibilization of the workforce in an increasingly industrialized agribusiness (1998a, 1998b). Key collaborators in the Tomasita Project included Maria Antonieta Barrón (UNAM), a pioneer in gender dynamics in the rural sector and Mexican migrant labour patterns (Barrón 1993), and Kirsten Appendini's (Colegio de Mexico) work on Mexican agriculture, food policy and the shifting roles of women in agribusiness (Appendini 2001).

I also address the complexity of the work and home lives of the women workers in the tomato food chain by considering particular social constructions of their relationship with nature, and, in Haraway's (1991: 195) terms, their situated knowledges. These are inevitably contradictory, given that the women workers featured here are immersed in diverse contexts where competing notions of development and globalization are at play. My analysis attempts to weave, like tangled roots and routes, an ecology of women and tomatoes that respects local contexts while acknowledging broader social and historical processes in constant interaction with them.

Mexican women workers – in Mexico

To illustrate this interlocking analysis, I will first introduce six women who work with Empaque Santa Rosa, the Mexican agribusiness at the production end of the tomato chain. The differences among the indigenous and mestiza workers, the pickers and the packers, will challenge any notion we might harbour in the north of a singular or monolithic Mexican woman worker.

Picking and packing for the north

Job categories and divisions of tasks within tomato production have evolved over decades (indeed, centuries) to reflect and reinforce institutionalized classism, sexism, racism and ageism. According to Sara Lara (1998b), the restructuring and technologization of tomato production during the 1990s – promoted by neoliberal trade policies – has not changed the sexual division of labour, but has, in fact, exploited it even further. By employing greater numbers of women, companies contract skilled but devalued labour that is not only qualitatively but quantitatively flexible.

A moving maquila: the 'company' girls

The packing plant is one of the places where entrenched gender ideologies clearly reign. Women are considered both more responsible and more delicate in their handling of the tomatoes; and because the appearance of the product is so critical to tomato exporters, there is at least some recognition of this work as a skill, even if it is considered innate rather than part of female socialization, as Lara argues (1998a: 29–36).

Women who sort and pack tomatoes for Santa Rosa are drawn from two sources: local girls living in the town and mostly young women hired permanently by the company and moved from site to site, harvest to harvest. The latter are the most privileged, and are clearly 'company girls', a kind of 'moving *maquiladora*'. They provide the flexible labour and the skills needed by Santa Rosa at the important stage of sorting and packing tomatoes for export.

Juana, packer

'I'm thirty-seven years old now, I've been following the harvests for twenty-three years. We go from here to the Santa Rosa plant in Sinaloa, and from there we go to San Quintin, Baja California, and then back to Sinaloa – every year we make the round. We are brought from Sinaloa with all expenses paid, the company covers the costs of transport, food, and, once here, we get a house with a stove, beds, mattresses. Our house is close to the plant, and we share it with sixteen other workers. In the end, we're all a family.'

Yolanda, sorter

'I'm twenty-one, and have been working for Santa Rosa for six years. My father was a manager at the packing plant in Sinaloa, and I began working there during school vacations. I liked packing work better than school. The atmosphere is different, it's more fun and you can make money. I came here from Sinaloa, and share an apartment with my mother, sister and brother-in-law. He works in the Santa Rosa office and gets special living expenses. I earn almost 1,000 pesos [$200] a week. I'm saving money for a house I'm building back in Sinaloa.'

Many young women Yolanda's age see this as temporary work, a good way to make some money, travel, and perhaps find a husband, so that they could then get on to the 'real' business of settling down and raising their own families. Older women like Juana, who do not marry and leave the job, have become virtually wedded to the company, with no time or space for creating their own lives. They move from harvest to harvest, like swallows, returning annually to their home base.

Sorters and packers are not drawn from rural indigenous communities, but rather from the mestizo communities in the towns where the production plants are located. They represent both racial and class privilege among the female labour force, and are also the women who are in greatest contact with the company management; the most privileged, in fact, seem to be women with close connections to men who have administrative jobs with Santa Rosa, like Yolanda's brother.

There is, however, a hierarchy of skills and of treatment between the two main jobs of sorting and packing, with the packers being the more privileged in several senses. 'The sorters have to sign in, but we packers don't. The sorters have to stand all the time. Packers can sit on wooden boxes.' The sorters start at 9 a.m., the packers at 10 a.m. Perhaps the biggest and most crucial difference is the wage level and form of payment. Sorters are paid by the hour, while packers are paid by the box. At 33 cents a box, a packer might average 200–500 boxes a day, or 66–150 pesos, or \$13–30 a day; a sorter, earning 5 pesos an hour, would average 35–60 pesos, or \$7–12 a day. Both of these far surpass the fieldworker's wage of 28 pesos (\$5) a day for back-breaking work under a hot sun.

Male workers in the packing plant are still the most privileged, however. On Saturdays, when workers go to the office to get their weekly pay, the queues themselves reveal the ultimate divisions. In the words of one of the packers: 'When we go to get our money, there are three lines: one for sorters, one for packers, and one for the men.' As stated above, sorters earn less than packers, have to sign in earlier than packers, and have to stand while working. The men's work is quite different, requiring strength that is more physical; this definition of 'skill', however, is highly gendered and so the differential salary levels can be challenged.

Factories in the fields: hi-tech greenhouse production

The future of tomato production in Mexico appears to be in greenhouses, which allows year-round production and almost total control of key factors such as climate, technology and labour. Greenhouse production can be seen as the epitome of the 'maquila' model which, since NAFTA, has now moved from the northern border to be applied to businesses throughout Mexico. In a greenhouse operation affiliated with Empaque Santa Rosa, the only Mexican inputs are the land, the sun (the company saves on electricity and heating), and the workers. And like most *maquilas*, 100 per cent of the produce is for export (10 per cent going to Canada but most to the United States).

In recent years young women have entered the labour force in increasing numbers and it has become more culturally acceptable for young women to work in the growing agroindustrial sector, which may take them away from home. Most young people have taken these jobs because they represent better alternatives than previous work and because their income is needed for the family wage. In the case of Empaque Santa Rosa, the greenhouse workers come from nearby villages and are not transported great distances from site to site as are the women packers and sorters described earlier.

Greenhouse work offers a new form of employment that combines planting and packing, and, in terms of wages and status, falls somewhere between the fieldworkers and the packers at the larger plants. For women, there are basically two different roles: working in the greenhouses planting and picking tomatoes, or working in the packing house in a more sophisticated process that combines selecting and packing. The next two profiles feature one woman in each area: Soledad who works in the greenhouse and Yvonne in the packing house.

Soledad, greenhouse planter

While Soledad is a feisty and sociable fifteen-year-old, her name means 'loneliness or solitude'. Ironically, when she was three years old, her parents moved to Los Angeles, and she hasn't seen them since. They have had five more children there, and they send money home, about $500 every two weeks, to support Soledad, her sister and brother, and grandparents, with whom she lives. This is not an uncommon family configuration, as relatives share childrearing on both sides of the notorious border, and those who remain in Mexico are tied both emotionally and financially to their families in the north.

Soledad has been working at the greenhouse since she was thirteen. She makes 180 pesos ($US26) a week, 30 pesos ($US4–5) a day for six days, or 4 pesos (under $1) an hour – only slightly more than the fieldworkers.

Yvonne, greenhouse packer

Yvonne, twenty, undertakes the other major task assigned to young women, work in the enormous packing house. In her three years working at the greenhouse, she has witnessed the move into hi-tech packing. The pressure that the computerized process on the lines creates within and among the workers is palpable. The French manager's strategy has worked on people like Yvonne who has succumbed to the competitive dynamic: 'I was depressed at first because they would tell me: "You're below the quota." I would be ashamed, because this means you're not worth anything. So I was very tense, concerned about getting faster, so they'd have a better impression of me.'

Yvonne's efforts to keep up with the new technology and to prove herself a productive worker also reveal the internalization of new work values. 'Good' workers are being shaped in Mexico by the combination of controlling technology and foreign management. Yet sexism reigns as once again the male workers are paid more: 'If we make 100, men make 175,' explains Yvonne.[4]

Into the fields

The women workers who are closest to the land, the plants and the tomatoes themselves are also the lowest paid and least skilled in the hierarchy outlined here. They are the most exposed to the hot sun and the rain, as well as to the pesticides sprayed incessantly in the fields. Two stories here will reveal two major sources of tomato fieldworkers: local peasants and indigenous migrants from the south.

Tomasa, local fieldworker

As an older woman (sixty-eight years old), Tomasa is perhaps not a typical fieldworker. But her story reflects many important characteristics of migrant labour in Mexico. First her personal history growing up as a mestiza peasant girl in rural Jalisco reveals the deeply rooted sexism that produces and reproduces the gendered division of labour in the agricultural sector. Second, like many other peasant families, she and her husband combine subsistence farming with salaried work for agribusiness. Finally, her story reveals the family wage economy that is the major strategy of survival for poor Mexicans.

'We raised ourselves, that is, my father died when I was two and so my mother was left alone to raise us, she had to work to feed us. As a child, I played around the house, but when I was eight or nine, my mother put me to work – sweeping, fetching water from a far-away stream. When I became older, I helped grind and mix the corn meal to make tortillas. Now my kids helped me with the housework and they still help. Two of my sons have gone to work in the USA and send money back. My other sons work in the lumber business, cutting pine trees nearby. The women don't work in the field, they stay at home with their family. I'm the only one who runs around like a fried chilli, picking tomatoes! My youngest daughter stays at home, and has food ready for us when we return from the fields.'

The unpaid domestic work that keeps Mexican peasant families alive is not accounted for in any of the official calculations. Tomasa, in fact, works a triple day: as a salaried worker for agribusiness, as a subsistence farmer on their family *milpa* and as the primary caretaker of her family.

In either case, they remain dependent on capitalist agribusiness, whether owned by Mexicans or foreigners; both take advantage of their cheap labour. And the companies benefit not only from their low wages, but also from the family wage economy, which incorporates family remittances, subsistence farming and Tomasa's domestic labour. While they may appear a triple burden for Tomasa, not even these options are open to most indigenous migrant women, the most exploited in the hierarchy of workers.

If gender discrimination is entrenched in the tasks offered women workers and in their double or triple days, racism is manifested against the indigenous migrant workers who are brought in packed trucks by contractors, with no certainty of getting work, and with even worse living and working conditions than local peasants. Housed in deplorable huts, without water, electricity, stores or transport, they come as families to work in the fields and move from harvest to harvest. The women bear the brunt of this lack of infrastructure – cooking and washing, taking care of kids (even while working in the field), and dealing with their own exhaustion and the poor health engendered by the conditions of extreme poverty. Because their own regions offer even less opportunity, they are forced to suffer these jobs and the racist treatment built into them (Lara 1998b: 210–15).

Reyna, indigenous migrant farmworker

'We're from Guerrero. Contractors came to our town to find people to work here. After we finish our contract, they take us back in trucks.

'Some women carry their children on their backs while they're working, because they don't have anyone who can take care of them.

'We earn 28 pesos a day [$5–6]. It's never enough to save anything. Sometimes the children need shoes and it's not enough. They give us some clothes, because 28 pesos is nothing. There's no union and no vacations.'

While working children (often as young as six or seven) are paid the daily rate, it is often the case that their parents, especially mothers, will rush to fill their own quota, so they can help their children complete theirs. This dynamic makes the fieldwork much more intense and more like piecework (Barrón personal communication, 2000). Mothers must also carry their babies on their backs as they work in the fields. In breastfeeding her child, Reyna passed the pesticides from the plants on her hands into his mouth, and almost poisoned him. Indigenous women and children are clearly in the most precarious position of all those who bring us the corporate tomato.

In the six stories above, the multiple strategies for survival become clearer. Women are key protagonists for their families, in their triple functions: as salaried workers (with varying status and wage levels), as subsistence farmers (when they have access to land) and as domestic labourers (with a wide range of living conditions, from the horrific camps of indigenous migrants to the better equipped but transient homes of the mobile packers). But no one woman's story can be understood in isolation from her family's story, nor separately from her ethnicity, age, marital status and experience. Globalizing agribusinesses such as Santa Rosa have built their workforces on these historically entrenched inequalities and differences.

Mexican women workers – in Canada

Early in the Tomasita Project, it became clear that neither the journey of the corporate tomato nor the movement of women workers on the tomato trail followed a straight line or a simple south–north axis. When co-researcher Maria Antonieta Barrón came to Canada in the mid-1990s for a project team meeting, I introduced her to the Foreign Agricultural Resource Management Services (FARMS) programme, that has brought Jamaican workers north since 1966 and Mexican workers north since 1974 as offshore seasonal workers on Canadian farms. Building on decades of research on the migration of seasonal workers in Mexico, Barrón conducted a survey in 1997 of a sizeable sample of the 5,154 Mexican workers in Ontario on the FARMS programme, fifty-seven of whom were women (Barrón 1999: 113–26).

In the context of the asymmetries of the three NAFTA countries (with per capita income in 1995 varying from US\$2,500 in Mexico to US\$26,000 in the USA and US\$20,000 in Canada), it's not surprising these migrant workers can earn five to six times as much a day in Canada as they can in Mexico. Barrón found that a Mexican woman working in Ontario on an hourly wage earned \$82 (in Canadian dollars) for an eleven-hour work day, while her Mexican counterpart earned about \$17.64 for a thirteen- to fourteen-hour day, all the more exhausting because of the pressure to fill the baskets that determined her piecework pay.

I befriended one group of these women and visited them over a five-year period. The story of Irena, the woman who introduced this chapter, can represent this important mobile labour force that has in-creased since NAFTA but is still invisible. While most people are aware that our winter tomatoes are planted, picked and packed by Mexican workers, few realize that our local summer tomatoes are also brought to us by Mexican hands.

Irena first came to Canada in 1989 among the migrant workers who are, in her words, 'rented by the Mexican government to the Ontario government'.[5] Most of the women who come are widows like Irena, who explains: 'They only accept single mothers, widows, divorcées, but not single women or married women. They're afraid that a single woman might stay in Canada, or that a married woman might leave her husband.'

The only reason that women like Irena can consider leaving home for four months is because they have an extended family to support them. Irena lives with her elderly father and mother, who are left with childcare and domestic work. Here again, the family unit is critical for the flexibility of these women workers who make the longest journey, ironically leaving their children behind in order to provide for them. With the economic crisis of the 1990s, most Mexican families cannot survive without combining the incomes of several family members; Irena's two adult sons are also seasonal workers in the USA and Canada.

In contrast to the women working for Empaque Santa Rosa or any large agribusiness, the Mexican migrant workers in the FARMS programme work for small and medium-sized family farms. Their employers are often struggling to survive in a context where small farms are on the brink of extinction and receive minimal support. But Mexican workers like Irena are totally dependent on the Canadian farmer who requests their labour. Migrant workers dare not displease their farmer/boss, or he may not request their return the following summer. Once in Canada, the farmworkers are totally dependent on the farmer not only for transportation but also for permission to leave the premises, and they thus live almost like indentured workers. They are housed on their employers' property, may depend on them for translation, filling out forms and communications home (Wall 1992: 261–75). Such a paternalistic relationship often incorporates classist, racist and sexist behaviours.

In general, Mexican migrant workers in the FARMS programme put up with the problematic labour relations, long hours of gruelling work, social isolation and often substandard housing conditions because they know it is temporary and lucrative (Basok 1997: 5). While they receive medical insurance, a Canadian pension and are covered by the Occupational Health and Safety Act, they have not been able to unionize. There have been efforts by the United Farmworkers of America office in Canada to respond to the needs of these workers, but it remains a very difficult population to organize, particularly because of its temporary seasonal nature, language barriers and employer pressures. In late 2001, however, the Supreme Court of Canada ruled, 'agricultural workers have a constitutional right to unionize without fear of reprisals' (Makin 2001).

After eleven years of seasonal work in Canada, Irena still makes only a minimum wage, but this remains a quick way for her to amass an income, because she is 'freed' from family responsibilities for those few months, has minimal costs and can work long hours. While the contract usually stipulates eight-hour workdays at six days a week, Irena and her co-workers not only agree to overtime and longer hours, but also seek it. Since her primary reason for being in Canada is to make money, she wants to use every waking hour for that purpose. And she still considers the working conditions in Canada better than those in Mexico:

> Agricultural work is harder in Mexico. Everything is done by hand. There, for example, we have to carry two boxes on our heads, full of tomatoes. In Canada, I can leave the tomatoes I've picked along the edge of the field and a truck will pick them up. In Mexico, if it's raining, we don't have anything to protect ourselves. But in Canada, they give us everything – a raincoat, a hoe, we don't have to buy anything. In Mexico, there's no protection from the fumes when they spray pesticides on the fields. In Canada, if you work for a good patrón, there is. In my case, the patrón even does the spraying himself and doesn't require us to do it.

I wondered what difference this job makes to Irena's life back in Mexico so, in 1997, I visited her during the eight months that she spends in a village in rural Morelos. In her living room were some of the immediate benefits of her Canadian earnings, new appliances she has brought back: a TV, stereo, sewing machine and fan. Her earnings mainly go to provide housing and security for her children. But far from living in luxury on her Canadian earnings, Irena must keep working in Mexico at two jobs to support her family, and ironically, for most of the week, she must leave her children again. 'I work on weekdays in Cuernavaca [one hour away] as a live-in domestic worker, taking care of two invalids. Then I make and sell tacos in my village on Saturday and Sunday.'

I was struck by the fact that Irena's survival depends on patching together work in different parts of the food system, whether as a migrant farmworker in Canada or cooking for a middle-class Mexican family in Cuernavaca, or selling tamales on the streets of her home town. She epitomizes women's centrality to the planting, picking, packing, preparing and selling of food. And, ironically, as a marginal Mexican woman worker, all of her food-related jobs take her away from her own land and family.

Fruits of injustice and seeds of hope

One of the environmental activists advocating for the human rights of indigenous migrant workers in the Mexican fields calls the tomatoes they pick the 'fruits of injustice'. Through the Tomasita Project, we began to realize that not only have the tomatoes become increasingly commodified in the neoliberal industrialized food system, but the most marginalized workers are also commodities in this new trade game. In fact, the tomatoes – a highly perishable and delicate fruit and one of the winners for Mexico in the NAFTA reshuffle – are often treated better than the workers.

Women predominate in the lowest waged work in tomato production, particularly in planting, pruning, sorting and packing. Managers claim that women are more skilled at intricate tasks (the famous 'nimble fingers' mantra) and are more efficient, productive and responsible than men. The vice-president of production at Empaque Santa Rosa reinforces this gender ideology: 'In selection, care, and handling, women are more delicate. They put up with more than men in all aspects: the routine, the monotony. Men are more restless, and won't put up with it.'[6] But these 'explanations' don't recognize the social construction of these gendered tasks. They also deny the women their own agency, or any recognition that they 'put up with' exploitative conditions out of necessity, sacrifice and a commitment to feed their families.

As has been clear in the stories above, these gendered roles are also mediated by differences in class and ethnicity, age and family status, tasks within the production process, and north–south asymmetries. The interlocking dimensions of power are even more complex than I was able to reveal here and are constantly changing. The women whose complex identities have been only glimpsed through this short essay also have multiple ways of responding to and resisting the conditions of their work in the tomato chain. As individuals, they create multiple strategies for survival on a daily basis. And there are groups in both the Mexican and Canadian contexts that advocate for their human rights and improved working conditions, ranging from unions in Ontario to community-based environmental and health organizations in rural Mexico, from Canadian networks acting in solidarity with *maquiladora* workers to transnational networks fighting pesticide use.[7] These stories are worthy of another chapter – within these struggles lie seeds of hope.

Notes

An earlier version of this article appeared in 'Women, Globalization and Trade', *Canadian Woman Studies*, 21/22 (4/1), Spring/Summer 2002. It draws heavily on research synthesized in Barndt (2002).

1. I borrowed the idea from a popular education story about 'Tomasito

the Tomato', but changed the name to 'Tomasita' to represent both Mexican workers and women workers as the most marginalized in the NAFTA food chain.

2. The stories of women in three different sectors – the agribusiness workers as well as Canadian supermarket cashiers and fast-food workers are featured in my book, *Tangled Routes* (2002).

3. Besides those referred to explicitly in this essay, feminist theorists I have drawn upon include Dorothy Smith (1987), Isabella Bakker (1996), Swasti Mitter (1986), Kathy Kopinak (1997), Ellie Perkins (1997), Patricia Hill Collins (2000), Donna Haraway (1991), Carolyn Sachs (1996), Rosi Braidotti et al. (1994), Vandana Shiva (1994), Bina Agarwal (1991), Cate Sandilands (1999), Egla Martinez-Salazar (1999) and Jaqui Alexander and Chandra Mohanty (1997).

4. Male work activities involve more physical strength such as carrying boxes and packing them into skids, but the issue of what skills are valued in the packing plant and the differential wage level is still to be challenged.

5. Irena's story is offered in more detail in Chapter 5 of my book, *Tangled Routes* (2002: 159–64). The quotes in this section are from interviews with Irena I carried out in 1997 in Ontario and Mexico, and in 2001 in Toronto.

6. Interview with vice-president of production, Empaque Santa Rosa, Guadalajara, Jalisco, 6 December 1996.

7. Chapter 8 of my book *Tangled Routes*, 'Cracks in the Corporate Tomato: Signs of Hope', offers stories of resistance from both Mexico and Canada, occurring at four levels: individual responses, local/global education, organized collective actions and transnational coalitional initiatives.

4 | Conservation or privatization? Biodiversity, the global market and the Mesoamerican Biological Corridor

LAURA CARLSEN

§   WITH the globalization of trade and capital, biodiversity has acquired a monetary value never before imagined. Transnational corporations in extractive industries, pharmaceuticals, biotechnology and energy, have fixed their sights on the remaining forests and 'biological hotspots' of the world, and are developing unprecedented ways to integrate these into the global market. Spurred by technological advances that revalue natural resources – from mushrooms to microorganisms – and environmental crisis in developed countries, corporations have joined forces with large conservation organizations to preserve areas of biodiversity in the third world while guaranteeing access to foreign investment. Corporate conservationism has proved to be an effective way to channel funds into conservation efforts. But this chapter argues that it harbours long-term perils for conservation and the equitable use of planetary resources. Above all, the strategy essentially leaves the wolf to guard the sheep.

This chapter begins with an analysis of the aims and efforts of conservationist organizations and identifies three perspectives on conservation that can be characterized as 'pure' conservation, corporate conservation and anti-conservation. The first section defines a trend towards conservationist–corporate alliances, based primarily on the interests of the latter. Here, the redefined market value of biodiversity in the global system is analysed, along with the growing alliances of multilateral organizations (World Bank, Inter-American Development Bank), international conservation groups and transnational corporations. The underlying argument is that the aim of these efforts is not conservationist in the traditional sense but the protection of *long-term, unrestricted access* for capital to natural areas and resources. This strategy repeatedly pits the conservationst–corporate alliances against the interests of local communities and regionally controlled sustainable activities.

The second section analyses the Mesoamerican Biological Corridor (MBC), a prototype of the 'new corporate conservation', designed to serve as a case study in the integration of biodiversity in the world market. The Corridor exemplifies many of the new forms of integration that are currently being developed by supranational programmes under the guise of conservation.

The MBC overlaps both geographically and organizationally with the more recent Plan Puebla-Panamá (PPP), and was its precursor. The Plan Puebla-Panamá is a regional policy instrument specifically designed to attract foreign investment, link the region with major international trade centres and facilitate transcontinental commerce. As such, the rapid absorption of the conservation-oriented MBC into the integration-oriented PPP reveals the central role given to international capital in biodiversity exploitation and management.

Finally, the third section outlines an alternative model of long-term biodiversity management – the peasant/indigenous stewardship model. Like the corporate conservation model, the stewardship paradigm also takes for granted the central *social* role of human societies in nature conservation. As opposed to the privatization practices of the corporate conservationists, however, the projects developed by small-scale farmers and indigenous organizations emphasize collective land and resource use, non-market incentives to conservation, local control and the indivisibility of cultural and biological diversity.

Conservationist thought and the birth of corporate conservation

Perspectives on conservation can be broken down into three models: 'pure' conservation, corporate conservation and anti-conservation. In recent years the lines between the three have blurred and hybrids have grown up that require close analysis.

Pure conservation

The first conservationists worked from the premise that nature had an intrinsic value to human life, primarily spiritual (Muir 1901). The goal of early conservationists in developed countries was to preserve nature for nature's sake – to maintain wilderness areas in a pristine state and protect animal and plant species in their natural habitat. Exploitation – particularly the extractive, polluting and despoiling ways of 'industrial society' – was viewed as the nemesis of conservationists. Conservation of nature represented the opportunity to maintain refuges from urbanization and industrialization, and to draw limits to the exploitation of resources and land.

Today, both biological and political theories emphasize the interconnectedness and intercausality of the globalized planet. In *The Risk Society* (1992), U. Beck states: 'Nature can no longer be thought of without society and society can no longer be thought of without nature' (cited in Toledo 2000: 18). The view that nature is outside of, or counterposed to, human society has become obsolete, both in the sense of those who viewed it as a refuge and those who saw it as an inert tool of progress.

As a result, nature management approaches now aim to balance use with conservation, and social with environmental factors. Conservation organizations have moved towards sustainable *management* of biodiversity, using a broad range of definitions of why and how to do that. Parks and reserves are now conceptualized in terms of multiple-use schemes that protect vital areas while allowing productive activities on large tracts.

Anti-conservation

At the other extreme, and explicitly anti-conservationist, are most corporations and pro-business interests. Although forced by regulations and public pressure to modify environmentally destructive practices in recent years, the historic and contemporary position of business has been to defend the bottom line. Typically, the arguments employed to resist environmental measures include citing responsibilities to shareholders to maximize profits, and questioning scientific data on environmental damage. An important example of the latter is the refusal of the major oil companies and the Bush administration to accept scientific data on global warming (see <www.greenpeace.org>).

Conservationists have routinely faced off with corporate interests that argue for unrestricted access to natural resources for development purposes and defend the business imperative to pollute. Environmental groups have often sued corporations and acted as gadflies for closer government regulation. However, a new trend is changing the traditional animosity between the two causes. Lately, heavily funded partnerships between large conservation organizations and transnational corporations are making bedfellows of former adversaries. This third school may be called *corporate conservation*.

Corporate conservation

Paradoxically, corporate conservation seeks to combine conservationist goals of preserving nature with the anti-conservationist defence of exploiting its riches. The underlying logic of this movement is unabashedly market-based. It hinges on four modern developments: the world ecological crisis, the need to expand markets, the growing importance of the corporate image and the new-found wealth in biodiversity.

The first rationale is well expressed in a report penned jointly by the World Resources Institute, UN Environment Programme and World Business Council for Sustainable Development: 'The world economy depends on a base of natural resources – our "natural capital" – that is showing signs of severe degradation. Without improved environmental performance, future business operations will be exposed to risks of rising prices for water, materials, and for waste disposal' (Doering et al. 2002). The report goes on to advise, 'the private sector has an interest – and an economic opportunity – in managing the natural capital portfolio wisely. Many of the goods and services supplied by ecosystems cannot be replaced at any reasonable price' (Shell Foundation 2003). Based on this analysis, corporations have begun to do long-range planning that includes assuring access to 'natural capital'. Corporate conservation projects oriented towards preserving planetary resources vital to industry and avoiding pressures to curb pollution and consumption patterns in developed countries include watershed protection, forest fire prevention and carbon sinks.

Closely related to this problem is the contradiction between the rapid depletion of resources and the need to expand markets, particularly as markets in developed countries become less elastic. Corporate conservation plans for biodiversity management imply integrating biodiversity-rich regions into the global market, breaking down traditional systems of subsistence farming, changing the consumer patterns of inhabitants and compelling local populations to migrate to cities – all of which increase the consumption of transnational products. Moreover, an important aim of bioprospecting activities is to develop new sources of energy and materials that may be successfully marketed to sustain growing demand.

Contaminating and image-sensitive industries have reasoned that alliances with name-brand conservation organizations can increase consumer acceptance. Through conservationist–corporate partnerships, corporations have calculated they can, in the words of the World Wildlife Fund (WWF) Business Partners Programme 'highlight support for nature conservation – a strategic marketing advantage for today's increasingly environmentally aware consumer audience' (<www.wwf.org>). In this logo-oriented world, the WWF offers use of its well-known panda logo to corporate partners. Starbucks has also launched a well publicized and brand-identified conservation coffee initiative in the Mexican Biosphere Reserve 'El Triunfo', in part to ward off an international protest campaign aimed at its corporate practices.

Finally, corporate interest in biodiversity management stems from the riches to be found there. Genetic engineering, biotechnology and systems of geographic information have redefined comparative advantages and redirected investment in bio-rich areas. Biotechnology has created the possibility of developing lucrative new products from biological materials, and global patent laws have enabled exclusive-use patenting not only of the products themselves, but also of their natural components.[1] Bioprospecting, along with ecotourism and tree plantations, can be extremely lucrative activities that appear on the surface to be environmentally friendly but entail severe environmental risks; all have been integrated into the corporate conservation model of biodiversity management.

Vanguards in the field of corporate conservation include Conservation International (CI), along with its Center for Environmental Leadership in Business with the Ford Motor Company; the World Resources Institute; the Nature Conservancy; the World Wildlife Fund; Wildlife Conservation Society and the World Conservation Union (IUCN). All are grouped in the Conservation Finance Alliance, which channels millions of dollars annually into biodiversity management. The 'conservation economy', comprised of funds from governments, multilateral development banks and conservation groups, is estimated at over half a billion dollars a year for biodiversity conservation in the tropics alone (Hardner and Rice 2002).

Conservationist–corporate alliances employ various strategies of bio-diversity management, including: (i) *land trusts,* the outright purchase of lands rich in biological resources for conservation purposes;[2] (ii) *conservation concessions,* a CI plan to pay local residents for conservation; and (iii) *direct administration,* a model in which the national government grants conservationist–corporate alliances management rights to bio-diversity areas.[3]

The critique of corporate conservation

The first question to be asked in designing conservation measures is: what is the nature of the threat? Under the corporate conservation model, the same transnational corporations that have intensified unsustainable and irresponsible resource-use are cast in the role of protecting them. For example, in the Center for Environmental Leadership in Business, Shell Oil co-led the working group charged with 'sensitive siting', at the same time as it was locked in a battle with U'wa Indians to exploit oil reserves on their lands in the Colombian Andes. The oil companies who fought the Kyoto Protocol to limit carbon dioxide emissions promote carbon sequestration programmes as a financial incentive to forest conservation, thus saving trees in the jungle in order to pollute air in the cities. In Mexico, the state-owned petroleum company, Pemex, inaugurated a conservation and environmental education project in the Centla Biosphere Reserve in Tabasco with the stated objective of 'making industrial development and environmental conservation compatible' (Pemex 2000). Pemex has been polluting agricultural lands and rivers in the region since 1952. According to local environmentalists, the programme – undertaken with the Environmental Ministry and the conservation organization Espacios Naturales y Desarrollo Sustentable – undermines Pemex's legal responsibility to pay for environmental damage by substituting voluntary conservation programmes for full compliance with indemnity and regulatory obligations.

Corporate conservation programmes seek to integrate bio-rich zones into the global market and relocate their management to precisely the same international forces charged with imposing the global market system. After years of experience with economic integration, such plans send up red flags in developing countries. Regional grassroots organizations and researchers have developed the following criticisms of the corporate conservation model:

- *The myth of market-based instruments.* The business logic imposed under this model argues that in a globalized commodity economy the most effective way to ensure biodiversity conservation is to assign it a market value. New forms of biodiversity integration emphasize developing market-based instruments to 'alter private costs and benefits so that any unaccounted social costs and benefits can be internalized to ensure the desired environmental improvement' (Cunningham and Young 2001: 7). These include pollution charges, tradable permits, market barrier reductions and economic incentives. Market-based instruments have become the axis of World Bank programmes, but researchers note that, when applied to biodiversity, 'market failure is pervasive, and results (inter alia) from externalities, the complete absence of markets for some aspects of biodiversity, and inadequately or incompletely defined property rights' (ibid.: 7).
- *Externalities.* The costs and benefits not taken into account in pricing goods and services include most social and environmental impacts of economic activities. In the Mesoamerican region, market-based instruments constitute a threat to agriculture-based indigenous and peasant cultures founded on communal subsistence farming, collectivity and territorial rootedness because they ignore the role they play in social and environmental protection. How does the market price culture? Economists do not have an answer and rarely even ask the question. Costs of market integration pertaining to loss of livelihood, chemical use, loss of agro-biodiversity and cultural genocide remain outside market equations. There is virtually no precedent for internalizing these in market assessments of natural resource use; indeed, such a process would collide with international market rules codified in the World Trade Organization and Free Trade Agreements.
- *Suspect multilateral actors.* The World Bank (WB) has been senior partner in the start-up of corporate conservation programmes. But WB structural adjustment, trade liberalization and austerity programmes have in the past brought many local ecosystems to their knees. Directly or indirectly, top-down policies have expelled indigenous populations and peasants from their lands and destroyed biodiversity through programmes such as the green revolution and hydroelectric dam construction (GRAIN 1996). The social and

environmental damage caused in Mesoamerican countries has led many developing countries to view current World Bank projects under the auspices of the Biological Corridor with a jaundiced eye – if not outright distrust.

- *The use of environmental information.* Corporate conservation activities rely heavily on the use of satellite mapping, geographical information systems, animal and plant inventories, traditional knowledge interviews and other sophisticated methods of gathering data on natural and biological resources. While these serve to indicate where conservation efforts should be concentrated, they also subsidize business by applying government and NGO funds to locate and identify natural resources.

- *Loss of local control over land-use decisions.* Corporate conservation management of biodiversity removes land-use decisions from local communities and national governments. In the conservation concession plan proposed by Conservation International, for example, communities lease out not only natural resource use (or non-use) but land-use rights. They thereby forfeit decision-making power over local economic activities and resource use. Communities also lose long-term rights over their own ecosystems and traditional knowledge through bioprospecting agreements and water and land-use decisions made beyond their reach.

- *The danger of delinking biodiversity programmes from sustainable development goals.* Most conservation mechanisms proposed under the corporate conservation model seem to have given up on regional sustainable development. Market-based instruments often imply one-time or short-term payments, and environmental service agreements that hand over control of resources to corporate–conservationist alliances reduce productive farmers to poorly paid employees. For example, the 'stimulation' of economic development in the form of conservation payments under the conservation concession plan (Hardner and Rice 2002) is just that; although it provides income, the plan amounts to little more than an environmental welfare payment.

- *Sovereignty.* Issues of sovereignty are raised in all the corporate conservation mechanisms, since biodiversity management passes from local and national control to transnationals, international conservation groups and multilateral organisms. Land purchases that place biodiversity ownership in the hands of foreign organizations, and land-use plans that emphasize biodiversity access and extra-national decision-making replace national and local policy. The voluntarist efforts of the transnationals seek to head off public pressure for greater national and international regulation of their activities, particularly in third world supplier countries. At the same time, World Trade Organization (WTO) and Free Trade Agreement (FTA) rules have been hacking away at governments' rights to enforce environmental regulations in cases of transnational investment, formally perceiving these as trade violations or expropriations of investment (Bejarano 2003).

- *Cultural diversity.* Studies by Conservation International and WWF show that of twenty-three biodiversity areas in the world, nine are also culturally diverse and of 233 ecoregions, indigenous communities inhabit 80 per cent. In Mexico, Indian peoples inhabit 60 per cent of priority areas for conservation in central and southern Mexico (Toledo 2000: 52). New models tend towards expulsion of local populations and the erosion of traditional collective organization. Where communities of endangered indigenous groups are expelled by force or by changes in land-use, the result can be genocide. Moreover, these populations are often a critical component of conservation efforts.

- *More consumption equals less conservation.* There is a fundamental contradiction between corporations' stated needs to broaden markets and world conservation objectives. The Shell Foundation defines a main focus of its Sustainable Energy Programme as 'the fact that 2 billion people living in poverty in developing countries lack access to the energy services which they need to improve the quality of their life and secure a sustainable livelihood' (Shell Foundation 2003). Currently, the USA with 4.73 per cent of the world's population has 22 per cent of the world's 'consuming population', while Mexico with 1.68 per cent of the world's population accounts for only 1.38 per cent (Toledo 2000: 239). While increasing access may be good for Shell Oil, to attempt to replicate US consumption patterns in developing countries would be a disaster on a planetary scale.

Although frequently presented as 'the role of corporations in the conservation agenda', the projects contemplated among the myriad corporate-funded conservation projects demonstrate the reverse: the increasing role of conservation or, more precisely, biodiversity management, in the corporate agenda. On close analysis, these programmes serve fundamentally to conserve long-term access to resources, promote the penetration of transnational interests in areas of rich biodiversity and expand markets.

The Mesoamerican Biological Corridor

The pilot project for the new insertion of biodiversity in the global market is the Mesoamerican Biological Corridor (MBC). Mexico and the Central American countries of the Great American isthmus share a land area that is geologically unique. Scientists calculate that some 60 million years ago two continents met and formed the isthmus, and that this confluence between the neoartic and neotropic plates produced unique unprecedented processes in the evolution of species (TVE Earth Report 2000). As a result, although the region accounts for only 0.51 per cent of the earth's land surface, it hosts over 8 per cent of world biodiversity. According to the MBC project of the United Nations Development Programme, the area defined as Mesoamerica covers half a million square kilometres and is host to 20,000 plant species.

Despite its wealth of biological resources, recent data on environmental deterioration indicate serious risks of extinction and biodiversity loss in the region. An estimated 44 hectares of forest are lost every hour, for a total of nearly 400,000 a year. At least forty-two species of mammals, thirty-one species of birds and 1,541 species of superior plant life are in danger of extinction (<www.undp.org.ni/cbm>). The loss of biodiversity and the fragmentation of habitat that has resulted from human activity have direct, long-term implications: on the sustainability of the region's natural resources; on the conservation of local, regional and global biodiversity; and on the quality of life of the inhabitants.

The Mesoamerican Biological Corridor was designed to protect one of the richest areas of biodiversity in the world. The MBC resulted from several previous studies, beginning in 1992 and including the Paseo Pantera project, carried out in 1994 by Wildlife Conservation, Caribbean Conservation and USAID; and a joint project of the Central American Commission on Environment and Development (CCAD) and the Central American Council on Protected Areas (CCAP) to design a Central American Biological Corridor, which was subsequently approved in the presidential XIX Summit meeting in 1996. Later, south-eastern Mexico was included and the project was launched as the Mesoamerican Biological Corridor on 11 April 2000 in Managua.

The MBC currently covers the seven Central American nations (Guatemala, Honduras, Belize, El Salvador, Nicaragua, Costa Rica and Panama) and four states of south-east Mexico (Yucatán, Campeche, Quintana Roo and Chiapas). Additional plans are expected to incorporate sub-corridors in the state of Tabasco (Boshier et al. 1999) and biodiversity 'hotspots' in Oaxaca (Los Chimalapas and Lower Mixe) (Delgado and Carlo 2002). A biodiversity hotspot is an area of extraordinary biological diversity; Conservation International and other conservation organizations have adopted the strategy of prioritizing hotspots for mapping and protection.

The Mesoamerican Biological Corridor is defined as a system of territorial ordering composed of natural areas under regimens of special administration. This includes core zones where natural resources are under strict protection, buffer zones where development and exploitation of resources will be permitted more broadly, multiple-use zones where different types of resources are used and organized and consolidated areas of interconnection. The main biological justification for the corridor is to connect Natural Protected Areas, and link these with other important fragments of forest in a multiple-use 'mosaic' (World Bank 2000b). The Corridor seeks to meet three ecological objectives: to (i) assure connectivity, (ii) conserve the biodiversity, or 'bio-quality' of the region, and (iii) improve the environment (Boshier et al. 1999).

The concept of a corridor was born of the theory of the 'biogeography of islands'. The theory posits that conserving isolated 'fragments' of biodiversity in reserves surrounded by environmentally threatening or degrading practices cannot guarantee the conservation of flora and fauna, and that connecting these generates a higher conservation value (Wilson and Willis 1975). Connectivity seeks to assure individual and species gene flow and ecological processes among the different reserves and spots of biodiversity, and protect sufficient habitat to maintain a stable population and migratory routes for threatened species. The corridor also seeks to preserve 'bio-quality' (biodiversity based on the rarity of endemic species) and to improve the environment through efforts to prevent forest fires, minimize erosion, protect water flows and buffer reserves (Boshier et al. 1999).

It is impossible to understand the complex plans and overlapping programmes of the MBC exclusively through conservationist goals, since the objectives go far beyond the environmental realm. In biological terms, the Mesoamerican region is host to an enormous variety of ecological conditions and territories that fall under all kinds of land-use patterns and are subject to a plethora of national, state and local policies. This diversity has led some scientists to question whether a biological corridor of these dimensions makes any sense at all and, indeed, the environmental projects of the MBC operate based on a set of national sub-corridors. In reality, the unifying principle of the MBC is not fundamentally conservationist, but is the development of a new model of economic integration for the region, and the need to attract international financing to carry it out.

Biodiversity and economic integration

The MBC defines a new form of insertion in the global market for a region that has been at once the bane and the promise of plans to impose a Free Trade Area of the Americas. Located at the hub of cross-continental trade flows, it has always been a particularly conflictive region – rich in natural resources and poor in the quality of life of its inhabitants, looted by foreign interests and shaken by homegrown rebellions. Throughout history, the geopolitical location of the American isthmus has provoked great interest in the modern world due to the possibilities of building interoceanic and intercontinental corridors. With globalization and the consequent increase in the transit of commodities, the isthmus takes on renewed importance as a nodal point in the world of economic integration (Barreda 2001: 166–85).

The programme set forth in the MBC also comes at a time when natural areas take on a planetary value, and – through bioprospecting and environmental services – capital begins to put a price tag on biodiversity. In this context, the proposal of the Biological Corridor addresses the challenge to capital of conserving the ecological value of the region while deepening its economic integration.

The identification of over 20 million hectares of territory that make up the MBC as a single entity for planning and external financing initiates a new style of intervention in the region. The project proposes to construct a 'new integral model' that serves to attract international investment, in the first phase from the public sector and in the second phase from the private sector. The various projects propose the creation of a *'shop window* to sell the concept of the biological corridor to decision-makers' (Boshier et al. 1999) and 'an investment vector' and 'a main integrator of the development priorities and environmental agendas of the whole region', according to the CCAD.

Up to now the strategy has been quite successful – millions of dollars committed from non-governmental organizations (WWF, Nature Conservancy, World Resources Institute, Fauna and Flora International, Conservation International, World Conservation Union [UICN]), multilateral organizations (World Bank, United Nations Development Fund, Global Environment Fund [GEF], Inter-American Development Bank) and governmental agencies (the Netherlands, Germany, USAID, and the environmental ministries of the Central American countries and Mexico). NASA, the US space agency, participates in a $12 million project to satellite map the natural resources and land-use patterns in the entire region.

Based on the strategy of private-sector involvement and market-based instruments defined by multilateral organizations and the corporate–conservationist alliance, mega-diverse regions of Mesoamerica are now seen as business opportunities in three senses: (i) to compensate for rampant processes of environmental contamination and deterioration in the developed world; (ii) to preserve *in situ* species or genotypes that can be privatized, patented and marketed in pharmaceutical, cosmetic or food products; and (iii) as the main attraction in the creation of a new service economy for the region. Economic activities that correspond to these forms are, respectively: payment for environmental services, bioprospecting and ecotourism. All three have caused debate within the countries of the Corridor.

Environmental services

Environmental services are activities that conserve or improve environmental protection, particularly watershed protection and carbon sequestration. The concept of 'carbon sinks' was pushed by the United States government as a way to avoid CO_2 emissions controls through compensatory mechanisms, before George W. Bush decided not to sign the Kyoto Protocol at all (US State Department 2000). In short, a community or organization 'sells' the capacity for carbon fixing of its lands to an entity of a developed country to compensate for excessive CO_2 emissions. The community promises to conserve forests and/or reforest, while the corporation or nation buys the right to pollute above internationally mandated limits. A study of PROARCA/CAPAS estimates that the Mesoamerican Biological Corridor has 5,721 million tons of carbon dioxide stored and the capacity to store 32 million tons of carbon dioxide a year if parts were reforested (CAPAS 2000). Critics of this scheme warn that the arrangement offers a 'licence to pollute' to those responsible for emissions in other parts of the world, since the scheme makes calculations on a 'business-as-usual' basis with no incentives for emissions reduction. In most cases, the sums paid to communities for the service are very low.

Bioprospecting

Although it constitutes a minor part of actual conservation financing, bioprospecting has gained wide attention because it represents the epitome of schemes to privatize biodiversity and traditional knowledge of the indigenous communities charged with the conservation and sustainable use of these resources. The patents give their owners exclusive property and marketing rights over the use, research and development of collected genetic materials. The social component of the MBC lists bioprospecting among 'viable environmental services/products' to permit the biodiversity management programme to 'achieve financial sustainability in the medium term' (World Bank n.d.). A recent study of bioprospecting contracts in Mexico concludes that they have caused disintegration and division in indigenous communities (only some receive payment for shared traditional knowledge and biological materials, some oppose the concept), little benefit sharing and inadequate consultation among local populations and the public. The activity also lacks a clear legal framework in Mexico (Barreda 2003). Moreover, the motor behind bioprospecting is the possibility of marketing biotech and genetically modified (GM) products. GM crops threaten local varieties, displace local producers and entail unknown environmental impacts. To employ an industry that threatens agro-biodiversity as a market incentive to protect biodiversity is a contradiction in terms.

Ecotourism

Ecotourism in theory provides tourist services with low environmental impact in areas of natural attractions. With integral planning of the social, environmental and economic factors, ecotourism offers a sustainable source of income to communities in protected areas. Problems occur with the privatization of lands considered national heritage areas and changes in land-use from agriculture to services. Development often leads to enclave economies where luxury hotels rise amid slums for employees that lack adequate infrastructure to assure minimum living conditions and ecological equilibrium. When planning omits local input, the ecological component is often diluted and local residents and the protection of ecological resources that do not generate income are considered dispensable.

The MBC and the Plan Puebla-Panamá

The Mesoamerican Biological Corridor established the paradigm that later would be used to develop the Plan Puebla-Panamá. First, it traced the geographic area (with the addition of Puebla, Guerrero, Oaxaca, Veracruz and Tabasco in southern Mexico) as the new target for investment. Second, it established new modalities for the exploitation of the biodiversity and natural resources.

Among the objectives declared in the presentation of the MBC programme in April of 2000 is 'to establish a new way of understanding environmental protection, integrating conservation and an increase in economic competitiveness' (Castro Salazar 2000). This objective coincides with the logic of the Plan Puebla-Panamá (PPP) announced in 2001. The base document for the PPP proclaims the motive of 'carrying out strategic investments in infrastructure that allow the region more connections and take advantage of the potentials inscribed in Free Trade Agreements ... utilizing its comparative advantages' (Presidencia 2002). It emphasizes the capacity to increase foreign trade and export-oriented production.

The PPP includes plans to build and improve infrastructure in roads and railways, development of industrial corridors and the new use of biodiversity. MBC conservation activities are absorbed in the PPP as its sustainable development component (IDB 2001).

The relationship between the MBC and the Plan Puebla-Panamá raises questions. Although the PPP contains reference to some 'projects for sustainable development', the latter is not among its primary objectives, nor an organizing principle of the plan itself. As discussed below, analysis of the projects proposed within the PPP indicate that many have negative environmental impact.

The overlap between the MBC and PPP subsumes conservation goals under economic integration programmes. The promotion of tree plantations in the MBC area illustrates the point. The monoculture of rapid-growth tree species (eucalyptus, Caribbean pine, African palm and so on) for paper production and derived products requires huge land surfaces and high chemical inputs to guarantee maximum profit. In the evaluation of use values for conservation and sustainability, tree plantations receive a zero on a scale of one to ten in biodiversity, and a zero in their ability to resist invasions of non-endemic (non-native) species (since they are themselves non-endemic species). Currently, large biotechnology companies are working to develop genetically modified rapid-growth species, which would increase the risk to biodiversity. Deterioration and pollution of soil, toxic wastes related to paper processing, and the expulsion of peasant communities are some of the consequences of this economic activity.

In spite of their environmental risks, plans for the MBC frequently refer to 'reforestation programmes' based on planting tree plantations that would serve to connect Protected Areas within the Corridor. The PPP considers the plantations exemplary investments because they imply conversion of land-use from subsistence agriculture to production for export, offer opportunities for foreign investment and supply the growing market for packing materials – all transformations that support the form of economic integration planned for the region. Tree plantations that already cover thousands of acres and several countries, including Mexico, actively promote further extension.

The missing social factor

On 29 July 1996, the Indigenous Peasant and Afro-American Coalition of Community Agro-Forestry (CICAFOC), an organization of over fifty Central American peasant and indigenous groups, wrote a letter to the directors of the Mesoamerican Biological Corridor: 'It would seem that this project is designed to strengthen conservationist organizations that many times forget that there are people who live in the territories that the Corridor passes through' (CICAFOC 1996). After consulting among affected populations, in 1998 the group proposed the creation of an Indigenous and Campesina Corridor as part of the Biological Corridor. In the words of the president, Alberto Chinchilla, the idea was to create 'living spaces balanced between human beings and other species of nature'.

The plan to include indigenous populations in the international megaproject of the MBC faced much resistance, and it was not until 1999 that organizers agreed to develop a 'social component'. The decision responded both to the pressure of groups living within the Corridor and from new theories based on a more integrated vision of biological corridors. In recent years, biologists and botanists have modified the basic concept of 'islands' by recognizing that the goal is not to protect 'pure' nature from contaminated (and contaminating) human beings, but to conserve biodiversity 'within a mosaic of land uses and habitats modified by human activities' (Boshier et al. 1999).

Even so, the role of local communities in planning and implementation has been limited. The MBC and Plan Puebla-Panamá have mobilized protest in many communities and regional organizations that view the plans as anathema to their own agendas for democratization, sustainable development, indigenous autonomy and cultural diversity. The top-down planning imposed by the MBC-PPP shifts the fulcrum of power in the region, leaving communities and organizations with less leverage in decision-making that affects land-use on their own lands. In most Mesoamerican countries, Indian peoples and peasants have had few opportunities to influence local, state and national policy and the ambitious projects of the Corridor set forth by international agencies and organizations further distance them from this possibility. The 'social component' that proposes the integration of communities came as an appendix to the Corridor project, and essentially proposes involving peoples in 'implementation and monitoring of the project', but not in the previous phases of planning and design.

Thirty million people live within the MBC, including approximately 6 million Indian peoples. To make decisions on land-use within the MBC without the determinant participation of Indian peoples not only tramples local rights but violates dictums of self-determination codified in international law, specifically, Convention 169 of the ILO. However, Mexico and the Central American countries involved lack adequate legal frameworks for the full recognition of the autonomy and collective rights of Indian peoples. The Mexican legislature recently passed a constitutional reform on indigenous rights and culture that dashed hopes of achieving real autonomy. The reform violates the terms of the San Andrés Agreements, signed between the federal government and the Zapatista Army for National Liberation in 1996, and Convention 169, ratified by Mexico. The new law denies collective rights by recognizing indigenous peoples as 'subjects of public interest' rather than public rights. It also stipulates the 'preferential use' of natural resources in the lands inhabited by communities, rather than collective access to indigenous territories (Carlsen 2002). The lack of an effective legal framework for Indian self-government, collective rights and property rights in biodiversity areas weakens their participation and strengthens the corporate conservation model of privatization and integration.

The resulting insecurity in land tenure and use for indigenous peoples undermines biodiversity conservation. As discussed below, the legal recognition of collective ownership and stewardship is basic to an alternative model. In the words of the Nurio Declaration of the National Indigenous Congress of Mexico:

> We demand the constitutional recognition of our ancestral territories and lands that represent the totality of our habitat in which we reproduce our material and spiritual existence as peoples, to conserve them integrally and maintain the communal tenure of our lands. Only thus is it possible to preserve our social cohesion, conserve the forms of unpaid collective labour in benefit of the entire community and assure the patrimony and the future of the next generations. (<www.foodforchiapas.net/History/cni/cnideclaration.html>)

An alternative model of indigenous/peasant stewardship

International coordination should be an important factor in protecting and managing biodiversity. In the area marked by the Mesoamerican Biological Corridor there is a real need for supporting projects that conserve biological and cultural diversity. But the answer to sustainable development in regions of mega-biodiversity cannot be conservation without people, nor biodiversity exploitation *à la* PPP. A viable alternative emerging from recent studies and grassroots movements is the native stewardship model.

This model does not reject all linkages between biodiversity areas and the global market, nor does it propose that transnational activity be barred from areas of high biodiversity. Some local communities have succeeded in retaining control over resource management while working with global partners in global markets. Shade-grown and organic coffee producing are examples of sustainable economic activity, linked to the international market, and with deep roots in the traditional cultures and the grassroots organization of indigenous and peasant communities. Shade-grown coffee is considered a good buffer for Natural Protected Areas by small growers, ecologists and economists alike (North American CEC 1999). Shade-grown coffee conserves biodiversity by maintaining both the tree cover and the undergrowth of family farm products and native plants that sustains indigenous families and preserves endemic biodiversity. The trees help assure bird migrations in the region. And culturally, although coffee is not a native plant it has become an integral part of the indigenous culture and a main source of livelihood. The native stewardship model reorients decision-making and biodiversity management from corporate–conservationist alliances to local communities, while at the same time granting a stronger role to national regulation.

The stewardship model factors in the people. The study of ethno-ecology has contributed important changes to conservation models and biodiversity management that are only now beginning to reach the sphere of public policy. Foremost among these is the recognition that human activities in areas of high cultural and biological diversity are often conducive and not hostile to conservation (Toledo 2000: 52). Indigenous peoples have made huge contributions to conservation and agricultural diversity through traditional sustainable practices adapted to local ecosystems, the preservation and development of native varieties of food crops and the conservation of natural sites with significance for spiritual practices. Toledo notes that research over the past three decades suggests 'the world's biodiversity will be effectively preserved only with the protection of the diversity of human cultures and vice versa' (World Bank n.d.).

Current legal frameworks for conservation may not be the best way to ensure sustainable development alongside conservation. The transformation of an area rich in biodiversity from indigenous communities to a Natural Protected Area under federal government control has often been a government tactic to break community resistance to privatization. Often, lands that are under the jurisdiction of dollar-hungry neoliberal governments, such as Mexico's, are more open to foreign investment than lands under the jurisdiction of Indian peoples or peasant communities that have agricultural, cultural and spiritual concerns. Various alternatives have been proposed, such as the creation of a peasant ecological reserve in the Chimalapas, a biodiversity hotspot on the Chiapas–Oaxaca border under direct control of the local communities.

Corporate–conservationist alliances have used Natural Protected Areas as excuses to remove local populations opposed to their activities. Such is the case in Montes Azules, in the Lacandon jungle of Chiapas. There, Conservation International, Espacios Naturales and other conservation organizations signed a declaration calling on the government to expel communities located within the perimeters of the reserve. The corporate conservation alliance working in the Lacandon includes Grupo Pulsar, a Mexican transnational with a huge biotech arm. Due to its high biodiversity, the area offers enticing opportunities for bioprospecting. The thirty to fifty mostly indigenous communities – including Zapatista-base communities – deny being the source of biodiversity losses and cite counter-insurgency and corporate interests as the motive behind expulsion and increased military presence. The threat of forced relocation has turned the already volatile area into a tinderbox.

Non-corporate conservationists have noted that involving local communities tends to be the most efficient way to conserve biodiversity. The Environmental Defense Fund working in the Brazilian Amazon found that tropical forest is better protected in Indian areas than in the conservation units, since the Brazilian government has only one guard for every 6,000 square kilometres. Governments could use the shared interest of native and peasant communities in curbing illegal exploitation (from which they receive little or no benefits) to redirect use patterns to small-scale sustainable activities.

For local populations to regain a central role in biodiversity management, prerequisites include strengthening indigenous autonomy and collective land rights, resolving agrarian conflicts, supporting integral regional development plans and providing training and support for community-run sustainable agriculture programmes.

The stewardship model returns to an emphasis on sustainable development as the only long-term solution to conservation needs. It urges support for the peasant economy, in the form of appropriate technology packages, training in organic production, the reconstruction and articulation of local and regional markets, gender equity and recognition of the value of production for consumption. The objective is not to preserve the situation as is but to defend and transform the peasant economy in the context of globalization. The Mesoamerican Peasant Conference in May 2002 reached consensus on some necessary conditions for strengthening the regional peasant economy: exempting agriculture from WTO regulations and any Free Trade Agreement of the Americas; declaring land, water, forests, biodiversity and traditional knowledge as collective goods and the heritage of humanity; rejecting privatization of biodiversity; and in favour of national food sovereignty (A. Bartra 2002).

The stewardship model vindicates and revises the role of the state. Whereas the corporate conservation model pushes the state out of the picture, the stewardship model of conservation requires federal, state and local policies to support it. The premise is that biological and cultural diversity form part of the national heritage, with complex market and non-market values to the country. This calls for major changes in the role of the government to regulate and fund conservation and promote sustainable development activities. Currently, the opposite is occurring. Under Mexico's decentralization plan for its Natural Protected Areas (NPAs), responsibility for biodiversity management supposedly devolves to state and local governments, but the fiscal inability of these to undertake management of NPAs means that the plan in effect delivers management to corporate–conservationist partnerships. The federal government is left with the role of policing private investment.

Under the stewardship model, the increase in militarization of areas rich in biodiversity and natural resources is seen as a direct threat to conservation. The director of Mexico's Federal Office of Environmental Protection (PROFEPA) recently announced that the Mexican Army will be assigned the task of policing natural areas, along with federal, state and local police forces. The PROFEPA justified the decision saying: 'To the degree to which we can offer the legal framework for inspection and vigilance, national and foreign organizations will be willing to place more resources,' and mentioned priority areas as the mountains of Guerrero, the Chimalapas (Oaxaca) and Montes Azules (Chiapas) (G. Guillén 2001).

Military presence destabilizes biodiversity zones and often protects private investment to the detriment of local communities. More vigilance is needed to break up organized crime in the form of black market resource exploitation, but the decision to put a lid on social conflicts in Natural Protected Areas by sending the army into indigenous communities can only lead to more intense conflicts, as the ten-year history of the Chiapas conflict has amply proven.

Government responsibilities should thus include: the revocation of public policies that work against conservation (subsidies to cattle-ranching, colonization of biodiversity-rich areas, support to local caciques and so on); crackdowns on illegal logging and biopiracy; and strict environmental protection legislation and enforcement, including control of biological risk factors such as the introduction of genetically modified and exogamic plants (not native to the place); bans on chemical pesticides and fertilizers that damage ecosystems; long-term plans for sustainable water use and enforcement of environmental regulations regarding industrial activity.

The stewardship model builds on human values ignored in market systems. The keys to the success of alternative conservation projects, the so-called 'environmentalism of the poor' that is gaining strength in developing countries, lie in building on millennia-old bases. Toledo lists these as: defence of traditional cultural values, maintenance or reproduction of communal structures, collective control of economic and exchange processes and conservationist use of natural resources. Indeed, emerging projects violate many dicta of market law: they emphasize diversified rather than specialized use of resources, collective accumulation of capital rather than individual, and small-scale enterprises over the large-scale production units generally encouraged by governments and financial institutions. A growing body of research and experience indicates that businesses with these characteristics can be efficient, produce high-quality goods and services, and compete in the market, while at the same time generating social and environmental value ignored in market equations (Toledo 2000: 79). For example, studies show that organic coffee cooperatives attain yields comparable to the plantation model at much lower costs. Organic production also generates a series of environmental and social benefits (Pérezgrovas et al. forthcoming).

Finally, international rural advocacy organizations have contributed to designing the new model through analysis and criticism of existing practices. A GRAIN critique of the failure of World Bank biodiversity practices concludes with recommendations that coincide with the model sketched above: recognize that local communities are the best stewards of biodiversity, reject monoculture agriculture that erodes agricultural diversity, incorporate biodiversity in environmental assessments, develop projects with the full participation of local communities and discontinue support for corporate bioprospecting.

The lines of battle between corporate conservationist plans for bio-diversity use and a native stewardship model of sustainable development have been drawn on the fields of mega-projects such as the Mesoameri-can Biological Corridor and the Plan Puebla-Panamá. The outcome has planetary ramifications.

Notes

1. Many books and articles have been written on 'biopiracy' and the implications of bioprospecting. The pioneering work and most complete to date has been done by the ETC Group (formerly the Rural Advancement Foundation International, RAFI), and may be found on their website: <www.etcgroup.org>.

2. In November 2000, the Nature Conservancy, Pronatura and private-sector partners bought 7,000 acres in Coahuila with desert springs that contain aquatic creatures found nowhere else on earth. The Nature Conservancy, with Amigos de Sian Ka'an, also purchased 64 acres of coastal land on the Yucatán peninsula in January 2002 for $2.7 million as a barrier between the Sian Ka'an Biosphere reserve and the Mayan Riviera tourist development area.

3. In Mexico, during President Ernesto Zedillo's administration the De-centralization Framework Agreement and the Commitment for Private Financing of Natural Protected Areas (both 1997) authorized international NGO direct involvement in biodiversity management.

5 | State corporatism and peasant organizations: towards new institutional arrangements

HORACIO MACKINLAY AND
GERARDO OTERO

§ MEXICO'S legendary political stability for the better part of the twentieth century has been largely attributed to the corporatist relations
between the state and a host of organizations of workers, peasants and
the so-called popular sector. The Partido Revolucionario Institucional
(Institutional Revolutionary Party, PRI) ruled from 1929 with tight political control and electoral support from its corporatist mass organizations.
Its longevity, until the presidential elections of 2000 when opposition
candidate Vicente Fox came to power, may be explained to a considerable
extent by the corporatist system of political control, which structured
important segments of the Mexican population. One of its accomplishments for the PRI regime was to delay the democratic transition that
started during the 1970s.

During Vicente Fox's presidential campaign in 2000, his discourse
included the promise that he would end all the vestiges of PRI-style
corporatism. Since the start of the Fox administration in December
of that year, however, it has taken good care to not confront the still-
powerful bosses of the PRI social organizations. Because of the inertia
that they imprint on several realms of the economy and society, they
still play an important role in the political control of their constituencies
(Singelmann, this volume). They also continue to have a considerable
power for social mobilization.

Corporatism became an indispensable concept in Mexico, not so
much because many intellectuals or academics used it, but because
it came to be a part of everyday language. It was often utilized in a
vague and imprecise manner, usually with a negative connotation and
associated with the party that had monopolized political life for decades.
Official organizations came to be called 'corporatist organizations', to
distinguish them from others regarded as 'autonomous' or 'independent'
of the state (Fox and Gordillo 1991). Other expressions such as 'corporatist practices', 'corporatist procedures', 'corporatist mobilization or
manipulation', 'corporatist vote' and so on became part of commonly
used political language.

Based on empirical work about tobacco producers, we will consider
some 'new institutional arrangements' in this branch, some of which

may still be regarded as corporatist while others are not. Depending on the extent to which Mexico builds on the non-corporatist type of institutional arrangements, its likelihood of moving ahead in the democratic transition process will improve. Our argument here is that Mexico is moving within a transitional moment in which the growth of organizations independent from the state and autonomous with respect to other political organizations, including political parties, is now more propitious than before due to the liberal-democratic political opening. Yet the new government's need for political control is encouraging the continuation of some corporatist relations. Which forces prevail will largely shape the future character of Mexico's regime and even the social and economic content of its development model. The post-revolutionary regime led by the PRI may be characterized as social-authoritarian in the sense that it tried to address issues of social justice within an authoritarian political context. Today's neoliberalism could merely do away with the social-economy content of the PRI regime of the past while reconstituting authoritarian corporatism, even if electoral democracy is respected. But another possibility is that social organizations under new, democratic institutional arrangements could be stronger to push in the direction of a social-democratic regime (i.e. with political democracy and a social economy, Otero 1996a: 237–44).

The purpose of this chapter is to describe the corporatist relations between peasants and the state during the PRI era and propose a conceptualization of emerging institutional arrangements in substitution or modification of traditional corporatism. In the first section we analyse corporatist relations both as an instrument of control and subordination of popular groups and classes, and as one of the main modes of political participation that existed in Mexico. The second section discusses the Mexican *ejido* and the ways in which corporatism works in the relations between leaders and constituencies. In the third section we suggest a renewed language that goes beyond corporatism, based on a case study of the tobacco industry. Finally, in the Conclusions we compare the old and the new conditions, and discuss the current uncertainties of the transition in more general terms.

Corporatist theory and Mexican authoritarianism

The concept of corporatism has been applied to political systems or governments which started to emerge from the crisis of the 1930s and became consolidated after the Second World War, in which the state assumed central functions in the conduction of the economy, as well as in political and social regulation. That is to say, the vast majority of states in the world encompassed corporatist structures.

Corporatist relations are those established between corporations that represent the various organized groups in society with the state, on one hand, and with political parties, on the other. These relations also encompass those inside corporations, between leaders and members. Two principal functions have been underlined as the most common of corporatist organizations: the exercise of *interest representation*, in exchange for corporations playing a role in the social and, eventually, *political control* of their constituents. An often-quoted passage is that by Philippe Schmitter, who wrote:

> ✗ Corporatism may be defined as a system of interest representation in which its constituent units are organized in a limited number of unique categories that are obligatory, non-competitive, hierarchically organized and functionally differentiated, recognized or authorized (if not created) by the state, which are given a representational monopoly, within their respective categories, in exchange for the observance of certain controls in the selection of their leaders and in the articulation of their demands and supports. (Schmitter 1974: 93–4)

From its initial formulations, corporatist theory distinguished between countries with more structured civil societies, in which organizations have greater negotiating power with the state, and countries which do not have such level of development in their civil societies, and in which the state has much greater authority. Two principal types of corporatism were thus delineated, apart from other refined variants: 'societal corporatism' and 'state corporatism'. Following Schmitter, *societal corporatism* is firmly rooted in liberal-democratic systems, whereas *state corporatism* is associated with authoritarian systems with a bureaucratic and centralized control of functional organizations, the political and electoral system is monopolized, and there is only one ideology and other political cultures are repressed.

Beyond this general definition, Schmitter's corporatist theory faces difficulties in characterizing concrete corporations in each system, and there has been considerable debate about its utility as a conceptual framework for analysing political reality (Ortega Riquelme 1977: 41; de la Garza 1994: 26). Rather than reviewing this debate, we will focus on our own interpretation of corporatism, with an emphasis on definitions that are useful for analysing the Mexican case.

To characterize the hierarchical relation between the state and corporatist organizations in developing countries where social inequalities are particularly acute, it is important to factor in the specific forms of subordination and subjection of corporatist organizations to the state. Although we can also use the concept of 'political control' to illustrate the state's capacity to ensure the conditions of governance, applicable to all countries with corporatist systems, the terms subordination and subjection are more appropriate to developing countries with state-corporatist systems in which subordinate classes are much more strongly under the control of the state apparatus. Another difference with advanced capitalist countries resides in the fact that subordinate classes in the latter enjoy relatively better standards of living due to a more developed social economy or welfare state, and this renders their subordination less hard to endure.

State corporatism, then, is defined basically by the fact that the level of subordination and subjection of corporations to the state is very high. This is so because, for the most part, corporations were created directly by the state or have been strongly subsumed under it, as has been the case in Mexico. It is thus preferable to speak about corporations not so much as interest representatives, despite the fact that they also fulfil this function to some extent, but as *demand transmitters* or as mechanisms of interlocution. These organizations may channel a series of individual and collective demands and grievances that are satisfied in a selective manner by the state, usually through its patron–client mechanisms. Decisions made by state officials depend on what concessions they see as valid and/or necessary, and to what extent they should be satisfied according to their estimation of the prevailing correlation of social forces.

In societal corporatism, by contrast, corporations maintain a greater degree of independence from the state. Their points of view are taken into account, and they have negotiation power by virtue of the fact that they can eventually withdraw their support for the party or state official, inducing their members to vote for another political party in the next election. In this case, we can properly speak of *interest representation* of civil society groups, rather than a mere interlocution to transmit the demands of subjected groups. On the other hand, emphasis should be placed more on political control than on subordination and subjection in societal corporatism. Subordination and subjection have obviously not disappeared in advanced capitalist countries, but their prevalence is less oppressive than in developing countries and subordinate classes there have better chances of having their voices heard; they are less marginalized from the political system.

The most important aspect in the definition of societal corporatism, however, is that the rule of law is more prevalent over arbitrary options in the exercise of political power. Therefore, those who occupy decision-making positions in societal corporatism must be less authoritarian because they are subject to clear rules. This environment eventually promotes a more democratic political culture, which affects the modes of doing politics.

Corporatism as a mode of political participation

Corporatist theory has highlighted the fact that in both types of corporatism – state and societal – a 'mode of political participation' was instituted (Schwartzman, cited in Mondragón 1994: 11). This amounts to the new form of doing politics, and this aspect of corporatism may be applied to all countries, given that party representation in elections cannot exhaust political representation on an everyday basis. It is nevertheless particularly suited to an understanding of countries like Mexico, in which the system of corporatist representation has coexisted with a highly deficient system of electoral representation via political parties. State corporatism has been overwhelmingly predominant in Mexico in spite of the theoretical existence of a pluralistic democratic system.

In fact, between 1940 and 1970, social organizations affiliated to the Institutional Revolutionary Party (PRI), with its three sectors – worker, peasant and popular – were practically the only channels for participating in organized political life, and for transmitting collective demands. Elections, which were highly controlled, only fulfilled a referendum role to sanction previously made decisions. The organizations that head each of these sectors are: the Workers' Confederation of Mexico (Confederación de Trabajadores de México, CTM), the National Peasant Confederation (Confederación Nacional Campesina, CNC), and the National Confederation of Popular Organizations (Confederación Nacional de Organizaciones Populares, CNOP), respectively. The first two sectors are comprised of several organizations each. The CNOP is an umbrella body that encompasses a broad set of organizations representative of several urban and rural strata, such as popular sectors, middle classes, professionals, small and medium merchants and entrepreneurs, private agriculturalists and so on. All of their organizations are affiliated to the PRI.

The role played by corporatist organizations throughout the PRI era in electoral politics has been overwhelming in shaping the results, whether by 'persuasion' or fraud. It was not until the July 2000 elections that the popular vote was duly respected. By this time, sufficient reforms had been introduced in the electoral system to afford relatively equitable opportunities for contending political parties. Between 1970 and 2000, then, there was a slow process of gradual change favourable to an electoral system of representation, combined with some setbacks. One core problem for democratic transition consisted in the control exercised by the government over the organization and qualification of elections, and its use of public resources to favour the official party (L. Salazar 1997). Another critical problem, though, was political control exercised by the corporatist system and its patron–client relations.

Authoritarian and patron–client traits

Let us now recapitulate the central components in the conceptualization of Mexican corporatism. There is no doubt that this system is of the statist type, but what are its specific features? There is consensus among scholars that Mexican corporatism has been imbued with authoritarian, patrimonialist and patron–client traits, at least during the PRI era (Bizberg 1990; Camacho 1988; de la Garza 1990; Luna and Pozas 1992; Mondragón 1994).

[Authoritarianism has to do with the presidentialist nature of the system.] Among other things, presidentialism has meant that the outgoing president had the last word in designating most of the important candidacies to electoral positions, including that of the incoming president, which was supposedly the responsibility of the party. Presidentialism filtered down its influence to the lowest levels of organizations, so that those in higher positions designated the leaders below them, especially when the positions had some strategic political import. This happened both inside party structures and in government institutions, within a hierarchy that came to be established as the years went by. If leaders in higher ranks did not intervene, then the usual practice was that incumbents delayed their replacement, or forced their re-election, or imposed one of their close allies in the leadership position, usually with the complicity of higher levels of authority.

Patron–client relations, as the name indicates, refer to those in which the establishment of personal links connect the client to a patron in a position of power. The patron uses his/her influence within an organization or institution in order to render favours or services needed by their clients (López Novo 1998: 117). The leaders, in turn, expect the support, loyalty and submission of their social constituency in exchange for some negotiation in their favour, or some concessions, or help in emergencies. Because leaders' decisions are usually discretional and arbitrary, the benefits obtained by social constituencies are usually partial: rarely are demands fulfilled adequately, or the agreements and promises satisfied in full. The acceptability of patron–client relations for subordinates lies in the fact that they could hardly attain better results outside instituted channels. Rather, they may face repression if demands and/or protest are organized outside official corporatist channels.

Patrimonialism in Mexico's political lexicon is vaguely associated with Max Weber's definition of patriarchal authority, a variety of traditional authority (Weber 1958: 296–7). It has come to signify the individual appropriation of the means of financial, economic and political power, which determined that certain leaders or officers could dispose of a certain part of public resources to their own benefit or for personal service, besides using them for the benefit of the PRI. In the case of social organizations patrimonialism has meant that leaders consider the organizations as their own property, so that organizational or material resources can be used for their own benefit. This practice has been facilitated by an extremely lax fiscal system for social organizations, which allows them to not carry proper bookkeeping of transactions conducted with members' funds. The practice of patrimonialism is not exceptional; organizations' constituents socially accept it with certain fatalism. Members have most likely reproduced or would reproduce such practices if they were in the position to do so. More than condemning the use of collective patrimony, what is condemned is that this is done in excess, especially when campaign promises are not even partially fulfilled.

The legitimacy of the corporatist system was consolidated thanks to the application of agrarian reform throughout most of the twentieth century. That is why this system enjoyed considerable consensus, even if this was a passive consensus in which constituencies lacked their own initiative in political matters. They did what had to be done, knew when to speak up and when to remain silent, whom to communicate with or not. The codes of conduct of the authoritarian order were thus established. Obviously there was a long historical background of authoritarian, patriarchal and paternalistic relations from prior epochs. The Mexican post-revolutionary state simply reshaped some of these traditions and adjusted them to an acquiescent national political culture. Corporatist relations could at times be less authoritarian and more inclusive, but generally they were anti-democratic and were impregnated with a strong component of subjugation of the masses to their leaders.

Corporatism has thus been a system of social participation and a conduit for group interest representation, except for some extreme cases in which organizations were used by their leaders to subjugate their members without participation and few benefits. Some examples of this include CNC caciques in indigenous areas, or the caciques of social organizations that have appropriated these as their own property and used their resources in an absolutely arbitrary manner. At the very least, however, corporatism has generally managed to transmit social demands and generate a space of interlocution with government institutions and other groups in society. In rural Mexico, the *ejido* system has been a prime realm of corporatist action.

The Mexican *ejido* system and corporatist authoritarianism

In the context of the strong predominance of corporatist relations, within the particular mode of political participation that developed in Mexico, the role of leaders or caciques (strongmen) was central. In this section, we describe this system of political participation to highlight the central features of power structure within *ejidos*, the core economic and political rural organization. We then describe how rural leaders became a central part of the recruitment ground for the formation of a bureaucratic elite in Mexico's politics.

The Mexican ejido and cacique power

Ejidos and agrarian communities are social and territorial organizations that were constituted during the agrarian reform process (1917–92). They first emerged from the proceedings of land redistribution to land solicitors, obtained on the basis of breaking down *latifundia* (huge extensions of privately held landholdings) that exceeded the limits allowed by the Agrarian Law, or via colonization of federal lands newly opened to cultivation. In the case of agrarian communities, technically this was not called land redistribution because they emerged from the confirmation of lands to which people had had a right from time immemorial. Between 1917 and 1992, the agrarian reform process constituted 29,162 *ejidos* and 2,366 agrarian communities on 103 million hectares of the total of 197 million hectares of national surface. In total, 3.5 million heads of family became beneficiaries of agrarian reform called '*ejidatarios*' or '*comuneros*' (SRA 1998: 313; DeWalt et al. 1994). This figure is on top of the land allotments granted in the form of private property, through proceedings established in the colonization laws (abolished in 1962) and the laws regarding vacant lands and the titling of national lands (property of 'the nation') (Pérez Castañeda 2002). On the other hand, although agrarian communities were legislated with the intent of giving back lands to Indian communities with ancestral rights to them, in the end many indigenous peoples received *ejidos*, and many non-Indians (*ladinos*) were awarded agrarian communities. In the latter case, legitimate Indian owners were often displaced (Mackinlay 1991).

The property regime of both *ejido* and agrarian community was defined by the rules of 'social property', which was a collective form of property. Their lands could not be sold, rented, or used as guarantee for loans, or be the object of any type of market transaction. The lands were given permanently to *ejidatarios*, however, and their rights could be transmitted by inheritance from generation to generation (Pérez Castañeda 2002).

In terms of production organization, a semi-collective regime predominated, in that most surfaces under cultivation were parcelled out and were held individually by *ejidatarios* and *comuneros*, while the common lands and resources such as forests, pastures, water sources, mining activities and so on were for collective use. Only some *ejidos* adopted a collective organization of production in agricultural land. This was the case during the administration of Lázaro Cárdenas (1934–40) for about 12 per cent of *ejidos*, but this type of organization came to be discouraged and, in fact, officially boycotted during and after the 1940s, with some resurgence in the 1970s (Warman 1980).

With the 1992 new Agrarian Law, the concept of social property disappeared from the legislation and the land controlled by this regime became subject to privatization. Before 1992, however, the only legal difference between *ejidos* and communities resided in the forms of organization and internal government structures. For *ejidos*, members had to follow procedures established in the law, while they were optional for communities, which could instead be ruled by their local uses and customs (*'usos y costumbres'*). The highest level of governance in *ejidos* is the General Assembly which used to meet at least once a month; and the executive organization is the *Ejido* Commissariat, looked after by the Vigilance Committee, comprising at least one president, a treasurer and a secretary (Mackinlay 1991: 117–30).

This type of political organization, in which a number of decisions were made by *Ejido* Commissariats or the Common Goods Commissariats, established a propitious space for government to intervene and for the development of power groups controlled by the strongmen or *Ejido* caciques. Among others, their task was to administer the resources and social welfare programmes that were channelled through the *Ejido* Commissariats. Caciques found a fertile ground to develop fully after the end of the Cárdenas era (1936–40) in close relation with the ruling-party structures. This does not mean that caciques did not exist before the Cárdenista period, but more than ever before they now found an institutional structure in which to thrive. In the post-Cárdenas years, the *ejido* sector lost its central character of articulating agricultural development, which it had during the ephemeral height of agrarian reform. Once relegated to second-order priority, leaving the main place from an economic development point of view to the business sector, the *ejido* became a component in the government's machinery to ensure political stability. The government's means for control became much more political than economic, which was another reason to reinforce the *ejido* as a power structure.

Ruling groups inside *ejidos* became the channel used by the official party to organize its political and electoral activities in *ejidos* and communities, which often favoured the PRI unanimously. They could not dispose of *ejido* land plots individually assigned so easily, for they were subject to regulation and control by official agrarian agencies. Yet they had some leeway to amass control, sometimes making arbitrary use of power, but especially using the illegal *ejido* land market that developed in the *ejido* sector, and also making personal use of *ejido* collective property (Hewitt de Alcántara 1978; Gordillo 1988a: 151–3).

Other types of caciques were also firmly established. These were not necessarily *ejido* members, but included those inserted in commercial and usurers' circuits in peasant villages, and many came from the former landowning classes, often linked to the PRI (R. Bartra et al. 1978; A. Bartra 1985). The relation between PRI caciques and government institutions was complementary, but sometimes contradictory given that the latter used the caciques but also represented a counterweight to their overwhelming, despotic power.

The mere membership in a corporatist organization could mean entering a sphere of relative privilege with respect to other members of the same subordinate class that were not organized. An example of such differences can be found in every *ejido* by the social stratification in their midst. *Ejidos* soon became populated with sons of *ejidatarios* and '*avecindados*' or neighbours that came from outside the *ejido* village and who had limited and poor access to land. Given the very small size of *ejido* plots, inheritance rules dictated that only one person or relative, generally the elder son, would inherit the land. Other sons of *ejidatarios* and neighbours were sometimes called *campesinos sin tierra* or landless peasants. Agricultural day labourers who sold their labour power also established residence in *ejido* villages. As time went by, all these individuals and families came to represent the majority in agrarian villages. Yet they were usually in an inferior situation with regard to those who enjoyed the legal condition of *ejidatario* (Paré 1979).

Ejidatarios thus became the materialization of the policy of social justice of the Mexican state. Their social distance from other strata within their villages became considerable. This does not mean that the difference between *ejidatarios* and caciques was dissolved, but shows that social stratification within the popular classes is significant. The sometimes fierce struggle for appropriating scarce resources allowed caciques to manipulate their subordinates, both the least favoured and the relatively better-off groups such as *ejidatarios*.

Leadership–constituency relations

Another sphere where cacique forms of power developed were the so-called peasant 'economic organizations'. In fact, given the exhaustion of lands susceptible to redistribution, during the 1970s the government promoted new institutions geared to improving the economic performance of small agricultural producers. Economic alternatives to land redistribution were sought also due to the crisis in peasant economy that started in the mid-1960s (Bartra and Otero 1987). During that decade, the state created or reformed numerous enterprises and state agencies, and a diversity of programmes for rural development through which a series of peasant organizations emerged, most of them affiliated to the CNC (Rello 1986). Of course, rural entrepreneurs also benefited from these economic institutions, even more than small peasant producers.

These new producer organizations, such as unions of producers of specialized crops, credit unions, *ejido* unions, insurance mutualities and several others, became intermediaries for channelling important financial resources. Certain producers' unions linked to powerful state-run enterprises, such as those of the sugarcane, coffee and tobacco growers, managed considerable amounts of resources thanks to captive union fees that the state-run firms charged union members on the union's behalf when buying their crops at the end of the harvest. As fundamental state instruments in the maintenance and reproduction of political mechanisms of subjection, peasant leaders enjoyed a multiplicity of economic and political benefits. For instance, they could negotiate loans, obtain export permits and get privileged treatment, especially in government institutions, but often also in private concerns inserted in agroindustrial activities or in the industrial transformation of agricultural raw materials produced by peasant union groups. In political terms, leaders enjoyed a whole series of privileges that allowed them access to the official party structures and popular election positions, at both the local and the federal levels.

The possibilities for social mobility for the members of corporatist organizations were considerable during the 1970s and, to a lesser extent, the 1980s. Some of them or their children managed to move up to positions of urban or rural middle class, often thanks to having acquired a university education. Their relations with the leaders were marked by a patron–client type of exchange, based on the granting by leaders of certain 'favours' in exchange for personal political loyalty and support. As mentioned, this attitude had been previously reproduced from higher circles of political power. Furthermore, it was not easy to escape the patron–client rules of the game because they were reinforced throughout the political system.

The various modes of patron–client relations already mentioned – in *ejidos*, peasant economic organizations and state-run companies – cannot be generalized for all corporatist organization in Mexico's countryside, but they do represent the most typical cases. Other producers not linked to economic organizations or state-run companies were engaged in lower degrees of patron–client relations, but were not altogether free of them. In the case of unorganized small property-holding peasants, for instance, patron–client relations have been less perceptible, but rarely non-existent, given that there were very few social agents that were not in some way related to the state. On the other hand, this does not mean that organizations that approached a participatory democratic and more egalitarian model, at least during some stage of their existence, never developed. In these cases, however, organizations had to be rather obstinate, given the continued opposition they faced from the overall system (Gordillo 1988b; Otero 1989b).

In most countries of the world, patron–client relations are present to a greater or lesser extent wherever there is a social organization, even in societal types of corporatism, as Gaetano Mosca, Vilfredo Pareto and Robert Michels perceived at the beginning of the twentieth century. In the Mexican case, however, this reality was exacerbated because it represented an institutionalized system organized by the state itself. Hence, the subordination of social constituencies to their leaderships and the state has been remarkable. This type of subjugation, especially *vis-à-vis* the leadership, prevailed both in PRI-affiliated organizations as well as in most of the independent and autonomous organizations that emerged during the 1970s and 1980s, given that it resulted from a political-cultural trait that goes beyond political affiliation.

Now, even if we use the terms 'corporatist domination', 'subordination' or 'subjection', members still had a degree of participation in the political life of their organizations. They viewed their *ejidos* and other producer organizations as intermediary bureaucratic levels through which they channelled specific individual or collective demands. In other words, they often identified the *ejidos* with a special kind of government office (Mackinlay 1996: 172). While social and political participation did not develop in an ideal democratic fashion, such relations enjoyed some degree of acceptance among the membership of corporatist organizations, depending on a variety of circumstances.

During the PRI era, open state repression was not excluded either and sometimes it could be quite severe. The greatest risk of repression was for those who actively opposed the system's rules. The risk was lower for those who did not actively support the system but also did not present a threat. Many *ejidatario* peasants and members of economic organizations managed to keep themselves from participating in organized life without being penalized. At most, they could be marginalized from certain benefits granted exclusively to those who showed good behaviour. This trait of Mexican authoritarianism distinguishes it from totalitarian regimes. In totalitarian regimes, simple dissent at the thought level can carry grave consequences. Another contrast with single-party countries, in which the party is virtually the sole channel of communication with the state, is that in Mexico there existed more than one organization affiliated to the PRI. There were even a few independent organizations, so that a certain degree of competition between different organizations developed over political clienteles. Furthermore, subordinate social groups had the chance of establishing a direct link with government agencies to channel their demands.

Party participation was, of course, expected from members of corporatist organizations. They generally had to attend activities, demonstrations and mobilizations of the government party and voted for its candidates in elections. With their non-questioning participation in corporatist life and their acceptance of the rules of the game, the PRI corporatist political culture reproduced itself. In most corporatist branches, political involvement was greatest for those that obtained the most benefits from state intervention. Conversely, participation was lowest and seen mostly as an obligation in those organizations that saw lower levels of state action in their favour.

The flexibility of Mexican corporatism was also manifested towards the urban middle classes. Sufficiently intelligent so as not to subject these classes to unbearable subordination, the system granted them a considerable margin of freedom of expression, did not submit them to the type of vigilance and espionage prevalent in Soviet-bloc state socialism, but it did restrict electoral access to power and affected democratic rights. Overt repression was resorted to only in situations deemed necessary to maintain order at critical junctures, such as against the student movement in 1968 and 1971, or the assault on *Excelsior* in 1976, then Mexico City's prominent independent daily newspaper. With regard to the peasant and working classes, however, while Mexican corporatism was authoritarian rather than totalitarian, it did exercise stern political control and seriously restricted organizational freedom. One could argue that Mexico's was a *sui generis* type of authoritarianism, one with totalitarian undertones with regard to political control of subordinate groups and classes, but closer to Western liberal democracies with regard to the middle classes.

Political-party participation and the bureaucratic elite

The PRI's division into three sectors was based on the idea that the party should assume the representation of the least favoured groups in society. These groups represented the 'social sector', and thus its organization expressly left out the economically privileged classes; they did not require such representation and were not to be incorporated into the political actions of the state (Córdova 1972, 1974). Only the organizations representing the middle classes that belonged to the heterogeneous CNOP could join the party, side by side with those of the social sector of this confederation and the workers' and peasants' sectors.

Political-party participation was centred on what has been usually called in Mexico the 'political class', whose peculiarity was that a good portion of it was recruited within the social sector. Instead of the popular label of 'political class', we have designated this group the 'bureaucratic elite'. Our intention is to establish a clear distinction between this concept and that of 'political-class formation' and its result: a political class (or 'class-for-itself') that is organized as a political subject that acts in civil society and, perhaps, in political society or the state as well. The bureaucratic elite was formed mainly by leaders of organizations who occupied posts of popular election through the party (e.g. municipal presidencies, members of the states and federal legislative assemblies, senators, governors and president of the republic). These leaders generally did not make their careers in public administration, as most did not have much formal education.

The speciality of these leaders was their contact with the popular masses and the mediation or brokering of their demands. The system rewarded them by giving them the chance to help themselves with public resources upon winning elections, which was practically assured. 'Helping themselves' also to positions in public administration to which they might have been appointed was common and expected. Leaders usually kept their posts within the corporatist organizations while occupying an elected position, specifically senators and members of the states and federal assemblies. The exceptions were cases when the new position required a full-time commitment, e.g. municipal presidents, governors and president of the republic. In both situations, incumbents would try to amass the largest sums of public resources, whether directly or through surrogates, or they could use their influence to make various types of personal businesses. The entire constellation of clients located under their leadership, but especially the people or constituents closest to them, could aspire to becoming part of the bureaucratic elite.

Another great source for recruitment of the bureaucratic elite was the public administration, whose cadre were usually recruited from the professional middle classes, trained primarily in public universities. These politicians mixed with the relatively few members of the economic ruling class that aspired to make a bureaucratic career within the system, or with relatives of already wealthy public officials from their own social background. Although numerically not as important inside the party structure compared to those who came from the party sectors, the public administrators and professionals occupied the most important positions of representation, including the presidency of the republic. Most Mexican presidents after Cárdenas had not occupied a post by popular election. When it was necessary to appoint public officials as candidates of the PRI, often without ever having been party members, they were affiliated to one of the party sectors, preferably to the one to which they had been related during their bureaucratic career.

In sum, a peculiar feature of Mexico's bureaucratic elite is that it did not have an oligarchic landed origin, given that the agrarian reform destroyed this class, and most of its cadres did not come from the industrial bourgeoisie either. This helps to explain why these two classes did not alternate in power through leading military coups as happened in various Latin American countries during the second half of the twentieth century. Individual members of the Mexican bureaucratic elite were definitely more obedient to the state institutions than to any particular faction of the ruling class, and they were well rewarded for this behaviour. Therefore, if we can question the results of the Mexican Revolution for the people, one cannot question its generosity towards the leaders of popular organizations and members of the professional middle classes who also became members of the PRI bureaucratic elite.

Towards new institutional arrangements

In order to illustrate the complexity of the new political situation, we will refer to the case of Tabacos Mexicanos, or Tabamex, a state firm that played a central intermediary role between agricultural producers and the private sector. Its privatization at the beginning of the 1990s produced quite diverse scenarios in the various regions where it participated, which made it very hard to keep seeing corporatism as a single system with common traits (Mackinlay 1999). Therefore, the new political relations emerging in this democratic transition are better theorized by transcending the corporatist concept, using instead the term 'new institutional arrangements' (NIA). In this concept, the corporatist relation has not disappeared altogether, but it stopped being the predominant relation between social actors and the market.

The definition we propose for NIA is as follows: new institutional arrangements are those representing new relations that have developed as a result of the reduction of state intervention in the economic and social spheres. NIA are emerging between a variety of social agents and the market, whether these involve organizations or individuals and their relations with various levels of public office. In studying the case of Tabamex, the concept of NIA worked well to incorporate a variety of regional and sub-regional situations that developed after its privatization.

We propose four types of NIA, without excluding the possibility that other types could be developed. First, there is a reconstituted corporatist NIA, in which corporatist subordination has been preserved through official organizations, although it has been adapted along two modalities. In one case, the corporatist relations headed by the federal government are now taken over by the state government, and a collective bargaining relationship developed between the corporatist organization and the new transnational cigarette firms that substituted the state-run company. The maintenance of such a corporatist relationship permitted the restructuring of the agroindustrial system in an overwhelmingly favourable manner for the transnational firms. In another case, the state was substituted by a regional cacique that had represented the growers' organization during the Tabamex era. He appropriated the growers' organization and the assets of the state firm that were transferred to producers as if it were his own private property. In this regional situation, the corporatist relationship became an even more authoritarian and personalistic corporatist relationship. Another example of a reconstituted corporatist NIA is the structure of the board of the new Financiera Rural, which has two producer organizations seats reserved, one for the CNC and the other for the CNPR (Singelmann, this volume).

The second type involves the absence of NIA, where tobacco production ceased to exist, along with growers' organizations. This took place either because the economic activity ceased to be profitable, or because the transnational private firms that were going to substitute the state-run company did not find it convenient to relate with the old corporatist organizations, which did not have a favourable approach towards improving productivity and efficiency. The latter case involves the emergence of individual market NIA, in which the state stopped being the linking element in the activity and social organizations disappeared. In their place, new individual contractual relations between tobacco growers and cigarette companies have surfaced. The individual small producers and even some medium-size producers that have started to operate in the activity have done so with no organization to defend their interests.

For the third type we have societal NIAs in which the state has withdrawn from the productive sphere and growers have managed to construct organizations independent of the state. This type of NIA involves the political formation of direct producers. That is to say, rather than simply being economic agents, existing objectively and at the mercy of the market, becoming politically formed signifies that they build organizational class capacities that will act in their interests. In contrast to corporatist organizations that functioned primarily for political control and cacique and state interests, autonomous organizations function primarily in the interests of direct producers. (Other examples of this type of NIA are discussed by Martínez-Torres for coffee producers, in Chapter 11, this volume.)

Our fourth NIA type is represented by a newly created firm that replaced Tabamex, owned cooperatively by direct producers. This firm is acting autonomously in the international market. It uses efficient entrepreneurial management of collective resources, and redistributes economic benefits to members in a considerably egalitarian manner (Léonard and Mackinlay 2000). This arrangement approximates what Otero identified as 'self-managed, democratic production' to describe previous struggles and accomplishments in Mexico's countryside (Otero

1989b, 1999), and what Gustavo Gordillo (1988b) called 'appropriation of the production process' by direct producers.

Conclusions

We have talked about the mainstream of the corporatist system related to the social sector and the middle classes. But it is important to underline that corporatism has also been present in the business sector, although with a different functioning modality. Corporatism in this sector was geared above all to promote the economic participation of entrepreneurs in agricultural production. The PRI state was the principal articulator of this whole system by linking the market with participating groups in society (Mackinlay 2002).

This corporatist system functioned according to a set of norms and procedures that were relatively uniform across the country. Although substantial differences can be seen from one organization to another, even within the same branch of economic activity, certain common parameters would allow us to speak of a corporatist system during the PRI era. When the state began to withdraw from its economic functions through the mid-1980s, the situation became much more varied and complex.

From the four types of NIA discussed above, types three and four point in the direction of invigorating civil society by the emergence of producer organizations that are both *independent* of the state and that are *autonomous* of political parties. These are critical ingredients for the political formation of subordinate groups, classes and communities. Nevertheless, this is a minority experience within the tobacco sector, made possible largely due to the international market niche in which this organization has inserted itself. But direct producers in other sectors are also making headway in creating new, democratic institutional arrangements, as exemplified in Chapters 10 to 14 of this volume.

From a democratic standpoint, it is only to be hoped that this type of NIA becomes more generalized and prevalent, thus consolidating a real democratic transition; that is to say, a transition that is not limited to the electoral political realm, but one that goes more deeply into the everyday practices of popular organizations.

Note

We are grateful to Jonathan Fox and Peter Singelmann for useful comments on a previous version of this paper.

6 | Institutional democratization: changing political practices and the sugarcane growers' unions of the PRI

PETER SINGELMANN

§ PEASANT mobilizations in post-revolutionary Mexico have shifted cyclically between 'independent' movements and (re)realignments with government policies and party discipline, in which union leaders ensured social 'guarantees' for their members in exchange for member loyalty to the leaders and accommodation to the regime (see Mackinlay and Otero, this volume; Córdova 1972, 1974; Meyer 1977; Brachet-Márquez 1996). The breakdown of both the political and the economic premises of this regime and similar developments in other societies during the last decades of the twentieth century have stirred new debates over the necessary, inevitable or problematic nature of the relations between economic and political liberalization. A central part of these debates focuses on the prospects for further transition towards democracies 'in the broad sense', i.e. transitions that go beyond institutionalized guarantees for free election (Przeworski 1989; O'Donnell and Schmitter 1986).[1] In the case of Mexico, these debates have had to address the implications of such transformation for the unique place the Institutional Revolutionary Party (Partido Revolucionario Institucional, PRI) and its confederations had assumed under the corporatist parameters of the post-revolutionary regime and under the regime's particular variant of patron–client relations. This chapter addresses these questions, with a focus on the challenges the two sugarcane growers' unions affiliated with the PRI's peasant and 'popular' sectors are facing in terms of reassessing their purpose, their political practices and their party affiliation under recent changes in the broader economic and political constellation.

The post-revolutionary regime and the cane growers' unions

The majority of Mexico's cane growers emerged as a new group of peasants with communal (*ejido*) landholdings under the post-revolutionary land reform. The dissolution of the sugar *haciendas* as agroindustrial units required new institutional arrangements to reconcile the interests of villagers and sugar mills and to ensure the production of industrial raw materials that had no direct commercial or use value for the growers. These requirements prompted increasing government intervention from 1943 on, through presidential decrees that obliged rural producers to cultivate cane in areas surrounding mills (*zonas de abastecimiento*). The decrees came to regulate the relations between the sugar industry and cane growers in the areas of financing, production and marketing (Villar 1976; Espinosa 1993; Espinosa and Aurrecoechea 1993).

In this context, the cane growers' unions played a central role in linking their members to the new economic and political parameters. Their mobilizations passed through cycles of conquests and subordination and through parallel cycles of subdivisions and fusions. These mobilizations reflected complex dynamics of social demands, ideological divisions, disputes over political strategy and confrontations between leaders over power and privilege in the corporatist political arena. Ordinary growers found their rationale for accommodating this dynamic in the ample opportunities it offered for articulating their social demands and in the possibility for upwards mobility that union membership provided for some growers. But the loyalty promoted by this rationale was inherently precarious, because it shifted readily with the flow of the benefits competing leaders could ensure or promise convincingly (Flores Lúa 1987; Iguarrúa and Mestries 1987; Paré 1987a; Paré and Morett 1987; A. Bartra 1993; Ronfeldt 1973; de Grammont 1979; Bonilla Macharro 1975; Gómez Carpinteiro 1998: 51–91; Cordero Díaz 1998).

During the 1970s, the sugar industry faced an accelerating economic crisis and the increasing takeover of bankrupt mills by the federal government. The period was also marked by dramatic growers' mobilization at the regional and national levels between 1972 and 1975 that made it increasingly difficult for the government to ensure the political 'discipline' of the four national and several regional growers' unions affiliated with the 'peasant sector' of the party, the National Peasant Confederation (Confederación Nacional Campesina, CNC). These factors prompted the government to increase dramatically its control over the agroindustry in 1970 and again in 1975 (Villar 1976; A. Bartra et al. 1993) and to limit cane growers' representations to two national confederations. While the landowning growers had already founded the National Cane Growers' Union (Unión Nacional de Cañeros, UNC) within the 'popular' branch of the PRI in 1973, the various unions affiliated with the CNC had to be integrated into the newly formed National Union of Sugarcane Producers (Unión Nacional de Productores de Caña de Azúcar, UNPCA) that began to operate in 1977 (Paré 1987b; Paré and Morett 1987; A. Bartra et al. 1993). This consolidation modified the distribution of power and strengthened the growers as a group; but it did not change the dynamics of political mobilization, the growers' rationale for affiliating with these unions and with the PRI, or the political customs of the union leaders.

The power and the legitimacy of the leaders in the rank-and-file remained directly dependent on their ability to make the government comply with its part of the post-revolutionary political contract through a wide range of social benefits and economic subsidies. The Decree that Declares the Planting, Cultivation, Harvesting and Industrialization of Sugar Cane to be in the Public Interest, commonly referred to as the 'Cane Growers' Decree' (*Decreto Cañero*), introduced in 1943 and revised many times under the premises of corporatist state control, provided an increasing range of state intervention in financing, industrialization and in continued market regulation until 1991. These policies were congruent with parallel developments that privileged the growers' unions affiliated with the CNC and the CNPP (A. Bartra et al. 1993; Singelmann 1990, 1993). They also reinforced peasant perspectives in the majority of the cane growers who, as *minifundistas* (Singelmann 2003), prioritized socioeconomic 'guarantees', minimized risks and personal investment, and who placed responsibility for success as much as for failure on mill administrators and 'the government' (Núñez 1995; Singelmann et al. 1982; Singelmann 1998; Gómez Carpinteiro 1998; on the current possibilities of changes in this orientation, see Otero 1998; 1999: 107–12). From this perspective, cane cultivation became a privilege under social conquests that included a secure crop buyer, crop price guarantees, inclusion of the growers in the social security system and regular cash advances (*avíos*) received for field labour as interest-bearing loans from the government. The repayments of these loans were deducted from the crop price, but the *avíos* were valued by *minifundistas* as the equivalent of a regular 'salary'.

In this context, government policies sought but ultimately failed to reconcile the need for adequate industrial and agricultural returns with the social demands of consumers for cheap sugar. By 1980, over 75 per cent of the mills could not pay their accumulated debts to the state-controlled National Sugar Bank (Financiera Nacional Azucarera, FINASA) and had been taken over by the government. But mere government control over financing, production and marketing did not resolve the problems that had resulted from low prices, outdated machinery and accumulated debts. It contributed, in fact, to new problems tied to the introduction of political criteria into business administration, including a dramatic increase in underemployment, accelerating corruption and the entrance of mill administrators whose primary qualification was of a political nature (see Villar 1976; Singelmann and Tapia 1979; Singelmann 1993: 67–79; Espinosa and Aurrecoechea 1998: 309–13).

With the breakdown of Mexico's national economy in 1982, the financial costs of this political compromise had reached a critical point in which recuperation mandated restructuring the national debt under the conditions stipulated by the International Monetary Fund. In the sugar agroindustry these conditions included the privatization or reprivatization of state-controlled and cooperative mills and the dissolution of the government institutions intervening in sugar production and marketing. These changes had direct implications for the growers' unions, whose leaders were now expected to redefine their responsibilities and become business administrators managing cane cultivation and financing.

Industrial crisis and new challenges

Mill privatization, sugar market liberalization and a 1991 reform of the Cane Growers' Decree were intended to resolve the financial crisis of the industry, increase field and factory productivity and adapt the sector to new market rules. With these reforms, the growers' unions were assigned the responsibility for coordinating cane cultivation at the regional level, but they had no control over the critical conditions of the sugar industry and the sugar market. As the growers could no longer look for a government bank to secure financing and payments, and their fate remained dependent on that of the sugar industry, they were exposed to previously unknown insecurities.

From the beginning, the cane price had been a central issue of contention for the growers. While the price was previously tied to government-regulated sugar prices, the 1991 revision of the Cane Growers' Decree weighted several factors to arrive at Mexican sugar prices. These included a weighted combination of prices in an unregulated national market, the favourable prices of sugar import quotas to the United States under high-tier tariffs, and the price of the remnants dumped at a loss in the unregulated international sugar market. The second key change in the cane price formula was crop quality. Whereas previously the price was determined only by the weight of sugar actually recovered and thus also depended on mill efficiency, the 1991 decree changed the formula to measure cane payment according only to crop quality, primarily in terms of sucrose content and geographically conditioned variations in sugar that *theoretically* can be recovered due to regional variations in soil quality and water supply (Chollett 1996; Singelmann 1993; García Chávez 1997). This reform was intended to separate the responsibilities of growers and mills and to replace the traditional priority of 'political returns' (Castellanos C. 2000) by the economic criteria of productivity and market competition. With these reforms, the returns of the growers became tied to the greater uncertainties of the sugar markets and to the ability of the sugar industry to adapt effectively to the new market conditions.

The new link of the cane price to crop quality and the rapid loss of the cane's sucrose content after its cutting generated the need for new mechanisms of agroindustrial collaboration. The 1991 Cane Growers'

Decree promoted such collaboration by assigning new responsibilities to the growers' union locals, whose leaders now had to collaborate with the field administrators of the mills through newly formed production committees. These responsibilities, however, became increasingly difficult to meet due to drastically reduced resources and services connected with the exit of the state from the industry, a corresponding reduction in resources and services, and from an accelerating crisis of the sugar industry (García Chávez 1997; Espinosa 1999; Mestries 2000; Singelmann 1993, 2003; *Azúcar & Fructosa*, 3[39], 2001: 3–7 and other issues between 1999 and 2003).

The crisis of the industry also represented a serious challenge to the growers' unions, whose legitimacy until then had been directly linked to their ability to mediate the distribution of benefits under the populist banner of the PRI regime. In response to the crisis, the national unions and their locals had to invest in joint-venture trust funds with industry and government institutions to finance part of the cane cultivation, ensure the cash flow for crop payments, in some cases keep bankrupt mills in operation, cover the costs of fertilizers and insecticides, and invest in agricultural machinery. On 3 September 2001, the government took over twenty-seven of the most indebted mills and assumed a new role in restructuring the industry's debt and in ensuring cane payments. These measures also strengthened its position in the push towards modernizing both industrial production and cane cultivation under neoliberal premises.

While these measures were accompanied by new securities for financing and payment in the field, the publicly discussed need for further adjustment through mill closures raised concerns in the unions about losing members. These challenges added to those resulting from the PRI's defeat in the 2000 presidential and legislative elections. While Mexico's economic transformation and the crisis of the sugar industry had already increasingly undermined the PRI's and its unions' ability to deliver the accustomed benefits to their members since the 1980s, the formal loss of the party's political hegemony also dissolved the second key component of its unions' power base. Now the growers' perceived conquest, which over time became manifested in the Sugarcane Decrees, also became precarious, since the decrees had no legal underpinnings but were merely a formal declaration of government policies and of rules that specified the application of these policies. Facing the prospects for change in these policies after the PRI's defeat in the 2000 election, the growers' unions aligned with legislators of their party and of the Party of the Democratic Revolution (Partido de la Revolución Democrática, PRD) to establish a legal basis of the 'rights' they had 'conquered' over time through the decrees. The pending legislation

(*Proyecto de Ley de la Agroindustria Azucarera*), initiated in December 2000, proposed the legalization of these conquests, new government involvement to modernize the sugar industry, measures to ensure the industry's survival under the economic changes stipulated by NAFTA, and opening the growers' political representation to unions not affiliated with the PRI (UNPCA 2001; interviews with leaders of both PRI-affiliated unions, June and August 2001, June 2002). In institutional terms, the pending legislation would reaffirm the government's intervention in cane cultivation, sugar production and commerce by integrating the numerous activities of intervening agencies under a single umbrella ('*ventanlla única*').

But the pending legislation met with resistance from both the government and the sugar industry, was revised several times and remains subject to unresolved disputes over the formula of the cane price, the cane payment calendar, penalties for cane containing other materials, the retention of a single national cane growers' contract, and over the direct link of cane and sugar prices under the new conditions of an unregulated sugar market and an industry in crisis. In general terms, the sugar industry rejects the pending legislation as incompatible with the new conditions of market liberalization because it 'artificially' raises cane costs to a level that limits its ability to compete effectively in the international market. This critique centres on the sugar value as a factor in the cane price formula. The industry considers the cane price formula, that factors in 66 per cent of the mean unrefined sugar value (*Ampliación del Reglamento del Comité de la Agroindustria Azucarera*, 27 July 1993), to be excessive in comparison with corresponding percentages as low as 35 per cent in other countries.

Related to that position is the insistence of industry representatives in corresponding changes in their contracts with the growers in terms of regional variations, greater flexibility and individualized crop payments according to cane quality (interviews with representatives of the industry, July 2001; *Azúcar & Fructosa*, 3[36], 2001: 6; CNIAA 2001: 7, 9). While the Cane Growers' Decree explicitly allows crop payment according to individual productivity as one option, cane quality has so far entered into the crop price only in terms of mean sucrose content and other mean quality factors for all growers contracted by a mill. This payment form favours the least productive growers and *minifundistas* at the expense of the mills and of growers with high production inputs, better land quality and/or better crop care. Many union leaders see the industry's insistence on such measures as a strategy to abolish their collective contract and to debilitate their national leadership (UNPCA and UNC representatives in Mexico City, interviewed June 2001).

The changing political parameters of the growers' unions

The transformation and crisis of the sugar agroindustry have established new conditions for both confrontation and collaboration between the industry and the growers' unions. In a few cases new forms of collaboration emerged between mill management, growers' unions and land cultivators (Singelmann 2002), but the crisis of the sugar industry has also made new forms of collaboration between mill administrators and union locals appear suspicious to the rank-and-file. In some cases such distrust is justified when union leaders and mill administrators reach fraudulent agreements at the expense of the majority of the growers, and the need to abandon such practices is recognized by many national and regional leaders of both unions. More generalized disputes among union leaders centre on union control, on changing political practices and on reassessing the unions' relations with the PRI and the government. In these disputes, leadership decisions and strategies played a central role in attempts to sort out contradictory options for redefining the vertical relations between the growers' unions, the CNC and the CNOP, the PRI, and the government of the National Action Party (Partido Acción Nacional, PAN).

Internal divisions

In the UNC, such disputes began to emerge in the 1990s between organized slates that competed for controlling the union's National Executive Committee (referred to in the following under its Spanish acronym, CEN). Initially, this conflict could be resolved only in 1993 when President Salinas de Gortari imposed a compromise in which the two slates shared power under the formal leadership of the entrepreneur Miguél Ortíz Junguitud. During his two regular three-year turns (1993–99), Ortíz explicitly aligned with the neoliberal government policies that sought to eliminate state subsidies and social 'guarantees' in favour of unregulated competition to promote increased productivity and administrative efficiency (Ortíz, interviewed in 1997 and 1998). But government, industry and growers' representatives of the UNPCA and even of the UNC agreed in interviews (June 2000 and 2001) that Ortíz showed no intention of changing the traditional ways of union administration, that he called for few national assemblies, and that these assemblies merely formalized decisions already made.

Ortíz's second term as the UNC's general secretary – the maximum permitted under union bylaws – was extended in 1999 in a special session of the union's general assembly. With this decision, the second slate in the 1993 leadership dispute, lead by Rolando Saavedra, felt deprived of its turn and occupied the central union offices in April 1999. Rejecting Ortíz's neoliberal agenda, this group assumed a populist stand, accusing

Ortíz in posters of being a 'crook' (*ladrón*) and surrounding his pictures with swastikas (Mexico City, June 1999). Informants from industry, government and the group loyal to Ortíz declared that Saavedra had merely pursued his personal interests through 'traditional' methods used by defeated political aspirants for demonstrating their remaining political assets.

When Ortíz organized an extraordinary general assembly to affirm his authority, the dissident slate succeeded in interrupting the event and in preventing the vote. In the end, Saavedra's group was expelled from the UNC under accusations of disloyalty and violation of union statutes. The government and the Chamber of the Sugar Industry then recognized the slate of Ortíz, and in July 1999 a sympathetic slate headed by Carlos Blackaller Ayala was elected without opposition or resistance. But at the end of 2002 the new CEN was still renting offices outside the union's headquarters under the expectation of a legal resolution.

Similar confrontations emerged in the UNPCA in 1994 when unresolved conflict between four slates led President Salinas de Gortari to impose Manuél Pérez Bonilla from the state of Veracruz as the union's general secretary. An official in the national union headquarters, interviewed in 1999, drew attention to 'some progress' in that for the first time Mexico's president had 'consulted' with the executive committee of the CNC before making his decision. The leadership of Pérez Bonilla (1994–99) was distinguished by his strong personality and his ability to neutralize his opponents in the union's CEN through strategies that opened up the national leadership to greater inputs from the general membership and from allied regional leaders. To mobilize regional forces, Pérez Bonilla increased the influence of local leaders on decisions made at the national level and promoted a more active and open participation of growers in regional electoral campaigns. These measures challenged the kind of manipulation that had traditionally been applied to ensure approval of decisions already made by the national union, CNC or PRI leadership. But greater regional input on the election of national leaders did not necessarily imply parallel changes in political *usos y costumbres* at any level. Indeed, this political opening was directly linked to the strong personality of Pérez Bonilla, to his political strategy for solidifying his leadership, and to the general political conjuncture of the early 1990s. During that period, Hugo Andres Araujo directed the CNC as the self-declared leader of a 'new peasant movement' that was fully embraced by the Salinas de Gortari government in its search for greater autonomy from traditional PRI control and in its promotion of increased agricultural productivity (Mackinlay 1996: 206–17). This conjuncture began to dissolve with a shift in the government's political strategy and with the subsequent fall of Araujo at the beginning of the

Zedillo government (1994–2000). In political terms, the position of Pérez Bonilla was undermined in 1999 when Miguél Alemán Velasco became the PRI candidate for the governorship of Veracruz, where twenty-two of Mexico's sixty sugar mills are located. Alemán's base of support in the primary election did not include the cane growers' unions, and informants tied to the UNPCA national headquarters (interviewed in June 2000 and 2002) have suggested that the victory of Alemán in the primaries was the main reason for Pérez Bonilla's resignation in 1999 – a year before his second term ended. These informants suggest that Pérez Bonilla sought new union elections without interference from the gubernatorial campaign and that he wanted to give a head start to the candidate of his choice, Francisco Castro González, against the potential resurgence of the three slates involved in the pre-1994 confrontations. But Castro did not have the charisma of Pérez Bonilla and, after he was elected, the chances of successful negotiations with the sugar industry were dramatically reduced as the industry was undergoing the most serious crisis in its history. Discontent with the leadership of Castro developed at the beginning of the 2000–01 *zafra* and promoted Jorge Schettino Pérez as the leader of a new group that insisted on stronger measures to press for cane payments and for financing land cultivation. Schettino also accused the union leader of having a purely 'political' agenda with no commitment to fight seriously for the rightful demands of the growers (interviews with opposition leaders, Mexico City, June 2001 and 2002; see also *La Jornada*, 7 August 2001).

The conflict in the UNPCA was also stirred by the methods Castro applied to ensure his 2001 re-election. Under Schettino, the opposition charged that Castro initiated his campaign in violation of the union's bylaws. He was accused of using the support of a minority in the union's executive committee to prevent the other slates from appearing on the ballots and of using traditional political methods to impose his re-election before the other groups could launch their campaign.[2] Specifically, these sources emphasize that not all union leaders were informed about the call for the extraordinary assembly, that in several regions Castro was selected by local political allies without being nominated or formally elected, and that Castro moved the union's electoral assembly at the last moment and against its bylaws from the state of Tabasco to Oaxaca without informing all of the union representatives. The seventeen dissidents – the majority of the twenty-four members of the union's CEN – found out about the assembly some five days before its opening.

This conflict was linked to a broader political realignment in progress. The Schettino faction of the UNPCA called for political democratization and demanded compliance with union bylaws. A representative of the Department of Agriculture recognized the doubts about the proper application of the union bylaws in Castro's re-election. He assigned greater priority to political considerations, however, than to legal statutes and union bylaws by emphasizing the support Castro had received from regional union leaders, indicating that the *legitimation* this support reflected was more important than the strict *legality* of the procedures. A representative of the industry took a similar position but emphasized the Chamber's need for political neutrality and for not intervening in internal union affairs (interviews, Mexico City, June 2002). For different reasons, Castro also gained the formal recognition of the government, specifically the Department of Agriculture as well as the Chamber of the Sugar Industry.

The conflict in the UNPCA at the national level was reflected in the regional elections of union leaders. While Castro received support from local leaders in fifty-three of the sixty sugar regions, his opposition claimed that these leaders were bypassing the sympathy Schettino's group found in the rank-and-file. In five regions, this conflict resulted in 'parallel elections' in which two or more groups claimed to be the authentic representatives of the growers.

Castro's victory in this conflict was, by September 2001, tied to a broader alliance with the 'traditional' factions of the CNC and the PRI that had sought to resolve similar internal conflicts over power and forms of operation since 2000. But the chances of 'closing ranks' under this vertical alliance are limited, because the alliance primarily entails accords over the distribution of power without addressing new pressures for changing the way union offices are obtained and administered. It is, furthermore, based on expedience more than on sympathy or shared convictions on the part of executive committees facing the need to present a united front in public for the 2003 legislative elections. This public image conceals, but does not resolve internal confrontations over power, organization and programmatic direction, and the opening of political space for new unions not affiliated to the PRI further confounds Castro's problematic position.

New links with the government [3]

The government takeover of twenty-seven highly indebted mills in 2001 again changed the cane growers' options for political alliances. The selection of the expropriated mills has been linked to political as much as to economic considerations, and dissidents in the UNPCA have questioned the legal and the substantive justification for the mill expropriations, emphasizing that many more than twenty-seven mills were in similar financial straits. They suggest that the selection of the mills for expropriation was tied to the long-term links of some owners with the PRI (UNPCA 2001: 5–9). A representative of the industry, interviewed in June 2002, had similar suspicions about the political motives behind the selection of the expropriated mills, arguing that it had no legal foundation while justifying it on the grounds of economic necessity. Owners of expropriated mills are disputing the legality of the mill expropriations. In a decision of 1 November 2002 that is being appealed by the government, a federal judge found that the 2001 state takeover of the Grupo Escorpión's nine mills had no legal basis.

The government also played a central role in directing conflicts within the UNPCA. The autumn 2001 re-election of Francisco Castro in violation of union statutes was directly linked to his ability to use the new political constellation initiated at the 2000 elections. In a political deal, the federal government bypassed union bylaws and recognized Castro as the union's leader. It increased the cane price for the 2001–02 *zafra* without corresponding increases in productivity and/or sugar prices, as stipulated by the Sugarcane Decree, and it ensured cane payments and new loans to the growers after a long period of uncertainty. In exchange, Castro, as head of the Chamber of Deputies' Special Committee of the Sugar Agroindustry, *de facto* abandoned the pending Law of the Sugar Agroindustry that the UNPCA had initiated under his leadership. While the pact with the government served to strengthen Castro's position within the UNPCA, his opponents were convinced that the government manipulated him 'like a spider [manipulates] a fly: it sucks out his blood and then throws him away' (a dissident UNPCA leader, interviewed June 2001) to ensure his support for future mill closures and for opening up the national market to massive imports of high-fructose corn syrup surpluses from the USA in competition with Mexican sugar.

These interpretations provide insights into the way union leaders and other informants tied to the sugar agroindustry assess their situation and the nature of the political playing field. Regardless of the undisguised agenda these understandings reflect, the developments examined in this section indicate that the 2001 confrontations in the UNPCA were tied to an emerging alliance between the new government and established union leaders who sought to maintain their control by adjusting traditional patterns of mobilization and cooptation to the new political constellation. But the future of the privileged position held by the UNPCA and the UNC is tied not only to such alliances but also to the general democratization of the political field that has opened new opportunities for mobilizations under the banner of other political parties or those without formal party affiliation.

Political reconfiguration

As the PRI began to lose its hegemony with its dubious victory in the 1988 presidential elections and with subsequent PRI defeats in gubernatorial and Congressional elections, cane growers' organizations not affiliated with the PRI emerged in the 1990s under the auspices of the PRD and the PAN. While the prevailing decree favours the two PRI-affiliated unions, eventual changes are expected by all groups involved as the government has explicitly emphasized that 'the decree is now obsolete' and requires 'an updated judiciary base' to 'eliminate corporatism ... so that the CNC and the CNPR are not in charge of the growers but that it be the free association of the cane producers' (Javier Usabiaga, Secretary of Agriculture [SAGARPA], as cited in *Azúcar & Fructosa*, 3[43], 2001: 8).

Like the confrontations within the UNPCA, these challenges have different manifestations at the regional level. A group of cane growing entrepreneurs associated with the Fundación Produce Jalisco represents an example of this new line of division. This group seeks to disassociate itself from the PRI-affiliated unions and to establish new forms of association through regional producers' circles. It is, furthermore, ideologically and politically tied to the PAN that won the 2000 gubernatorial election in the state of Jalisco. But the group is also linked to traditional political strategies chosen by a slate that had lost its bid in the 2000 election of the UNPCA local of the Tamazula mill in Jalisco. The two competing groups accused each other of having manipulated the election either by fraud or by running candidates who falsely pretended to be cane growers (interviews with members of the losing slate in Jalisco and of the national UNPCA leadership, December 2000 and June 2001).

A similar conflict emerged in the UNPCA at the national level when Isidro Pulido Reyes, the leader of the union in the early 1980s, announced the foundation of a new cane growers' organization that was not tied to political parties and was opposed to 'the political corporatism of the [PRI's] organizations' (see *Azúcar & Fructosa*, 2[21], 1999: 13). But Pulido Reyes has no significant political base today, and his association has never been active. Such contentions reflect new possibilities for shifts in union affiliation. Shortly before the UNPCA's political rupture, 'working papers' by various members of its CEN discussed the need to separate the union from the PRI, to dissolve the different growers' confederations within a single professional chamber, and to ensure the freedom of unions to negotiate their interests with any political party (see Rodríguez Sosa 2001; Spinoso Foglia 2001). This change would also ensure minority party representation in local production committees and be founded on the transformation of the Sugarcane Decree into law (Spinoso Foglia 2001: 6–7). The proposal to incorporate the UNC and the UNPCA into a single national chamber or association was not shared by other UNPCA leaders, and the agenda was ultimately put on hold because it was presented by members of the union's executive committee who lost the subsequent conflict with Francisco Castro. Nevertheless, the need to open space for other unions was generally recognized. A new version of the pending legislation, by the PAN in 2002, also opens the entrance for other unions. But, unlike the PRI and the PRD, it proposes the separation of the growers' unions from all political parties, the formation of a single professional cane growers' chamber, and decentring the negotiations with the sugar industry according to regional conditions (interview with a federal deputy of the PAN; Zacatepec, Morelos, June 2002; see also *Azúcar & Fructosa*, 4[51], 2002b: 4; ibid., 4[55], 2002: 10). The debate over these issues has also raised new questions about the contradictory principles of individual liberty and common interests, the response to these contradictions, and over the costs or benefits of different strategies of mobilization. While the PRI's union leaders 'read the signs' of equal institutional rights for other unions, representatives of the sugar industry have critiqued this project because they prefer a single partner in efficient negotiations or, given the perceived political reality, no more than three national unions. On the other hand, Mexico's Supreme Court decided in favour of a dissident mill workers' union in a 2001 benchmark decision, declaring that the exclusionary clause that had privileged a single national mill workers' union under the auspices of the Workers' Confederation of Mexico (Confederación de Trabajadores de México, CTM) was unconstitutional and violated the higher right of free association (*Reforma*, 18 April 2001: <www.reforma.com/justicia_y_seguridad/088193>; *La Jornada*, 19 April 2001: <http://www.jornada.unam.mx/043nlsoc.html>). This decision has parallel implications for the corporatist organization of the PRI's cane growers' unions.

Conclusions

This chapter has addressed the relations between economic liberalization, the democratization of political institutions and changing political culture. Pressures for political democratization from the late 1980s on were rooted in mobilizations within the political and civic spheres under the banner of resistance to the social implications of economic liberalization. The government none the less enforced its neoliberal economic reforms between 1985 and 2000 with the support of the non-democratic parameters of the post-revolutionary regime. Perceived economic requirements under the premises of market liberalization were not the cause of political mobilization in search for democracy.

In the case of Mexico's PRI-affiliated cane growers' unions, economic liberalization and institutional democratization have had no immediate or direct effect on changing *usos y costumbres políticos*. Economic conditions constitute part of the context in which mobilizations emerged, evolved and provided feedback for structural and cultural 'elaboration' (Archer 1988). In this context, economic, political, legal or cultural fields have operated under different principles, and social groups within these fields pursued both common and opposing goals. Reasonably integrated relations between these fields and their groups are necessary but inherently problematic and subject to dispute. Such disputes and their outcomes reach high degrees of uncertainty during periods of transition 'from contingent choice to structured contingency' (Karl 1990: 6–9; see also Przeworski 1989; O'Donnell and Schmitter 1986).

Recognizing such complexity confirms a variety of more general social theories that since the late 1960s have assessed the 'relative autonomy' of different social forces or 'fields', or the contradictory relations between the 'autopoietic' forces of different 'systems' that operate within a society or between societies and different elements of their environment (Poulantzas 1987 [1968]; Bourdieu 1989; Habermas 1981; Luhmann 1984). Among analysts of rural Mexico, Gerardo Otero (1999) has offered a comparable argument that emphasizes the significance of social class, personal leadership and regional culture as forces in their own right whose reconciliation is necessary but inherently precarious and subject to contention.

The findings of this chapter suggest the utility of such arguments in general terms to explain the dynamics of the transformation faced by Mexico's PRI-affiliated cane growers' unions as they have to reassess the interests of their members and their political options in redefining their relations with the sugar industry, the government and the federal legislature in a transforming broader economic context. This reassessment is currently in a transitional phase whose eventual outcome also hinges on the resolution of confrontations within each of these groups. Assessing the forces that promote or hinder changes in organizational goals and forms of operation in the two established cane growers' unions, the findings indicate that such changes entail a dynamic in its own right that responds to, and feeds back on, broader changes in the macroeconomic and institutional political fields. Political mobilizations and countermoves are a central intervening factor in determining the directions of structural and cultural reconfiguration. Mexico's cane growers' unions reflect an exemplary case of such processes in progress and without a definite direction of structural changes in the broader economic and political fields. Contestations are frequently presented here in terms of divisions between 'traditional' and 'modern' orientations. But demands for clean elections or administrative practices in the union headquarters may reflect genuine convictions or obvious options for election losers who challenge the legitimacy of the winners but have no intention of going beyond rhetorical declarations. Under the same principle, relations between formal institutional democratization and political practice are more complex, as is reflected in the case of Francisco Castro and his faction in the UNPCA. While Castro is formally recognized as the UNPCA leader, his group seeks to hold unresolved confrontations at bay in a precarious alliance with the leaders of the CNC and of the PRI, who face similar unresolved divisions and challenges. This alliance, in turns, is rooted less in mutual sympathy than in a political necessity for the PRI and the CNC, given Castro's unspoken albeit precarious agreement with the new government. The democratically elected government here is able to enlist support for its 'modern' economic agenda through an alliance in which it readily supports 'traditional' political leaders and, in the process, appropriates some of the political practices on which the hegemony of the PRI had been founded.

Notes

This chapter is a partially translated and partially revised version of Singelmann 2003, with permission from the *Revista Mexicana de Sociología*. I am indebted to Gerardo Otero and Horacio Mackinlay for critiquing previous versions. The final draft and any errors are my own responsibility.

1. On these debates see Singelmann (2003) and MacKinlay and Otero (this volume). Apart from the issue of democratization 'in the broad sense', the major issues of contention in this literature include the 'necessary' or contingent nature of the relations between economic liberalization and political democratization; between formal institutional democratization and changing political practices at all levels; and specifically the dissolution of different types of intersection between corporatist–authoritarian structures and political cultures marked by patron–client relations.

2. The following interpretation is based on internal documents of the UNPCA's dissident faction (UNPCA 2001) and on confidential documents obtained from that group in June 2002; interviews with leaders of the dissident slate (June 2001 and 2002), with representatives of the union's Board of Arbitration (August 2001, November 2001), and on newspaper articles appearing daily in *La Jornada* and *Excelsior* 10–25 June 2001. See also *Azúcar & Fructosa*, 4(41), 2001: 12.

3. Unless cited otherwise, this section is based on the reconstruction of information and interpretations provided in June 2001 and 2002 by representatives of the Chamber of the Sugar Industry (Cámara Nacional de la Industria Azucarera y Alcoholera, CNIAA), the Secretary of Agriculture (Secretaría de Agricultura, Ganadería, Desarrollo Rural, Pesca y Alimentación, SAGARPA), and from members of the dissident faction of the UNPCA lead by Jorge Schettino.

7 | Manufacturing neoliberalism: industrial relations, trade union corporatism and politics

ENRIQUE DE LA GARZA TOLEDO

§ BEFORE 1982, the Mexican socioeconomic structure was considered to be an import substitution system characterized by a strong and authoritarian state that promoted industrialization. The state protected industrialization against external competition, providing industrialists with soft credits and favouring them by controlling agricultural prices. From an economic point of view, this structure facilitated the transition from light industrialization in the 1930s and 1940s to heavy industrialization in the 1950s and 1960s. In the 1970s, however, economic and political turbulence led this socioeconomic structure to crisis point and it was replaced by neoliberalism.

A turning point for the Mexican socioeconomic model was 1982 and, in spite of imbalances and unsteadiness, it was also a turning point for the industrial relations system. The contradictions that had been accumulating for more than ten years exploded in the form of the state's financial crisis in 1982, specifically as a foreign debt crisis. Superficially, the drop in oil prices that had taken place a year before (Mexico being a large oil exporter) coincided with an increase in international interest rates. Deep down it was a conjunction of different problems – the weakness of an agricultural sector that could no longer grow given a government price policy that favoured the industrial sector; the state's fiscal crisis, in addition to deficit expenditures with which it had been subsidizing industry for decades – coinciding with the new policy of the transnational corporations based in Mexico, which were now prioritizing the international market over the domestic market. Under these conditions, the state initiated a change in the economic model. This implied widespread privatization, the state's withdrawal from productive investment, deregulation, opening up the external market, an end to the industrial promotion policy, the pre-eminence of the financial sector and using the exchange rate to anchor the economy. Since this turning point, however, economic growth has been low on average, with many fluctuations and crises: a childhood crisis in 1987, a youth crisis in 1995 and a maturity crisis in the year 2001 (de la Garza 2001).

As part of the import substitution model, labour and trade union relations in Mexico were subordinated to the economic and political needs of both the state and the firms. In this sense, the backbone of the industrial relations system has not been based on the labour law but, among others, on the following elements:

1. Most trade unions were considered to share with the state the responsibility for maintaining the economic model and the political system. In spite of recurring tension, the state's economic policy was commonly imposed on the trade unions' demands in order to save the economic model. This shared responsibility worked during the import substitution period and is also working during the current neoliberal model. Trade unions in Mexico, rather than being private bodies representing specific interests, are public bodies at the same level as political parties and have public policy functions.

2. Labour relations in Mexico were subordinated to public policies, whereby trade unions did not contribute as external bodies, but rather as part of the state structure itself. The subordination of the labour sphere to the public policy arena did not always act against wages or working conditions. During the economic boom (in the 1960s), wages increased, as did workers' legal protection and collective agreement provisions.

3. Labour relations have mainly been negotiated in the public policy arena, thus establishing a system of exchanges. That is, wage increases, benefits or social security are granted in exchange for support of public policies and elections.

4. Trade unions and the political system overlap heavily. Trade union leaders are at the same time important political party leaders. In exchange for this, they receive a quota of popular election posts or positions within the government's administration.

5. In other words, the official trade unions in Mexico have traditionally intervened in the design of economic and labour policies, although always subordinate to the logic of the state's economic policy. They participated in the political system, in elections and the government, in the management of the social security system by creating tripartite administration boards related to institutions of health, supply and housing. Official unions also participated, of course, in labour relations. But it must be noted that these labour relations are constantly permeated by the political and governmental spheres and thereby turned into political relations.

The historical conversion of trade unions into state bodies also implied the state's support in maintaining this system and its leadership. The labour laws as well as extra-legal practices are used for this purpose. This system implied the state's control over trade union registration and over the trade unions themselves, and over strikes and collective bargaining (de la Garza 1990). In the face of this alliance between corporate trade union elites and the state, the opposition, often from the Left, came across many legal and extra-legal obstacles. It was by no means a peaceful system. Since the 1930s there had been recurrent workers' eruptions in search of union democracy. The state, however, always managed to reduce them to minor expressions of discontent.

This cluster of relations and mutual support between trade unions, the state and entrepreneurs, with its implications for labour relations, has been called corporatism in Mexico (on rural corporatism, see Mackinlay and Otero, this volume). Mexican corporatism has been characterized by a lack of democracy in the trade unions, because their function of representing the workers' interests has been subordinated to political functions. Besides, this corporatism has established exchange, reward and punishment systems between leadership and the rank-and-file which, having persisted for sixty years, have become part of the workers' culture. This culture includes a combination of the following features: statism (problems get solved only within the state's realm), decision-making is delegated to the leaders, patrimonialism (the leaders seen as the boss in the trade unions), and bureaucratic rules that are not effective without the leaders' personal interventions, thus implying the favour to and commitment of those receiving them. Considering that corporatism is hardly interested in improving production in the firms, it may have helped to consolidate the workers' instrumentalist culture with regard to work and a favour system within the productive process that, in effect, acts contrary to productivity (de la Garza 1993). This form of corporatism was a vital part of the import substitution model because it ensured social and labour peace, and voters for the ruling Institutional Revolutionary Party (PRI) and its sinecures. It was also seen as a lever of aggregated demand that would encourage investment and production.

The import substitution model, however, went into crisis in the early 1980s, and the consolidation of the neoliberal model in the 1990s implied important tensions for corporate trade unionism in its practices, exchange systems and ideology. This form of trade unionism nevertheless continues to prevail in Mexico in its mutual support of the new state, in spite of being immersed in many contradictions that have been pressuring it towards transformation since the 1990s and particularly under the new Fox administration.

The macroeconomy in the 1990s: the neoliberal transition

We shall first analyse some of the important changes in the economic model related to the new production models geared towards work flexibility, and how the different trade union trends have faced these changes and how these trends have changed as well. We will try to explain why trade union corporatism persists in spite of the consolidation of the neoliberal model.

Economic policy under the neoliberal model applied to Mexico has focused on fighting inflation. Besides, the state has largely withdrawn from direct productive investment. In the fight against inflation, close attention has been paid to the mass of money placed in circulation by the Bank of Mexico. A restrictive wage policy has also been in place, and the overvaluation of the peso has been permitted in order to maintain cheap imports. High interest rates have been required to attract foreign investment.

In this neoliberal economic policy context, the manufacturing industry has become the pivot around which the economy grows. In the year 2000, manufactured goods accounted for 28.7 per cent of the total production, surpassed only by commerce, restaurants and hotels. The manufacturing sector has experienced the most accelerated growth after the great crisis in 1995, responsible for 87.3 per cent of total exports in the year 2000. Economic opening, however, has not only translated into an accelerated increase in manufactured exports. As it turns out, this model has also resulted in a substantial increase in the imports of raw materials and capital goods for the export sector. The import-intensity of the export sector has been so sharp that manufacture's trade balance in the 1990s has always been in a deficit. The export-oriented *maquiladora* industry is one of the main causes of this imbalance. In the 1990s, the *maquiladora* exports increased in importance and reached 47.9 per cent of total exports and 34 per cent of total imports in 2000 (V. Fox 2001).

There is also a strong concentration of Mexican exports by consortium, and by industrial branch. Since 1996, when exports shot up, three industries accounted for 67.3 per cent of all exports: auto and auto-parts, electric goods and electronics, and machinery and special equipment. Seven hundred firms, representing only 2 per cent of all export-oriented firms, export 80 per cent of the total (de la Garza 2001).

Neoliberal economic policies jointly resulted in a reduction in inflation and an increase in exports. This situation, however, reached its limit towards the end of 2000. The deterioration of the domestic market, low wages in particular, the dependence on imported inputs, the decreasing presence of governmental expenditure in the aggregate demand, and the overvaluation of the Mexican peso had negative effects on both economic growth and the trade balance during the Zedillo administration. This deficit was mainly financed with foreign direct investment in the second half of the 1990s. It was secondarily financed by the external debt and portfolio investment, as opposed to the first half of the 1990s when portfolio investment played the main role (Otero 1996b). The deficit of the balance of payments has none the less grown considerably since 1998.

The growth of the industrial sector has had its succession of ups and downs. After a pronounced drop during the 1995 crisis, it started a slow recovery in 1996, with greater growth in 1997 and 1998, deceleration in 1999, a new high level of growth during the year 2000 and a new drop during 2001, reaching negative figures towards mid-2002.

Although, in general, the physical volume of manufactured production increased considerably in the 1990s, its repercussions on the personnel employed in the manufacturing industry have followed a different trajectory. Towards the year 2000, the 1993 employment levels had not recovered, in spite of the fact that employment was showing sustained growth in the *maquiladora* industry up until the new 2001 crisis. This could be due, on the one hand, to an increase in labour productivity, which grew 46.3 per cent between 1993 and 2000, or, on the other hand, to the fact that workers had been expelled from the non-*maquila* sector by competition with imported products and the dismantling of the old chains of production (Dussel Peters 1997, and this volume).

Remuneration to personnel employed in the manufacturing industry between 1988 and 1998 decreased in real terms by 45.9 per cent. This decrease took place in firms of all sizes, although disproportionately in small firms, and workers' incomes tended to grow in real terms after reaching rock bottom in 1996. By the year 2001, remuneration had not yet reached its 1994 level. The highest wage levels ever were reached in 1976. Between 1976 and July 2002, deterioration was approximately 75 per cent in real terms (*La Jornada* 2002).

The fact that wages were kept low throughout the last administration can also be explained by the persistence of trade unions that did not actually represent the workers. Although in 1997 official trade unionism suffered splits and the National Union of Workers (Unión Nacional de Trabajadores, UNT) was founded, most workers continued to be under the control of trade union corporatism.

Since November 2000, production, employment and manufactured exports have decelerated. This crisis did not start as a financial crisis, but rather originated with Mexican industry en route to improving productivity and competitiveness through a policy of intensifying work together with lower wages, either in its Taylorist–Fordist or Toyotaist style. Taylorism–Fordism is a form of work organization based on separation between conception and operation that translates into work methods that are standardized, simplified and routinized, where time and movement are measured and where the assembly chain may be incorporated. Toyotaist methods are based on task reintegration, greater worker autonomy in the working post, multi-skills, teamwork and a supposed labour culture of identification with the firm's goals. This path of increased productivity and competitiveness, however, has its limitations: first, in the workers' physical resistance to the deterioration of their labour power; and second, in social resistance, which in Mexico is not expressed through collective action headed by the trade unions, but through the workers' individual claims filed in court, and especially through the high, voluntary external turnover.

Furthermore, the viability of a production model implies an explicit or implicit agreement between capital and labour in order to be able to work. The state seemed to understand this throughout most of the 1990s and encouraged trade unions and firms to sign productivity agreements. Establishing productivity agreements from the top resulted in low trade union representation, reinforced by the fact that for a long time trade unions tended to be excluded from the discussion of production-related issues in Mexico. Besides, the productivity agreements hardly contributed to the workers' income. Especially in the firms restructured along Toyotaist lines, which assume workers' participation and engagement in production issues, it was not possible to harmonize capital and labour in the face of low wages. In any case, capital offered labour ambiguous guarantees of stabilization in the labour posts which did not convince the 'new *maquiladora* working class' who responded with high external turnover. In the *maquiladora* industry, the external turnover rate towards the end of the twentieth century was close to 80 per cent per year (Carrillo and de la O 2002).

In fact, towards the end of 2001, mean real wages in the manufacturing industry (average wage provisions in collective agreements and *maquiladora* wages) had not yet reached the level they had before the great crisis in 1995, and were lower than in 1976. Productivity in manufacturing industry, however, increased considerably (Dussel Peters, this volume). To summarize, the macroeconomic policy of the Zedillo administration did not succeed in eradicating the economic crisis. By the last months of 2000, the economy decelerated and went into an open recession in the first few months of 2001. Neoliberalism in Mexico has been associated with production models based on low wages and labour intensification, which may well have reached their limit with the current crisis.

Close to 10 per cent of all large establishments (firms with over 250 workers) in the manufacturing industry were restructured by 1994 (de la Garza and Melgoza 1994). This segment included firms that have been favoured by NAFTA. These are firms with middle to high technology that partially apply total quality and just-in-time processes, without extreme levels of labour flexibility or important articulations with their economic zone (de la Garza 1998). 'Backward' socio-technical configurations are, on the one hand, the middle-sized and large industry that have not been restructured with Taylorist–Fordist processes (such as traditional assembly with simple, repetitive, standardized tasks) and, on the other hand, small and middle-sized firms with unscientific work administration (de la Garza 1998). The firms that have articulated with the US economy and, to a lesser degree, with the Canadian economy have been restructured at least partly with Taylorist–Fordist processes. Contrarily, most micro- and small firms do not export or act as outsourcers of the export-oriented firms because their technological and organizational conditions, their market knowledge, labour relations, labour force qualification, productivity, quality and just-in-time production do not allow for this linkage, and neoliberal governments have systematically refused to design an active industrial policy to support this important segment of the economy. Restructured firms in Mexico have also resorted to the Toyotaist model, but to a lesser degree. Most firms would find it difficult to comply with conditions such as a high investment in training, an educated and qualified labour force, and the management's willingness to share decision-making about production with the workers (de la Garza 2001).

Changes in the industrial relations system

The concept of the industrial relations system was created for societies in which the rule of law and legal labour norms are the backbone of relations between employees, employers and the state. It is assumed that the actors have accepted and internalized the system's norms (Dunlop 1958). In societies like Mexico, legal labour norms are only part, and perhaps the least important part, of the relations between trade unions, the state and entrepreneurs. In other words, unwritten rules and negotiations are often added and laid over the labour and industrial relations, which are the most important. Furthermore, these latter relations have been modified much more in the last twenty years than the legal norms.

The process of change in the industrial relations system in Mexico during the neoliberal model, instated as of 1982, can be divided into four periods. First, from 1982 to 1992, when flexibilization of the collective bargaining agreement was initiated; second, from 1992 to 1994, when there was an attempt to restructure trade union corporatism; third, from 1994 to 2000, the period that witnessed the failure of efforts to turn productivity agreements into the basis of a new worker–employer agreement; and, last, the period initiated in 2001 with the new Fox administration that made way for the possibility of corporate restoration.

Unilateral flexibilization: 1982–92

It was not the state that gave the signal for a change in labour relations to be initiated in Mexico, although it later played an extremely important role in inducing and supporting this change. Rather, the change was spear-headed by multinational corporations, which in the early 1980s decided to be no longer oriented to the domestic market in Mexico and instead to orient themselves to the international market. The new auto plants in the north were thus born flexible (Arteaga and Carrillo 1990) and opened a new era in labour relations. Since then, 'flexibility' has become a key word that has crossed the different forms of productive restructuring in Mexico in the past twenty years. For management, however, this notion has acquired two polarized meanings. On the one hand, it means labour deregulation, allowing management to do as it pleases with the labour force according to the needs of production and, on the other hand, flexibility is linked with new forms of work organization that incorporate the idea of identity with the firm.

The former meaning is likely to prevail among Mexican firms: labour deregulation as a means to increase management control. Between 1982 and 1992 management doctrines regarding labour flexibility to gain competitiveness *vis-à-vis* the opening of the economy spread throughout Mexico. In this period, flexibility tended to be identified with deregulation and the trade unions were seen as rigidities that needed to be minimized. Many collective bargaining agreements of the large-scale firms were consequently modified to marginalize trade unions from decision-making regarding changes in technology or work organization. The flexibilization of collective agreements in particular took place in the firms that were in the process of being privatized. This period was characterized by repeated confrontations between firms and trade unions, even the corporatist trade unions (de la Garza and Melgoza 1994). However, with regard to the scope of flexibilization in Mexico, we must not forget that, although in a primitive way, most workers in the micro-enterprises were already flexible to start with and that the flexibilization processes have been concentrated above all in the large corporations.

Both corporate and independent trade unions came up with different responses to the shift in the economic model and the role of the state. Yellow unions (i.e. management-oriented unions) have not yet come up with a collective reaction. When the first adjustment in the economy was initiated in 1983, it was mainly the nationalistic sectors with both a corporate and independent expression that reacted. The resistance of these sectors reached its peak with the strikes that took place in June 1983, when a large number of conflicts broke out demanding wage increases, although in the end they were actually questioning the shift in the role played by the state. Both official and independent strikes were defeated and it took the Workers' Confederation of Mexico (Confederación de Trabajadores de México, CTM) two years to repair its relations with the state. It was not until 1987 that large-scale negotiations between official trade unions, the state and entrepreneurs were resumed with the so-called economic pacts that were reaffirmed in the 1990s. Through these tripartite economic pacts, annual wage increases and public service rates were fixed.

In the 1990s, the CTM was still defending its 1978 programme, heavily based on state control. In 1988, the more congruent nationalists of the PRI found refuge in *neo-Cardenista* (which refers to a renewal of the nationalist trend in the 1930s during the administration of Lázaro Cárdenas) approaches together with other left-wing sectors. This situation had a deeper effect on the sectors that had been relatively modern in the 1970s and which had already reconverted in the 1980s (the auto industry, iron and steel works, the telephone service, the banking system and so on). It was in these sectors that productive restructuring mainly took place, which converged with the industry emerging in the 1980s. In this sector, the effects of restructuring have not been reduced to wage decreases or staff cutbacks, but have been combined with changes in work organization, technological changes and changes in labour relations with amendments to collective bargaining agreements. In this sector, the trade unions' responses have gone from resisting the changes to policies of negotiation with the firms or *laissez-faire* management.

In the case of the independent trade unions, priority has been given to confrontation and resistance to change, with a few exceptions, such as the Authentic Front of Workers (Frente Auténtico del Trabajo, FAT) and the Telmex workers' union. Corporatist trade unions have gone from trade union passivity to an attempt to negotiate. In the period from 1982 to 1992, an important part of the trade union conflicts was related to the unilateral flexibilization of collective bargaining agreements, without underestimating wage and unemployment issues. Struggles of dismissed workers sprouted in the oil industry, the sugar industry, iron and steel works, railways, ports, aviation, insurance companies and banks.

To summarize, in 1982–92 work flexibility became an integral part of the new management doctrine. The large collective bargaining agreements were made flexible, giving rise to serious conflicts with the trade unions. In general, the workers' struggles resisting flexibilization were defeated through joint action between firms and the state. This, however, does not imply that most collective bargaining agreements in Mexico became flexible, probably because an important part of the small and medium-sized firms had already been flexible and the technical and social conditions of production did not always advise entrepreneurs to promote it (Covarrubias 1992). With regard to the relations between the state and the trade unions in this period, the latter lost influence over state policies, corporatism as a system of exchanges was weakened, and the trade unions did not generate any projects towards change.

The 'new trade unionism': 1992–94

Corporate trade unions in Mexico were never interested in productivity issues because they prioritized negotiations with the state. At best, they took on protecting the workers in the work processes, establishing client systems, defending the lack of internal mobility (changing a worker to a different post, category, department or establishment, depending on the production needs of the firm), and took stands against lay-offs, work intensity and protecting promotion due to seniority. In this sense, Mexico does not have a tradition like the European strategies and institutions, such as industrial democracy and factory councils or committees. Towards 1988, at the beginning of the Salinas administration, state and entrepreneurial sectors referred to the crisis of corporatism as a form of trade union that is no longer functional with the new economic model. The luck of these organizations between 1982 and 1988, and their main collective bargaining agreements seemed to justify this idea. With regard to trade unions, the Salinas administration began by striking a blow to two of the most powerful corporate leaderships: the oil workers' union and the teachers' union. In 1990, however, President Salinas outlined a change in the government's strategy towards trade unions. Instead of weakening or destroying them, the government was to press them towards restructuring in agreement with the new economic model and transformation of the state. This strategy was called New Trade Unionism and implied that trade unions would be more representative and democratic; decision-making regarding labour relations in the firm would be decentralized; the historical alliance between trade unions and the state was to be maintained; trade unions would collaborate with management; the new labour culture among the workers would be geared towards productivity. After endless conflicts, the government got the trade unions and employer organizations to sign the National Agreement to Increase Productivity and Quality in 1992, essentially containing the most updated version of the Total Quality doctrine recognizing the trade unions' right to participate in the discussion of these issues. In October 1993, for the first time, the Economic Agreement for Competitiveness and Employment, introduced by the government, and signed by the trade union and entrepreneurial leadership, foresaw that the wage increase in 1994 would be equal to the rate of inflation expected that year plus the increase in productivity in 1993.

Since January 1994, the director of the Department of Labour through the Board of Conciliation pressured the firms and unions that signed collective bargaining agreements or reviewed wages to establish productivity agreements. The number of agreements signed in 1994 thus increased considerably, headed by the CTM.

Throughout these years, the most important conflicts have been:

1. In declining industries confronting the opening of the economy (textiles, rubber and sugar, for example), with the most important conflicts taking place around amending the collective agreements covering a whole industrial branch. In 1992, for example, there was a large strike within the cotton branch. Other conflicts revolved around staff readjustments or flexibilization of the collective agreements of reconverted firms or those undergoing restructuring (Montiel 1991).
2. The great conflicts within the oil industry, steel and iron works, mining, the auto industry, the metal mechanic industry, insurance companies and banks, and the cement industry. In some of these conflicts, collective bargaining agreements had already been partly flexible during the 1980s. This trend deepened in the 1990s. In many of these cases, there were confrontations between trade unions and firms, but in general the workers' resistance did not succeed.
3. Strikes in modern and flexible firms, such as Ford in Chihuahua and Hermosillo, and General Motors in Ramos Arizpe, that did not imply staff cutbacks or additional flexibility, but were struggles for wage increases mixed with trade union democracy struggles.
4. Trade union struggles that have known how to negotiate the restructuring of the firms they work for, such as the telephone and electricity workers' unions.
5. The struggles of the workers in the public sector, particularly elementary and junior high school teachers, as well as in the social security and health sector, who have staged large-scale movements throughout the decade. Without doubt, the teachers are those who mobilized the most frequently during the 1990s.

The struggles around the new economic model and the change in the role played by the state have also been crossed by inter-trade union conflicts: confrontations between the large official confederations for control of the collective bargaining agreements, mainly between the CTM and the Revolutionary Confederation of the Workers and Peasants (Confederación Revolucionaria Obrera y Campesina, CROC); the conflict between the Federation of Trade Unions in Goods and Services (FESEBES) and the CTM; and, recently, the conflict between the UNT and the Labour Congress.

Failure of the productivity bonus strategy: December 1994–2000

In December 1994, the Mexican economy went into a deep crisis. The Gross Domestic Product decreased by 6.2 per cent in real terms in 1995 and the rate of real mean remunerations in the manufacturing industry dropped by 8 per cent that same year. In the face of this great crisis, during which inflation reached 50 per cent, productivity agreements were granting only a 1.4 per cent wage increase. In 1996, inflation was 25 per cent and productivity bonuses gave a 2.2 per cent increase. In other words, in the face of this great crisis, the government and firms chose to depress real wages and the corporatist trade unions accepted this situation. The macroeconomic policy imposed itself once again over the productivity bonus strategy: it attempted to control inflation through depressing real wages, among other measures.

Beyond this impasse, in this period there are three novelties in the panorama of large-scale negotiations and readjustments of the industrial-relations system in Mexico. First, in the context of a full-blown economic crisis in mid-1995, the CTM and the Employers' Confederation of the Mexican Republic (Confederación Patronal de la República Mexicana, COPARMEX) negotiated the introduction of a new labour culture. This negotiation was closed in August 1996, and involved the recognition that economic globalization and integration forced the firms to increase their competitiveness. The document that the CTM and the COPARMEX signed presents the ethical principles that should rule worker–employer relations: good faith, loyalty, justice, truth, responsibility, equity, dialogue and harmonization in labour relations. The whole document, however, revolves around the core idea that labour relations should focus on the human being and not on the social class and that the firm is a com-munity and must be based on solidarity. There is therefore space for conciliation but not for class struggle. This document states that what a human being is worth is due to his/her capacity to transcend. Like a Christian adaptation of Toyotaism, it claims that the core cultural change that must be made is shifting from confrontation to collaboration. This agreement breaks away from the rhetoric of 'class struggle' nourishing the discourse of corporatist trade unions in Mexico during the twentieth century. For these unions, their interests coincided with the state's, but not necessarily with the firms'. Although the Agreement for a New Labour Culture had few practical effects during the 1994–2000 administration, the Fox administration has taken up these ideas. In fact, Carlos Abascal, the former COPARMEX president who originally crafted the agreement, was appointed Secretary of the Labour Department.

The second ground-breaking event was the organization by the most radical segments of independent unionism of Coordinadora Intersindical Primero de Mayo (the May First Inter-Trade Union Coordination) in 1995. Third, in February 1995, and in the context of the deepest crisis in Mexico since 1929, some large trade unions critical of corporatism and the neoliberal model organized the first 'Forum on Trade Unionism before the Nation and in the Face of the Crisis'. By the end of 1997, these trade unions constituted the National Union of Workers (Unión Nacional de Trabajadores, UNT). We will proceed to summarize the strategies followed by the three main trade union lines: the Labour Congress, the Inter-Trade Union Coordination and the UNT in the 1990s.

The CTM and the Labour Congress (CT)

In the 1990s, official trade unionism continued, within its traditional support of government policies, to sign all the economic agreements that have contributed to keeping wages depressed. It is a kind of unionism that has lost its capacity to improve workers' wages and life conditions. Fidel Velásquez, the historic CTM leader, died while the CTM was experiencing this apparent full stop. His successors have no new strategic proposals for the trade unions, except to show their lack of expertise in trade union and national policy issues. The CTM and the CT are immersed in a credibility crisis that also has electoral implications, since they are no longer capable of ensuring future PRI voters. When the time comes to open the state up to other political forces, this process can mark the decline of a type of organization that focused on costs and benefits for workers in a subordinate alliance with only one state.

The May First Inter-Trade Union Coordination (Coordinadora Intersindical Primero de Mayo)

Heir apparent to the independent unionism of the 1970s, but with different actors, the main actors in the Coordination can be divided into three groups: those who swung back and forth between the Coordinadora and the UNT, such as the National University Union and the Authentic Front of Workers (Frente Auténtico del Trabajo, FAT); those who aim to lead the new trade union insurgency, such as the leadership of locals IX and X of the National Education Workers' Union (Sindicato Nacional de Trabajadores de la Educación, SNTE), the Autonomous Metropolitan University Union (Universidad Autónoma Metropolitana, UAM), and the Mexican Oil Institute Union (Instituto Mexicano del Petróleo); and the third group who could be considered the resurrected fundamentalist cadres of the 1970s, currently represented by the Socialist Workers' Party (Partido Obrero Socialista), the Socialist Union League (Liga de Unidad Socialista), the Workers for Socialism League (Liga de Trabajadores por el Socialismo), the journal *El Machete* and the Committee for a Workers' International (Comité por una Internacional Obrera) (information provided by Sergio Sánchez). Leaving aside the sectors that participate in both the Coordination and the UNT at the same time, the majority of the members of the Inter-Trade Union Coordination had a Marxist background and claimed that the contradictions between capital and labour and the class struggle were core issues. The different groups constituting this organization, however, entered into an unsolvable ideological confrontation that led to their dissolution in 1999.

On several occasions, some of these unions tried to reorganize around the Mexican Electricians' Union (Sindicato Mexicano de Electricistas) creating the Front of Mexican Unions (Frente Sindical Mexicano).

The National Union of Workers (Unión Nacional de Trabajadores, UNT)

The UNT trade unions have tried to occupy new labour areas in competition with the Labour Congress and the Coordination. First, they tried the area of negotiation of firms' restructuring, aiming to gain competitiveness. The Coordination refused to look into this problem because it was considered exclusively an issue of the firms and because of the risk that the trade unions might become *reformist*. The Labour Congress and the CTM, although talking of a new labour culture, marginalized its main initiator, Juan S. Millan, and in the face of a CTM leadership that felt obliged to give support to the government during both good and bad times, the force of this discourse subsequently declined. The UNT does not waste time. The moment it was founded in January 1998, it started negotiating the new labour culture with employer organizations without the government's mediation. In electoral policy, UNT trade unions propose not to be affiliated to a political party, but also not to abstain from participating in the electoral process. This differs from the Labour Congress that corporately belongs to the PRI or the Coordination whose hegemonic faction refused to participate in elections. It is nevertheless possible that important UNT masses will have voted and will continue to vote for the Party of the Democratic Revolution (Partido de la Revolución Democrática, PRD). With regard to the new social movements, like the Zapatistas, the UNT immediately protested the killing of indigenous people in December 1997 and sought to act as a witness to the pacification process in Chiapas. Congruent with its traditional support of the government, the Labour Congress remained silent, and the Coordination did not express a stance because of doctrinarian disagreements with the Zapatistas. Internationally, the UNT has established public relations with the American Federation of Labor-Congress of Industrial Unions (AFL-CIO), and both organizations coincide in their critical view of the North American Free Trade Agreement (NAFTA). The CTM has supported the government, declaring that the agreement must not be modified, and the Coordination's criticism of the agreement had minimum effect due to its limited capacity to establish relations with trade unions internationally.

Although the UNT is a workers' organization with an up-to-date trade union discourse and good conditions for development, it will not act as the spark that sets fire to the priority of labour relations. The problem begins with the working class itself, which has not up to now shown any mass-level incendiary intentions. In an attempt to move through this context of political, productive and social readjustment, the UNT is creating alternative discourses. These capacities, however, are marked by both the authoritarian attitudes of the leaders of the main UNT trade unions, and the top-down attitudes of their intellectual advisers. The rank-and-file have had little to say about this, beyond endorsing in assemblies what the new elites have decided beforehand.

The PRI defeat and the change of government: 2000–?

When Vicente Fox came to power, he promised he would put an end to trade union corporatism. He nevertheless appointed Carlos Abascal, former entrepreneurial leader and author of the New Labour Culture corporate agreement in 1995, as director of the Labour Department. His performance throughout the first three years of his administration would point to renewed restoration. This consists of the creation of *Christian Corporatism*, which implies the continuation of the old regime in the labour sphere, with the support of entrepreneurial organizations that are little interested in trade union democracy and fearful of the potential danger that the workers might go beyond the workers' organizations due to the serious condition of labour issues in Mexico. Apart from providing continuity to the labour question, Abascal's line can provide a new labour discourse, that of the Christian right wing, which was suspended in the 1920s with the defeat of the 'Cristeros' (Catholic 'guerrillas' against the governments of the Mexican Revolution). This discourse prioritizes the concept of the immutable human essence over the idea of the existence of workers and employers with different interests: human essence and dignity versus the conflict of interests. More than a century ago, movements within the social sciences abandoned this concept of human essence and substituted for it the concept of the socially and culturally constructed subject. This Christian view states that the worker cannot be understood as a cost to be minimized, but rather as a person who should be dignified. This ideology, however, crumbles in the face of the principle of production models based on labour intensification and low wages. The conservative Christian doctrine in relation to labour relations has thus been unveiled as harbouring the labour crisis in Mexico. This crisis is threefold: in people's capacity to survive by selling their labour, an increasingly more intense depletion of the labour force, and an anomie reflected by an extremely high voluntary turnover. One would expect the Christian ideology's effectiveness to be limited in view of the actual conditions and traditions in Mexico.

The discussion around the New Federal Labour Law based on Christian principles, such as those mentioned above, was resumed in 2001. The government invited the creation of a Central Decision Board in which the main trade union and entrepreneurial factions participated with a view to producing a condensed Labour Bill. By 2003, differences became important. The UNT, favouring a democratizing and anti-corporate reform that includes chapters on flexibility and productivity, has presented its own project. The Labour Congress unions were willing to accept labour flexibility so long as their spheres of influence were respected. The independent trade unions that once affiliated with the May First Coordination were against any amendments to the law. Following their tradition of not participating in politics, the company trade unions (directly controlled by employers) hardly participated. The Fox administration favoured flexibility of the law and possibly some democratizing reforms. In the face of the danger of trade union democratization, the entrepreneurs bet on flexibilization. The National Action Party (Partido de Acción Nacional, PAN) supported the Fox administration's reforms. The PRD opposed the reform generated in the Labour Secretariat and presented a reform of its own, while the PRI tampered with the corporate trade unions.

These are not all the actors involved, however. There are also the ordinary workers who have personally suffered the Mexican-style labour crisis and might find expression outside the leaders' joint manoeuvring. To what extent would the impression that the state can no longer control the workers' organizations, that trade unions would not have the support of the state's superstructure, alongside a weakened PRI and divided official leaders generate the necessary distrust to initiate a period of conflict like that of the 1970s?

Conclusions

The new economic model has been through several structural economic crises: it started with the crisis of the import-substitution model in 1982, then a childhood crisis in 1987, followed by a deeper youth crisis in 1994–95, and an adulthood crisis in 2001. The balance for the workers in terms of employment, wages, contractual protections and social security has been negative so far. Trade union organizations have also lost legitimacy and influence in core areas, such as developing economic and labour policies, managing social security and negotiating the ups and downs of the political system.

Although trade unions have weakened with the neoliberal model, this does not imply corporatism will tend to disappear. The Salinas administration tried to reconstruct the old State Corporatism into a corporatism that would participate in a productive agreement with management. It nevertheless failed in the face of personnel policies that did not really wish to share the decision-making related to the productive process with the workers' organizations, or did not wish to place enough resources into productivity bonuses. The second attempt to combine neoliberalism with corporatism turned out to be weaker than the first. It is the agreement for a New Labour Culture, which in spite of its limited results established the principles of the Fox administration. In the exceptional situation of having a PAN federal government, there is a new attempt at corporatist restoration, first of all providing the trade unions with a doctrine. (The 1910 revolutionary doctrine of social justice, as well as Salinas's incipient doctrine of Social Liberalism and New Unionism, have become history.) Now is the moment for the Church's social doctrine in its corporate version. What is missing, however, are the institutions that support the practice of these actors, since it cannot be sustained on ideology alone. In the old corporatism, the figure of the President, with his highly concentrated power, was the main institution. Under current conditions, however, the presidency appears to be weak and corporatism survives thanks to the networks woven in the past between trade union leaders, government officials and entrepreneurs at both micro- and macro-level. Corporatism also survives thanks to at least two factors: (i) the conviction of most entrepreneurs that corporatism has played a historical role useful for controlling workers' demands and eradicating dissidents, and (ii) that opening trade union democracy under conditions of low wages and the workers' lack of identity with the employers can be a risky venture. The experience of the PAN governments in the states proves that it is possible to continue with the labour and trade union *modus vivendi* between a party that is not meant to be a corporate party and the old PRI corporations. In other words, trade union corporatism can coexist with economic neoliberalism under certain conditions and in states with a strong interventionist tradition in the labour sphere. A political party change-over is not enough to seal its destiny.

All this will happen unless the workers are determined to take another path. For a long time, low wages and bad working conditions have prevailed for most workers in Mexico. Determination for change requires several conditions, however. Workers would need to have organizations and activists that, as in the 1970s, help to provide union-oriented training, to link discontented workers with Non-Governmental Organizations (NGOs) and trade unions, and to create resistance networks to avoid protesters being laid off immediately. Recent cases, like the Kwon Dong *maquiladora*, in the state of Puebla, show that workers can break away from labour control by creating broad national and international support fronts. These strategies would have to move away from state corporatism and be firmly rooted in civil society.

8 | Who reaps the productivity growth in Mexico? Convergence or polarization in manufacturing real wages, 1988–99

ENRIQUE DUSSEL PETERS

§ SINCE the 1990s, Mexico's economic liberalization strategy has become a model to follow for many institutions and schools of thought. From their perspective, Mexico's development since then has been a success in terms of macroeconomic stabilization, integration to the world market and export-orientation, mainly since 1994, after the North American Free Trade Agreement (NAFTA) came into effect. Free trade agreements' preferential trade access until 2002 with thirty-two countries and unilateral import openness are part of this new development strategy.

This chapter goes beyond these issues to analyse the effects of Mexico's new development strategy, since 1988, on productivity performance. In addition, it examines the distribution of productivity increments in real wages, emphasizing the periods before and after 1994, although, in some cases, analysis begins at the end of the 1980s and covers the years up to 1999 or 2002, depending on data availability. The chapter is divided into three sections. The first presents conceptual issues regarding the distribution of productivity growth and examines the pillars of liberalization strategy in Mexico since 1988, providing an overview of a number of indicators of the Mexican economy. Going into more detail, the section also presents some of the main variables and tendencies for productivity growth and employment, and compares Mexico's data with those of other countries. The second section analyses the main features of the most successful branches of Mexico's manufacturing sector for 1988–99 regarding labour productivity, real wages, trade and production, among others. Labour productivity is understood as the relationship between value-added or Gross Domestic Product (GDP) and employment. This relationship is measured at various levels of aggregation: the economy as a whole, manufacturing and/or a group of specific branches. The final section summarizes the main findings of this chapter.

Concepts and overall tendencies in Mexico's labour market and productivity

Assuming a relatively elastic supply of labour, neoclassical economic theory – as well as most multilateral agencies in the context of the 'second generation of reforms' since the mid-1990s (Edwards and Burki 1995) – expects that countries that supply and demand labour will reach a full equilibrium regarding employment and wages (Dornbusch and Fischer 1978; Kerr and Staudohar 1994; Layard et al. 1991). That is to say, real wages will fall whenever there is an excess supply of labour and will rise whenever there is an excess of demand. As a result, most of the discussion related to neoclassical economic theory has focused on the flexibility of labour markets, particularly on the supply side, i.e. unions, wage inefficiencies and minimum wages, social institutions, and laws and labour market inefficiencies generated by public institutions that allow for slow or no adjustment in the respective markets.

Other authors have posited productivity as the key for industrial and economic development, particularly by favouring export-oriented industrialization (EOI), since the latter generates greater capacity utilization and learning-by-doing effects and results in internationally competitive prices and higher quality of products (Krueger 1978, 1983). In the EOI view, policies have to be envisioned within an overall liberalization process and free development of market forces, based on macroeconomic stability, and including goods and labour markets (Balassa 1988; Bhagwati 1991).

Several schools of thought have been critical of this perspective of socioeconomic development and the functioning of labour markets (Dussel Peters 2000). For the purposes of this chapter, however, the view of the French regulation school is useful. Contrary to ahistorical automatisms, as developed by neoclassical economic theory, Glyn, Hughers, Lipietz and Singh stress that some of the main institutions generated during the 'Golden Age of Capitalism' in OECD (Organization for Economic Cooperation and Development) countries (1950–70) referred to social security and labour markets (Glyn et al. 1989). That is to say, the socioeconomic and political sustainability of Fordism during this period was validated by sharing the growth of productivity and profits through increases in real wages. This 'Fordist Equation' – i.e. a stable relationship between productivity growth and real-wage growth – allowed for an endogenous growth process and virtuous cycle in growth, employment, investments, capital intensity, profits and real wages (Boyer 1990; Michl 1988). From this perspective, a positive relationship between real wages and productivity growth reflects an institutional strategy of sharing the growth in productivity. Without this virtuous cycle, the regime of capital accumulation would become socially and economically unsustainable in the medium and long run and it would add to growing income and territorial-distribution disparities.

The liberalization strategy in Mexico: 1988–

Along the theoretical guidelines of EOI, the respective governments in Mexico since 1988 have consistently followed a new development strategy: economic liberalization. As a result of the crisis of Keynesianism internationally, as well as of import-substitution industrialization (ISI) in Mexico since the end of the 1960s, a new breed of politicians, mainly economists, departed radically from prior decades of social and economic policy-making related to ISI. The period prior to the implementation of liberalization strategy, 1982–87, was one of profound socioeconomic instability: the political system was in general disarray, the Mexican government was under enormous pressure to service an external debt of more than 70 per cent of GDP (Gross Domestic Product), while inflation rates and the fiscal deficit, as a percentage of GDP, accounted for levels above 160 per cent and 16 per cent, respectively (Villarreal 2000).

Since December 1987, when the first Pacto de Solidaridad Económica (Economic Solidarity Pact, PSE) was implemented, liberalization strategy has proposed the following core macroeconomic goals:

1. To transform Mexico's productive sector from import-substitution to export-orientation. The private manufacturing export-oriented sector should become the motor of socioeconomic development.
2. Public economic policy should focus on macroeconomic stability, i.e. to bring inflation rates and the fiscal deficit under control, and to attract foreign investment, the latter as the main source to finance the new development strategy.
3. A 'minimalist state' was to reduce investments and market distortions substantially. This represents a sharp contrast with the mixed economy that had prevailed since the 1940s, in which the state had played an active role in promoting the private sector, infrastructure and the social sector, among many other functions.

As a result of this strategy, the fiscal deficit was substantially reduced, and a surplus was achieved for several years. The overall retreat of the public sector, however, had significant effects; for example, in institutions such as development banks and in price guarantees and sectoral programmes in the agricultural and manufacturing sectors. To facilitate macroeconomic stability, the government has used the exchange rate as an 'anti-inflationary anchor', i.e. it will not allow devaluation of the peso, since this would have a negative impact on inflation as a result of imported inputs. The guarantee of cheap labour power to both domestic and foreign investors has been one of the main priorities of the respective PSE since 1987. Annual negotiations on minimum wages between corporatist unions and the government resulted, in most cases, in wage increases *below* inflation rates. Cheapening wages, in fact, was one of the main objectives of several PSEs (Aspe Armella 1993; J. Córdova 1991; Dussel Peters 2001; Salinas de Gortari 2001).

Strictly in its own terms, then, the liberalization strategy has been relatively successful. Inflation rates have decreased substantially since the end of the 1980s to reach single figures during the second part of the 1990s. The fiscal deficit has been controlled and in several years during the 1990s a surplus was achieved. Furthermore, Mexico was one of the most successful of the developing countries in attracting foreign investments during the 1990s: in terms of gross capital formation, foreign direct investment increased from levels below 6 per cent to more than 20 per cent during the 1990s, while, as a percentage of GDP, it more than doubled its share, to almost 3 per cent by the end of the 1990s. Finally, one of the most profound changes in Mexico's productive sector has been the increasing share of exports: from levels below 10 per cent of GDP at the beginning of the 1980s to more than 30 per cent by the end of the 1990s (Dussel Peters et al. 2003). As discussed in what follows, the percentage of GDP of total economy for exports is significantly lower than for manufacturing.

Several economic results stand out strictly as a result of the liberalization strategy. Independently of a worsening of income distribution, in 2000, minimum and manufacturing real wages represented 29.4 per cent and 76.4 per cent, respectively, of what they were in 1980 (CEPAL 2001). Another key result is a 'lean and anaemic' state, in which the public sector has withdrawn significantly from educational, institutional, social and territorial programmes, among others, in order to reduce the fiscal deficit. On the one hand, there has been an increasing overvaluation of the exchange rate, which has reached levels of around 40 per cent at the end of 2001, even by official estimates (PEF 2001: 244). The latter is substantial, since imports are significantly cheaper and exporting firms get significantly fewer pesos for exporting their products and services. On the other hand, financing of the commercial banking system to the non-financial sector, as a percentage of GDP, declined substantially in 1994–2001. In 2001, this financing represented less than 20 per cent of what it was in 1994.

These two outcomes of liberalization strategy added to a rapid tariff reduction for imports during 1985–87 and again in 1994 as a result of NAFTA have affected Mexico's manufacturing sector substantially. These outcomes represent the broad framework with which manufacturing established in Mexico is confronted: overvaluation, practically no availability of credit, and increasing competition from cheap imports as a result of tariff liberalization.

Additionally, the annual average growth rate of GDP was 3.3 per cent for 1988–2001, which is significantly lower than the 6.6 per cent achieved during the import substitution industrialization period of 1940–80. On the other hand, gross capital formation and total savings, both as a percentage of GDP, did not increase for 1988–2001. Total external debt, in contrast, has increased substantially. Private debt increased from $9.04 billion in 1990 to more than $54 billion in 2001, while total debt service more than doubled to $34.693 billion in 2000. As a result, liberalization strategy has been able to control a few macroeconomic variables, but has achieved limited performance in other macroeconomic aspects.

Real wages, productivity and employment: international comparisons and national performance

The average annual growth rate in monthly wages, measured in US dollars, shows that manufacturing wages in Mexico have outperformed other nations such as Chile and France. For the period December 1993 to December 2001 (INEGI 2002), wages observed an average annual growth rate (AAGR) of 2.4 per cent, 2.9 per cent, 0.3 per cent and 1.3 per cent respectively for Mexico, United States, France and Chile (see Figure 8.1).

Table 8.1 shows that Mexico's performance in terms of productivity growth for 1993–2001 has also been outstanding internationally. In fact, by the beginning of 2002, the manufacturing sector showed an increase of 51.7 per cent for 1993–2002. Only Korea's performance was higher (see Table 8.1).

Finally, with regard to the labour market, the open unemployment rate – measured as all those persons twelve years of age and older who

Table 8.1 Productivity in selected countries (hours worked per person in manufacturing, December of each year), 1993–2002 (1993=100)*

	Mexico	USA	Canada	Japan	Korea	Germany	UK
1993	107.2	101.5	105.5	99.6	106.5	115.3	101.3
1994	116.1	106	115.8	105.9	117.7	132	105.1
1995	126.3	111.3	110.6	109.8	127.4	140	101.6
1996	134.7	116.8	109.4	115.7	140.2	158.8	102.6
1997	138.1	123.4	114.2	115.7	147.1	168.5	102.6
1998	141.9	130.8	117.2	112.3	179.5	162.6	103.3
1999	143.3	139.3	121.2	120.4	204.8	169.7	108.6
2000	147.2	145.7	117.3	126.1	213.2	189.1	115.1
2001	149.3	147.7	113.5	116.9	222.8	196.9	112.3
2002†	151.7	149	113.5	118.5	230.5	–	–

* Index of hours per worker. † Refers to the January of 2002 for all countries, with the exception of Mexico (February 2002).

Source: Author's calculations based on INEGI (2002).

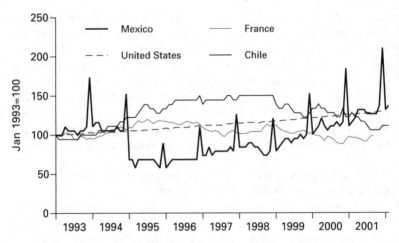

Figure 8.1 Manufacturing: wages per hour in US$, 1993–2002 (1993=100)
Source: Author's calculations based on INEGI (2002) <http://
www.inegi.gob.mx>.

were looking for a job during the period of the poll and who worked for
less than an hour a week – was, with few exceptions, the lowest among
seven countries of the OECD during the second half of the 1990s, and
even earlier, with the exception of Japan (see Figure 8.2).

These international trends reflect, on the one hand, that Mexico's
performance in these variables has apparently been outstanding. On
the other hand, and as discussed above, some of these comparisons
and results are significantly distorted by the high overvaluation of the
exchange rate in Mexico, which reached levels of about 40 per cent by
2001. So, independently of these international trends, what are the basic
conditions of Mexico's employment, real wages and productivity?

The economically active population (EAP) increased during the
1990s by 1.3 million persons annually, while the general population
increased by 1.9 million (see Table 8.2).

These are the latest estimates according to official sources. Other
estimates have calculated an annual increase of the EAP between 1.2
and 1.5 million people annually (Dussel Peters 2000). This is the basis
for understanding Mexico's labour market, because at least 1.3 million
persons attempted to enter the formal labour market during the 1990s
annually. For 1990–2000, however, only 600,000 jobs were generated
annually on average, and less than 450,000 jobs were insured annually on
average. That is to say, around 850,000 persons annually had to search
for a job in the informal market.

The labour market in Mexico is highly segmented. The most formal
segment, which is insured and registered at the Social Security Institute

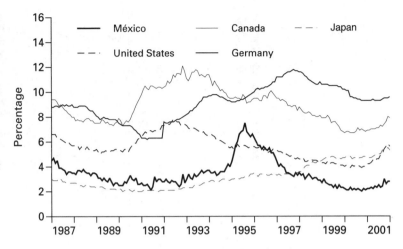

Figure 8.2 Open unemployment rate in selected countries, 1987–2002

(Instituto Mexicano del Seguro Social, IMSS), represented 35.2 per cent of the EAP in 2000. From this perspective, the challenge for generating employment lies in the informal labour market. Clearly, this is not reflected in the open unemployment rate, which is by definition not significant in Mexico, given that Mexico has no social or public safety-net that allows for unemployment. In fact, in this context, it is quite surprising that the open unemployment rate has reached such high levels as those reflected in Figure 8.3: for 1990–2001 the non-insured segment of the labour market represented 66.76 per cent of EAP in 2001 and has fallen for the period. That is to say, the formal labour market segment has not been able to absorb the increasing EAP. Thus, Mexico's labour market is segmented into three main components: (i) the economically active population (EAP); (ii) a formal and insured employed sector (of around one-third of EAP); and (iii) the rest of the EAP, which is employed, given that Mexico has no unemployment benefits, but not insured. This latter segment explains the large size of the so-called informal sector and contains a huge potential for migration, particularly to the United States.

Added to these structural limitations of Mexico's labour market, the recent recession in the US economy, as well as domestic difficulties, have led to a deep crisis in Mexico's labour market: permanent insured employment has fallen significantly, particularly for manufacturing, accounting for an annual growth rate since October 2001 and until March 2002 of minus 10 per cent. That is to say, more than 400,000 jobs were lost, the worst decline since data exist for insured employment.

Furthermore, real wages and productivity for manufacturing and

Table 8.2 Mexico: general information on population and employment, 1990–2000 (in thousands)

	1980	1985	1990	1995	1996	1997	1998	1999	2000	2001*	2005*
Total population	66,847	74,048	81,250	91,158	93,571	95,127	96,648	98,132	100,300	101,500	106,306
Economically active population (EAP)	21,996	25,853	30,164	36,637	37,541	39,422	40,770	42,057	43,299	44,507	49,149
Official employment	–	–	–	33,578	35,006	37,043	38,363	38,939	38,785	–	–
Insured†	6,368	8,149	10,764	10,932	11,895	12,714	13,611	14,560	15,240	15,131	–
Employed**	20,282	21,956	25,958	27,347	28,270	29,347	30,635	31,407	32,000	31,000	–
Open unemployment rate (%)	–	–	2.6	6.2	5.5	3.7	3.2	2.5	2.2	2.8	–
Insured / EAP (%)	29.0	31.5	35.7	29.8	31.7	32.3	33.4	34.6	35.2	34.0	–
Employed / EAP (%)	92.2	84.9	86.1	74.6	75.3	74.4	75.1	74.7	73.9	69.7	–

* Estimates

† Total insured employed population according to Instituto Mexicano Seguro Social (IMSS), December of each year.

** Employed population according to INEGI (2002). Sistema de Cuentas Nacionales.

Source: Author's calculations based on CELADE (2001a, 2001b); CONAPO (1999); INEGI (2002) and Partida Bush (1999).

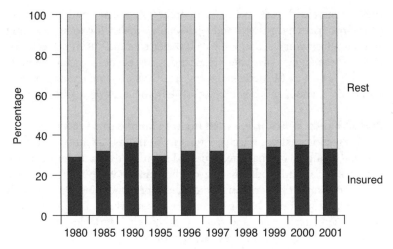

Figure 8.3 Labour market conditions, 1980–2001 (as a percentage of economically active population) *Source*: Author's calculations based on Table 8.2.

the total economy in Mexico reflect various performances for 1988–99. On the one hand, real wages for the total economy and manufacturing declined significantly during 1994–99, by 8.41 per cent and 12.61 per cent respectively. Such decline is a result of the fall in real wages during 1995–96, but it also contrasts with an improvement in real wages during 1988–94. On the other hand, and this is contrary contrary to what would be expected by neoclassical economics, productivity for

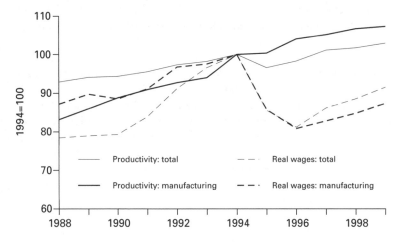

Figure 8.4 Real wages and labour productivity, 1988–99 (1994=100) *Source*: Author's calculations based on INEGI (2002).

1994–99 increased, particularly in manufacturing. The resulting gap between productivity growth and real-wages growth for total economy and manufacturing accounted for 11.37 per cent and 19.90 per cent for 1994–99 (see Figure 8.4). These respective gaps, particularly for the most dynamic sector of Mexico's economy since 1988, manufacturing, reflect a lack of an endogenous source of development, as discussed above.

Performance of branches with highest labour productivity

This section analyses the characteristics of those branches of Mexico's manufacturing sector that have reflected the most dynamic performance in terms of labour productivity growth during 1994–99. The objective is to understand the performance of these branches since 1994 – with the implementation of NAFTA – and their specificities in terms of GDP, employment, real wages and trade, among other variables, and in the conceptual context of our previous section.

Mexico's National Accounting System of INEGI consists of nine large divisions, one of which is manufacturing (*Gran División* 3). Moreover, the economy is divided into seventy-three branches, of which manufacturing includes branches 11–59, or forty-nine branches. Given the higher disaggregation of data, by the beginning of 2002 information was available only for 1988–99. As a result, I have divided the forty-nine manufacturing branches into three groups. Group 1 includes all those branches that displayed a labour productivity growth rate of 30 per cent *above* that of manufacturing during 1994–99, while Group 2 includes all those branches with a labour productivity growth rate of 30 per cent *below* manufacturing, but above the labour productivity growth rate for the total economy. Finally, Group 3 includes those branches with a labour productivity growth rate below that of the total economy's performance during 1994–99 (see Table 8.3).

Based on this typology at the level of branches, what are the main characteristics of the created groups, and particularly those branches in Group 1, with the highest labour productivity?

In summary, the main results presented in Table 8.4 are as follows: first, the surprises. Group 1 branches include some 'old industries' from the ISI period such as cement, steel and iron, sugar, tobacco and basic inorganic chemicals. Previous analyses (Dussel Peters 2000; Hernández Laos 2000) would have expected Group 1 to be comprised of other branches such as electronic equipment, glass and products, non-electrical machinery, electrical equipment and motors and autoparts, among others, in addition to automobiles and machinery and electric equipment, which belong in Groups 2 and 3. Also surprisingly, petroleum refining and basic petrochemicals are both in Group 3 and show some of the worst productivity performances for 1994–99. These surprises

Table 8.3 Typology of Mexico's manufacturing branches by growth rate of labour productivity, 1994–99 (1994 = 100)

	Total economy	102.96	32	Printing	114.89
	Manufacturing	107.29	41	Rubber products	113.04
	Group 1		17	Fats and oils	110.46
44	Cement	156.91	24	Cotton, wool, synthetic textiles	110.31
46	Steel and Iron	147.32	29	Lumber, plywood	110.28
16	Sugar	147.22	28	Leather and footwear	109.38
37	Plastic resins, synthetic fibre	141.27	42	Plastic products	108.91
56	Automobiles	140.61	36	Pesticides and fertilizers	108.80
52	Machinery and electrical equipment	139.61	53	Household appliances	108.42
23	Tobacco	138.99	51	Non-electrical machinery	107.52
35	Basic inorganic chemicals	135.79		*Group 3*	
	Group 2		48	Metal furniture	106.59
40	Other chemicals	129.30	14	Corn milling	103.93
39	Cleaning and toilet prep.	128.12	26	Other textile industries	103.60
38	Medicinal products	127.01	15	Coffee	103.33
58	Other transportation equipment	124.70	11	Meat and milk products	103.21
19	Other food products	124.27	13	Wheat milling	103.02
49	Structural metal products	124.22	57	Motors and autoparts	101.33
50	Other metal products	122.47	30	Other wood products	100.65
45	Ceramics	120.23	18	Food for animals	99.61
54	Electronic equipment	120.04	55	Electrical equipment	98.51
47	Non-ferrous metals	119.68	59	Other manufacturing industries	97.98
12	Fruits and vegetables	119.44	25	Jute, rough textiles	92.68
22	Soft drinks and flavourings	118.97	20	Alcoholic beverages	91.66
21	Beer and malt	118.46	33	Petroleum refining	90.48
31	Paper and paperboard	117.53	27	Apparel	76.89
43	Glass and products	115.23	34	Basic petrochemicals	74.13

Source: Author's calculations based on INEGI (2002).

can also be a result of the definition of labour productivity and its shortcomings. As defined earlier, labour productivity is the coefficient of GDP and employment. Although a growth in productivity is generally assumed to be positive, it can be the result of several tendencies, even a 'perverse' growth in which both variables decrease, but employment decreases even more than GDP.

Second, as expected by the definition of the typology, Group 1 presents the highest growth of labour productivity during 1988–99: it increased by 33.93 per cent during 1994–99, as compared to growth of 14.92 per cent and –25.08 per cent for Groups 2 and 4, respectively. Even manufacturing's productivity as a whole increased by only 7.29 per cent for the period.

Table 8.4 Results of typology of Mexico's manufacturing branches selected by productivity growth, 1994–99 (1988–99)

	1988	1989	1990	1991	1992	1993	1994	1995	1996	1997	1998
Exports (1994=100)	61.22	63.12	67.55	72.55	75.67	83.19	100.00	148.48	179.30	194.49	207.59
Group 1	45.91	48.88	55.17	64.94	72.08	83.72	100.00	151.52	199.66	211.66	214.32
Group 2	67.88	74.56	76.02	78.39	75.63	82.24	100.00	169.22	190.28	208.74	230.46
Group 3	72.49	68.30	73.56	75.60	79.94	83.54	100.00	123.81	144.14	159.75	176.41
Exports (% over manufacturing)	100.00	100.00	100.00	100.00	100.00	100.00	100.00	100.00	100.00	100.00	100.00
Group 1	27.58	28.21	30.51	35.60	36.79	37.15	36.96	40.16	43.00	41.31	39.91
Group 2	36.94	38.73	34.81	33.68	32.56	31.43	31.17	33.49	30.51	31.29	32.28
Group 3	35.49	33.07	34.68	30.72	30.65	31.42	31.87	26.35	26.49	27.39	27.81
Imports (1994=100)	35.79	43.77	54.54	67.01	82.84	83.14	100.00	72.26	89.69	114.88	133.24
Group 1	37.91	46.31	61.45	69.22	82.15	76.55	100.00	71.94	92.93	117.53	143.54
Group 2	35.23	41.02	51.62	65.08	82.22	82.12	100.00	71.37	91.85	120.54	141.67
Group 3	35.78	46.36	55.89	68.67	83.83	86.59	100.00	73.47	85.93	106.96	119.35
Imports (% over manufacturing)	100.00	100.00	100.00	100.00	100.00	100.00	100.00	100.00	100.00	100.00	100.00
Group 1	13.10	13.26	14.39	13.33	12.37	11.83	13.08	13.01	13.37	13.19	13.86
Group 2	47.49	46.00	45.75	46.80	48.10	47.73	48.62	48.67	50.78	51.82	52.72
Group 3	39.41	40.75	39.87	39.87	39.53	40.43	38.30	38.32	35.84	34.99	33.43
Exports/GDP (%)	31.63	30.43	30.84	28.66	26.28	29.56	34.49	66.30	69.05	66.07	65.97
Group 1	49.08	50.30	54.77	56.57	55.94	64.50	75.34	138.19	144.14	136.63	133.12
Group 2	23.96	23.49	21.73	20.25	18.12	19.10	21.86	46.03	45.01	43.85	44.65
Group 3	33.55	30.70	32.00	25.67	22.71	27.04	32.44	53.76	56.13	55.07	56.42
Imports/GDP (%)	47.04	54.12	61.00	63.50	69.98	68.80	79.39	79.98	86.75	92.49	99.61
Group 1	34.67	42.05	51.07	46.93	50.06	47.82	61.38	54.02	56.31	61.06	69.78

Group 2	45.80	49.62	56.50	62.34	71.27	67.54	78.47	80.69	94.11	101.64	110.78
Group 3	55.40	67.30	72.76	73.83	77.97	80.97	89.73	94.32	95.42	98.48	102.37
Trade balance/GDP (%)	-15.40	-23.70	-30.16	-34.84	-43.70	-39.24	-44.90	-13.69	-17.20	-26.42	-33.64
Group 1	14.42	8.25	3.70	9.64	5.87	16.68	13.96	84.17	87.83	75.57	63.34
Group 2	-21.84	-26.13	-34.76	-42.09	-53.15	-48.43	-56.61	-34.66	-49.10	-57.79	-65.45
Group 3	-21.85	-36.60	-40.75	-48.27	-55.27	-53.93	-57.29	-40.56	-39.29	-43.40	-45.95
Gross formation of capital (1994=100)	52.91	59.60	71.76	85.66	99.54	91.18	100.00	63.80	78.47	105.03	122.76
Group 1	59.22	73.55	88.49	113.75	128.73	106.90	100.00	43.15	54.79	86.87	107.35
Group 2	49.40	52.77	65.11	75.73	90.62	86.14	100.00	68.63	80.78	110.10	128.54
Group 3	54.58	61.13	70.00	79.84	90.22	86.72	100.00	73.81	97.50	111.92	125.17
Gross formation of capital (% over manufacturing)	100.00	100.00	100.00	100.00	100.00	100.00	100.00	100.00	100.00	100.00	100.00
Group 1	24.70	26.53	35.92	30.29	29.97	27.71	23.92	14.13	14.73	18.74	19.69
Group 2	54.13	51.91	53.40	49.63	49.84	50.48	53.61	60.04	57.34	57.09	57.08
Group 3	21.17	21.56	20.68	20.08	20.19	21.81	22.47	25.82	27.93	24.17	23.23
Gross formation of capital/GDP (%)	39.50	43.00	46.61	50.08	53.88	48.95	51.35	40.17	45.37	51.42	56.80
Group 1	55.01	65.31	70.30	84.10	93.44	79.69	72.58	29.46	32.45	48.25	56.55
Group 2	43.94	43.45	50.40	52.14	56.85	50.81	55.95	50.00	55.57	62.25	67.98
Group 3	25.05	27.63	28.84	29.33	30.66	31.08	34.05	31.92	38.89	37.82	40.57
Employment (1994=100)	93.69	97.81	101.12	102.11	104.35	102.19	100.00	94.68	101.22	110.10	116.50
Group 1	123.52	122.00	118.59	116.57	113.44	106.77	100.00	92.35	95.78	102.15	107.79
Group 2	94.16	97.69	101.50	103.88	103.81	101.97	100.00	93.31	98.06	105.71	110.36
Group 3	86.80	92.90	96.93	96.65	103.17	101.53	100.00	97.04	106.65	117.73	126.66

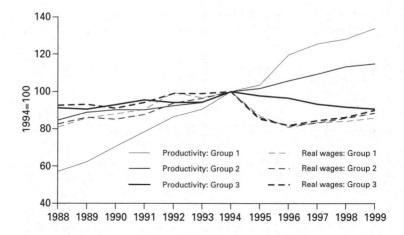

Figure 8.5 Typology of manufacturing branches: real wages and productivity, 1988–99 (1994=100) *Sources*: Author's calculations based on Table 8.4.

Third, the share of Group 1 over manufacturing's GDP has remained relatively constant during 1988–99, at 17.77 per cent in 1988 and 18.96 per cent in 1999. Particularly in 1994–95, its share increased substantially, but has fallen since then. Groups 2 and 3 accounted for more than 80 per cent of manufacturing's GDP during 1988–99.

Fourth, in terms of gross-capital formation (GCF), the performance of Group 1 has underperformed branches in Groups 2 and 3, both in terms of growth rates during 1994–99, as well as in terms of GDP. Regarding the latter, for example, GCF represented 57.70 per cent for Group 1 and 69.50 per cent for Group 2. As a result, Group 1's share of GCF over manufacturing has fallen from 24.70 per cent in 1988 to 23.92 per cent in 1994 and to 19.08 per cent in 1999.

Fifth, branches in Group 1, particularly automobiles, have been very dynamic in terms of trade. Exports increased by more than 135 per cent during 1994–99, although less than export growth in branches of Group 2; their share over manufacturing's exports increased from 27.58 per cent in 1988 to 39.35 per cent in 1999. Significantly, much of this growth took place before 1994. Most impressively, however, the exports/GDP coefficient has been higher than 100 per cent since 1995, and it almost tripled for 1988–99. This surge in the exports/GDP coefficient in automobiles reflects a significant structural change in the production and specialization pattern. The rest of the manufacturing sector and its groups display coefficients below 65 per cent. The imports/GDP coefficient is lower than the rest of the manufacturing sector. As a result, branches in Group 1 account for an increasing trade surplus, from 14.42 per cent of GDP in 1988 to 13.96 per cent in 1994 and 64.23 per cent in 1999. This performance is outstanding, since the rest of the Groups, and total manufacturing, reflect increasing trade deficits, from −15.40 per cent of GDP in 1988 to −34.16 per cent in 1999 for total manufacturing.

Sixth, and contrary to expectations, employment in the most dynamic branches in terms of productivity has continuously fallen for the analysed period until, in 1999, it reached 1988 levels. As a result, the employment share of Group 1 over manufacturing represented only 7.31 per cent in 1999. This result indicates that the most dynamic branches in terms of productivity have achieved these results by increasing GDP since 1988, and by reducing employment.

Seventh, one of the most striking features of the most dynamic branches in terms of productivity is that they have widened their gap between productivity growth and real-wages growth substantially. Therefore, while the gap has shortened for Groups 2 and 3, as well as for manufacturing as a whole, this gap accounted for almost 50 per cent for Group 1, as a consequence of increasing productivity and falling real wages. Although branches in Group 1 account for the highest wages in absolute terms, 66.01 per cent higher than manufacturing's average in 1999, its performance in terms of growth has been the worst: wages in Group 1 branches experienced the most significant decrease during 1994–99 of all groups, by 14.25 per cent (see Figure 8.5). Branches such as automobiles account for a gap of more than 60 per cent as a result of real wages declining by 20.4 per cent and productivity increasing by 40.61 per cent.

The typology is relevant from several perspectives. On the one hand, it shows that activities related to the highest productivity growth in Mexico's manufacturing sector have underperformed other branches in terms of gross capital formation, GDP and employment. The latter is particularly significant because, in terms of the conceptual discussion above, productivity growth has not been positively associated with employment growth, but rather by its fall in the most dynamic branches. On the other hand, branches that outperformed the rest of the manufacturing branches in terms of productivity reflect a high dynamism in foreign trade, particularly in exports. As a result, branches in Group 1, as a whole, are the only ones that have generated a trade surplus, in contrast to Groups 2 and 3 and manufacturing as a whole. The positive association between productivity growth and export growth is relevant for manufacturing as a whole, considering that its trade deficit has become one of the main sources of macroeconomic and balance of payments instability since 1988. A final and fundamental point for understanding the growth strategy since 1988 is that activities associated with high labour productivity have been the weakest in terms of real-wages growth: the gap between both variables has widened substantially for 1988–99 and also since 1994. As a result, the gap accounted for almost 70 per cent for 1988–1999, i.e. labour productivity increased by 71.1 per cent, while real wages only by 3.4 per cent.

Conclusions

Who reaps the benefits and fruits of productivity growth in Mexico? This article has shown in detail that, thus far, real wages have not been the main beneficiaries, particularly since the implementation of NAFTA in 1994. Although the Mexican economy has achieved substantial productivity increases since 1988 and 1994 – also in comparison to other countries – real wages have continued to fall. This increasing gap since the start of the liberalization strategy is relevant in terms of the sustainability of the economy, as well as in social and political terms, because the increasing gap affects both income distribution and the political sustainability of Mexico in the short, medium and long term.

Changes in the exchange rate, such as the devaluation in 1995–96, have no doubt had a negative impact on real wages. A deeper analysis would be required in the future to distinguish and weight the effects of devaluations, among other variables, on real minimum wages, real wages in manufacturing and the total economy. As discussed above, however, wages have in general declined continually since the start of the liberalization strategy in the 1980s, with no significant recoveries.

The resulting socioeconomic polarization has been analysed at the branch level of the manufacturing sector. In this case, branches that have achieved the highest productivity growth have also resulted in the highest gap between productivity and real-wage growth. Cortéz (2001) has identified similar results. Rather surprisingly, branches in Group 1 – those with the highest productivity growth – have also achieved the lowest performance in terms of employment, gross-capital formation and real-wage growth since 1994. Nevertheless, branches in Group 1 have been very dynamic in foreign trade, particularly regarding exports, i.e. these branches have been able to account for an increasing trade surplus, in contrast to the rest of Mexico's manufacturing sector and the economy as a whole.

These findings are relevant from several perspectives. On the one hand, they show some of the contradictions of the liberalization strategy and export-oriented industrialization followed in Mexico since 1988 (Dussel Peters 1996). The liberalization strategy has not been able to generate competitive conditions for the productive sector in Mexico, particularly with regard to financing and the overvaluation of the exchange rate. Although exports are positively associated with branches with high productivity growth, they are far from resolving some of the main challenges of Mexico's economy, particularly those of employment generation and improving real wages. As a result, by the end of the 1990s, high-growth branches in terms of productivity have not been able to establish links to the rest of the economy to overcome one of its weakest conditions: its increasing dependence on imports to produce exports and to grow in terms of GDP, as reflected in the trade-balance/GDP coefficient. On the other hand, the liberalization strategy and NAFTA have been far away from achieving positive effects on employment and real-wage growth, particularly in those branches that have increased productivity. Furthermore, these branches have deepened the socioeconomic polarization in Mexico.

These issues are relevant economically for Mexico as well as for the United States and Canada, in terms of the sustainability of the liberalization strategy. Socially and politically, the model has contributed to an increase in overall polarization. Several authors and business chambers have proposed to link productivity to real-wage growth in Mexico. In the context of the Mexican discussion of the 'New Labour Culture' and the reform of the Labour Law since the beginning of the 1990s, the Confederation of Mexican Workers, closely linked to the government, and the Employers' Confederation of the Mexican Republic (Confederación Patronal de la República Mexicana, COPARMEX) proposed linking real wages to productivity, among other variables. Will employers really be able and willing to increase real wages by more than 60 per cent to close the gap between both variables, only for the period 1994–99?

9 | Labour and migration policies under Vicente Fox: subordination to US economic and geopolitical interests

RAÚL DELGADO WISE

§ THE treatment of migration issues clearly represents one of the most important changes to have taken place in Mexican foreign policy during President Vicente Fox's first year in office (Castañeda 2001: 89). Above and beyond the anecdotal and symbolic fact that the first official ceremony he held at the president's official residence, 'Los Pinos', involved representatives of the migrant community, the National Development Plan for 2001 to 2006 identifies migration as a 'priority issue for Mexico', one that must be addressed under 'a new long-term approach' within the framework of 'comprehensive negotiations [with the United States] that address the structural roots of the phenomenon, its manifestations, and its consequences, and that sees dealing with migration as a shared responsibility' (Castañeda 2001: 61).

In line with this position, in the Annual Report he presented on 3 December 2001, Foreign Minister Jorge G. Castañeda noted that for the first time in the history of the bilateral agenda, the question of migration was taken on board on the basis of joint responsibility and with a long-term outlook aimed at 'making good use of the synergies that exist between the two countries'. After the hiatus caused by the attacks on the United States of America on 11 September 2001, he added, negotiations had recommenced in full, and the two governments had recognized the need for the migration question to incorporate security concerns and for a wide-ranging agreement to be struck at the earliest possible juncture.

In addition to the Mexican Foreign Minister's 'optimistic' view of progress in the bilateral negotiations, the migration issue is also emerging as a priority question for the government in Washington, albeit for very different and contrasting reasons. The growing US interest in the matter is due to a range of factors, including the following: (i) the presence of a population of Mexican origin that already numbers over 23 million and is consolidating itself as the 'hard core' of the largest minority in the country, the Hispanics; (ii) the ebullient dynamism that has been characteristic of recent emigration from Mexico; and (iii) the obvious problems and challenges posed, from a 'national security' viewpoint, by the USA's southern border, which is more than 3,000 kilometres long and the busiest in the world, with more than a million crossings a day. As a result of the progress made in the negotiations, five broad areas for discussion have so far been placed on the bilateral agenda:

- Straightening out the legal status of the more than 3 million undocumented Mexican migrants who live in the United States.
- Establishing a temporary worker programme, to allow the Mexican workforce authorized access to specific regions and sectors of the US job market.
- Agreeing on a special migratory relationship between Mexico and the United States and, consequently, increasing the number of visas available to Mexicans, to bring them more into line with the real migration levels currently prevailing between the two countries.
- Strengthening border security through joint Mexico–US actions, with particular emphasis on efforts to combat trafficking in human lives and to prevent migrant deaths along the common border.
- Promoting regional development programmes in the areas of Mexico with the highest levels of migration, and combining those efforts with the future implementation of a temporary worker programme between the two countries. (Tuirán et al. 2001: 4)

While recognizing the unprecedented nature of this agenda, which has fuelled great expectations in government circles and in some sectors of the migrant community, it should be noted that none of the proposed issues has been dealt with in full and that conflicting reactions still prevail in the different forums where they have been discussed (presidential summits, foreign ministries, parliamentary meetings, the bi-national commission and so on). It is clear from the onset that the agenda excludes the proposal that Fox made during his presidential campaign: the demand for the free movement of labour. Important questions thus remain unanswered: What is the nature of the Fox administration's change of direction on the migration question? Is it a strategic shift in Mexican foreign policy or merely a short-term superficial change? Is there a hidden agenda behind the trappings of the government's new position? And, if so, what are its thrust and its likely consequences?

Using those important questions as a starting point, the main objective of this chapter is to offer a critical overview of the Fox administration's migration policy, taking into account the broad and intricate spectrum of labour relations that has arisen between Mexico and the United States under the influence of neoliberal globalism. Our primary interest lies in penetrating the content and scope of that policy and in revealing what lies behind the official rhetoric and constitutes the true face of relations between the two countries.

Our principal hypothesis is that, beyond the partial achievements that have been attained, the shift in Mexico's migration policy under President Vicente Fox represents *the country's greater subordination to the strategic geopolitical and economic interests of the United States*. This, in turn, is tied in with the strategic role that Mexican labour has been given in the context of US industrial restructuring, both within and beyond its borders.

For the purpose of this analysis, the chapter is divided into four sections. The first examines the nature of trade between Mexico and the United States under the aegis of neoliberalism. Next, attention is paid to the particular dialectic that has arisen in that context between the country's export growth and international migration. Third, the content and scope of the migration issues on the bilateral agenda are studied. The final section briefly describes the responses and alternative approaches that have emerged from the rank-and-file of the migrant community itself.

The true face of trade between Mexico and the USA

Two background factors are of relevance in addressing this first topic. The first of these is the creation of three blocs characterized by different configurations of capitalism following the dissolution of the post-war 'order' and the emergence of a strategy for stepping up the US hegemony in this continent. The second is the USA's need to tackle its shortcomings in competitiveness and technological innovation *vis-à-vis* Germany and Japan, and thereby resolving – or at least mitigating – its severe external debt problem. It should be noted that the United States has gone from being the world's leading creditor to become its biggest debtor. Since 1987, the United States has been a net debtor. Faced with this new dynamic in the global economy, US multinational companies have adopted a strategy aimed, *inter alia*, at drastically reducing their labour costs.

Part of this has been the neoliberal reforms and painful structural adjustment programmes imposed on Mexico and on the rest of Latin America by the ruling classes acting in concert with the different international agencies that serve the United States and the powerful interests it represents: the multinational corporations and banks (Otero 1996c; Valenzuela Feijóo 1996; H. Guillén 1997; Veltmeyer 2000). At this point we offer an analysis of one of the strategic goals at which those measures are aimed: *the transformation of the country's export sector, making it the centre point of the reoriented Mexican economy and placing it at the service of US imperialist power.*

Because of this and because of the optical illusion created by the country's repositioning as Latin America's leading export power and the eighth largest exporter in the world, it is vitally important that we reveal exactly what the country exports and who exactly is involved in and benefits from this export 'boom'. The first noteworthy element that emerges from an examination of Mexico's exports is the elevated dynamism and specific weight of *maquiladora* companies: assembly plants associated with internationalized productive processes that are not highly integrated with the national economy. Between 1982 and 2001, the *maquiladora* industry's sales abroad increased twenty-five-fold, ultimately accounting for almost half of all manufactured exports (48.5 per cent). Moreover, that proportion rises to 54 per cent if the export surplus alone – that is, the difference between the value of the exports and the import requirements – is taken into account (Cypher 2000: 16). In addition, spectacular growth also took place in non-*maquiladora* manufacturing, exports from which rose twenty-fold over the same period. And, even more significantly, in some of its more dynamic segments, such as the automobile industry, trends toward *maquila* patterns can be seen, based on segmentation and industrial delocalization processes, with an exceedingly high import component. Imported components generally account for between 85 per cent and 95 per cent of vehicles exported to the United States (Unger 1990: 77). Gerardo Fujii (2000: 1014) highlights this phenomenon in the following terms: 'The dynamism of the export sector does not pull the rest of the economy along with it; instead, it escapes abroad, chiefly to the United States.' Two very dynamic export sectors provide good examples of this: automobiles and electronics. Both are dominated by multinational companies, which carry out final assembly of their products in the country, using mostly imported components. And so the industrial sector is beginning to resemble the assembly industries along the border with the United States. Supporting this same line of analysis, James Cypher holds that: 'Mexico's export "miracle" can be largely explained by globalization strategies drawn up in Detroit – the U.S. auto industry accounted for approximately one out of every five dollars of Mexico's non-oil exports during 1997' (Cypher 2001: 12).

Another important piece of this peculiar structure is the overwhelming presence – estimated at between 65 per cent and 75 per cent – of intrafirm trade within US corporations (Baker 1995: 402). In addition to contravening the 'free market dynamics' preached by neoliberal orthodoxy, this underscores the exceptional plundering of the Mexican economy that is taking place. The concept of shared production inherent in intrafirm trade does not, of course, mean shared profits. Export prices in commerce of this kind are set artificially by the companies without declaring 'profits', which not only allows a net transfer of earnings abroad, but also enables each job created to be subsidized and the bill for those subsidies to be passed on to the Mexican economy.

Paradoxically, in spite of the Mexican economy's dedication to exports – the total volume of which rose from US$22 million to $158 billion between 1982 and 2001 – this does not help mitigate the country's severe external deficit problems; on the contrary, it translates into an ever-increasing volume of imports. It is particularly revealing that between 1988 and 1994 manufactured exports grew at an average annual rate (5 per cent) that was less than half the rate of growth recorded for imports of those same products (12 per cent). So pronounced are these tendencies that Enrique Dussel Peters (1996: 80) has called this model of industrialization 'import-oriented'. And although this import dynamic was momentarily interrupted by Mexico's 1995 economic crisis, it soon picked up again, with deficits of slightly over US$6 billion in 1997 and $16 billion in 2001.

All of this casts a diminished light on the scope of the new export dynamic and puts it into perspective. It becomes clear that this process, contrary to what might be expected from its evolution towards a model of secondary exporting (i.e. a specialization in manufactured exports), bears little relation to the domestic economy and has a minimal multiplying effect on it.

In addition to showcasing the fragility and volatility of the export dynamic, the comments made above require that we accurately assess the nature and scope of what the country actually exports. In this regard, it is clear that 'manufactured exports' is too grand a title for most of Mexico's foreign trade, which takes place within the realm of intrafirm commerce and primarily involves the *maquiladora* sector. As Carlos Tello (1996: 50) has correctly pointed out, what Mexico essentially sells abroad is its *labour force*, without ever having it leave the country. Thus, the veil of supposed progress in secondary exports conceals the contraction of a part of the Mexican economy, which is reduced and compelled to serve as a reserve of labour power for foreign capital.

Perhaps it is not superfluous to point out that this export specialization bears some relation to Mexico's direct exports of labour to the United States through labour migration, which indelibly marks the nature of commercial exchanges between the two nations. Both cases mean *net transfers abroad of potential earnings*.

This analysis of the nature of the Mexican economy's reincorporation into the sphere of US capitalism leads to at least two conclusions. First, *labour* is the country's chief export good, with a net contribution to the balance of trade in excess of US$28 billion in 2001. This estimate includes both the added value of the *maquiladora* industry – intended as an approximate indicator of indirect labour exports – and the remittances sent home by directly exported workers. Mexico also exports *natural resources* (primarily oil) and *assets*. This latter area – the acquisition of the assets of privatized public companies at knock-down prices – is where most direct foreign investment has been channelled, helping to concentrate and centralize the capital of large multinational companies. It is worth adding that these investments have been channelled into acquiring the country's financial sector through the purchase of Mexico's largest banks: Bancomer, bought by Banco Bilbao Vizcaya, and Banamex, bought by Citibank.

Secondly – and perhaps the best illustration of the extremely restricted nature of the process of capital accumulation in Mexico – is the transfer (or, perhaps more correctly, the plundering) of surpluses that takes place in the neoliberal context, under the aegis of US imperialism. The total amount of surpluses transferred from the country, chiefly to the United States, between 1982 (when the shift towards neoliberalism began) and 1997 has been estimated at US$457 billion, expressed in constant 1990 prices (Saxe-Fernández and Núñez 2001: 150–1). This calculation includes two types of transfers: those intended as debt service, and those that can be considered trade losses (either through the trade balance or rent, or to pay for franchises, concessions or patent rights). The true dimensions of this figure, which does not include transfers of potential earnings through direct and indirect exports of labour, become apparent if we consider that Latin America is the underdeveloped world's leading tributary region and that, within that region, Mexico is the leading country.

Dialectic between export growth and international migration

The other side of the Mexican economy's export orientation – and what gives it the appearance of an enclave (Delgado Wise and Mañán 2000) – is the impoverishment of most of the population. 'Enclave' is not used here in its classic sense, but rather to refer to the plundering and expropriation of a portion (and not necessarily a small one) of the nation's territory and its workforce by foreign capital, through a construct that brandishes highly destructive 'macroeconomic conditions' that restrict the domestic economy and pull down wages. In such an enclave, social inequalities become more acute and there emerges an ever-increasing mass of workers unable to find a place within the country's formal labour market, as a result of which one-third of the economically active population situates itself in the 'informal sector' (see Dussel Peters, this volume). This is the breeding ground that fuels the current vigorous process of cross-border migration.

To give an idea of the dimensions the phenomenon has acquired, the following figures are more than eloquent:

• the number of people born in Mexico and who live in the USA totals

8.2 million, of whom slightly more than one-third are undocumented migrants

- the flow of temporary migrants ('sojourners') accounts for between 800,000 and one million journeys per year
- each year, some 300,000 Mexicans establish their permanent residence ('settlers') in the USA (Tuirán 2000)

Even though the phenomenon of Mexico–US labour migration has a lengthy history dating back to the second half of the nineteenth century, unprecedented levels of intensity and dynamism characterize its current phase. For instance, the net annual international migratory flow over the past decade was ten times higher than the one recorded twenty years earlier (Tuirán et al. 2001: 6). This dynamic also implies major qualitative transformations, in terms of the geography of migration (diversification of points of origin and destinations, and greater numbers coming from urban areas), the occupational spectrum of cross-border workers (new fields for insertion into the US job market), migratory patterns (age, sex, schooling, place in the family, duration of stay, legal status and so on), and the amounts of remittances, the mechanisms used to send and receive them, the uses to which those funds are put and the impact they have.

The following figures from the year 2000 underscore some of the new aspects of the phenomenon:

- Although the intensity of international migration varies on a geographical basis, 96.2 per cent of the country's municipalities report some form of a link with migratory phenomena. Something similar occurs inside the United States, where residents of Mexican origin, while they are mostly concentrated in a handful of states, can be found in practically all parts of the country, including Alaska and Hawaii, where slightly over 100,000 Mexicans live.
- 55 per cent of all Mexico-born residents of the United States aged fifteen years and older completed their secondary schooling or some higher level of education. This figure drops to 40.7 per cent among the core group of temporary or circular migrants and rises to 71.8 per cent if the full spectrum of the population of Mexican origin in the United States is taken into consideration. The corresponding national average is 51.8 per cent; in general terms and contrary to common belief, this means that more qualified workers are migrating than remaining in the country.
- Another form of migration that does not fit the traditional stereotypes involves Mexican residents in the United States who have university degrees or postgraduate qualifications. The numbers in question stand at around slightly more than 250,000 people.

Table 9.1 Importance of remittances in foreign exchange earnings ($US million), by sector of origin

	Remittances	Tourism	Oil	Manufacture	Agriculture
1991	2,660	4,340	8,166	32,307	2,373
1992	3,070	4,471	8,307	36,169	2,112
1993	3,333	4,564	7,418	42,500	2,504
1994	3,475	4,855	7,445	51,075	2,678
1995	3,673	4,688	8,423	67,383	4,016
1996	4,224	5,287	11,654	81,014	3,592
1997	4,865	5,748	11,323	95,565	3,828
1998	5,627	6,038	7,134	106,550	3,796
1999	5,910	5,869	9,920	122,819	4,144
2000	6,572	5,953	14,884	145,261	4,263
2001	8,895	6,538	12,801	141,346	4,007

Source: Bank of Mexico's Annual Report for 2001; INEGI, Economic Indicators, 2001.

- The employment rate among the economically active Mexican population in the United States is fifteen percentage points higher than the corresponding level in Mexico.
- The number of Mexico-born migrant workers with formal jobs north of the border stands at around 5 million – a figure equal to one-quarter of the workers employed in the formal sector in Mexico.
- 36.2 per cent of migrants are employed in the secondary sector (i.e. industry), while the corresponding figure in Mexico is only 27.8 per cent. This situation contrasts with the stereotypical view of migrants as agricultural workers (in reality, only 13.3 per cent of Mexican migrants work in the primary sector) and points to a fundamental change in the cross-border labour market.

Along with these characteristics, there has been a significant increase in the flow of remittances sent from the United States to Mexico, which increased three and a half times over the past decade to reach, in 2001, a historical maximum of US$8.89 billion (see Table 9.1). Not only does this consolidate the country's position as the number one recipient of migrant remittances in Latin America and number two in the world (Waller Meyers 2000: 275, Lozano 2000: 160–1), it also makes labour exports Mexico's third most important source of foreign exchange earnings, making a greater contribution to the balance of payments than either tourism or agricultural exports.

The vital importance of these remittances in offsetting external imbalances becomes even clearer if each sector's net contribution to foreign

Table 9.2 Contribution of remittances to the net external trade balance ($US million), by sector of origin

	Agri-culture	Oil and gas	Minerals	Manu-facture	Tourism	Remit-tances
1991	242	7,030	395	-14,660	1,905	2,660
1992	-746	6,896	360	-22,066	1,788	3,070
1993	-129	6,054	319	-19,068	1,948	3,333
1994	-693	6,265	291	-23,350	2,305	3,475
1995	1,373	7,507	-133	-117	3,028	3,673
1996	-1,079	10,469	74	-124	3,327	4,224
1997	-345	9,227	758	-6,023	3,710	4,865
1998	-976	5,406	544	-9,881	3,760	5,627
1999	-554	8,954	-446	-10,363	3,768	5,910
2000*	-161	9,385	1,388	-12,969	2,854	4,564
2001*	-843	11,006	-483	-13,356	2,981	6,700

* Data for the third trimester.
Source: Bank of Mexico's Annual Report for 2001; INEGI, Economic Indicators, 2001.

exchange earnings is analysed. In this case, remittances constitute the second largest source of net income after oil. Moreover, following the decline in international oil prices in 1998, incomes from remittances managed to secure the top position.

The fact that migrant remittances have attained this status – becoming the source of foreign exchange with the most consistent levels of growth over the 1990s – not only makes them more visible and attractive to international financial capital, it also places the apologists of the Mexican exporting 'miracle' in a decidedly difficult position: faced with such overwhelming evidence, how can they continue to conceal the underdeveloped nature of the Mexican economy or the profoundly asymmetrical character of the trading relations established with US capitalism?

Moving on to the social arena, the strategic importance of migration is not only reaffirmed, it is redimensioned: as Rodolfo Corona so rightly points out, the 'migration phenomenon and its remittances are generalized aspects in the country's life, in that they involve one out of every five Mexican households' (Corona 2001: 38). The phenomenon is even more accentuated in the rural areas of nine states in the centre and west of the country, where that figure rises to one household in every two.

The contradictory dynamic between migration and economic growth under the aegis of neoliberalism can be summarized in the following four points. First, although migrant remittances are enormously important as a source of foreign exchange for the country and of subsistence for countless Mexican households, they also represent a net transfer abroad of potential earnings.

Second, unlike labour that is exported indirectly (through *maquiladoras*), workers who emigrate and settle in the USA consume a very significant part of the wages in that country, whereby the potential multiplying impact of their earnings is transferred to the US economy. Note that the incomes of workers of Mexican origin in the United States totalled, during 2000, some US$250 billion, $87 billion of which were earned by Mexican-born emigrants. These amounts contrast sharply with the remittances sent back to Mexico, which, impressive as they may seem, accounted for a total of US$6.57 billion during that same year.

Third, from a fiscal point of view, international migrants contribute more to the receiving economy than they receive in benefits and public services. Through transfers of resources, migrants contribute to the mass of social capital available to the US state. According to data from the National Immigration Forum, during 1997 the migrant population in the USA contributed US$80 billion more to that country's coffers than they received in benefits from the US government at the local, state and national levels; with contributions at this level, migrants introduce dynamism in the receiving economy.

Fourth, although this aspect is difficult to quantify, by bringing pressure to bear on the job market, migrants tend to have an adverse affect on wage increases in the receiving economy, particularly in the areas and sectors in which they are employed. In connection with this, a recent study by Jean Papail (2001) points out that the gap between the average income of migrant workers and the US federal minimum wage has been decreasing for the past twenty-five years. Measured in constant 2000 prices, the minimum wage fell by 38 per cent over that period, from US$11.70 to $7.20 per hour. The paradox of this situation is that it is taking place alongside the changes in migrant profiles described above – in other words, that migrants now have higher education standards and greater presence in the manufacturing sector. This clearly indicates the vicious circle within Mexico's migration patterns, whereby the dice are clearly loaded in favour of the hegemonic interests of the United States.

Mexico's migration policy: from 'no policy' to open subordination

Using strict cost-benefit calculations – with the clear aim of avoiding a confrontation with the United States, particularly as regards undocumented migrants – from 1974 and until very recently the Mexican government chose to follow a peculiar strategy that García y Griego (1988) calls 'the policy of no policy', entailing the absence of any explicit policy on migration matters.

The negotiation and enactment of the North American Free Trade Agreement (NAFTA) served as a fundamental point of reference for the subsequent course of bilateral relations and, in particular, of international migration. The Mexican government's agreement to exclude the issue of migration from the negotiation agenda and adhere uncritically to the principle of free movement for investments and goods reaffirms not only its lack of commitment towards the migrant sector, but also its frank and, in this instance, open subordination to the hegemonic interests of the United States.

The same attitude can be seen in the Mexican government's lukewarm stance *vis-à-vis* Washington's ferocious assault on the human and labour rights of Mexican migrants. Among the many measures introduced by the United States to instal a regime of terror along the border with Mexico are the countless operations deployed by its Immigration and Naturalization Service (INS) to curtail, at any cost, the growing flow of labour migrants. Bearing in mind that Mexico ranks as the United States' number two trading partner, this is far from a civilized 'good neighbour' policy between partners. One clear indicator of the vehemence with which the anti-immigration policy is being pursued is the increasingly generous (some might say exorbitant) budget given to the INS, totalling US$4.18 billion in 1999. In line with the xenophobia behind the failed Proposition 187 of California Governor Pete Wilson, on 30 September 1996 the Illegal Immigration Reform and Immigrant Responsibility Act came into effect. This legislation (which is still in force) was important in that it institutionalized the *criminalization of labour migration* through a series of arbitrary procedural provisions that violate the human and labour rights of cross-border workers (Mohar 2001: 51). One of the most reprehensible outcomes of this 'hard-line' approach within US immigration policy has been the proliferation of Mexican deaths along our northern border, totalling 1,236 between 1998 and 2000 (Villaseñor and Morena 2002: 13); recourse is thus being made to 'death as an element in dissuading migration', ratifying the predisposition towards state terrorism as an essential ingredient in US foreign policy and domestic security.

Significantly, the Mexican government's chief response to those challenges was the enactment of legislation whereby Mexican nationality could not be lost. This was, essentially, a measure intended to help Mexicans in the United States defend their rights, allowing them to acquire US citizenship without losing Mexican nationality (Martínez 1999: 251). However, one area of constant conflict is the fact that the law still does not grant sufficient guarantees to those who use it and wish to enjoy full exercise of their Mexican citizenship, i.e. the right to vote and to run for public office. It should be noted that the law in question, which came into effect on 20 March 1998, has been taken up and reinterpreted by the organized migrant community in the United States who are demanding, with increasing vehemence, full political rights.

The onset of Vicente Fox's presidency in December 2000 brought on a reassessment of the migration question, placing it for the first time ever in the history of Mexican–US relations as a priority issue on the bilateral agenda. How should the change in positions on the part of the two governments be interpreted? What reading should be made of the negotiation agenda they agreed on? What interests does it serve? And what are its real implications? Moreover, returning to the main issues on the agenda – straightening out migrants' status, a temporary worker programme, increased visa numbers, strengthening borderland security and promoting development programmes in high migration areas – what assessment can we make of the progress of the negotiations?

First, the change in the governments' positions regarding migration is based on their recognition of a reality: the burgeoning growth of the migration phenomenon (contradicting the predictions and preachings of neoliberal doctrine) and the United States' inability to contain it (or, better put, to regulate it) on a unilateral basis using strict police and military measures, such as those provided for in the 1996 Act (Mohar 2001: 54). Because of the recession affecting the US economy and its knock-on effect on the Mexican economy, these problems are accentuated and redimensioned from the perspective of the hemispheric security of the world's leading capitalist power.

Second, even though these five issues on the bilateral agenda address matters of interest to the migrant community, they avoid one issue of key importance to Mexico's strategic interests: the liberalization of migratory flows. The agenda is therefore structurally limited in that it fails to address a key aspect of the root causes of international migration and that, on the contrary, and as the Mexican government itself has stated, it is aimed at 'evolving toward a regime of ordered flows' or regulated migration. It is not difficult to see that the negotiating dice are loaded in favour of the United States' strategic interests and that, in the worst-case scenario, they will continue to benefit from a reserve of cheap Mexican labour. Consequently, President Fox's comment, made in his first State of the Nation address and reiterated in Foreign Minister Castañeda's annual report, that 'for the first time in history, the United States has agreed to negotiate the migration issue on a comprehensive basis with another country', is inaccurate.

With respect to the 'progress' made with each of the items on the bi-national agenda, the following comments and observations are of relevance. First, to date there has practically been nothing of importance to report regarding the migratory status of the 3 million Mexicans stigmatized as 'illegals'. The only information available notes that any possibility of an 'amnesty' (a term proper to the criminalization of labour migration) has virtually been dismissed by the US government and replaced by a more modest programme of 'acquired adjustment' (Miller and Seymour 2001: 1). Thus, in February 2002, the INS announced that the so-called 'amnesty' could benefit some 300,000 Mexicans.

Third, the question of temporary workers is clearly one that has fuelled keen interest among US authorities and law-makers alike. Everything points towards the launch of a programme that will allow a given number of Mexicans to work legally in the United States for a guaranteed minimum wage and access to some health benefits, provided that they return to Mexico after one year and that the number of workers allowed to register is annually adjusted in response to the conditions prevailing in the US economy, particularly unemployment rates (G. Roldán 2001: 85). This programme, which has been styled as involving *guest workers* – perhaps in an attempt to disassociate it from the discredited Bracero Program – clearly demonstrates one of the basic pillars of Washington's position in the negotiating process. With its 'generous' offer of extracting millions of Mexican labour migrants from under the 'shadow of illegality' and 'granting' them minimum labour rights, the programme proposes, in the words of its chief advocate, Senator Gramm, 'strengthening the US economy and stimulating [through the remittances sent back to Mexico and the skills acquired by the 'guest workers' in the programme] Mexico's long-delayed economic development'. In accordance with this idea, a pilot experiment was carried out in the state of Zacatecas, involving the US companies LEH Packing Company, ACME Brick, Kanes, San Angelo and Marcus Drake (García Zamora and Moctezuma 2001). And although everything indicates that the programme has President Fox's blessing, the United Conference of Mexicans Abroad (an umbrella group representing some twenty political organizations) has stated its flat-out 'rejection of the guest or temporary worker program' and its disagreement with the fact that the migrant community's representatives were excluded from the negotiations (*El Universal*, 5 January 2002).

Fourth, no information is available on possible progress in the numbers of visas allotted to Mexicans. The INS's per-country information gives updated figures for 1999 only, as does the webpage of the US Embassy in Mexico. The only figure we have is that in the H-2a visa programme (temporary farmworkers), Mexico's share in comparison to other nationalities fell between 1995 and 2000.

Fifth, of the five issues on the bilateral agenda, the matter of *border-land security* is by far the one that has received the most attention from both governments and regarding which the greatest common ground has been identified. In this case, as with the guest worker programme, the vision and interests of Mexico's northern neighbour have been imposed. A clear example of this can be seen in the Plan of Action for Coopera-tion on Border Safety, signed on 22 June 2001, which includes: 'stopping people up to three kilometers to the south of the border; having the Border Patrol and the Grupos Beta carry out operations to '"dissuade" migration; and exchanges of information between the Office of the Attorney General of the Republic (PGR) and the Naturalization and Immigration Service (INS) to combat smuggling gangs' (Sandoval 2001: 252). This is a set of coordinated operations, through which Mexico's police forces are placed at the service of US security and assigned tasks in combating undocumented migration, under the aegis of a supposed commitment towards protecting the human rights of the citizenry. The 377 Mexican migrants who died during 2001, the 29 per cent increase in the INS's budget (announced by President Bush on 29 January 2002), and the decision to increase by almost 800 per cent the number of National Guard members deployed along the border (divulged by the White House on 6 February 2002) are unequivocal signals that human rights do not feature among Washington's priorities.

At the same time, the Mexican authorities' lukewarm reaction to the violence and terrorism unleashed by the US government reveals that human rights are not a priority for the Fox administration either. And, worse still, in exchange for certain concessions *vis-à-vis* Mexican labour migration – which, to date, have been nothing more than empty promises – the Mexican government has agreed to serve as the US sentry on its own southern border under two complementary programmes: the Plan Puebla-Panamá (see Carlsen, this volume) and the Plan Sur.

This latter programme, launched on 1 July 2001, was designed to reduce the porous nature of Mexico's borders with Guatemala and Belize, through a heightened police and military presence within the framework of the commitment the Fox administration made with Wash-ington to reduce the flow of undocumented immigrants reaching the common border (Sandoval 2001: 252). This is, above all, an operation to seal off Mexico's southern border through police and military controls, which reproduces within the country the security system designed by the United States and assigns to the Mexican government the 'dirty work' of curtailing migration from Central and South America, in a unprecedented demonstration of servility and subordination. President Fox's recent offer to tighten up controls on flows of migrants explicitly reaffirms that position (*La Jornada*, 14 February 2002).

The sixth issue is regional development in the areas of highest migration, where progress has been practically non-existent. So far there have been no signs of any such initiatives involving the governments of the two countries. All that exist are mechanisms run by state governments, such as the 3x1 programme in Zacatecas, 'My Community' in Guanajuato, and, most recently, with backing from the Fox administration, 'Adopt a Community' (*Reforma*, 20 January 2002). The aim of the first two programmes is to channel collective funding from migrants into social projects (F. Torres 1998). The peculiar feature of the third programme – to be put in place in five Mexican states – is that it has been designed as a strategy for fighting poverty. This approach, however, is based on a mistaken view of the relationship between marginalization and international migration. The severe structural restrictions imposed by the neoliberal context notwithstanding (Veltmeyer and O'Malley 2001), none of these programmes seriously addresses the possibility of using the potential offered by remittances – and other resources available to the migrant community – to further local and regional development (Delgado Wise and Rodríguez 2001).

From what has been said it is clear that the results of the bilateral negotiations on migration issues have exclusively favoured the US strategic interests in the arenas of geopolitics (hemispheric security) and geoeconomics (availing itself of the advantages Mexico offers in terms of cheap labour and natural resources). The agenda emerges as a zero-sum game wherein what is gained by one side is lost by the other. In this asymmetrical negotiation process that has nothing to do with the principle of shared responsibility, the dignity that for so long characterized the foreign policy pursued by the Mexican government has ultimately been disfigured and replaced by *open subordination*.

The migrant community and the challenges of neoliberal globalism

In conclusion, it should be pointed out that today's migrant community appears much less isolated, dispersed, and disorganized than in the past. As a contradictory by-product of the historic evolution and maturing process of migratory social networks, individual migrants have embarked on an increasingly perceptible and significant evolution towards becoming what Miguel Moctezuma (2001) has called bi-national and transterritorial collective agents. This process is taking shape through the emergence of a wide array of clubs (currently totalling more than 500), associations of clubs, state-based federations in several US states, and multiple alliances and coalitions between organizations from different states with a national and bi-national outlook. The migrant community is progressing towards higher levels of organization, characterized, *inter alia*, by: (i) having a relatively permanent formal organization; (ii) using it to strengthen ties of cultural identity, belonging and solidarity with their places of origin; (iii) opening up the potential for dialogue with different public and private agencies, in both Mexico and the United States; and (iv) enjoying a not inconsiderable financial potential – through collective funds that transcend the limitations and constraints inherent in individual or family remittances – for undertaking public works projects and, ultimately, local and regional development efforts.

One of the demands that has stirred up the most interest among migrant communities is for them to be able fully to exercise their rights as Mexican citizens while abroad. This demand, which is an immediate consequence of the 1998 constitutional amendment whereby Mexican nationality could not be lost, brings together three claims that go severely against the grain of the ideology and practices of neoliberal globalism: (i) strengthening national identity, the opposite tendency to the disintegration and fragmentation inherent in globalism; (ii) collective support for local and regional development, in opposition to the destruction of the domestic market and the country's productive base caused by neoliberal restructuring; and (iii) bottom-up democracy, attacking the separation between the political class and civil society that neoliberal 'democracy' has exacerbated (Petras and Veltmeyer 2001b: ch. 6).

On the other hand, the demands of the migrant community in the United States are directed towards straightening out their legal status, securing full rights as citizens and creating a multicultural society, in contrast to political exclusion, social marginalization and the constant formation of ethnic minorities and ghettos (Castles and Miller 1998). And we could also add their demand for open borders, which is directed at one of the key elements in the strategy for imperialist domination that guides relations between Mexico and the United States (Wihtol de Wenden 1999).

10 | Community, economy and social change in Oaxaca, Mexico: rural life and cooperative logic in the global economy

JEFFREY H. COHEN

§ MICHAEL Kearney (1996) and Gerardo Otero (1999) characterize Mexico's rural populations as 'post-peasant'. What they mean is that rural folks are no longer in the process of proletarianization (becoming workers in wage labour markets); rather, they are fully part of the capitalist market system (for the history of this process see Feder 1978; Hewitt de Alcántara 1984). The reliance on small-scale agriculture where it continues to exist is squarely rooted in an expanding labour market that links the most isolated communities in the most rural parts of Mexico with centres of business and commerce. Tamar Wilson argues that this system benefits employers in the United States who turn to temporary rural migrant workers, because the workers' home base subsistence economies bear the cost of family reproduction and household maintenance and act as a safety-net for migrants who cannot find work in receiving communities due to economic downturns, poor health or lack of knowledge (Wilson 2000: 195; Delgado Wise, this volume).

Rural communities in the central valleys of Oaxaca are engaged in this expanding and complex system of changing social and economic realities. The challenge is to understand how rural Oaxacans make sense of the social and economic structures they encounter. In this regard, I concentrate on the *usos y costumbres* (practices and customs) that define social, economic and political space in the central valley community of Santa Ana del Valle, a village of 3,000 Zapotec speakers located 35 kilometres to the east of Oaxaca City (the state's capital) and 4 kilometres north of Tlacolula. My goal is threefold: to define the structures rural Oaxacans create to answer the forces of globalization, to note the positive and negative results of the encounter and, finally, to speculate on the trends that may arise from this.

The community

Santa Ana del Valle is a rural village with a history rooted in the region's pre-Hispanic past. It was resettled as a *congregación* (ecclesiastical settlement) by Dominicans following the conquest. The community gained its independence from Teotitlán del Valle in the eighteenth century, though it remained little more than an agrarian satellite of its more powerful neighbour. Over the last century small-scale agriculture was supplemented by an increasing reliance on the production of woollen textiles for sale locally and for tourism. Since the 1970s, the production of textiles for the tourist market has become crucial to the success of most households (Cohen 1999; Cook and Binford 1990; Stephen 1991).

A rise in out-migration has characterized the last two decades as Santañeros (the people of Santa Ana del Valle) cope with Mexico's economic decline (see Cohen 1999), the reorganization of the state along neoliberal lines and the collapse/decline of small-scale agriculture resulting from the withdrawal of state subsidies (DeWalt et al. 1994). Migrants have left Santa Ana throughout the community's history. In the 1970s only eight men left for work in the United States. The 1980s and 1990s saw a rapid increase in migrations: the number of people leaving for the USA increased to include 68 per cent of the fifty-four households surveyed in 1996, or sixty-seven individuals from thirty-seven independent households (see Cohen 2001b: 957).

At the same time, development policies have sought to capitalize on the indigenous roots of the communities by organizing craft cooperatives to market locally made wool textiles to Oaxaca's growing tourist trade (García Canclini 1993). These policies work rather well for Santa Ana where government funds are joined with the support of NGOs (including the Union of Oaxacan Community Museums, UMCO) and the local population to develop the community. Town leaders organized a series of projects and programmes that began in the 1970s with the arrival of electricity, the paving of roads and the purchase of a village bus with an hourly service to Tlacolula. The most important of the more recent projects (at least in terms of outside involvement) was the founding of the Museo Shan Dany in 1986 by Instituto Nacional de Antropología e Historia (INAH) and community leaders. The success of that project led to many others, including the creation of a sewer system for the town, the installation of telephone lines, the reforestation of village lands, and an effort directed at eco-tourism (Cohen 1998, 2001a).

Usos y costumbres: some ways to cooperate in Santa Ana

Santañeros have maintained a sense of independence and uniqueness that belies their involvement in global markets and the increasing importance of migration to the community. I argue that the continued importance of cooperation and, more specifically, *usos y costumbres* are crucial to Santa Ana's continued success as a community. It is the sense of commitment, identity and independence that Santañeros hold that allows the community to maintain itself even as it is embraced by (and embraces) the global ecumene. However, two caveats are important. First, even as Santañeros organize themselves, there are growing social and economic inequalities that divide village households in profound ways, particularly in terms of wealth and of differences that separate migrant from non-migrant households (Reichert 1982). Second, even as Santa Ana embraces and is embraced by the global ecumene, gross inequalities between parts of the system (in other words, between the centres of power and commerce and the rural community) mean that there is little equality, and the linkages between centre and periphery are far from transparent. In other words, while Santañeros in general want the goods and services that come with the arrival of Western-style markets and wage labour, they have little or no control over the shape and structure of this global system. To contextualize my example, I begin with a few examples of cooperative relationships in Santa Ana.

Tequio

Village leaders will put out a call for men to participate in *tequio* (communal labour) throughout the year, for a myriad of reasons. All household heads are asked to serve from one to several times a year in work crews, as representatives of their households and in the name of village tradition. For example, on a particular day five men arrive to join in clearing brush and trash from the *arroyos* that cut through village lands. The *arroyos* fill during the rainy season and bring water from the Sierra Madre del Sur to the community's fields. These individuals participate in *tequio* for two days clearing the *arroyos* in preparation and anticipation of a new season's rains. When they are finished they have the satisfaction of knowing their *tequio* contribution to the village is covered for the next year.

What makes a Santañero participate in *tequio*? There are several reasons. First, as a rule, *tequio* is a requirement of residence. Those who cannot or will not participate can be fined. Failure to serve and to pay can also land a person in jail. A single jail cell stands in the centre of town as part of the village's office complex. Jail time is served quite publicly and there is no way to hide the fact that one is in jail. But *tequio* is more than simply a community obligation. It is also an opportunity to earn status and to show leadership. Thus, a second outcome of *tequio* is to earn or reaffirm the status of an individual and his or her family. In general, a household's male head or the senior son of a family serves in a *tequio* crew. Women can serve and are serving in growing numbers as men leave the community. This status can translate directly to community support and standing in cargos (positions in the political and religious hierarchy of the village) and committees and status *vis-à-vis* the community as a whole. A crew member can also benefit directly from service. It is common for members of *tequio* crews to 'find' a bag of cement that has 'fallen' off a truck carrying supplies to a project.

Similarly, crews clearing brush have first rights to the firewood they collect, so a third outcome is direct remuneration for crew members.

A second level of association and cooperation similar to *tequio* is organized around ritual cargos and community service committees that define Santa Ana's local political and religious life. *Servicio* is important in the reproduction of the community not simply as a social space, but as a political space as well. The civil–religious hierarchy accomplishes these goals by, first, establishing a local system of ranked positions that administer to a village's political as well as ritual life. Second, the many committees working in the village also confirm the status and rank of local individuals and their families, thus indicating a form of local prestige that does (and does not) conform to Western notions of wealth and power (Cancian 1965; Watanabe 1992). This hierarchy of status, while tied to state programmes and market economics, is locally defined and therefore a structure around which a community can formally organize a response to the paternalism (or neglect) of the state (Fox and Aranda 1996).

Tequio and the cargo system are going through changes. Some households (about 12 per cent) contract others to fulfil their commitments. In Santa Ana the going wage for a day of *tequio* is between 50 and 70 pesos (depending in part on the job). The minimum wage in the state remains extremely low (around 30 pesos a day);[1] thus a day's *tequio* is not a bad alternative for an unemployed or landless villager. What is problematic is the shift from a social to an economic contract. Recognition for work, whether it is in *tequio* or the cargos, continues to go to the family that is paying for *tequio*. For the person who is hired as a stand-in, there is nothing but wages to earn. In at least one community we have visited in this project (San Juan del Estado), there is a growing group of young men who make their living as replacements for *tequio* among other community required services. In the long run, this shift may mean increasing class differentiation as wealthier wage earners hire stand-ins who lack the resources to find wage work (or to migrate) and therefore take the positions as the only potential job.

Basketball

Most afternoons older men congregate around the central plaza of the village to play basketball on a court constructed in the late 1980s. As usual, younger boys and girls drift off the court as the older players converge. Older Santañeros are members of two village teams, Los Lakers and Shan-Dany among others. Shan-Dany is the Zapotec name for the community and translates as foothills, referring to Santa Ana's location at the base of the Sierra. The Lakers are named for the Los Angeles Lakers, a popular team among villagers in 1992. For about two hours the teams will play a physical and aggressive version of the game, entertaining onlookers, some of whom have wagered on the outcome. The game ends when there is too little light to continue. If the Shan-Dany team wins it will maintain its status as a premier team (out of about a dozen squads of varying ages) in the village.

Casa del Pueblo

A final example of cooperation in Santañero life relates to the Casa del Pueblo. Most evenings during the school year teenagers congregate at the Casa del Pueblo (a division of the state-run folk arts and perform-ing arts programme, Casa de la Cultura). The youngsters change into costumes and practise a variety of folk dances native to various parts of Mexico, including Vera Cruz, Sonora and Oaxaca. Perhaps surprisingly, few of the dances are indigenous to Santa Ana. The group performs at state events, and tours the valley on weekends and holidays competing with dancers from throughout the region for small prizes and honours. The Casa also supports one of the two village squads that perform the *danza de la pluma* (feather dance), which retells the story of the Spanish conquest, during fiesta celebrations and *mayordomías* (family-sponsored saints' day celebrations).

Tequio, basketball and folk dancing are three different social institu-tions. *Tequio* is informed by village traditions, framed in shared history, and a key element in the construction of communal identity. These are important markers of Santañero-ness and a sign of an individual's responsibility to his or her village. *Tequio* exists as part of a large set of cooperative and reciprocal relationships that define local morality and commitment. In comparison, basketball seems quite trivial, an intro-duced sport played for fun. There is no tradition to playing basketball, it has existed for only a few generations and lacks any historical precur-sor in the community. There is little about the game that would make outsiders think basketball informs communal identity. Nevertheless, players tend to turn to one another for support and team members hold important formal reciprocal relationships off the court. Finally, there is folk dancing at the Casa del Pueblo and the replacement of local traditional practices with generic Mexican expressive culture. The danc-ing and parallel classroom training (which often includes programmes tied to state development goals and health projects) take children away from their parents, housework and textile production, and place them in schoolroom settings or workshops where they learn according to state-defined expectations. In the Casa del Pueblo programmes new social relationships are highlighted, defining the teenager as Mexican first and Santañero second. Yet, even in this example we find the roots of traditional cooperation reproduced. Dancers join the Casa del Pueblo squad to fulfil *promesas* (ritual promises made to saints to ensure good fortune for an individual or family), thus following traditional patterns of association in a new setting. Furthermore, the connections forged among the dancers can become a basis for long-term personal relationships.

Approaching identity

Anthropologists often approach the idea of identity in an essentialist or historicist fashion and emphasize shared cultural traits and social institutions. They assume native populations are 'fundamentally passive – either the stoic survivors of a fading past or hapless victims of an unjust present' (Watanabe 1992). Certainly, for the casual visitor to Santa Ana it is easy to essentialize the natives. Community members suggest their identity is defined first and foremost by their place of birth. In addition, most Santañeros will mention their traditional clothing (which few people wear), the local weaving industry, the practice of many forms of cooperation and their language (valley Zapotec) as markers of identity.

However, birth does not guarantee identity; it establishes only the most basic of boundaries around which an identity can be constructed. This is particularly true as the national and international pull of wage labour makes it easy to leave the village and deny connection. However, in general, migrants remain in touch with their homes and only about 8 per cent of the households visited in this study reported that members had left and severed all ties. Additionally, we should not mistake the utility of the primordial structures we use to create relationships in an alienating system as equal to the foundation upon which a social identity is built (Nash 1989). Rather, as the Santañero example reveals, identity is founded in historical processes of political, economic and social change; and it is only in a Santañero's participation in the social life of his or her family, networks, neighbourhood and community that identity comes to life (Barth 1969, 1992).

I am not suggesting that Santañero identity is now established apart from traditional patterns of cooperation and reciprocity. Rather, traditionally cooperative and reciprocal relationships are a measure against which villagers constantly judge one another (on the conventions of community see Watanabe 1992: 104). Santañeros regularly point out where people fail in their commitments to family, friends and community. On the other hand, while traditional relationships remain at the core of Santañero-ness, it is in fact new patterns of associations that create settings where identity and cooperation are reproduced, updated and reinvented to meet the challenges of the new economic and social realities of Mexico.

To understand the place of cooperative relationships in this new

order, I focus on four areas: the foundation of contemporary cooperation, the current economy and the place of reciprocity in local society,
a discussion of new patterns of association among Santañeros and an
analysis of the ways in which new cooperative structures and relationships meet the challenge of a changing world, defend the community,
and create a powerful sense of local identity.

For rural peasant and indigenous communities throughout the
world, the ability to balance and reinvent local traditions in the face
of global change is a growing challenge to local cultural, social and
natural resources. Taken as a whole, the examination of Santañero
identity affords an opportunity to follow the ways in which indigenous
peoples creatively respond to global change and the importance of an
anthropological perspective that moves away from static definitions of
identity based primarily upon place and attributes, to a dynamic analysis
of the ways indigenous peoples, like Santañeros, reinvent themselves,
their identities and their communities, and the social relationships that
are the foundation upon which the material expression of identity is
constructed.

Santañero past and present

Santañero identity is organized around cooperative and reciprocal
relationships that work at many different social levels, from the most
intimate of familial relationships to the community at large. They include
the close bonds (often organized around dyadic contracts) that unite
parents and child, join siblings, create *compadrazgo* (godparent relations)
and link friends to one another (Wolf 1966). Beyond the immediate
family, relatives and close friends, there is a series of ever-widening cooperative structures at work in Santañero society 'cross-linking' (Nader
1990) families and embedding individuals and families into the social life
of the community (El-Guindi and Selby 1976).

Guelaguetza (reciprocal exchanges of goods and services between
individuals and families) links families in contracts of delayed reciprocity to support ritual feasting and celebration. *Tequio*, as noted above,
builds a sense of communal identity through the physical support of
the village. So, too, *servicio* (participation in the village's political and
religious hierarchy – or cargo system) and *cooperación* (the contribution
of funds to communal projects, to cover the costs of fiestas and to
develop and improve the community's infrastructure) bind individual
Santañeros, as representatives of their families, to the village through
their participation in local government and their financial support of
community development.

The logic of cooperation also extends to new settings and situations.
The migrant working away from his or her natal village can choose to

maintain close, reciprocal ties with family and friends (Hulshof 1991; Mountz and Wright 1996) and will often use the logic of cooperation to organize for action and survival in his or her new home. New patterns of association that are organized at home (including basketball teams and state-supported dance troupes) re-create the logic of cooperation and in the process establish a framework for the construction of shared identity, but do so in new ways.

The reader might intuitively assume the issue at hand is one of a world where the past made sense and it is only the present that is problematic. Perhaps if we look at Santa Ana before the economic crises of the 1980s (which collectively brought a meteoric rise in out-migration, the arrival of new markets and goods locally and new social contracts), we would find that life in rural Mexico most likely did follow primordial patterns, revolving around cooperation, because there was no other way to survive. In other words, we would assume that twenty or thirty years ago, identity in Santa Ana was less problematic as the community was more or less isolated from the overwhelming impact of global change. But this assumption is patently wrong. Santa Ana's past is part of a region's (if not the globe's) history, and the village is embedded in economic and political processes that reach well beyond the local. In relation and response to these forces, it is likely that cooperation in the community has gone through more changes than we as scholars can be sure of or count.

Today the village boasts a population of nearly 3,000 people. The red-tiled roofs and adobe walls, the sound of hand-driven looms and the trappings of family farming all bring with them an image of bucolic harmony and long-lived seclusion. However, if we go back just seventy or so years, the span of only a few generations (a period that older Santañeros still recall), we find a fundamentally different place. The village, with a population of approximately 1,000 people, was caught in fierce fighting associated with the Mexican Revolution (CMSD 1992). This was not an isolated settlement. Rather it was a small village that, because of its location on trade routes into the Sierra, became a battleground. In fact, Santañeros were forced to abandon the village for six years during the most intense period of fighting between the nationalist army following President Carranza and Serrano guerrillas dedicated to Oaxacan independence (1914–20). The force of fighting was such that the village did not fully recover its pre-revolutionary population until the 1950s, and only in the 1960s did Santañeros as a group move fully back to the central community (CMSD 1992; Cohen 1999).

A few decades earlier (the late nineteenth century), Santa Ana was the site of three silver mines owned by English businessmen and home to a population that included workers from throughout Europe and North

America, according to the children of local mine workers (now some of the oldest members of the village). One informant recalled her father earning a peso a day (well beyond the local wage of 15 centavos) in the mine. The wages produced a short-lived boom in the local economy, driving home building and limited economic expansion. Furthermore, identity was not framed as a question of indigenous roots. During the years preceding the Revolution, officials of the *Porfiriato* recognized people like Santañeros not as indigenous, but rather as peasants. State economic and educational policies were aimed at the proletarianization of the population and in no way sought to celebrate or commemorate Indian roots (Cockcroft 1983). To muddy the waters even further, over a hundred years ago craft production (what is today described by villagers as traditional production rooted in pre-Colombian motifs and technologies introduced at the conquest) was organized around colonial technology (the vertical loom), market capitalism and tourism (Clements 1996; Cook and Binford 1990).

Our immediate impressions of Santa Ana today, while rooted in historical processes like the conquest, colonialism and the Mexican Revolution, remain problematic, and to believe that the past was less chaotic or more coherently organized than the present, while making for a more convincing explanation, is to project our own myopic reading of the present backwards. Thus, as we consider the structure of cooperation in the village, we must remember that while locals frame their practices as traditional, they are decidedly not primordial practices. Traditional patterns of association are really nothing more or less than relationships imbued with a sense of the past (which may be real or created) by actors following shared systems of belief, practice and morality. The key is to place traditions into a framework that will explain their social meaning.

Economy and identity

The maintenance of community in Santa Ana is organized around three key household strategies: farming, weaving and migration. Agricultural production is perhaps the most traditional, and long-lived, means of meeting the costs of family life in the community, and Santañeros who own land (78 per cent of the households in the community) grow the typical Mesoamerican crop of maize with the addition of some beans and other vegetables. The families with larger holdings of more than 3 hectares (about 10 per cent of households) grow alfalfa (if they have access to water) or garbanzo beans, among other crops, for sale to area markets. The problem facing many families is a lack of land. The rapid increase in the village's population (doubling between 1970 and 1990) and land speculation now permitted by agricultural reform laws has shifted the way people use and think about land (Otero 1999).

Additionally, most of Santa Ana's lands are of a poor quality, neither overly fertile nor irrigated, making production difficult and dependent on good weather. One way younger Santañeros who have little or no arable farmland are able to gain land is to trade services or money for plots, or to assist family members with farm work in the hopes of a share once a crop is harvested.

In addition, to compensate for, or more often in place of, dwindling land and the difficulties of farming, most households (83 per cent) also weave. Textile production has grown in importance since the 1970s and the development of tourism in Mexico. Santa Ana is part of a four-village complex that produces goods for international tourism (Cook 1984; Stephen 1991). Weaving is an anachronistic business (Cook and Binford 1990); producers control the means of production – hand-driven looms – but they do not control their product; and most Santañeros weave on contract for buyers and exporters following a style of production called *mano de obra* (a putting-out system) in which designs, wools and quantities are contracted and when the work is completed a new contract begins (Cohen 1998; Littlefield 1978).

The structure of production, and the state of the economy – one in which competition is fierce and the market appears to be shrinking – means there can be a high degree of self-exploitation production (see Cook and Binford 1990). One way weavers mediate the costs of production is by using family members as an unremunerated or underpaid workforce. Young children spin bobbins and clean finished weavings. Older children typically work alongside their parents (and today both men and women weave), producing *tapetes* (rugs or tapestries) for little or no pay. Funds earned are pooled and controlled by one or both family heads in the name of the entire familial group.

Migration, present as the strategy of a few Santañeros throughout the last century is currently one of the most important avenues towards earning a better living (Cohen 2001b). More than one-half of Santa Ana's households have migrants as members, and these men typically make between one and three trips to the United States over their lifetimes. In the United States they work in restaurants, construction and agriculture to finance house improvements, cover ritual obligations, pay for schooling or start a small business. Most migrants go to enclaves in Santa Monica or Los Angeles, California, where they live with friends and relatives.

For Santañeros who continue to farm (more than three-quarters of the households), it is more than simply work. Farming creates a series of reciprocal relationships. Individual Santañeros establish dyadic contracts around farm work, and assist one another in the preparation, planting and care of their fields. Children help their parents, and brothers aid one another. There are villagers who pay others to work their fields; however, it is more typical to find Santañeros turning to their social networks to succeed at farming rather than building contractual and wage relationships with workers. Part of the logic lies in the low return that comes from farming. With the marginal nature of Santañero land it is difficult to justify using a family's cash reserves to cover production costs.

What is clear from this brief description of work strategies is the important place cooperative relationships have in the practical maintenance of family and household. And while wage work, contract weaving and migration have changed how reciprocal relationships are organized, they have not destroyed the logic of cooperation, or devalued the importance individuals place on their models of shared identity. However, to be an effective structure of the organization of communal identity and the definition of community, these patterns of association must reach beyond the family, and among Santañeros we find that the logic of cooperation is re-created at ever more abstract levels of society.

The connections that exist between individual Santañeros, their families and the community at large are more than metaphors that describe a world that does not exist. Cooperative and reciprocal relationships reach beyond the family to include extended kin, friends, neighbours and others, from the individuals living in nearby compounds to the migrants living quite far away (Kearney 2000). Associations are also established around fictive kin networks and *guelaguetza* exchanges that often link Santañeros into odd asymmetrical pairs from very different strata of local society. The result at a functional level is the creation of intense support networks. But cooperation and reciprocity provide more than networks. The logic of cooperation and the enactment of reciprocal ties establish a measure against which practices can be judged and changes evaluated. For example, the problem with migration is not that it takes individuals out of the community – because the community is much more than a physical place. The key is whether individuals who migrate remain in networks when they are not present and when or how they choose to remove themselves from those networks. At this point, few Santañeros (about 8 per cent of households) noted that their households had lost members. Furthermore, it is common for Santañero migrants to return from the United States and other parts of Mexico specifically to fulfil commitments to the community, most notably taking a position in the community's cargo system.

Santañeros describe their role in the communal life of the village in ambivalent terms (as something they would rather not do) and it is only in abstract that most realize that their participation in the committees, their support of community initiatives and their contribution of time, energy and money into cargos, *tequio* and other local development projects mediates the influence of state programmes. *Cooperación* takes the place of formally sanctioned state taxation and is an effective means to the continued maintenance of the community in a physical as well as spiritual sense. On the other hand, men get angry when they are chosen for a difficult or a particularly onerous cargo.

The number of committees is increasing as new demands are placed on village government. The state demands new committees to manage growing bureaucracies, and as social life becomes more complex (people want more services), there is a local need for new committees. One example is the bus committee, a group that sees to the maintenance of the village's two mini-buses, their routes and schedules. This committee eats away at its members' free time, yet there is little prestige to be gained by men who serve. On the other hand, as Santañeros slowly work their way up through the ranks of different committees they do accrue definite identities based upon the status of their positions, the prestige of their families and their wealth. For these individuals, and their families, cooperative logic is important as their standing in the community becomes more and more closely linked with traditional patterns of association.

Cooperative traditions and change

The relationships reviewed above form the foundation for new patterns of association to meet the demands of social, economic and political change. Needs within the community are changing, and villagers are likely to be tied to market-driven economics. Links to the market remove, or at least mitigate, the survivalist explanation of local traditions. In other words, Santañeros no longer cooperate in order not to starve; they cooperate because they choose to cooperate. In terms of encouraging cooperation there are limited sanctions that the community can impose, including fines and jail for non-compliant citizens.

Given this change, we can ponder how cooperation is maintained as a logical construction and how relationships are updated and reproduced among villagers. The quick answer is simply that cooperation does more than define the parameters for survival. It is an effective structure for the organization of community hierarchy, and at the same time it defines a set of relationships that mediates difference. In basketball we see this logic and patterning literally played out. The teams are organized by Santañero men (among younger villagers there are both male and female teams) who come together to meet a particular goal – winning a game. However, the relationships extend beyond the court and competition to create social networks among the players. There are also families that become associated with particular teams, supporting the players by purchasing jerseys and equipment.

The teams also mediate class and status differences among players. On any given team the individual players may represent a variety of strata from the community, rich and poor, the prestigious and the inconsequential. On the team, everyone works for the good of the group and differences are put aside, creating what Nader (1990) describes as 'harmony ideology'. Skill on the court also becomes a new measure of ability, taking the place of wealth, ritual knowledge and age. In the game the issue is athletic ability not social skill, creating yet another measure of personal ability. The support networks created around basketball endure as Santañeros migrate. Players from Santa Ana play in tournaments in places like Santa Monica, California. These games become settings where Santañeros can meet and celebrate their shared identity. The teams are also a rallying point for villagers at home. There are frequent tournaments throughout the valley and during these competitions dozens of teams may show up to compete for what are sometimes hefty prizes.

A similar process is occurring in the programmes of the Casa del Pueblo. As described above, the Casa programmes train Santañero children in the expressive arts and crafts traditions of a generic Mexico. There is some debate as to the positive and negative effects of these programmes. Garcia Canclini (1993) argues such efforts diminish native traditions, corrupt indigenous world-views and become yet another forum through which native peoples are dominated by the state. On the other hand, Brandes (1988), describing 'Day of the Dead' rituals and the influence of tourism in Tzintzuntzan, notes that state support is welcomed as it reduces the need for locals to fund ritual performance (although in Santa Ana costs are shared by state programmes and local households). Additionally, the publicity and support increases outside awareness of local practice, increasing tourism and, therefore, increasing money entering village and family accounts.

The situation in Santa Ana sits between the extremes of the above examples. Many Santañeros, in interview, voiced their discomfort with the changes occurring in the structure of ritual practice and with the validity or purpose of the Casa del Pueblo programmes, but no one suggested the programme should be ended. Part of what mediates animosity and tension is the important role older Santañeros play in Casa programmes. While the dances, songs and arts that are taught are generalized to most of Mexico, local traditions particular to the community (the *danza de la pluma* for example) are also encouraged.

Cooperation and solidarity in contemporary Santa Ana

I have noted the interactive process through which reciprocity and communal identity create a sense of belonging for Santañeros. However, while our examples are all in general quite positive, cooperation is not always described as a benefit. The migrant son or daughter who sends money home to support parents and cover expenses that cannot be met through textile production will likely do so only grudgingly. Weavers use the vocabulary of cooperation to control the labour power of their children. Furthermore, those individuals who decline to participate in the social life of the community risk heavy sanctions that can lead to the expulsion of families. Thus, it is clear that there is a coercive dimension to cooperation. The rhetoric and practice of reciprocity tie children to parents in an indentured structure from which they cannot break. This is a relationship that can last a lifetime. There is also ongoing debate among Santañeros over where new programmes, including those of Casa del Pueblo, will end and how best to deal with new patterns of association like those found among migrants.

In a more clearly economic sense, cooperative relationships are changing as Santañeros become part of the global economy. As villagers find employment in wage labour (whether locally in Oaxaca City or in the United States) the constraints on their time and energy increase. Some households have begun to hire other villagers to cover their commitments to *tequio* and *servicio* (although as noted above this is a small group, about 12 per cent). Thus, one of the fundamental forms of community-wide cooperation is replaced by a formally contracted labour agreement between individuals. Poorer households, and in particular poor, non-migrating households are in increasingly marginal positions in such a system. These households typically lack the funds to cover commitments, they often lack the manpower to cover service and they may even lack the social networks that might create new opportunities. It is around these inequalities that I am focusing at the present.

Conclusions

Cooperation works at a number of levels to create a sense of identity for Santañeros in the new world order. It establishes the parameters of behaviour for individuals as members of families and of the community in general. It also becomes a framework for the control of family labour and for building political authority and prestige. Cooperation mediates differences and builds cross linkages between the strata of Santañero society. Finally, cooperative relationships as they are updated – for example, through dance or basketball – become a framework through which Santañeros can cope with the state and the shifting identities that come with migration to the United States.

The way in which identity is created in the village works to define and set parameters for local social action, they also demarcate and differentiate Santa Ana as a social setting that stands apart from and independent of other populations (whether neighbouring villages, nation-states or market systems). Today, cooperation continues as an important way to define local identity in the face of rapid social and economic change. Concentrating on the practice of these relationships moves us away from the judgemental approach of the primordialist who pins identity to a set of attributes and attitudes that cannot change. The approach advocated here is one that frames identity in social and economic history. Cooperation is part of a meaningful system that is created in the continuous modification, reinterpretation and reproduction of tradition in social practice and ever changing situations. And as we see among the Santañeros, maintaining a sense of local identity becomes a way to filter the pressure of migration, of increasing dislocation and of growing incorporation into global markets. Communal identity is not about an escape into a world of indigenous harmony, but is a structure that, in its reproduction and reinventions allows individuals to embrace the chaos of the moment and deal with the issues of change while maintaining a coherent body of shared ideals.

Notes

Support for this project came from the National Science Foundation grant #9875539, the Department of Anthropology, Pennsylvania State University, and the Instituto Tecnológico de Oaxaca. My thanks to Sylvia Gijon and Rafael Reyes for their assistance in the field. Any errors remain my responsibility.

1. The exchange rate during this work hovered between 9 and 10 pesos to the dollar.

11 | Survival strategies in neoliberal markets: peasant organizations and organic coffee in Chiapas[1]

MARÍA ELENA MARTÍNEZ TORRES

§ THIS chapter describes how small-farmer cooperatives (re)organized themselves to respond to neoliberal restructuring and survived – and in some cases even prospered – in the reconfigured marketplace. Coffee producers, most of them small peasant farmers, have been among the hardest hit by neoliberal reforms. The key features of the neoliberal economic policies that have buffeted all Mexican farmers since the early 1980s have included massive cuts in support prices and subsidized credit, a generalized market opening to competition from cheap imports, and the privatization of technical assistance and support services including the supply of subsidized inputs, and the collection, transport, processing and marketing of crops. For peasant producers of coffee a key manifestation of neoliberal reform was the privatization of the Mexican Institute of Coffee (INMECAFE), which had previously provided them with exactly those services. This national-level neoliberal impact on Mexican coffee farmers was part of the larger global neoliberal restructuring of the coffee industry after the 1989 collapse of the International Coffee Agreement (ICA). In addition to losing access to a vast array of services formerly provided by the state, peasant coffee growers also had to negotiate the reconfigured terrain of the world coffee market.

In this chapter I will first review neoliberal market changes for coffee producers. In the second section, I present some general responses to these changes. Finally, in the third section I describe three case studies of small-peasant-farmer coffee cooperatives in the state of Chiapas. These cases are typical of an isolated but fairly large bright spot on the generally negative canvas of neoliberal rural Mexico – a boom in small-farmer production of certified organic coffee, centred in Chiapas. What these case studies highlight is that those communities that met two conditions – organizational capacity and natural endowments – have in many cases been capable of successfully navigating this reconfigured terrain. 'Organizational capacity' has to do with Otero's (1999) notion of political class formation, although it is here applied to more localized situations, at the community and regional levels. It focuses primarily on economic aspects of livelihood rather than the political constitution of a class. In fact, the key goal of the organizations described in this chapter has been to 'appropriate the production and commercialization processes' (Gordillo 1988b; Otero 1989b, 1999). These cases offer a glimmer of hope, an alternative vision of a countryside organized around principles of solidarity and the sustainable management of natural resources.

Coffee, neoliberalism and international markets

Mexican coffee is an important export commodity with an average annual value of US$800 million. Federal government programmes targeted coffee production after the First World War since coffee prices were particularly high and the land most suitable for coffee was considered to be marginal for most other commercial crops (Hidalgo Monroy 1996). There are almost 300,000 coffee farms in Mexico (Harvey 1994; Plaza Sanchez et al. 1998) occupying approximately 800,000 hectares and involving about 2 million people (Celis et al. 1991). Coffee is the second most important source of income for rural economies after the remittances migrant workers send to their families. An important characteristic of coffee production in Mexico and Chiapas is that the majority of the producers (70–90 per cent, see Table 11.1) are relatively small.

Historically, in national and international markets, demand has determined how financial, material and human resources have been allocated for expansion and changes in technology and quality. However, producer-country power grew within the coffee industry when the nature of production became oligopolistic (controlled by a few producers). This meant that only a few countries contributed to the production of more than half of the world's coffee. The principal producing countries have made tremendous efforts to maintain high prices in the coffee market for many years. Brazil, for example, destroyed its entire harvest in 1906 to prevent coffee prices from dropping, and from 1921 to 1944 burned 74 million sacks in order to maintain relatively high prices (Junguito and Pizano 1993). The high prices then provided an incentive for producers in Africa, Central America and other countries to produce more coffee (Dicum and Luttinger 1999). However, during the Second World War demand for coffee dropped drastically and the competition for sales forced prices to drop as well. The downward trend continued after the war and reached a low of 30 cents per pound in 1960, which severely damaged the economies of those countries dependent on coffee as a source of income (Arenas Melo 1981).

The coffee market eventually became oligopolsonic, with only four large buyers internationally: Nestlé, Maxwell House, General Foods and Kafee Harz account for 60 per cent of total coffee purchases worldwide (Lombana Mejia 1991). The bilaterally oligopolist nature of the world coffee market lent itself to an agreement between producers and buyers that gave coffee a fairly unique governance structure in the form of the

Table 11.1 Coffee producers in Mexico and Chiapas by amount of land planted to coffee

Hectares planted with coffee	Chiapas producers no.	%	Mexico producers no.	%
up to 2	48,762	66.1	194,538	68.9
2–5	18,248	24.7	64,377	22.8
5–10	5,102	6.9	17,881	6.3
10–20	1,202	1.6	4,291	1.8
20–50	208	0.3	808	0.3
50–100	104	0.1	246	0.1
over 100	116	0.2	178	0.1
Total	73,742	100	282,319	100

Sources: Hidalgo Monroy (1996); Harvey (1994).

International Coffee Quotas Agreement, signed in 1940. In the context of US President Kennedy's 'Alliance for Progress' approach, driven by the fear of another Cuban-style revolution, it evolved into the International Coffee Agreement (ICA) in 1963, which established production quotas for each country (Dicum and Luttinger 1999). The ICA agreement more or less stabilized prices and the implementation of the quota system guaranteed each country access to the market. Furthermore, the price of coffee rose as much as 200 per cent after the ICA was established. The agreement eventually grouped fifty producing countries, representing 99 per cent of world production, and twenty-five consuming countries, or 90 per cent of world consumption. The ICA's purpose was to balance the competing interests of buyers and sellers.

One of the results of the ICA was the strengthening of the government institutions that existed in almost all coffee-producing countries to support coffee production. Marketing and distribution 'Coffee Institutes' or quasi-governmental coffee producer associations were established in Latin American coffee-producing countries such as Brazil, Colombia, Central America and Mexico. These agencies established a guaranteed minimum price and, in some countries, growers could sell to the national institute or to private exporters at the free market price. In other countries such institutes had, until recently, a monopoly over exports, as in the cases of El Salvador and Mexico. Coffee institutes may also have been in charge of collecting export taxes and of the distribution of export quotas, allowing them to obtain revenue and thus finance the state apparatus (R. G. Williams 1994). The coffee market was thus not self-regulating; rather, the state played a continuous role in the changes that took place within the industry.

Evidence of this role appeared in the 1960s when international financial institutions and donors adopted new development policies in response to the major social and political movements that were sweeping Latin America at the time. The World Bank and the US Agency for International Development (AID) promoted limited agrarian reforms, access to credit and new research to promote higher productivity in rural areas (Parra Vazquez and Moguel Viveros 1996). The state took on a regulatory role in Mexico in order to protect the peasant economy from market forces. World Bank funds were channelled into Mexico's Rural Development Investment Programme (Programa de Inversion para Desarrollo Rural, PIDER) (Parra and Moguel 1996) in response to peasant and other social mobilizations. Official policy supported production-oriented projects throughout Mexico from 1976 to 1982.

The governmental development programme required that coffee producers be organized in groups suitable for receiving credit (*sujetos de crédito*) in order to transfer funds. Laws were implemented to create various legal constructs for this purpose, including the Unión de Ejidos (UE), the Unión de Uniones de Ejidos (UUE), and the Asociaciones Rurales de Interés Colectivo (ARIC). The Mexican countryside was reorganized under these forms of association and peasants learned to manage and organize their production, to deal with the market and with the state. This earlier change in state policies helped to strengthen the peasants' organizational capacities in that their self-directed reorganization gave the small organizations a new purpose and confidence in themselves, as well as a stronger trust in the organizational levels above them. Rural development policies tended to support the sectors that would provide higher revenues for the state, and, as coffee fell into this category, the Mexican Institute of Coffee (Instituto Mexicano del Café, INMECAFE) was created.

Responding to market and state reconfiguration

The birth of INMECAFE had a great impact on the technification, support, commercialization and research of coffee production in the 'social sector', or the organized rural poor. It was in charge of research, support prices, credit, storage and distribution. Changes in production technology made by the medium and large producers forced many small operations to seek loans in order to keep pace with them. This led many into debt and eventually bankruptcy as the market was reconfigured.

At a global level, the International Coffee Agreement produced a constant struggle between producers and buyers. The agreement periodically disintegrated when one or the other found itself in a weakened position, only to be renegotiated later (Restrepo 1990), and in fact the ICA was suspended twice during its twenty-seven years of life (1962 to 1989). In 1989, after many negotiations, the agreement finally col-

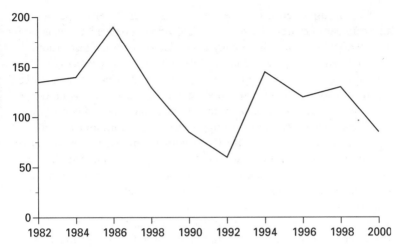

Figure 11.1 Price of Mexican Santos 4 coffee in New York Exchange Market, 1982–2000 (US cents per lb). *Source*: ICO composite indicator prices.

lapsed and the futures market set world prices that have been in effect ever since. Prices then dropped dramatically and stayed low for five years. Countries dependent on coffee exports had drastic cuts in their export earnings within a few months and there was an overall drop of $5 billion worldwide (Dicum and Luttinger 1999). During the next few years Colombia led an attempt by producer countries to forge a new agreement. Once again new proposals were made and the United States' request to veto was denied (Junguito and Pizano 1993).

In 1993, after another failed attempt to re-establish the ICA, the main coffee-growing countries without the participation of the consuming countries established a coffee cartel. Members agreed to withhold stocks so that world supply could be controlled. The producing countries wielded their power in the continuing struggle between buyers and producers. World prices doubled in 1994 due to frosts in Brazil but fell again a few years later to reach the historical low that matches the prices of today (Figure 11.1).

The role of the state in Latin America changed with the entrance of neoliberal policies after the 1982 economic crisis. The state withdrew from its regulatory role and the market protection offered to the peasant economy gradually disappeared over the course of the 1980s. The neoliberal solution was to privatize, cut social expenditures, and all the groups engaged in productive projects with the governmental institutions had to restructure or disappear (J. Fox 1994). INMECAFE was also cut as part of structural adjustment policies. The government thus left the area of production totally in the hands of the producers.

This brought serious consequences for small farmers, particularly those in remote areas such as the Lacandon Jungle in Chiapas (Collier 1999) which had traditionally depended on national institutions for technical assistance, credit and subsidized transport and processing. The retreat of government support throughout Mexico and Chiapas forced them to reconfigure their activities to confront their new condition of rural marginality in a global context. Peasant families and communities had various responses. Some groups with strong communities responded to the economic crisis of the 1980s with formal structures based on tradition and kinship or religion (i.e. the Majomut and ISMAM coffee cooperatives described below). For instance, in the assemblies of these organizations the presence of the traditional authority is required to take decisions. Many other groups chose to explore migration as an alternative (Craipeau 1993) or opted to change their practices and cut the external dependence that had developed during the prime years of the Mexican developmental state. In this context, emergent Non-Governmental Organizations (NGOs) had an important place in accompanying organizations of rural civil society in their transition to becoming more autonomous.

During the 1980s two distinct but interlinked sets of demands from peasant organizations took shape. The first set of demands was agrarian and derived from the continued struggle for land together with farm-workers' demands for better conditions of work and salaries. Organizations focused on these demands were more political in their outlook and strategy. The second set of demands was agricultural and came in the 1980s from peasants who had already won access to land and sought support to produce on their land. Some agrarian movements converted into *sujetos de crédito* in order to obtain resources mainly in the form of loans and support for their production practices. Many continued along both lines for some time, although the movements eventually separated into specific struggles. Small producers could no longer rely on the support system of the state; they were forced to take action themselves. The resulting organization within the communities served to strengthen the already existing social and familial ties of solidarity.

The productive objective of the agricultural group was known as 'the appropriation of the production process'. The central goal was now to control all stages of the production and commercialization process of their products (Gordillo 1988b; Otero 1989b, 1999; A. Bartra 1999; J. Fox 1994; Celis et al. 1991). Peasant organizations shifted away from the militant tactics of their land-seeking counterparts in negotiating their demands for economic development. Instead, they relied on non-violent mobilizations and strategic negotiations with different official institutions for concrete policy ends. Many of these regional organizations merged in 1985 to form the National Union of Autonomous Regional Peasant Organizations (Unión Nacional de Organizaciones Regionales Campesinas Autónomas, UNORCA) which later gave birth to sectorally focused national networks of peasant-managed credit unions, fertilizer distributors, and corn, coffee and lumber producers (J. Fox 1994). UNORCA was founded in 1985 as a union of twenty-five peasant organizations with different political affiliations.

Coffee producer organizations were part of this peasant movement focused on production issues. Because the agrarian reform had been *de facto* over since 1979, they became the most dynamic and important sector among peasant organizations during the 1980s and early 1990s. In this context, the coffee producer organizations were among the most successful examples of peasant-organization-managed production. The state support for this sector was strong during this period but it focused on organizations rather than the coffee sector as a whole.

The new cooperatives formed in Mexico during this period included: CEPCO (State Coordinator of Coffee Producers of Oaxaca), UCIRI (Union of Indigenous Communities of the Isthmus Region), UPCV (Union of Coffee Producers of Veracruz), UCIZONI (Union of Indigenous Communities of the Northern Sierra of the Isthmus), CARTT (*Tosepan Titataniske* – 'We shall overcome', Regional Agricultural Cooperative in the Sierra Norte of Puebla) and ISMAM (Indigenous People of the Motozintla Sierra), among many others.

Coffee prices in Mexico hit the floor in 1989 because of the breakdown of the commodity agreement; the international price for coffee fell below the high cost of production for technified coffee. This meant that many large and medium-sized technified growers went bankrupt and had their land and machinery confiscated by the banks. Some of the largest growers were able to survive by relying on outside sources of funds to make their payments. However, in Chiapas, most of the mid-size technified farmers were foreclosed (Meda 1995). Organic farmers and traditional growers lost substantial income but managed to survive the crisis, unlike the technified growers. As conventional coffee prices dropped, the organic market boomed. Many small farmers in Mexico saw an opportunity to market their traditionally grown coffee as organic – which it often is – and a strong movement for organizing in organic cooperatives sprang up (Meda 1995). Most of the farmers converted to organic coffee and now many are certified by the Organic Crop Improvement Association (OCIA) in the United States or Naturland in Europe. In many cases Alternative Trade Organizations (ATOs) in the United States and Europe such as Max Havelaar, Royal Blue Organics or Aztec Harvest, which is locally owned in Mexico, have played key roles in getting organic coops of small farmers up and running. Spurred on by economic necessity and the lure of higher prices (Toledo 1989, cited in Carruthers 1995), growers who had traditionally used sustainable practices (Bellon 1995) sought to convert to organics. Organic certification is a way in which peasants can get a financial return from investing in their natural endowments (land), slowing or reversing degradation and building up soil fertility, as well as receiving higher prices for the harvests.

A key feature of the current market system developed after the 1989 breakdown of the coffee agreement: the freeing of quality-based pricing from the six narrow categories previously imposed on the coffee market. Today, quality designations or labels such as 'Guatemala Altiplano' or 'Pluma Hidalgo' constitute significant-content information that adds to the quality component of value-added. This new labelling practice opened a slew of fresh opportunities to market coffee from small producers, organic coffee, coffee from cooperatives and 'shade coffee'. It is also one of the key features of the reconfiguration of coffee demand that has impacted small farmers in Mesoamerica as dozens of new ATOs have appeared to help them market their 'specialty' coffees (Medea 1993).

Alternative trade was born in developed countries to use 'consumer buying power to help producers in developing countries'. This movement takes advantage of the boom in consumer interest in 'specialty' coffees (Greenfield 1994). The idea is to address the inequity of the terms of trade in which the north sets prices and producers in the south are forced to take them. As Raynolds put it: 'the overall goal of alternative trade is to counter the organization of production and trade around abstract market principles that devalue and exploit disadvantaged peoples and the environment, particularly in poorer regions of the South' (Raynolds 2000: 2).

Greenfield (1994) reports that ATOs have focused on coffee as their lever of change and that this is the export crop in which fair trade can make the most difference. Efforts to include other products have been growing recently, for example bananas (Murray and Raynolds 2000). Most ATOs are linked to notions of alternative or 'sustainable' rural development (Luttinger and Dicum 1999). They seek to transform conditions of poverty in rural areas by providing poor peasants with new marketing channels, technical assistance and new products, e.g. organic coffee, which may result in higher prices for their coffee (Nigh 1997; Meda 1995; Greenfield 1994). These organizations often run small rural programmes where recipients are trained in alternative production and marketing techniques.

A political movement emphasizing social responsibility in the marketplace evolved in Europe during the 1960s. Fair Trade, as it was known, established a chain of 300 small stores called 'solidarity' shops all over Western Europe to sell socially responsible products (Murray and Raynolds 2000). The shops were privately owned or run by local organizations or NGOs (Nigh 1997). The Mexican organic coffee cooperatives ISMAM and UCIRI marketed their products in these shops.

Today, one of the more important European solidarity markets that follow the idea of 'fair trade not charity' is the Max Havelaar initiative. It was formed out of a meeting of Unión de Comunidades Indigenas de la Region del Istmo (UCIRI) in 1986, where coffee producers told 'Solidaridad', a Dutch Development Aid Agency, that they would not need grants if the coffee price covered the cost of production and offered a decent life for their families (Max Havelaar 1995, cited in Hidalgo Monroy 1996). Max Havelaar is a Europe-wide ATO created to assist producers with growing and exporting organic products.

Fair Trade calculated a minimum price of US$1.26 per pound that took into account the cost of production (Rice and McLean 1999: 21). Producers cannot receive less than this floor price when buying under Fair Trade conditions.

The last few years have marked the appearance of coffee label initiatives within the market. Labels give information to the consumers about the conditions under which commodities are produced. These conditions focus on environmental or social issues, or sometimes a combination of both. Many coffee labelling initiatives and brands emerged as part of the highly specialized coffee market. 'Organic', the first label created, is the most recognizable but 'conservation coffee', 'shade grown coffee' and 'sustainable coffee' all compete with it. Every one of these labels establishes a process of certification that producers have to meet.

The International Federation of Organic Agriculture Movements (IFOAM), founded in Germany in 1972, promotes organic farming and has developed certification criteria for coffee. There are detailed agro-ecological requirements that producers must complete so that their coffee may be certified as organic. Currently IFOAM has accredited twelve certifying organizations rather than certifying directly (Raynolds 2000: 5). IFOAM opened its Latin America chapter in Colombia in 1989. Mexico has made important advances in local certification with the Association of Organic Certifiers and is the only country that has established an in-country certifier organization. OCIA also opened a Mexican chapter. Certification criteria, however, vary according to different labels.

The formation of certification organizations has been just one example of the organization within the coffee industry. Coffee organizations also show that peasants are organizing successfully to enter the global market. Fox observes that: 'The indigenous movement of organic coffee farmers has the skill, experience and sophistication to process and market their crop to Europe and the United States. Since the late 80s, the movement has become a major progressive political force, comprising more than 60,000 families in Chiapas, Oaxaca, Guerrero y Veracruz' (J. Fox 1997).

The opening of coffee shops in the form of coffee cooperatives such as La Selva, and later by the Chiapas chapter of the National Coordinator of Coffee-growers' Organizations (Coordinadora Nacional de Organizaciones Cafetaleras, CNOC) as a group, has been a development strategy based on the local and national market. This strategy used by other producers in Latin America, as in the case of wine in Argentina (Posada and Velarde 2000), has been an attempt to change the urban consumption preference to locally produced coffee via high standards of quality and taste. It is an interesting proposal to revitalize marginalized zones by changing urban preferences for coffee. This tactic also opens up the national market for the consumption of coffee and makes the producer less dependent on the international coffee market. Coffee producer organizations are strengthened and, at the same time, they may have the chance to retain more value-added as the organization also handles the roasting, packaging and retail selling.

Regional coffee producers' organizations founded the CNOC in 1988. This was a national organization created as an independent alternative to the government's State Coffee Council (Consejo Estatal del Café), which the larger producers controlled. CNOC began to sell coffee under its own label, Aztec Harvest, with an office in Emeryville, California, although the experiment lasted only a few years due to the high costs of maintaining the office.

The Mexican Coffee Council (Consejo Mexicano del Café) estimates Mexico's internal coffee market to have consumed one million bags in 1995 with Nestlé dominating the market (CEC 1999). Mexico's internal market has been significantly low compared to those of industrialized countries although the growing presence of cafés owned and run by producers selling high-quality coffees in Mexico is paving the way for expansion. This initiative allows direct selling by producers like CEPCO in Oaxaca City and Union de Ejidos de la Selva with four cafés in Mexico City and one café in each of the cities of San Cristóbal de las Casas, Guadalajara and Monterrey. La Selva, now selling franchises in Mexico and abroad, has the first international café in Barcelona, Spain. There is also negotiation underway to open a café in Atlanta, Georgia. The commitment of the franchises is to buy all the coffee they sell from La Selva, a cooperative of more than 1,500 small peasant producers.

Another example of an organization of small coffee producers in Chiapas is Café Museo in San Cristobal de las Casas where coffee from members of CNOC Chiapas is sold. This space has become a centre of cultural events, a meeting place for activists, NGOs and researchers.

They also set up a remarkable, museum-type exhibition on the coffee production process and the lives of the coffee-growing families.

On the consumer side, a recent study (North American CEC 1999) shows coffee drinkers in Canada and the United States to be more interested in environmental conservation through canopy-grown and environmentally protective techniques than in health protection by the avoidance of the use of chemicals. Consumers in Mexico City have also expressed an interest in possible internal market expansion by small Mexican coffee producers if the product is mainly grown in an environmentally friendly manner.

Case studies
ISMAM

The cooperative of indigenous farmers Indígenas de la Sierra Madre de Motozintla (ISMAM) was founded in 1987 to provide an alternative marketing channel avoiding the middleman, and became the most successful organic coffee cooperative in Chiapas in the 1990s. The Catholic Church played an important role in its formation and the support of the government and international NGOs has been critical to its development and growth. The Catholic dioceses of Tapachula are organized in *Foraneas* or regions. The *Foranea* of the Sierra has five commissions, which address health, women, youth, human rights and cooperatives, the last of which is in charge of helping in the organization of agricultural cooperatives. The cooperative commission promotes alternative agriculture and aquaculture, develops new models of commercialization and production, and promotes savings plans and credit programmes.

Father Jorge Aguilar Reyna, coordinator of the Sierra *Foranea*, was crucial in the formation of ISMAM. Towards the end of 1985 the Sierra *Foranea* organized a coffee producers' meeting in which a sub-group was named to look into the best way to start a production and marketing organization. The group, accompanied by Father Reyna, went to Oaxaca and established contact with the union UCIRI, an organization that was already producing certified organic coffee. It began experimenting with compost, and had a general meeting in mid-1986 to elect representatives and leaders by region. It defined its principles as an organization 'of Service not Business', and decided to use only biological agriculture methods to produce a better-quality product and to protect the environment and its members' health. ISMAM was one of the organizations that promoted the TCO (Trabajo Común Organizado) programme, in which producers organized themselves in groups to exchange labour. This was a revitalization of the indigenous tradition, known as *tequio* in central Mexico, of working collectively. TCO implied extra work, little credit, a lot of meetings and heavy service requirements. Many farmers did not accept this burden and, of the 250 producers that originally met, only ninety-nine decided to continue with the organization.

This organization, as well as the other coffee organizations, was spurred on by the 1989 collapse of the ICO agreement and the subsequent 30 per cent price drop over the following three days. Coffee producers were forced to look for alternative ways to sell their coffee. At the same time the market for organic products in Europe was growing and would continue to grow. The ISMAM consultants soon learned of this growth potential in the organic market from the meetings of the International Federation of Organic Agriculture Movements (IFOAM) that they attended.

The initial development of ISMAM was supported by a grant from SOS Werdenhandel in the Netherlands. In these initial efforts, UCIRI supported ISMAM by selling part of ISMAM's harvest. With the help of the Europe-wide Max Havelaar Fair Trade Association to commercialize its product, ISMAM soon overcame its initial membership loss and had 490 members by 1990 (Sanchez Lopez 1990). IFOAM also contributed with training in organic practices and principles. A Mexican NGO known as Maderas del Pueblo provided training in composting, erosion control and intercropping of other crops with coffee. Today, ISMAM coffee is certified as organic by Naturland in Germany.

The fundamental goal of the cooperative is to concentrate the production of its many members in order to facilitate direct export, eliminate intermediaries and recover greater value-added for their product. ISMAM had the good political connections and obtained one of the largest and most modern coffee mills in Chiapas in 1992 when the government sold it to them on credit as a part of the privatization of INMECAFE. In fact, the government has treated ISMAM with great favouritism on a number of occasions, in a way that has led other organizations to distance themselves from ISMAM for fear of cooptation. Luis Donaldo Colosio, the 1994 PRI presidential candidate who was assassinated before the elections, was the guest of honour at ISMAM's annual meeting in 1993, in which the head of the Rural Development Bank (BANRURAL) announced a credit line for ISMAM of US$2.1 million. It was thus no surprise that ISMAM responded to the Zapatista uprising in early 1994 by calling them delinquents (Meda 1995). This illustrates both a lingering corporatism in the Mexican countryside and the fact that the state can be a key actor in supporting peasant organizations. The key question for them is how to garner such support while retaining their political independence from the state, or how to generate enough resources to be self-sufficient.

ISMAM sales rivalled the government largesse. In 1990 sales were estimated at US$900,000. They rose to US$1.5 million in 1991, to US$2.4

million in 1992, to US$3.2 million in 1993, and in 1994 they totalled US$4.8 million. By 1995 they had 1,529 members and the average annual income for these members was US$1,850, an exceptionally high income in indigenous, rural Chiapas (Meda 1995).

ISMAM's structure reflects a commitment to democratic principles. Its members attempt to reach a consensus in decision-making, but are open to a vote when there is no consensus. The cooperative was organized to give local members some degree of autonomy, so each community has two representatives that attend general assemblies. The structure of the cooperative consists of six committees: executive, controller, finance, education, technical assistance and *other* committees (Sanchez Lopez 1990).

The collective decision to adopt organic farming had profound impacts on ISMAM members. Organic farming requires a strict internal control of all phases of coffee production in order to maintain certification. Thus ISMAM established a form of control where each bag could be traced to its origin. Its own agronomist (hired so as to be independent from the government extension agent) makes monthly visits to the members' farms and takes notes about fertilization and the condition of the groves, which are archived in a computer in the central office (Nigh 1997). This process helped ISMAM perfect its levels of internal organization and independence.

Majomut

In 1980 and 1981, a number of local coffee farmers' groups, which had been formed in conjunction with a couple of government programmes, came together to request that the project resources be given directly to the communities. In the process of holding these meetings it was suggested that a storage shed be built to store the members' products, to then be sold at a better price on the local and regional markets. The building of this storage area was also a response to INMECAFE's faulty coffee collection practices. Apparently, INMECAFE had an agreement with local middlemen in Panthelho, under which INMECAFE would mysteriously be closed on certain days, so the middlemen could buy all the coffee. The following day the middlemen would sell the coffee to INMECAFE for a better price. The shed provided a place for producers from very distant towns to leave their coffee cargo until the INMECAFE store reopened.

Eighteen communities from two municipalities were selected to begin the negotiations with regional representatives from PIDER and, in 1982, they agreed to build the storage shed in the town of Majomut, in the municipality of Polhó (which means 'place where the birds fight' in Mayan Tzotzil). A recognized legal incorporation was needed to receive the facility, so the federal Secretariat of Agrarian Reform (Secretaría de la Reforma Agraria, SRA) and the Chiapas state Secretariat of Indigenous Affairs (Secretaría de Asuntos Indígenas) created the Union de Ejidos and Comunidades de Cafeticultores del Beneficio Majomut, S. de R.L.

The four main objectives of the organization were:

1. The cultivation, industrialization and commercialization of coffee and its derivatives on an international and national level.
2. To build, acquire and establish industries and services, use renewable and non-renewable resources, distribute and commercialize the products, manage credits, and in general engage in all classes of industries, services and rural activities.
3. To promote the economic improvement and material progress of the members, as well as the capitalization of the *ejido* and the community.
4. To carry out all economic or material transactions to improve the collective organization of work, as well as to increase crop productivity, and use of available resources.

Three agrarian communities (Chenalhó, Panthelo and Cancuc) and two *ejidos* (Los Chorros and Puebla) legally form the Unión de Ejidos y Comunidades Majomut. The members are represented by two delegates from each of the thirty-two towns that participate and conduct monthly meetings and annual assemblies.

The cooperative structure is based on a three-person executive committee (president, secretary and treasurer) and an oversight committee. Their principal adviser is also a key person in the cooperative itself. The executive committee is in charge of commercialization and the oversight committee is in charge of collecting the harvest and looking after the fixed assets of the organization (machinery, trucks, coffee mill, storage facilities). Usually both committees have three-year terms, although circumstances can vary. For example, in the uncertainty in the wake of the Acteal massacre, in which forty-five unarmed indigenous people (mostly women and children) were killed by paramilitary forces while praying in a church in 1997, the assembly decided to extend their terms of office for another cycle.

Majomut sold its first shipment under a contract from another cooperative, La Selva. The idea was that it would cooperate and learn from La Selva's experience until it could become self-sufficient and create its own roster of clients, which it was soon able to do. Over the years the cooperative has managed to survive despite setbacks, as when coffee prices fell in the late 1980s and when two buyers declared bankruptcy in 1988 owing money for the coffee that Majomut had sent them. Majomut almost disappeared because of this crisis. Despite false accusations that he was stealing money, the president of the cooperative helped keep the faith of the members, and the organization forged ahead.

In 1992 Union Majomut began to seek alternatives to the crisis brought on by the disappearance of ICA and INMECAFE (Perezgrovas 1997). This led to the promotion of conversion to organic technology on the mostly communal lands of the Majomut members in 1993, following the path taken by other coffee organizations in Oaxaca and Chiapas. The transition to organic took less time than it did for other organizations, because the lack of economic resources among the Majomut membership had prevented most of the producers from applying agrochemicals for many years.

This organization has taken on a role more typical of an NGO. It has an independent professional staff and advisers and grant support from the Rockefeller and the Inter-American Foundations. In recent years, Majomut emphasized diversification away from a single focus on coffee production, expanding to include planting food crops for self-sufficiency. Members now have a family garden, reforestation programme, housing construction, transportation and nutrition programmes. Majomut members have dedicated more of their land, in comparative proportional terms, to the cultivation of maize, than have members of other coffee organizations. Currently, 50 per cent of the 1,500 Majomut members are completely organic, 30 per cent are in the process of converting to organic, and 20 per cent use traditional/natural technology.

There is a range of political affiliations within the membership of Majomut, and the relationship with the autonomous Zapatista authorities is cordial. All *ejido* members can be part of Majomut without regard to political affiliation as the community's economic interests are put ahead of politics. This continues to be the case even after the formation of the Zapatista autonomous municipality of Polhó in 1996 and the consequent division of municipal authorities. Currently, 65 per cent of their member communities are Zapatista bases. As the organization is relatively strong, and because it was helped by other organizations early on, Majomut has a general policy of helping other, smaller and newer organizations to enter the market. Its members have also learned that exporting together with other organizations lowers export costs, so this is an added incentive for cooperation.

MutVitz

MutVitz (Hill of the Birds) is a coffee producer organization that formed after the 1994 Zapatista uprising. It was founded by Zapatista support bases that split from another peasant organization in the Western Highlands. Although the previous organization was also on the left (Partido del Trabajo), it found the hard and clear-cut Zapatista line

– 'We will have nothing to do with the state' – very difficult to accept. Because the Zapatistas are completely divorced from the current government, consistent with their principle of autonomy, MutVitz is allied with international Zapatista solidarity groups. Although the split was not particularly confrontational, members of the former organization criticize the Zapatistas for the armed struggle and for wasting work time in demonstrations and marches.

The 1,000 members of MutVitz, mostly Tzotzil, come from sixty autonomous communities in the Highlands of Chiapas, spread across the municipalities of El Bosque, Simojovel, Bochil, Jitotol, San Andrés Larrainzar and Chenalhó. They have almost fifty peasant promoters who teach organic farming practices, similar to the formula now used by many peasant organizations. They say that the switch from professional technicians to peasant promoters gives more continuity and ensures that the promoters know the local area well, rather than having school knowledge with no context to back it up.

Earlier, the Zapatista coffee farmers in this area had worked without formal organization for a number of years, selling their coffee to local middlemen. In 1997, during a period of good prices, they organized the MutVitz coffee cooperative, which made it possible to export directly. Their fruitful entry into the export market facilitated the consolidation of the organization, and they have followed the organic conversion path that other coffee organizations have followed in the Highlands. Members that are in transition to organic farming first experiment on small plots and then apply the technology to the rest of the grove. Now, with coffee prices at a low point, most MutVitz members have completed their conversion to organic. They sell through the solidarity and organic markets, often at better prices than the other coffee organizations in the area, and better than unorganized Zapatista coffee producers. Recently they sold their first two containers of coffee under Fair Trade certification.

Conclusions

Neoliberal restructuring in Mexico and the world has presented the rural poor with diverse challenges and some opportunities. While most have seen their situations worsen, some have tackled the challenge of creating capable organizations, some of them built with earlier state support, to take advantage of certain opportunities. This has been the case of a number of small-farmer and indigenous peoples' coffee organizations in Chiapas. Most, but not all, of these organizations had earlier benefited from significant state support, giving them the organizational capacities needed to respond when the terrain of the coffee market shifted. The elimination of INMECAFE forced them to appropriate the productive and commercial process, in partnership with emerging ATOs, thus taking advantage of new niche markets opened by the otherwise negative collapse of the ICA. In the process they often underwent technological change towards more ecologically sustainable production systems and organic certification, an investment in their own natural endowments that may pay off in greater sustainability of production in the future.

If we can highlight some key lessons of the relative success stories presented in the case studies, they might be the following:

- A minimum requirement has been a favourable resource or natural endowment, in the form of access to land suitable for coffee production.
- Developing sufficient organizational capacity, to take advantage of the opportunities that inevitably open when major restructuring takes place, has usually required state support early on. But this has not been the case with MutVitz, of course, which has a strong, alternative ally in the Zapatistas. This case shows that creating autonomous alternatives is possible even in the absence of state support. Were the state to become more democratized and responsive to its constituents, without attempting to coopt their organizations for political purposes, opportunities for small peasant farmers could be multiplied dramatically.
- When state support was withdrawn, organizations had to 'wean' themselves, and here the role of external allies has been critical: UCIRI and the Catholic Church for ISMAM, La Selva for Majomut, and the Zapatista solidarity movement for MutVitz. For all of them, combinations of ATOs, organic certifiers and alternative buyers have also been critical allies.

Strategies for developing the political formation of communities (organization and allies), as well as investing in their natural endowments (organic farming and certification), have combined effectively in the emergence of a new survival strategy for small farmers in Chiapas. It remains to be seen what the larger impact of this 'bright spot' will be. Will it prove to be an exception made possible by the favourable resources endowments of a relative small number of communities? Worse yet, will their integration into the global economy convert them into supporters of the status quo and opponents of movements for broader change, as ISMAM may have been at some points in the past? Or will organic cooperatives ally themselves with other forces fighting for broader social change through the further political formation of their communities, as in the case of MutVitz? Only time can answer these questions, which are critical to resolving the larger issues of rural inequality and poverty.

Note
This chapter is based on various sections from Martínez-Torres (2003).

12 | The binational integration of the US–Mexican avocado industries: examining responses to economic globalism

LOIS STANFORD

§ THE 1990s witnessed a fundamental expansion in world trade, restructuring of national economies and political confrontations in response to expanded economic globalization. The growth and integration of commercial food systems resulted in a profound commodification of land and labour to the extent that great numbers of growers and consumers now rely on international food markets. By the early 1990s, scholars identified certain trends in the reorganization of international agricultural markets and national agricultural systems, and associated trends with the globalization of food production, distribution, and consumption (McMichael 1994). In Latin America, the international agricultural industry experienced a rapid expansion in non-traditional export crops, particularly in fresh fruit and vegetable export for the United States and European markets (Friedland 1994; Llambí 1994).

In Mexico, incorporation into the international market has not been smooth; it has been marked by tensions between a rapid economic liberalization and retarded democratization of political processes. During the 1980s Mexico's new agricultural policies distinguished between those sub-sectors that faced challenges in an open economy, e.g. basic grain producers, and those commodities, such as fruits and vegetables, where policy-makers attributed a greater competitive advantage to Mexican growers (Lara Flores and Chauvet 1996). Under a neoliberal economic regime, the government instituted essentially a triage approach to its agricultural sector, abandoning more marginal agricultural regions in favour of those that showed greater competitive advantage in the international market. Fresh fruit and vegetable production for the export market, particularly the US winter fresh market, has displayed phenomenal economic growth despite Mexico's national economic sluggishness, representing 48 per cent of the total value of agricultural exports between 1995 and 1997 (de Grammont et al. 1999). Examining the impacts of neoliberalism and local-level responses to economic restructuring thus requires analysis of specific regions and agricultural commodities to understand accurately the potential for challengers and alternatives.

This chapter examines the case of the avocado industry in Michoacán, focusing on the economic and political process of market integration as Mexican avocados enter the US winter market. In order to study this bi-national integration, I employ the methodological model of a commodity chain. Using this model, the fresh fruit and vegetable industry, as a series of international commodity chains, can be conceptualized as a 'dumbbell' (Friedland 1994), in which Mexican and US fresh fruit and vegetable products are channelled through a narrow sphere of distribution to be subsequently marketed through retail chains. Theoretically, commodity-systems analyses cut an even wider swathe, ranging from the more traditional political economy approach, in which transnational companies exert control over the international market (Friedland et al. 1991), to actor network theory, in which individuals and/or institutions may introduce changes that restructure an existing production or distribution system (Busch and Juska 1997). Drawing on anthropological discussions of power, this chapter proposes to bridge these two perspectives, by citing discussions of agency within the context of economic transformation. The theoretical analysis here draws on Eric Wolf's delineation of different levels of power, specifically focusing on the relationship between the two highest levels of power – structural and organizational (Wolf 1990). The highest level of structural power, that is, the political economy, is defined as that which 'organizes and orchestrates the settings themselves, and that specifies the distribution and direction of energy flows' (ibid.: 586). Yet, analysing power as structure precludes analysing globalization in a way that fully captures the tension, struggles and uneven nature of its expansion. Wolf next distinguishes the level of organizational power in which agents use strategic tactics to constrain, influence and control others in their quest for structural power. As well, Wolf calls for analysis of power as sets of relations, examining how power is played out through social and political interaction: 'how power operates on different levels and in different domains, and how these differences are articulated, becomes an important research question – something to be demonstrated, not assumed' (ibid.: 67).

In distinguishing two levels of power in the bi-national avocado commodity chain, analysis turns to how more powerful agents jockey and struggle to exert their organizational power. In turn, these struggles by the powerful create the political and economic conditions at lower levels which represent the structural power and constraints faced by less powerful actors at a lower level in the commodity system. Yet if we recognize the potential for agency by all actors, powerful and less powerful, then there remains the question of whether less powerful agents can affect structural power or influence themselves, through alliances with similar actors or with more powerful agents higher in the system. Their potential to defend their interests often reflects external factors beyond their control, and we should not romanticize their potential agency. Nevertheless, global processes are not inevitable economic changes and reflect powerful human behaviour. Searching for alternatives requires demystifying these processes and identifying specific human behaviour.

Establishment, growth and economics of the avocado industry in California and Mexico

From the beginning, both Mexican and Californian entrepreneurs played critical roles in shaping the development of the avocado industry in the two countries. In the early 1900s, United States Department of Agriculture (USDA) researchers embarked on exploratory trips to Mexico and Central America to identify avocado varieties suitable for US production. Concurrently, property and agricultural developers in southern California promoted the growth of suburban lifestyles and the 'gentleman farmer', thus linking a Californian suburban lifestyle to the establishment of small avocado orchards (Charles 1999: 6–7). In 1914, the USDA imposed federal legislation banning Mexican avocados in the US market. In 1924, California avocado growers organized the Californian Avocado Growers' Exchange and, by 1926, had adopted Calavo as its official name. By 1930 more than 95 per cent of state avocado growers marketed their fruit through Calavo packing houses (ibid.: 15). As California's avocado industry expanded, many new farmers marketed their product independently or joined other avocado associations. Californian growers expanded avocado orchards dramatically during the 1950s, flooding the market and reducing prices. In 1962, growers established the California Avocado Commission (CAC), a private association that represented different growers' organizations, of which Calavo was the largest. The CAC has been funded through a state marketing order by which the state treasurer's department collects quotas from packing houses and turns over the funds to the CAC. As an association representing all California growers, the CAC developed generic advertising programmes, provided funding for avocado research, and collected production and marketing information. In the 1970s California experienced its second avocado orchard expansion phase, increasing by over 200 per cent to nearly 80,000 acres (University of California 1988: 3). Export markets provided some solution to the market challenges faced by Californian growers. In the early 1990s, California began to export avocados to Europe and the Far East, primarily Japan. As US and Mexican trade negotiators initiated the North American Free Trade Agreement (NAFTA) talks in the early 1990s, California avocado growers did not express much concern. They trusted that phytosanitary problems in Mexican orchards, specifically the avocado seed weevil, precluded the USDA from lifting the 1917 quarantine restrictions.

California's avocado industry is concentrated in southern California, in the areas near San Diego, Riverside, Santa Barbara, Ventura and, more recently, the San Joaquin valley. As of 2000, there were 58,987 acres of avocado orchards in production, with a remaining 739 acres not yet bearing. The California Avocado Commission reports a total of 5,500 California avocado growers. Despite the challenges faced by these avocado growers, in 2000 the industry reported a production total of 321 million pounds (equivalent to 146,000 tons). This production resulted in a crop value of US$339 million. California avocado growers see their industry and economic survival threatened by Chilean and Mexican avocado growers who compete directly with domestic growers in the US winter market from November to March.

For Michoacán, avocado production now represents the most important legal commercial crop. Mexico is the world's leader with an estimated avocado production of 900,000 tons/year. Of that, Michoacán produces 797,000 tons (83 per cent of national production, and 35–40 per cent of world production), concentrated within the districts of Uruapan, Peribán, Tacámbaro, and Zitácuaro (Cano Vega 1995). Estimates are that avocado orchards cover approximately 90,000 hectares, almost all in production by 1997. The varied topography of Michoacán's temperate region produces a wide range of microclimates, suitable for growing avocados almost year-round. The land tenure system is extremely heterogeneous, with an estimated 75 per cent of the production area in private property and only 25 per cent in the *ejido* or communal sector. The avocado industry's production profile is equally heterogeneous. Orchard size varies greatly, ranging from small orchards of 1 to 5 hectares (both private and *ejido* producers) to large commercial operations of 500 hectares. Given the range of orchard size, of the estimated 6,000 producers, few have commercial operations and produce for the export market. Despite their limited numbers, large avocado growers have played an important role in shaping the political and economic environment of Michoacán's avocado industry.

In Michoacán, state programmes encouraged the rapid expansion of avocado growing in the 1970s, resulting in overproduction, market saturation and low prices throughout the 1980s. Wealthy avocado growers turned to the example of the Californian marketing boards, discussed above, as a possible solution to their marketing problems (Paz Vega 1987); Michoacán also initiated the first exports to the European market in 1982.

NAFTA negotiations
In the late 1980s, Mexico's financial crisis, economic liberalization and expanded trade opportunities presented great challenges for the

Michoacán avocado growers. Wealthy commercial avocado growers in Michoacán turned to the US market as a market alternative and supported NAFTA negotiations in the hopes that NAFTA's passage would permit Mexican avocado exports into the US market. By 1987 the Regional Union of Avocado Growers began holding meetings with growers and government representatives to initiate a phytosanitary campaign against the banned insect pests. Despite the passage of NAFTA, Californian avocado growers successfully maintained the US phytosanitary ban on Mexican avocados and thwarted Mexican efforts to enter the US market.

The Michoacán phytosanitary campaign and political negotiations

In 1992, Michoacán avocado growers furthered organizational efforts to negotiate their entry into the US market. Through technical and political efforts, they strengthened strategic alliances with both Mexican federal authorities and US agencies, specifically the United States Department of Agriculture (USDA) and its respective agency, the Animal and Plant Health Inspection Service (APHIS). First, in the technical realm, wealthy producers, state representatives and federal agricultural technicians joined together in a state-wide phytosanitary campaign to combat US concerns about quarantine pests. This complicated and sophisticated technical organization required coordination among federal agencies, state representatives and the growers themselves. Following several years of detailed technical surveys and pest eradication throughout the regional districts, the Mexican government then submitted a request to USDA to allow Michoacán avocados into the US market. The proposal was supplemented with supporting documentation from specific orchards proposed for Mexico's export programme (Stanford 2002). Despite public protests by Californian growers, Michoacán avocado growers and technicians continued to cultivate the trust and confidence of USDA/APHIS representatives through technical documentation of insect pests and their eradication.

Second, paralleling the phytosanitary campaign, Michoacán growers and packers expanded political lobbying efforts and established the Avocado Commission of the State of Michoacán in 1994. The association was comprised primarily of wealthy commercial growers and packers situated in Uruapan. By May 1995, the commission began operations with three primary objectives: (i) negotiation of the US market opening, (ii) coordination of producer organizations to seek additional export markets, and (iii) coordination of producer organizations to solve common problems (Sierra Reyes 1997: 26). The commission also mounted its own publicity campaign and published editorials in US produce publications, addressing the concerns of Californian avocado growers. By July 1995 APHIS published the initial ruling that would allow Mexican avocados from registered orchards to be imported into the approved nineteen north-eastern states, opening a public comment period from July until October. During 1995, commission representatives met with US authorities and Congressional representatives to discuss Mexico's petition. Mexican representatives pitched Californian growers' counter-attacks as attempts to maintain trade barriers and prevent competition in the US domestic market.

On 31 January 1997, the USDA reversed the 1914 ruling, and APHIS approved the final ruling to allow Hass avocados from Michoacán to be imported into nineteen north-eastern US states from November to February inclusive (USDA 1997). In its decision, USDA cited the net economic benefit to US consumers, although the agency acknowledged the potential negative impact on domestic avocado growers. Michoacán growers were required to coordinate with USDA field inspectors to survey orchards for insect pests, carry out adequate field sanitation procedures, and inspect packing houses in a whole series of restrictions (USDA/SAGAR 1997). Registered packing houses were required to modify their structures, enclosing the entire packing house in netting and constructing double doors to prevent the entry of quarantined insect pests (García Guzmán 1997). For those avocado growers left outside the US export programme, the Mexican government held up the promise of future exports.

The USDA guidelines imposed strict conditions, yet the Michoacán growers recognized that they had won their initial battle against the Californian growers. United States federal agencies had sided with Mexican export producers over the protests of US growers. For Michoacán avocado growers, the USDA ruling represented an exceptional organizational success on a scale that the growers themselves acknowledged had never before occurred in the avocado industry. For the first season, 1997–98, only sixty-one avocado growers from four districts with a total of 1,499 hectares met the phytosanitary requirements to enter the US export programme (SAGAR 1998). Yet this initial success opened a small window to exports and set the conditions for developments in the avocado industry in recent years.

In summary, these actions represent what Wolf identified as organizational power, a specific set of actions by which the Michoacán avocado growers moved to alter US national policy, i.e. non-tariff trade barriers, through strategic tactics. Important as well is the recognition that their organizational efforts were successful both because they worked at the local level, that is, they successfully eradicated banned insect pests in their orchards, and because they established strategic political alliances with more powerful actors in the avocado industry, particularly the state, as represented by federal agencies from both countries.

Mexican entry into the US market, 1997–2002: impacts of globalism

Mexico's entry into the US market holds consequences not only for the small group of exporters but also for the region as a whole. Now analysis turns to examine changes in the US avocado market from 1997 to 2002, in an attempt to understand whether or not this organizational power has coalesced into structural power. That is, after negotiating entry into the US market, do Michoacán avocado export growers and packers continue to exert influence in the market?

From 1997 to 2002, Mexico has exported avocados for five seasons during the winter months between November and February to nineteen approved north-eastern US states. The export programme has earned the grudging respect of importers and wholesalers in the US produce industry, although Californian growers express persistent concerns about pest problems. On 1 November 2001, the USDA approved expanding the shipping area to twelve additional states and the marketing window to two additional months. Despite recent expansion, this analysis focuses on the winter market, November to February, from 1998 to 2002.

Market integration

In Michoacán, the number of avocado orchards in the US export programme expanded from sixty-one in the 1997–98 season to 252 the following season and to a total of 497 orchards in the 1999–2000 season. As well, the number of hectares expanded from 1,499 in the first season to 6,758 hectares in the 1999–2000 season, increasing the volume exported from 6,000 tons in 1998 to 11,729 tons by 2000. As more avocado orchards entered into the US export programme, technicians from the USDA and the Mexican Ministry of Agriculture and Rural Development (Secretaría de Agricultura, Ganadería, y Desarrollo Rural, SAGAR) expanded surveys of newly registered orchards and packing houses (Facultad de Agrobiología 1999). As Michoacán has expanded its total export volume and export window in the US market, the Californian and Michoacán avocado industries have become more closely intertwined. Californian, Michoacán and Chilean avocado growers channel their product into the US market during the same approximate period from November to March. From the perspective of Michoacán's avocado growers, Mexico represents a major player in the international avocado market because of its dominance over world production. Yet analysis of the US winter market from 1998 to 2002 suggests a more complicated situation, reflecting differential power relations in the market.

Tables 12.1, 12.2 and 12.3 present economic data from the US winter market (November to March) that indicate differences in power and economic benefits across these three sets of producers during this

Table 12.1 Volume marketed during winter season by California, Michoacán and Chile in the US avocado market, 1998–2002 (recorded in 1,000 cwt)

	1998–99	1999–2000	2000–01	2001–02
California	543	644	770	982
Michoacán	202	194	190	395
Chile	246	188	449	554

Table 12.2 Number of weeks in the winter season market for California, Michoacán and Chile in the US avocado market, 1998–2002

	1998–99	1999–2000	2000–01	2001–02
California	17	19	19	24
Michoacán	16	16	17	19
Chile	7	11	20	20

Table 12.3 Average price in US$ received for size 40 box during winter season by California, Michoacán and Chile in the US avocado market, 1998–2002

	1998–99	1999–2000	2000–01	2001–02
California	48.78	39.5	30.83	30.90
Michoacán	19.13	26.13	27.28	23.42
Chile	31.40	41.33	28.91	25.50

Source: 'MarketScope', *The Packer*, weekly reports, 1998–2002. Shipments, i.e. volume, recorded in 1,000 cwt on weekly basis. Table 12.2 estimates the number of weeks different producing regions ship to the market, overlooking some weeks when shipments are noted as 'too light to count'. Prices recorded by different-sized boxes, including 36, 40, 48, 60, and 70 avocados per box. (Table 12.3 reports averages for only 40s boxes.) Table 12.2 also estimates the number of weeks different producers are in the market. Original source is USDA Agricultural Marketing Service.

four-year period. In Table 12.1, the total number of avocado boxes is reported over four seasons for California, Michoacán and Chile. On a week-by-week basis, actual volume reported varies significantly, but, in general, the total number of boxes has increased dramatically. Californian and Chilean volume more closely responds to market conditions than Michoacán volume since the USDA/APHIS programme controls Michoacán exports. Despite Mexico's public rhetoric and presentation of the Michoacán avocado growers as if they had won a great battle in their entry into the US market, it is the Chileans who have most rapidly expanded their exports to the US market. On a weekly basis, Chilean exports respond more quickly to market changes, adjusting avocado exports rapidly if market volumes decline or prices increase. The Chilean avocado industry is dominated by a small group of wealthy commercial growers. Despite the fact that their domestic avocado production pales in comparison to Mexico's, Chilean avocado growers export a higher percentage of their avocado production; they do not have a domestic market like Mexico's. As well, Chilean exporters have a longer experience of the US winter market. In the trade newspapers, industry experts cite problems first encountered by the Chileans, before they 'learned' to work with established avocado importing companies, such as Mission and Calavo. Since 2000, Chilean growers have pursued joint ventures with US companies and have participated in shared advertising campaigns. Experts now cite this history as a lesson to the Mexicans who initially attempted to export directly to the US market.

The last four seasons have witnessed changes in the season's length. Table 12.2 provides an estimate of the number of weeks in the winter market for each of these three avocado-producing regions. While Mexican avocado exports are limited by USDA/APHIS restrictions, Chilean and Californian growers are restrained only by market prices and product availability. Although Mexico has recently negotiated a two-week increase, Chile has tripled the length of its seasonal presence during the same period (see Table 12.2). For both California and Chile, increased production and seasonal presence help explain the dramatic increase in product volume.

Finally, Table 12.3 presents four years of data on the average price paid in US dollars for a box of medium-sized avocados. Consistently, Californian and Chilean avocados net higher prices; according to US wholesalers this price differential reflects the lower quality of Mexican avocados. On a weekly basis, these data suggest a three-tiered market in which Mexican avocados consistently receive lower prices across all sizes. Over four years, prices have come closer together, although Mexican avocados continue to receive the lowest prices. Market integration has impacted most negatively on Californian growers, who have seen their prices decline.

In general, Michoacán exporters made small inroads into the US market but have not earned projected economic benefits. Nor has the US export market provided a practical outlet for large numbers of Michoacán's small avocado growers. Understanding the impacts of binational integration in these two avocado industries requires a closer analysis of the political acts of powerful actors in the binational commodity chain.[1] This discussion documents the political aspects of power relations that Wolf identified as critical to explaining neoliberalism as a political process even within the economic arena.

Company operations at the local level

The international fresh fruit and vegetable industry represents an economic and political arena within which transnational companies and other agents jockey to defend their economic profits. Examining specific practices by companies and/or organizations involved in the international trade of avocado provides insights into politics in the global arena. It further demystifies the inconsistencies and contradictions of these organizations' operations at different levels of the avocado commodity chain. In the avocado industry, the companies carry out these acts at the level of production (Michoacán and California), at the state level and within the international market itself.

In Michoacán, avocado producers grow alarmed as foreign companies expand into the regional avocado industry. Gaining entry into the US market represented a success that demonstrated Mexicans' capacity to organize and defeat Californian growers in a battle for an economic market. In the public discourse, Michoacán growers express a deep mistrust of Californian growers, fuelled further by the presence of two Californian avocado companies, Calavo and Mission. From their perspective, Calavo represents Californian growers' interests. Michoacán avocado producers espouse a conspiracy theory in which the Californian companies intentionally planned the takeover of the regional industry.

Calavo did not participate in Mexico's first US export season, but in 1998 Calavo constructed the largest packing house in Mexico. As well, Calavo has operated in a different manner in Mexico. Originally maintaining itself as a producer cooperative in California, it operated as a private company in Michoacán. Calavo purchased fruit at the level of the packing house from growers and would not allow Michoacán growers to join the California cooperative. Calavo aggressively expanded its operations during the first season, and by 1999 its vice-president announced plans to ship at least 25 per cent of Michoacán avocado production by the 1999–2000 season. During the 1999–2000 season, Calavo shipped 2,780 boxes of avocados from its Uruapan packing house, representing 24 per cent of the total volume exported to the United States from Michoacán. Combined with other companies, including Chiquita Frupac, Fresh Directions, Mission and West Pack, in reality, foreign companies already control Mexican avocado exports to the US market (Bartra, this volume). In Michoacán, avocado industry experts distinguish between packing houses that export directly to the United States under their own-brand label and packing houses that are *maquilando* fruit. These are packing houses that merely pack the fruit and sell the avocados to a US importing company that actually exports it under the company's name. These sources estimate that 63 per cent of the Michoacán avocado volume to the United States is exported under the brand-name of these identified companies (unnamed brokers, personal communication, 2000). Thus, at the regional level, all Californian avocado companies aggressively expanded their operations and participation in the Michoacán avocado industry to the extent that, within a few seasons, they control and market the bulk of Mexican avocado exports under their own brand-names.

Company operations in the market

At the market level, importing companies shape the conditions that export growers face both through economic practices and industry discourse. As noted in Tables 12.1, 12.2 and 12.3, Mexican avocado exports have expanded slowly, while Chilean exporters aggressively increased export volumes during the same period. A three-tier price market was initially established, reflecting quality differences. Yet, in the industry discourse, experts also shape the image of different exporting countries, often distinguishing between Mexican exporters and Chilean companies. During the third export season, 1999–2000, when Mexican avocado prices declined, Michoacán growers imposed a moratorium in early December 1999 in order to restrict export volume and drive up prices. According to US importers, the Mexicans 'tried to manipulate the market', and US shippers maintained that Mexican shippers should have honoured contracts despite lower prices and maintained their presence in the market. The episode exacerbated suspicion and distrust between the two groups. US produce industry experts also contrast Mexican exporters with Chilean exporters, noting that when the Chileans first entered the US market, they worked with general export/import companies rather than avocado importers. However, after 'several years of difficulty', the Chileans switched to US companies, specifically Calavo and Mission Produce, Inc. These representatives allege that Mexican avocado growers contracted with inexperienced wholesalers who dumped large volumes of poor-quality fruit on the market.

Company reorganization practices

Companies as well may reconstitute their legal status. In the case of Mission or Fresh Directions, these operations are already transnational companies, but Calavo presents important insights into the nature of organizational transformation. Calavo's Michoacán operations mirrored those of a transnational company expanding its export operations in one of its 'source' regions, yet Calavo was founded legally in 1926 as a Californian producer cooperative. Inconsistencies between its Mexican operations and those in California reflect an internal struggle over Calavo's future. In May 2001 Calavo filed a petition with the US Security and Exchange Commission (SEC) to change its legal status from a co-operative to a for-profit corporation. In October 2001 the SEC approved its request, and Calavo members voted to reconstitute themselves as Calavo Growers, Inc. Calavo's chief executive officer commented that for-profit status provided Calavo greater financial flexibility, allowed for broader shareholder investment and facilitated global marketing of US and foreign avocados.

Local-level impacts in Michoacán and California

Michoacán's regional phytosanitary campaign represented an alliance between federal agencies and a small group of avocado growers who wanted to enter the US export market (SAGAR 1998). Since 1997 Mexico's avocado export programme to the USA has increasingly shaped the nature of production and commercialization in Michoacán's regional avocado industry, even for those growers who produce for the national market. Regional technical efforts were further strengthened by legislation, specifically the publication of NOM-066-FITO-1995 on 26 August 1996, a Mexican federal order that established the legal requirements and phytosanitary specifications for commercializing avocados in national and international markets. This order also established a regional system of phytosanitary control that required all avocado growers to enrol in the state pest control programme and obtain certificates to sell their fruit. The regulations established the procedures that growers should follow for orchard maintenance, harvesting techniques, initial transport to the packing house and orchard registration with SAGAR (García Guzmán 1998). SAGAR recognized that phytosanitary conditions and banned insect pests remained the principal factor preventing export expansion in the US market, but technicians also contended that pest eradication would improve avocado quality for the national market. General benefits thus justified the imposition of quotas on all avocado growers in order to carry out the campaign in their orchards and integrate even the smallest growers into the phytosanitary campaign (García Guzmán 1999).

Avocado growers enrolled in the US export programme perceive the SAGAR programme as evidence of state support for their efforts to expand the avocado market. In contrast, small-scale avocado producers interpret state regulation and checkpoints as attempts to force them to comply with standards that enable wealthier growers to export to the United States without providing apparent economic benefits to small producers. They resent increased numbers of state agricultural technicians and imposed quotas to subsidize an export programme they cannot enter. Small avocado growers have resented state attempts to expand the programme from 1998 to 2002 and to impose quotas to eradicate insect pests that never precluded avocado commercialization in the national market (Paulsen 1999). What started as a phytosanitary campaign for a select group of growers and orchards has expanded into a transformation of a regional production system supervised by state technical personnel (Stanford 2002).

Mexican export impacts on California's avocado industry have been mixed. Californian growers have experienced four productive winter seasons, albeit at declining prices. Growers call for state intervention to limit Mexican avocado expansion in the US market. While acknowledging Mexico's continued presence, the California Avocado Commission polices the export situation, searching for a significant breach of the USDA phytosanitary regulation. Now the California growers shift strategies in support of the Hass Promotion Act of 2000, approved by the US Congress, which imposes a tax on imported avocados to provide financial revenues to promote US avocado consumption. Recognizing the permanent status of imports, Californian growers now argue that importers should help finance the promotional campaigns and market studies that have expanded US domestic avocado consumption.

Challenges and alternatives to neoliberal globalism: state alliance with elite producers

Within the process of bi-national integration, Michoacán growers have adopted different strategies or responses to neoliberal globalism. These different strategies reflect the industry's heterogeneity and continued state presence in the regional agricultural economy. In general, these practices fall along a dimension that lies between political actions that challenge neoliberal globalism, on the one hand, and practices that seek alternatives to the globalization process as imposed by foreign companies, on the other. Analysing these specific actions falls into the arena identified by Wolf as organizational power, in which power is played out through social and political interaction and different actors attempt to shape the avocado industry's future.

Despite reduced federal support for agriculture, Mexico's federal and state agencies continue to intervene in Michoacán. In 1997, the state of Michoacán introduced a new Law of Agricultural Organizations (Gobierno del Estado 1997). Through this legal statute, state authorities proposed to restructure the local agricultural organizations (Asociaciones Agrícolas Locales, AALs) and bring them under the legal jurisdiction of a newly created State Union of Agricultural Producers (Union Agricola Estatal de Productores, UAEP). The state governor argued that 'organization' was needed for the modernization of Michoacán's agriculture and this legal framework would enable agricultural organizations to cooperate (Tinoco Rubí 1997). By 1998, the UAEP reported ninety-six member associations comprising an estimated total of 3,500 individual producers, although regional sources allege that this organization exists primarily on paper. UAEP officials detailed new programmes and plans, including a certification programme, a research and documentation centre, and new credit programmes (Recio 1998; M. Campos Díaz, personal communication, Morelia, Michoacán, 1998).

Producer alliance

In Michoacán, regional experts consciously recognize the historic failure of formal organizations encompassing large groups of different types of growers. By 1990, most cooperatives and associations established during the 1970s and 1980s had disbanded. As these folded, small private enterprises, often consisting of former members, acquired each association's operations, trucks and packing facilities. These companies possess an internal cohesion, grounded in kin ties, but lack a broader collective appeal that would draw in large numbers of avocado growers. Outside this small group of 100–200 avocado growers and packers, the remaining estimated 5,000 avocado producers operate individually and sell their fruit in the national market. With the reduction of agricultural extension programmes, most avocado producers have reduced inputs, do not adequately maintain their orchards, and resent government mandates and phytosanitary campaigns they cannot afford (Paulsen 1999). They also object to the industry's increased segmentation and wealth concentration with a small group of elite producers.

Regional leaders recognize the importance of broadening membership and linking the avocado industry's commercial expansion to increased membership in organizations. In an address to members, one new association president noted: 'my first lines serve to express my appreciation for your trust and my commitment to continue the work carried out and to strengthen our association more each day. For this, I ask that we work together and join our forces so that we can achieve the great and strong association that we want to be' (López Luján 1998).

Yet leaders in these traditional agricultural associations also recognize the growing influence of the local phytosanitary boards in the avocado industry. Given that membership in the local phytosanitary groups is mandatory, many commercial avocado growers belong to several organizations. Tentative alliances between voluntary and state-imposed organizations require revision of earlier traditional views of agricultural organization. Two recent examples serve to demonstrate the dynamics of current organizational responses. First, during the 1999–2000 season, members in both sets of organizations jointly carried out weekly meetings to discuss prices, reach a consensus on volumes to be sent to the market, and establish their opinion of a minimum guaranteed price in the packing houses (Ayala Aceves 2000a). Participating growers viewed their efforts during the 1999–2000 export season as successful enough to extend the weekly meetings and collaborative efforts through the 2000 season for the national market.

Second, during the national market's 2000 season, leaders moved to establish a specialized division of avocado growers under the political jurisdiction of the newly established Regional Union of Agricultural Producers (Unión de Regional Agrícola de Producores, URAP). Through these efforts, avocado growers proposed to establish a semi-autonomous avocado organization, technically under the state union's legal jurisdiction yet financially autonomous. Advocates contended that this new association would provide services for the entire industry by bringing together a wide range of new organizations. As noted in one editorial:

> There is no doubt that this project will benefit the entire avocado sector of Michoacán. The recently created 'Specialized Section – Avocado' asks for the support of each and every avocado grower in Michoacán to cooperate with this project. We ask them to give 100 percent support to the leaders of their associations and of their local phytosanitary boards so that together we can increase the avocado's value to the Mexican consumers. (Ayala Aceves 2000b)

Thus, in response to state efforts to impose a new agricultural union, avocado growers complied, yet they revived historical attempts to introduce a marketing board, along Californian lines, by advocating financial autonomy (Ayala Aceves 2000c).

Dissemination of information and training

Leaders moved to have organizations play a wider role in the general community of avocado growers. During the 1996–97 season, one avocado association initiated a series of weekly radio spots, identifying the location of the current best prices for avocados and recommending that growers not harvest when prices dropped too low. Also, in 1997, one local agricultural association, the AAL Uruapan, began publication of a local bulletin, *El Aguacatero*, designed to disseminate technical, market and current information about the avocado industry to the public. Technical staff began to disseminate production advice, ranging from investment recommendations to advice on ideal harvesting conditions (Ayala Aceves 1999a, 1999b).

Regional efforts to organize growers reflect conscious and public recognition of the need for organizational cohesion despite increased numbers of growers and foreign companies' expansion. This challenge reflects the legacy of organizational problems and regional conflicts that characterized Michoacán's avocado industry from its early days. At the local and regional level, these organizational strategies contrast sharply with those of the previous period (1990–95) by which Mexico initially gained entry into the US market. Earlier efforts were successful since, combined with political alliances established with US and Mexican federal agencies, efforts led to a reversal of the US 1914 phytosanitary ban. Now, continuation of the phytosanitary campaign results in greater numbers of avocado growers entering the US market. This undermines the elite growers' capacity to maintain control over their constituency and over the avocado volume entering the US market. Regional avocado leaders, primarily wealthy commercial growers and government officials, publicly distinguish between export growers, whom they recognize as capable of collective organization, and those growers who tradition-ally have not exported, known as the 'disorganized'. Wealthy avocado growers participating in the US export programme complain bitterly about US companies, particularly Calavo and Mission, who undermine temporary moratoriums by offering higher prices to avocado growers. Their accusations are often true. Calavo and Mission, however, purchase their avocados from Michoacán avocado growers, and large numbers of avocado growers continue to sell their fruit to these 'foreign' companies despite vehement protestations by avocado leaders. That is, the small group of elite growers who negotiated US market entry now has its position of economic power undermined by small avocado growers who willingly sell to their competitors. If Michoacán proposes to maintain a united front in the international market, then elite growers must face the industry's heterogeneity and meet the economic needs of small producers.

Bi-national producer alliances

The bi-national integration of California's and Michoacán's avocado industries means that both growers' groups produce for the US winter market. In public discourse in California and Michoacán, this integra-tion is presented as if it were a competition between producers from two countries. This myth exacerbates tensions between Californian and Michoacán avocado growers and suits the companies' financial interests. Several commercial avocado growers in Michoacán expressed resentment that, as Mexicans, they were not allowed to become members in Calavo, a producer cooperative in California, although they had broached the subject with Calavo representatives in Michoacán. They observed that bi-national alliances with the California avocado growers would be critical to resolving difference and confronting the large companies. Now that Calavo has established itself as a company, member growers continue to hold shares, which may be purchased by outsiders some time in the future. Calavo is also exploring the option of offering public shares. At that point in time, Michoacán growers and respective associations could purchase stock and invest in the company. Undoubtedly, Calavo's governing board plans to transform Calavo into an import/export company, but Calavo itself has experienced internal conflicts that do not bode well for Californian member growers. Thus, Californian and Mexican avocado growers have common interests that might be used to develop bi-national alliances, if they could confront the historical legacy and mystification of bi-national competition.

Conclusion

In conclusion, this period of bi-national integration of the avocado industries of Michoacán and California has been marked by significant changes in company operations and rancorous battles between growers from these two regions. This case also contrasts important differences in respective strategies, i.e. attempts to effect organizational power, between growers and the importing companies. Growers in both countries have attempted to defend their market interests in the US fresh avocado market through political actions that limit the volume of fruit in the market. Californian growers call for US federal intervention to limit Mexican export expansion, while Mexican growers call for harvesting moratoriums when market prices drop. In these instances, the importing companies simply expand their imports from existing source regions or import from new regions, thus thwarting any attempts by producers to influence the market. At the same time, these companies vertically expand their presence and influence over the market by establishing commercial operations in source regions. The actions and their respective consequences demonstrate that growers cannot effectively confront the market through their individual linkages to the companies that buy their product. The international competition among the Michoacanos, Californians and Chileans has suited the economic interests of importing companies such as Calavo, Mission and Chiquita. New alternatives must be sought if growers have any remote hope of surviving in a globalized market. International horizontal linkages among growers from different countries may provide the producers some small hope of retaining a degree of market influence. If the companies now conceptualize themselves as global, or transnational, the producers themselves must broaden their self-image. Elite growers also need to recognize their regional responsibilities and the consequences of respective business decisions. Operating as individual entrepreneurs has provided short-term benefits, but failing to address and resolve regional heterogeneity and the needs of small growers has long-term consequences that undermine the viability of the regional avocado industry. Finally, despite Mexico's move to privatize its agricultural sector, the state has an important role to play in searching for market alternatives, providing options for different types of growers, and supporting the development of multiple market strategies for an important regional agricultural industry. Neoliberal globalism must be faced in Michoacán, as in other rural regions, and the economic strategies adopted will have long-term political consequences.

Notes

The author expresses her appreciation to Ing. Eugenio Treviño García, Jefe de Planeación, SAGAR, Morelia, Michoacán, for access to information and statistics. I am also grateful to Lic. Daniel Sánchez Pérez, Uruapan, Michoacán, for sharing unpublished reports and his insights with me. Funding for this research during May–December 1998 was provided through the Council for International Exchange of Scholars (Fulbright-García Robles Scholar Program, 1998) and the US Department of Education (Fulbright-Hays Faculty Research Abroad, 1998). During this period, I lived in Uruapan and collected the documentary material and interviewed exporters and growers who provided the information upon which this chapter is based. The author assumes full responsibility for any errors and/or misinterpretations of the material provided.

1. The discussion of events and strategic activities within the US produce industry is based on articles from *The Packer*, the weekly business newspaper of the US produce industry from 1996 to 2002. Due to space constraints, the author cannot cite each article, but specific citations may be obtained from the author if desired.

13 | Convergence: social movements in Mexico in the era of neoliberal globalism

HUMBERTO GONZÁLEZ

§ NEOLIBERAL globalism and its policies have brought about protective movements in sectors of the population whose livelihoods and chance of achieving higher levels of development are threatened. These sectors have not been passive, nor are their actions purely defensive, immediate or restricted to the local level. This chapter analyses a social movement formed by bank debtors with overdue loans that emerged through the consolidation of a heterogeneous 'web' of rural and urban organizations which questioned and disputed the state's exclusive right to represent the national interest in processes of global change. This movement influenced the course of the nation's political economy – particularly in the financial sector – and abetted Mexico's transition towards a more participatory, democratic society.

This chapter is organized in five sections. In the first, I present the explanatory richness that the concept of 'convergence' offers for analysing recent social movements in Latin America. The second section is devoted to identifying those elements of neoliberal policy that explain why this particular movement attained a national scale as it questioned the legitimacy of the Mexican state. In the third part, I analyse the activities that the movement developed in the civil arena, followed by a deeper analysis of the factors that led to the actions of this social movement becoming concentrated in the juridical-political arena. In the fourth part, I explain why this social movement – originally defined as independent of political parties – eventually became organically articulated with one party through the acts of its leaders. Finally, I present my conclusions.

New social movements: convergence, participation and equality

The study of the movement of bank debtors allows us to stress three features common to other current social movements in Latin America: first, the capacity to incorporate highly diverse sectors of the population (Matos 1993); second, the strength that arises precisely from the capacity to encompass groups and organizations in different areas of the country that represent different classes, and to form networks of social relations among people with similar interests, independent of political parties (Foweraker 1988); and, third, existing loyalties and identities – primarily local and regional – do not constitute the principal support of such movements (Collier 1995) but, rather, their support comes from their ability to unite and mobilize groups and institutions at the local, national and international levels. These movements have introduced novel elements into the state–civil society relationship and given new meanings to the notion of citizenship that go beyond the narrowly defined sphere of what was once understood as 'political' to propose changes in the entire complex of society (Alvarez et al. 1998).

The study of the bank debtors' movement allows us to identify new forms of shared experience in the globalization process, in which social and cultural heterogeneity neither disappear nor present obstacles to the formation of organizations with broad bases of support. Though pluralism appears to be a fundamental feature of emerging social movements, in this new era of globalization it is more than just a feature of an increasingly powerful social structure at the world level. It is the collective purpose of aligned individuals and groups who define common objectives and interests and undertake actions designed to achieve them, according to current, structural circumstances. With Jorge Alonso (1991), I call this process of social construction 'convergence'.

As the result of a collective will, the duration of 'convergence' can vary and manifest itself in one or more actions through tactical or strategic agreements. The scale of 'convergence' (local, regional, national, international) and the degree of institutionalization or formality it attains can also vary (Alonso 1991). This is so because 'convergence' may or may not evolve into an institution or, alternatively, because the 'converging' actors may articulate with other institutions. Based on Alonso's proposal and the analysis of the case presented here, I outline the most important characteristics of 'convergence', the first of which is plurality. 'Convergence' integrates clearly heterogeneous elements that agree to unite to gain greater strength and projection for their actions, but without eliminating their differences, decision-making capacity, possibilities for independent action or their specific identity. The second feature is the particular dynamic of growth and consolidation of 'convergence' that implies both openness and the flexibility to enlist new members, to integrate the different projects of all participants, to adapt the nucleus of 'convergence' to changing internal and external circumstances and, finally, to resolve the conflicts that often characterize such heterogeneous collectivities. On the other hand, this dynamic is related to what Alonso calls the 'culture of convergence', in reference to the need for leaders and members to experience a learning process in the art of 'converging' based on consensus. This flexibility and the process of cultural learning explain why convergences can attract new members as the movement grows.

An additional feature of 'convergence' concerns the implications of this collective will for the political system in which it emerges. The nature of convergence (plural, inclusive) leads it to criticize all forms of 'integrationism' and transforms it into actions that challenge all dogmatisms (economic, in this specific case) and authoritarian power. Convergences also allow wide-ranging networks to develop, create new symbols and identities, and elaborate imaginative actions and organizations that fight for a more participatory, equitable society. Thus, convergences gained the sympathy and support of national and international groups and institutions that fought for a more democratic, egalitarian global society and, above all, tried to minimize the possibility of violent repression by the state.

The El Barzón social movement developed among people who were unable to repay their bank loans according to the scheduled terms and thus faced repossession orders against their property, including agricultural fields, farm equipment, buildings, materials, industries and services, not to mention family homes. All of them were from the middle and higher economic strata of Mexico's population and enjoyed access to private or official credit. This feature of the movement explains the limited participation of subsistence peasants, indigenous peoples, workers and the urban poor.

Although this movement of bank debtors has not received the same national and international attention as the armed mobilization of indigenous people in Chiapas, it has come to include the active participation of a broader range of sectors of the population in most states and has had direct repercussions on the electoral–political system. As this analysis demonstrates, the movement has promoted a broad mobilization and organization of the population in rural areas and cities that has replaced or redefined the role of local and regional political, corporatist organizations. Also, it has affected local and state elections in several states where opposition party candidates have triumphed. Finally, it questions the government's centralism and the independence and impartiality of the judiciary, and takes action at the local and national levels intended to revalidate federalism and the rule of law.

This study is based on interviews with members and leaders of the movement in several states during mobilizations and meetings held between 1993 and 1997. I reviewed the national press and, for Jalisco and Michoacán, followed the local newspapers closely. Finally, part of the study is based on research by other scholars who have analysed this movement.

Neoliberal policy in Mexico

Neoliberal policy has three main traits that explain why debtor organizations have emerged in almost every state and formed a national confederation. First, it excludes all economic actors who lack the capital, technology, economies of scale and knowledge of commercial relations necessary for them to compete in an open economy with modern global corporations. Many small and medium-scale businesses lost markets in this attempted 'modernization' that offered them little opportunity to increase technological sophistication or 'reconvert' (González 1993; Chauvet 1994; Girón 1994), and that pushed landowners to take on excessive debt, move their operations to the informal sector, become unemployed or seek work in the United States.

After 1990, the number of bank debtors with overdue loans grew at an ever-increasing pace, bringing with it decapitalization and failing confidence in Mexican financial institutions at the international level. In 1990, overdue loans constituted only 2.1 per cent of all credits. In 1992 this figure rose to 5.3 per cent, and in 1994 it reached a high point of 10.6 per cent. Though these National Banking Commission figures reflect the critical condition of Mexico's financial sector, they actually underestimate the real percentage of debtors with overdue loans (Calva 1994; Girón 1994). In the first trimester of 1995, over half of all banks experienced capitalization problems due to the burden of overdue loans. At least six of these eighteen financial groups had to resort to state-sponsored bail-outs for amounts that averaged 71 per cent of their capital assets (*La Jornada*, 4 July 1995). Later (October 1996), the amount of such loans reached an all-time high of 49.1 per cent ('Securities Auction Capital', *El Financiero*, 11 December 1996).

The second important feature of neoliberal policy is its unevenness. It supports and privileges only those corporations and financial groups with a higher probability of responding favourably to the challenges of new commercial opportunities and economic deregulation. Legal frameworks were modified to attract private domestic and foreign investment capital in almost every economic domain, while many public-sector enterprises were sold, and the financial sector was reprivatized (Calva 2000). This last measure was a concession granted to certain very powerful domestic financial groups. Compared to other sectors of the economy, the state gave owners of reprivatized banks privileged treatment by slowing and regulating the entry of foreign banking interests. It also allowed them to conduct operations that in terms of financial sector regulations can only be called 'shady' (Fentanes 1995).

A third important feature is neoliberalism's centralization of federal government decision-making with no increase in participation by state and municipal governments; a clearly authoritarian approach. Though centralization has long been a feature of political practice in Mexico (Meyer 1977), it was accentuated in the Salinas administration. In 1987, a clique of young financial sector executives who shared a remarkable ideological cohesion began to occupy positions in the country's political and economic hierarchy. This included the presidency, important cabinet posts concerned with economic regulation, and the chairmanship of the Institutional Revolutionary Party (PRI), which governed Mexico after 1929 and organized the corporatist integration of the principal sectors of Mexican society, including peasants, workers and the popular classes (Hernández 1994). This new elite led by President Salinas implemented the components of the neoliberal programme on a broad basis. This explains why demonstrations against state economic policy were directed at the federal government (especially the President) and debtors' actions also ignored corporatist organizations of businessmen, workers and rural producers linked in varying degrees to the PRI (see Mackinlay and Otero, this volume).

In summary, neoliberal policies intended to resolve long-standing national problems also generated broad opposition in the country. The debtor movement that developed from the convergence of heterogeneous groups initially made demands related exclusively to problems with banks, but soon began to demand profound changes in state economic policy and the creation of new forms of popular participation in matters that affected the nation's future.

Bank debtors opposed to state policy: the civil arena

To explain the emergence of a social movement of debtors, it is not sufficient only to examine the economic and political implications of the adoption of neoliberal policies, as mentioned above. We must also understand the conditions in which a specific collectivity considers the consequences of change as illegitimate and unacceptable (Scherer-Warren 1989), and the political opportunities it perceives for changing them with the resources within its reach (Tilly 1999).

The first public mobilizations of bank debtors against state economic policy were isolated incidents in the northern state of Chihuahua in 1992 (de Grammont 1994). In the following year, a mobilization took place in Jalisco (western Mexico) that in effect initiated the movement at the national level and gave it the name by which it became known: El Barzón. Demonstrators were mostly agricultural producers with different scales of production linked to national and international markets (González 1995).

The situation of financial insolvency among producers affected states with more dynamic agricultural sectors. In 1993, 77 per cent of all overdue agricultural loans were concentrated in states with more advanced farming oriented to national and international markets (de Grammont 2000, based on data from the Ministry of Agricultural and Water Resources, SARH). The largest amount of overdue loans in this sector (62 per cent) was held by commercial banks that had loaned money to solvent agricultural businessmen representing 27 per cent of the total number of debtors. Finally, the majority of debtors with problems (73 per cent) were small and medium-sized producers with credits from official banks or development banks (de Grammont 2000).

Before the public mobilizations in southern Jalisco, debtors from the region called on municipal and state governments, state and national-level leaders of trade organizations, and their networks of political influence, in an attempt to persuade high-ranking federal politicians to create support and capitalization programmes for producing areas. Since 1993, the debtors' main demands have been: (i) government financial support to restructure debts with private banks; and (ii) a halt to bank foreclosures and auctions of debtors' properties, together with a support plan for people so affected. Local governments and leaders of corporatist groups linked to the PRI bowed to federal government's plans and in some cases even blocked organizational initiatives by debtor groups.

In 1993, when local banks began to foreclose on loans and auction off debtors' property and agricultural equipment in southern Jalisco, one group occupied government offices in the provincial capital of Autlán by parking farm equipment on the streets and blocking entrances to the city square. The impact of this apparently isolated incident was felt in neighbouring areas, where agricultural producers with overdue loans or crushing debt burdens decided to participate, or sent messages of support. The demonstrators elected a committee to speak on their behalf to the local and state press and negotiate with debtor delegations from nearby municipalities that urged them to march with their tractors to the capital.

Although the participants in these demonstrations – *ejidatarios* and private landowners – had long-standing political rivalries over land tenure, all of them shared crushing debts with private banks and lacked access to the new credits they needed to finance their operations. This 'alliance of convenience' among previously rival groups (in varying degrees of intensity) became characteristic of most mobilizations and debtor organizations in the agricultural sector at the local and regional levels (González 1995; H. Williams 2001: 154–5). It was this common interest that allowed diverse groups to 'converge', create ties and form a basis for collective action among distinct productive sectors that may well have been bitter rivals dating back to the agrarian reform period that began with the 1917 Constitution and that was implemented selectively in the entire country over the course of a half century (Otero 1989a, 1999).

Several weeks after the first demonstration in Autlán, the debtors prepared their tractors, harvesters and trucks and 'marched' to the state capital, paying no heed to warnings from the governor of Jalisco. On the way, the demonstration grew by absorbing debtors from nearby municipalities who wished to participate. Together they occupied the central square, called 'Plaza de Armas' (or Square of Arms, a symbol of state political, religious and military power), where they remained for fifty-seven days (Rodríguez and Torres 1994; González 1995). News of this incident reached the national and international press and the organizers received delegations of debtors who spoke of public protests in other states.

Debtors from Jalisco who sought to identify with similar groups and carry out joint actions at the national level called their movement El Barzón. This name was adapted from the title of a popular revolutionary era song about a peon who lives in misery, working from dawn to dusk to pay the interest on his debt to the *hacendado*. One fine day, at the urging of his wife, he decides to join the revolution. A *barzón* is the ring on the yoke to which a traditional team of oxen was tied. The song says the 'ring was broken', so the peon no longer has to obey his *amo* (master) and is free to join the revolt against the supreme government.

To assert unity in the midst of substantial differences, common symbols were created, including the popular song that is both the movement's name and its anthem, and the logo of a tractor. In creating this symbolism, debtors used popular tradition without resorting to 'national' symbols such as the flag or to revolutionary heroes who legitimize the state.

The local press and, to a lesser extent, the national and international media, reported public actions including blockages on highways and private toll roads, newspaper ads, hunger strikes by debtors in front of banks, municipal office buildings and buildings in state capitals, and the takeover of local radio stations by debtor groups. Demonstrations in state capitals and smaller cities in several states were one means of founding and consolidating local debtor organizations that absorbed individuals and existing groups from distinct social strata, political parties and religious affiliations. They also represented a new form of protest against the state, political parties and other associated organizations, and established the right to organize public demonstrations in the interests of the nation. It became clear to the debtors that their strength and their chances of negotiating with bankers and the state would increase as they forged links with other such organizations. On the other hand, as we will see, other groups saw in this movement of agricultural businessmen an opportunity to present their own demands, which were fundamentally convergent with those of El Barzón.

In October 1993, producers from Jalisco attempted to take their farm equipment to the nation's capital, where they were to be joined by contingents of debtors from other states. At that point, however, the federal highway police broke up the march and jailed its leaders. When the leaders from Jalisco were freed several weeks later, they called a meeting of agricultural debtor organizations to form El Barzón (National Confederation of Bank Debtors, NCB). This group of agricultural producers soon became the point of convergence for new debtor groups from the industrial and service sectors, and for many urban consumers with unpayable mortgages or credit card accounts. The organization defined objectives and proposed that the actions of different groups be coordinated at the national level, including direct negotiations with cabinet ministers and important bank stockholders.

At the end of 1993, in the regional city of Fresnillo and later in the capital of the state of Zacatecas, debtors organized a 'sit-in' that lasted sixty-nine days. During this time they contacted other debtor groups in Zacatecas and neighbouring states (H. Williams 2001). At first, organizers recognized an El Barzón national confederation and perceived the possibility of integrating into a single organization. Ideological disagreements and mistrust among the leaders, however, soon made it clear that no such integration would be possible.

The respective positions of the leaders of the two El Barzón groups were clearly defined when, in 1994, Maximino Barbosa – the leader of the NCB and a man with political experience linked to the PRI – announced his candidacy for a seat in the Federal Congress representing that party. The same year, two of the three leaders of the Zacatecas movement – Manuel Ortega and Alfonso Ramirez, the latter a militant in leftist movements when younger – were presented as candidates for the Party of the Democratic Revolution (PRD), a centre-left party. All three lost their respective elections and then announced that political parties were not viable alternatives for assuring continuity and greater strength for the debtor movement. Nevertheless, the differences between the directors and their mutual attacks intensified to a point where the separation of the two movements was openly acknowledged (H. Williams 2001: 175). The debtor movement in Zacatecas formed an independent organization called the National Union of Agricultural Producers, Merchants, Industrialists and Service Providers, El Barzón (NUB), uniting debtor groups from Oaxaca, Michoacán, Durango, Sinaloa and Chihuahua. Meanwhile, the NCB merged debtor organizations in Michoacán and Chihuahua (where the other group also had organizations), and soon spread to Guanajuato, Tabasco, Oaxaca, the state of Mexico and Puebla.

The metaphor that best describes this articulation is a 'web', as it allows us to '... more vividly imagine the multi-layered entanglements of the movements' actors with the natural-environmental, political-institutional and cultural-discursive arenas in which they are embedded'

(Álvarez et al. 1998: 16–17). This 'web-like movement' spread information and programmes of action, provided the organization with bases for contention and for recruiting new members and was soon transformed into a collective actor. The strength of national-level organizations rested precisely on their role as articulators, capable of achieving the convergence of state and local-level groups. At this stage, decision-making rested upon the participation and commitment of local representatives who nurtured the movement and breathed life and continuity into it with their resources and initiatives. In the case of the NUB, H. Williams observed: 'Where differences of opinion existed between local and national leaders over specific issues or strategies, local leaders would most often prevail, simply because the organization had little power to censure rogue local chapters' (H. Williams 2001: 198). This description matches the situation I found at state and national NCB meetings in 1994 and 1995.

The split between these two organizations that competed to represent the movement at the national level has not resulted in constant confrontations designed to defeat the adversary, due to two underlying factors. First, the movement's resilience and continuity are deeply rooted in local associations that have always sought to be inclusive and to present a broad front to their main adversaries; that is, the bankers and the federal government. These groups adopted the slogans of the national leadership and used them to gain tangible advantages in the local media. If they considered that larger-scale mobilizations in state capitals could have local effects, they joined in. If the legal defence strategy in the courts yielded results, it was often adopted by all. If some other confederation offered better solutions and greater support, local groups might adhere to it.

Second, the rivalry between the two El Barzón groups has not seriously affected the debtor movement because of the importance of presenting a united front to obtain support from, and establish a consensus with, national and international political and civic organizations. The best-known case (see below) is the alliance of both groups to act jointly with congressmen from the three main opposition parties. To achieve this support it was necessary to formulate a common political agenda. Thus, both El Barzón groups played a unifying role among competing parties that saw in this 'mass movement' an opportunity to increase their respective political clienteles.

Debtors followed the actions of the Ejército Zapatista de Liberación Nacional (EZLN), in Chiapas on 1 January 1994 with great interest, and on more than one occasion publicly threatened to change the non-violent nature of their own political struggle. The leaders of both El Barzón groups had individual interviews with the leaders of the EZLN in Chiapas and announced the points on which they coincided, though they also clearly established the independence and autonomy of each movement (Mestries 2000b and below).

Neither the state nor the bankers agreed to negotiate the debtors' demands. Bankers in particular systematically refused to negotiate the problem of overdue loans with the leaders of this movement. They limited their response to sending representatives with no decision-making power to meetings of debtors and public officials.

The devaluation of the peso in December 1994 exposed the fragility of the Mexican economy and sparked an acute crisis. Rising interest rates and unemployment, together with stagnation in the productive apparatus, explain why in the first nine months of 1995 overdue loans at Mexican banks grew by 112 per cent, while loan portfolios grew only 11 per cent ('CNV', *El Nacional*, 12 April 1995). With the increase in interest rates, the number of debtors unable to pay rose at an accelerated rate. Facing the real threat of losing their property, even some who distrusted debtor groups or attacked them publicly found them to be a viable means for defending their interests.

Debtors converged around the conviction that the so-called 'modernization project' was frustrating their participation as economic actors and depriving them of wealth and the means of making a living that they felt was part of their family heritage.

As the number of debtors and unemployed people in the agricultural, industrial and service sectors grew, it became clear to all that the state was defending interests that were contrary to those of most Mexicans. In this context, we can discern what G. Torres (1997) calls the '*Derecho de Barazonear*' (roughly, the right to resort to the same actions as the El Barzón movement), and H. Williams (2001: 193) termed the 'Culture of *Barzonism*'. This consists in calls for the solidarity and mutual support of all members of civil society affected by the authoritarian implementation of neoliberal economic policies, and also in a commitment to non-violent confrontations and civil disobedience.

Debtors from the industrial and urban sectors formed individual or group relationships with these local agricultural producer organizations. Non-agricultural debtors promoted groups that could respond more specifically to their particular problems, and founded chapters in various cities around the country, including the Association of Bank Customers, the Family Heritage Defence Front, the Debtors' Association, and the National Credit Card Holders' Association. All these groups had a certain base of local power, while many emerged through initiatives of non-governmental civil and religious organizations that sought alternative solutions to an increasingly widespread problem among their members and the population as a whole.

An unprecedented situation arose in November 1995, when a group of 500 'small' and 'medium' bank shareholders opted to change sides because, ironically, the weight of their overdue loans had turned them into debtors! During the reprivatization of the banks, these investors had purchased stock and received loans to increase their holdings, assets that appeared to represent a safe and profitable investment at the time. Moreover, they had ways of obtaining loans that they could then invest to develop and modernize their own firms. Rising interest rates and economic stagnation, however, affected their ability to pay, especially because they had enjoyed certain 'privileges' in obtaining loans and had managed their banks on the very edge of the law and banking regulations.

The NCB received these stockholders with open arms because: (i) they were irrefutable evidence of the failure of the government's economic policy; (ii) they exposed the privileges and irregularities in the management of privatized banks; and (iii) they constituted indisputable proof that the organization of corporate bank stockholders was ultimately controlled by large financial consortiums with few qualms about sacrificing their partners.

In summary, the El Barzón movement grew, mobilized and absorbed enormously diverse groups located in rural and urban areas, linked to other organizations (governmental and non-governmental) and to ecclesiastical and lay institutions and corporations located in almost every sector of the economy. The meetings and debates essential to the formation of El Barzón allowed it to define binding objectives and the means of achieving them. The actions that made this collective actor into a concrete force and produced experiences of convergent collective action among its members provided continuity and strength. The rivalries, divergences and divisions among *Barzonistas* have not disappeared nor ceased to influence the movement, but members have overcome or tolerated them in the interests of shared objectives and interests, and this has led them to form a coalition to confront the alliance of state and private bankers.

The struggle in the juridical and political arena

In most areas, the El Barzón movement managed to postpone embargoes and legal proceedings initiated by the courts against debtors (Rodríguez and Tórrez 1994; González 1995; Mestries 2000b; de Grammont 2001). Debtors have acted to denounce corruption publicly and have developed tactics to block the carrying out of judicial initiatives, including satirizing local judges and magistrates – public acts in which biased and corrupt judges are ridiculed – and even mobilizing contingents of debtors to 'honey [not tar] and feather' bank lawyers.

As of 1996, demonstrations and public actions by debtors were complemented by a new strategy; they began to present demands in local courts and later to the Supreme Court and Congresses at the federal and state levels. These demands questioned laws and sponsored legislation to defend their interests. Through these actions, debtor groups questioned the legitimacy of the state as an institution that defends the rule of law and the national interest.

The actions carried out by this mosaic of debtor organizations throughout the country and in most economic sectors now include launching suits in local courts. Thus, debtors no longer go before the courts as defendants, but rather as plaintiffs in suits that accuse credit institutions of resorting to illegal practices and demand the cancellation of credit operations. These suits have bogged down local courts and revealed a series of dishonest practices – common even before the nationalization of the banks – designed to push clients' debts to unpayable levels. One such practice (*anatocismo*) consists of including unpaid interest as part of the principal of the loan, thus allowing banks to charge interest-on-interest; a procedure that the Mexican constitution clearly prohibited.

Between 1995 and 1996, lawyers in most states were specially trained to comprehend the illegal operations in which banks had participated, and their violation of the terms and dispositions of mercantile law, and to prepare suits for presentation in local tribunals. The work of training these lawyers was initiated by a jurist named Fentanes (1995), who published a study on bank procedures that documented clearly and in great detail the illegal operations banks had used in their attempt to increase the debt burden of their clients. This research was widely disseminated and the author prepared and distributed the pertinent legal documentation so that debtors, or their lawyers, could present suits in local courts. As I was able to verify with the leaders and lawyers of the El Barzón movement in Jalisco, Tabasco, Michoacán and Chihuahua, in some cases local tribunals found in favour of the debtors and saved or recovered properties including industrial plants, houses, agricultural machinery and ranches. The first legal victory of this nature spurred many other debtors to present their own suits and led to a virtual saturation of local tribunals that lacked sufficient personnel to deal with the number of complaints filed. This tactic allowed debtors to succeed in neutralizing, at least temporarily, the bankers' principal weapon.

The level of activity by debtors and banks in the legal arena was intense and severely tested the judicial system's operating capacity and efficiency. By July 1996, El Barzón had presented 400,000 suits in courts, and debtors had sent 900,000 letters to banks manifesting their intention to pay the principal of their loans, but not the accumulated interest (de Grammont

2001: 157). On the other hand, banks had presented 1.145 million suits in tribunals, many of which involved debtors with mortgage loans (ibid.).

From 1994 to 1997, the federal government (for clearly political motives) introduced a series of programmes that offered those debtors who had the capacity to pay back their loans legal alternatives to restructure debts and continue paying. These programmes, however, were overtaken by the country's grave economic situation and did not fulfil their announced objectives. Negative factors included a substantial increase in interest rates after 1995, the persistent lack of solvency and profitability among small and medium-sized businesses that pushed them into moratorium, the decline in the real value of family income, and increasing unemployment in the middle classes and urban areas (González 1995; de Grammont 2001; Mestries 2000b). Finally, in the medium and long terms, these programmes actually increased the burden of many debtors, as loans were indexed to the annual inflation rate (Garrido and Leriche 1998: 24)

These circumstances clearly demonstrated the veracity of one affirmation that the *Barzonistas* had espoused from the beginning: the joint responsibility of the federal government and the banks for the unjustified amount of debt (Mestries 2000b). The problem of overdue loans continued to be critical, as was the situation of the financial sector which, to avoid insolvency, needed more state intervention in the form of the indiscriminate buying up of overdue loans (Garrido and Leriche 1998: 24).

In the face of the juridical actions initiated by debtors in the courts and the critical situation of the financial sector, the federal government responded with a series of measures sent to Congress in 1996. In the opinion of debtor groups, these initiatives reduced their margin of defence and made it much easier for the courts to proceed against them. The central arena of this struggle shifted to the National Congress and state Congresses, where debtors found allies among congressmen from the PRD and other parties, including the PRI, who were sympathetic to their interests and critical of federal economic policy. The linkage with political parties should come as no surprise, given the important role that parties play in the structure of political power (Craig 1994), and the fact that parties allowed these debtor organizations to launch a decisive battle against the federal government in the juridical-political arena.

The strategic alliance with political parties was also based on 'convergence' and spurred a wider discussion of initiatives in the federal Congress concerning debtors' interests and demands. It meant that proposals more damaging to their interests were eliminated (de Grammont 2001: 158). In the case of state Congresses, debtors enjoyed greater success, as fifteen states approved legislation or dictated measures that favoured them. These included the establishment of moratoria for debtors with overdue loans, prohibitions on auctions of debtor properties and on embargoes of tractors and transport vehicles, and the prohibition in some states of *anatocismo* (Mestries 2000b). Through these actions, El Barzón not only reaped the benefits of the support it received in state Congresses, but also reaffirmed the principle of federalism.

Due to controversies among different state legislations concerning *anatocismo*, the legal advisers of debtor organizations, with the intervention of the PRD, argued before the Supreme Court that it was necessary for that court to rule on the unconstitutionality of this practice. Such a ruling would allow them to invalidate all debts in which the use of this practice could be demonstrated and so oblige the banks to reduce considerably the amount of interest owed. On 7 October 1998, however, the court decided against the debtors and recognized the legality of the capitalization of interests.

Political action and political parties

For the national debtor organizations it soon became clear that in the long term the objectives of the struggle could be achieved only through fundamental changes in the national economic and political system. Thus, they opted for the electoral route, but what made it possible for them to orient their actions to this route was precisely the opening of the Mexican political system that resulted from a historical process involving many other social groups and institutions. The reform of the 1996 electoral law, after a political–electoral struggle that lasted several decades, offered Mexican citizens greater guarantees of free and impartial elections, and limited electoral corruption and coercion of the corporatist vote. The 1997 electoral campaign was one result of this change, as for the first time in seventy years the PRI failed to win a majority in Congress and coalition-building among representatives from different parties became the key for modifying, rejecting or approving proposed legislation.

It is in the context of this political system that the growing integration of El Barzón organizations with political parties should be understood; especially in the case of the PRD, which was more interested in and accessible to debtors' demands. This process was facilitated by the fact that NUB leaders had been militants in leftist movements and had links to members of this party. In addition, during the debate concerning the first package of laws sent to Congress by the executive in 1996 (see above), the *Barzonistas* sought to integrate representatives from other parties who were sympathetic to their demands. In contrast, in the 1997 debate over the package of initiatives for the financial sector, the PRD actually presented proposals, as two national leaders of the Barzón – Maximino Barbosa (NCB) and Alfonso Ramirez (NUB) – had won seats in the Chamber of Deputies and Quirino Salas (NUB) in the Senate through proportional representation.

In 1997, the executive branch sent Congress a new series of legal initiatives affecting the financial system. These measures contained important reforms for this sector, the most far-reaching of which was the proposal to transform the liabilities of the Fondo Bancario de Protección al Ahorro (FOBAPROA) into public debt. In 1996, this fund had absorbed the debts of banks and other large debtors valued at some $40 billion. By 1998, when the initiative was passed, the value of this fund had grown to $60 billion; a figure that represented 14.4 per cent of Gross National Product (GNP) (CNBV, cited in Garrido and Leriche 1998: 24). The legislation passed thanks to the efforts of the two largest parties in Congress (PRI and PAN), though it was opposed by the PRD, the party that has leaders of El Barzón among its members.

Also in 1997, with the support of the leaders and state representatives of both El Barzón organizations, the PRD presented a proposal to resolve the problem of FOBAPROA. This initiative was less costly than the executive branch's proposal, but above all it insisted that official support be channelled to the debtors, instead of having the country absorb the banks' unpayable debts, as was finally determined by the PAN–PRI coalition. According to Mestries (2000b), this was the final card that the Barzón movement played as an organized group.

The close relationship between the PRD and NUB leaders meant that the chances of the other organization (NCB) acting in the national political arena were weakened and limited. From the PRD's point of view, then, the only organization that represented debtors was the NUB.

The cooptation of this movement by the PRD and its subsequent subordination to party electoral strategy and plans of action caused local and state organizations (the source of the movement's previous vitality) to weaken and become disarticulated (Mestries 2000b; de Grammont 2001; H. Williams 2001). Though today we occasionally read information in the national press concerning the actions of a debtor group called El Barzón, its force, identity and capacity have been lost.

Conclusions

Despite the fact that the Barzón movement includes no significant participation by the most marginal sectors of the society, it became one of the most highly integrated and pluralistic movements in contemporary Mexican history. We find no other social movement of the same size and geographic scale in Mexico in which so many individuals and such socially and culturally heterogeneous groups have succeeded in coalescing to this degree.

The study of the El Barzón movement allows us to consider 'convergence' as a central component of current movements and to explain the transforming role that they play in the national political system and culture. This movement arose and became strong thanks to socially and culturally heterogeneous debtor groups that, by 'converging', looked to give their actions greater impact and transcendence.

Through this process of convergence, the movement contributed to redefining the forms and spaces of political participation at the local, state and national levels. Debtors clearly point out the effects of greater commercial freedom and economic deregulation on their immediate reality and take a well-defined position with respect to them. They organized and acted at the local level, but also promoted the formation and articulation of national webs of rural and urban debtor groups. These webs were coordinated by two national committees that allowed debtors to participate in the national legal–political arena. The El Barzón movements were not opposed to the idea of change in the nation or to the country confronting globalization processes. Rather, they objected to the fact that their opportunity to participate in processes of change had been nullified and that the coming generation would have to face such an uncertain future. This reaffirmation of their presence in national and international processes was thus projected and remains firmly rooted on the local scene. In this sense, El Barzón moved in the opposite direction from the state and transnational corporations and institutions.

During its existence, El Barzón was an instrument for defending debtors, for uncovering the corruption and illegality with which local and federal courts undertook actions designed to enforce the law, for assuring that justice was done. This movement became stronger without losing its collective, plural nature that allowed it to resolve disputes and rivalries among its members and to implement effective forms of internal participation in decision-making that contradicted state authoritarianism and the control exercised by political corporations linked to the official party. On the other hand, the movement opened channels of political participation that permitted the presentation of alternatives to resolve at the local and national levels the problems of debtors and the financial system, as well as the critical economic situation that confronted small and medium-sized businesses and a wide sector of the urban population who found it impossible to pay off their mortgage loans.

These elements allow us to consider El Barzón as a movement that generated changes not only in the political system and culture of its participants, but also among all those who followed it and showed solidarity with the actions carried out at the local and national levels to promote a more participatory, inclusive society with less inequality. Thus, we can conclude that El Barzón contributed to the development of convergence as a form of citizen participation; one that brought concrete results when electoral reform opened the way to greater political participation that in the year 2000 led to an opposition candidate occupying the presidency of the republic.

Note

Research for this chapter was conducted with support from Mexico's National Council for Science and Technology (Consejo Nacional de Ciencia y Tecnología, CONACYT).

14 | Contesting neoliberal globalism from below: the EZLN, Indian rights and citizenship

GERARDO OTERO

§ THE purpose of this chapter is to offer a conceptualization of the ideological and normative challenges to neoliberal globalism posited by Indian peasant mobilization as represented by the social movement around the Zapatista National Liberation Army (Ejército Zapatista de Liberación Nacional, EZLN). I argue that this mobilization challenges hegemonic definitions of nationhood and directly opposes neoliberal globalism on the ideological terrain: the liberal ideology behind neoliberal globalism focuses on the goal of equality of individuals, but indigenous struggles demand respect for and legal recognition of group cultural difference. Furthermore, Indian struggles also include demands for land and self-government, which include collective forms of property and are considered central for the cultural reproduction of indigenous identity. These demands go directly against the neoliberal drive towards the privatization and individualization of social life. The vigorous Indian peasant movement from below is bringing to the fore a post-liberal conceptual and normative framework that may provide the basis for expanding the nation from within. Such expansion could not only accommodate the demands of Indian peoples; it could also be the basis on which to reformulate the very definition of the Mexican nation and to reform the state itself. The long-term goal is to create a 'world where all the worlds fit'.

My more general argument is that the new Indian peasant mobilization also results in the strengthening of civil society *vis-à-vis* the state, specifically based on the growth of organizations of subordinate groups and classes. This amounts to what Jonathan Fox aptly termed the 'thickening of civil society' (1996). Therefore, even if some particular movement goals are not achieved, the resulting solidarity and organization will none the less reinforce future struggles and citizenship.

Furthermore, in contrast to some recent theorization about social movements in Latin America, which emphasize either a class-based approach (Petras and Veltmeyer 2001a) or an identity-based perspective (Alvares et al. 1998), I will argue that, in the case of indigenous peasant mobilization class and identity struggles are actually inseparable. Emphasizing one or another determinant or 'variable' will necessarily lead to an incomplete and one-sided analysis. If there is any subordinate social group in Latin America for which both class grievances and identity-rights issues are similarly important in their constitution as political subjects, this is the indigenous population. Paradoxically, this population was constituted as 'Indian' by the conquering forces from Europe. By the late twentieth century, Native Americans began to use this same label, historically used to exploit and oppress them, to liberate themselves. In many cases, they are using colonial documents to demand land rights, and they are adopting the term 'Indians' to designate themselves.

In the first section, I further elaborate the theory of political-class formation (PCF) introduced in Chapter 1 as an alternative framework for explaining Indian peasant mobilizations. This theory combines regional cultures, state intervention and leadership types to explain the links between class structural processes and political outcomes in a systematic manner. The focus of the second section, however, is narrower. It traces the ways in which material grievances have been articulated to ethnic demands, given the regional cultures and the processes of collective identity formation that prevail in Mexico. The next section discusses the conceptual and normative issues involved in redressing Indian rights and citizenship in emerging democracies. It juxtaposes what can be seen as an establishment-friendly, yet post-liberal conceptual and normative perspective on Indian rights and citizenship with the bottom-up theory of political-class formation. The final section outlines the main theoretical, substantive and policy conclusions.

Political-class formation (PCF) and civil society

As outlined in Chapter 1, PCF proposes regional cultures, state intervention and leadership types as the key mediating determinations between class structural processes and political outcomes. Regional cultures form the basis for articulating an organization's demands. State intervention shapes the initial contours of the resulting character of a class organization. Finally, leadership types and modes of participation determine its alliances with other movements and organizations, and its chances of remaining independent of the state and autonomous in terms of other political organizations.

This chapter focuses primarily on how regional cultures and collective identity construction have worked in the shaping of the EZLN's demands, and only a brief discussion will be made as to how state intervention and leadership types work in PCF theory. When state intervention helps the material reproduction of subordinate classes, but the initiative of such policies comes from the state itself, the political result is usually a coopted organization that loses its independence from the state and reinforces bourgeois hegemony. We could say that the more coopted organizations there are, the more civil society becomes 'confiscated' by the state or political society. Within an authoritarian regime, this entails that the realm of domination grows over the realm of hegemony.

Negative state interventions, in contrast, like those that Indian organizations have most often faced, may result either in demobilization or the formation of independent and oppositional organizations for resistance. Repressive state policies, for instance, usually involve the loss of state legitimacy and a decline in bourgeois hegemony; but they can also result in genocide and/or subordinated assimilation for Indian peoples. It is only when favourable state interventions are the result of the independent pressure and mobilization from below that oppositional organizations enter a 'subjective moment of struggle', i.e. when they become the political subjects constructing their future. These are 'popular-democratic' organizations and promote an alternative hegemonic project.

Leadership types and modes of participation matter a great deal in the process of constructing organizations for struggle. They determine the formation of alliances with other social movements and organizations in civil society, as well as whether the organization will remain (or not) independent of the state and autonomous (or not) from other political organizations (such as political parties). Unfortunately, this 'variable' also has considerable dependence on state intervention, for the state usually has the possibility of attempting to coopt the leadership of oppositional organizations. But the ease or difficulty with which cooptation and/or corruption takes place will depend largely on the modes of participation of the leadership's constituency: the more democratic and accountable a leadership, the less likelihood there is for its cooptation and/or corruption (see Otero 1999 and Chapter 1, this volume).

There is no doubt that collective identity construction and the production of counter-hegemonic meanings and symbols play a significant role in social movement formation (Pichardo 1997). This fact has been clear in Marxist theory since the seminal and classic work of Antonio Gramsci (1971) on hegemony and revolutionary strategy in the West. The problem is that too many Marxists have remained in a Leninist, Stalinist, Trotskyite or Maoist, but otherwise pre- or non-Gramscian, stage in their thinking. Identity construction is a particularly crucial process for members of indigenous movements, whose legitimacy as political actors hinges on their ability to gain recognition of their shared identity and social position in relation to those of dominant groupings (Van Cott 2000). Yet, that social movements are influenced by culture and collective interpretation should not be understood as an indication that class structural processes are either ineffectual or obsolete as stimuli of social movements, nor should it be taken as evidence that culture and meanings 'trump' structural causes in the process of social-movement formation.

Because indigenous struggles in Mexico and elsewhere are inseparable from struggles for autonomy, self-governance and the control over natural resources (Assies et al. 2000; Comaroff and Comaroff 1985; Wearne 1996; Otero 2003; Sieder 2002), we cannot see them through the lens of identity politics alone. The economic conditions for Indian cultural reproduction must be contemplated. Similarly, we cannot diminish in importance the ethnic-identity component of the mobilizations in favour of strictly class-based interpretations, because Indianness (as the participants of indigenous mobilizations conceive of and frame it) constitutes a central challenge to emerging liberal democracies in Latin America. I propose a theoretical synthesis in which both class and identity are core constituent parts in the political-class formation of Indian peasants (Otero 1999; Otero and Jugenitz 2003).

The question of how indigenous peasants become constituted into a political class could conceivably be answered from a strictly economic class perspective, or from an identity-based point of view. Nevertheless, the distinctiveness of the theory of political-class formation (PCF) presented here is, precisely, that both economic and cultural issues are integral parts of what constitutes classes *politically*. A politically formed class involves elements of both material interests and cultural aspects of identity that result from the relations of production and the relations of reproduction, respectively. Relations of production are defined as primarily relations between exploiters and exploited, while relations of reproduction are above all those among the exploited.

For Indian peasants, a key component of the relations of production comprises their relations with other ethnic groups, namely with the dominant groups of *mestizos* and *ladinos*. Now, for predominantly subsistence peasants, it may well be that the key relation with the dominant groups takes place through the market, and not through production. In either case, ethnic relations within asymmetrical production or market relations will tend to either reinforce ethnic identities, or force the subordinate ethnic group into assimilation. In Laclau and Mouffe's terms (1985), the antagonism between the two subject positions constitutes their respective identities. The remarkable fact about many Indian ethnicities is that they have resisted assimilation for about half a millennium, despite the reality that they have always occupied a subordinate position as a group.

Regional cultures, collective identity construction and indigenous demands

In contemporary Mexico, ethnicity is part of regional cultures and to this extent it plays a role in shaping demands or objects of struggle. In much of southern Mexico, a large proportion of the population is indigenous and, in some areas, people with indigenous ethnicities are actually the majority. One could thus ask: What constitutes the basis of political mobilization for indigenous peasants? Is it their class situation as peasants or their ethnic status as Indians? Once again, my response is that we cannot really separate the two issues, except analytically. That is to say, the full package of demands posited by the EZLN intends to redress both material and cultural or identity grievances. Let us turn to how this organization has articulated its grievances.

The EZLN as political-class organization

The EZLN started out as a typical guerrilla organization by launching a frontal attack on the state on 1 January 1994, as the North American Free Trade Agreement (NAFTA) went into effect. After only sixteen days of battle, however, it responded favourably to the government's proposal for peace negotiations. Its first communiqué did not even mention the right to indigenous culture as a demand; it focused on economic and political issues that included: 'work, land, housing, food, health care, education, independence, freedom, democracy, justice and peace' (EZLN 1994). (For a chronology of the EZLN dialogue with the government for the first four years, with web-links to crucial communiqués, see Paulson 1999.) Yet, in an interview given on 1 January 1994, EZLN spokesman Subcomandante Marcos indicated that NAFTA represented the death sentence for indigenous ethnicities in Mexico. It was also clear from the outset that the vast majority of the EZLN militia and community support bases were Indian.

During the first month after the uprising, most indigenous and peasant organizations in the state of Chiapas and beyond manifested their support for the EZLN and their agreement with its goals, if not its means. Soon the EZLN began to reshape its goals and programme explicitly to include the demand for Indian rights and culture. In fact, out of four major themes that were to be negotiated with the Mexican government, Indian rights and culture was the first to be addressed. Other major themes included land and economic issues, reform of the state, and women's rights (Harvey 1996, 1998; Gilbreth and Otero 2001). In preparation for these negotiations, the EZLN launched a national call for an indigenous forum to be held in Chiapas. Thirty-six ethnicities of a total of fifty-seven were represented at this forum in January 1996. Its resolutions were reflected, if not in full, in the San Andrés Accords signed between the EZLN and the government on 16 February 1996. Another resolution of the forum was the formation of a National Indigenous Congress (Congreso Nacional Indígena, CNI), which was organized in October 1996.

The massive backing of the EZLN by Indian peasant organizations throughout Mexico was shown once again during its leadership's march to Mexico City between February and March of 2001. Travelling through the most populous Indian regions between Chiapas and Mexico City, the EZLN leadership was received by crowds of thousands of people, and in each case they received the symbolic '*bastón de mando*', or command baton, from the chiefs of each regional Indian people. They were on their way to have their hearing before the plenum of the national Congress, which was about to discuss the legislation on Indian rights and culture (more on this later) (see Mexico's newspapers of those months for coverage, especially *La Jornada*, whose website goes back with daily issues to March 1996: <http://www.jornada.unam.mx/>).

Regional cultures and types of demands

The types of demands or objects of struggle that we can observe in rural Mexico are primarily: peasant, proletarian, peasant-entrepreneurial, indigenous-communitarian and post-capitalist. Certain cultural orientations correspond to each of these primarily economic labels (Otero 1999: Chapters 5–7). With regard to the indigenous-communitarian demand, some would argue that this is a post-modern type of struggle, to the extent that it centres on the issue of identity (Esteva 1999). Nevertheless, because the existence and reproduction of indigenous identity depends largely on access to land, I would argue that the indigenous-communitarian demand has an economic class base in the peasantry. Indianness as an identity clearly conditions this demand in that it incorporates at least a partial preference for a communitarian form of production and a specific ethnic identity. This is not an argument for the traditional Marxist primacy of economic-class relations as the basis for political-class formation. Rather, it is an assertion that economic interests are shaped not only by experience in production relations, but also by relations of reproduction (which include household, kinship and community relations). The ensemble of these relations has considerable bearing on regional cultures and processes of collective identity formation. In PCF theory, regional cultures primarily shape the objects of struggle or demands.

Subordinate groups, communities and classes in the indigenous areas of Mexico have sustained ethnic cultural differences for centuries. This does not mean that all current normative systems in indigenous communities are pre-colonial. Anthropologists and historians have demonstrated conclusively that people shape and reshape values and traditions interactively through contact with people from other ethnic groups, especially in resisting dominant groups or classes. Therefore, many or most cultural 'traditions' in an indigenous area could be of a recent fashioning (Assies 2000; Kearney and Varese 1995; Kicza 2000; Stern 1987; Wearne 1996; Zárate Hernández 2000). Yet they will still be specifically indigenous to the extent that such traditions emerged partially or wholly as ways of resisting the dominant groups in society. Sandstrom (2000), for instance, has concluded that 'Indianness' can be summed up in a few features (five in his ideal type), none of which is biological. This emanates from the fact that ethnic identity, like most other forms of cultural identity, is socially constructed (Assies 2000). As Sandstrom puts it:

> Ethnicity is often situational in that people decide when and how to assert their identity using different strategies at different times. An added complicating factor is that over time a group's self-definition changes to meet new challenges, and the symbols people choose to represent their identity may be modified, created anew, intentionally eliminated, or resurrected from a previous period. (Sandstrom 2000: 272)

Contrary to a traditional Marxist view on the subject, then, we cannot regard ethnicity as merely an ideological conception that involves 'false consciousness' (e.g. R. Bartra 1993). To the extent that ethnicity and its associated cultural values and traditions have real effects on social action and social life, they should be taken as important social determinants. In the case of the Zapatista struggles, fighting for the right to Indianness became central soon after the uprising, even if the EZLN started primarily as a class-based, typical guerrilla organization fighting for state power. Given the overwhelming support by Indian groups to the EZLN, the symbolic fight for Indian rights and culture became a key rallying point in its struggle.

In turn, this Indian-identity focal point functions as the main rationale behind the fight for autonomy and control over natural resources. Such an arrangement would allow indigenous communities to deal with their own affairs in governance and management of their natural resources (Burguette Cal y Mayor 2000; van der Haar 2001). This would be done in accordance with their own normative systems. Autonomy is thus seen as the condition for redressing and sustaining indigenous cultural identity. Hence liberal states feel threatened by contemporary Indian mobilization. Because Indian culture emphasizes community identity and values, it goes well beyond the values of individual rights and individual private ownership. As Rodolfo Stavenhagen has put it: 'Demands for the right to autonomy can only be fully understood in relation to a long history of oppression, exclusion and exploitation. Such has been the case of indigenous peoples' (Stavenhagen 2000: 13).

Expanding national borders within: Indian rights and citizenship

The discourse on citizenship has rarely provided a neutral framework for resolving disputes between the majority and minority groups; more often it has served as a cover by which the majority nation extends its language, institutions, mobility rights, and political power at the expense of the minority, all in the name of turning supposedly 'disloyal' or 'troublesome' minorities into 'good citizens'. (Kymlicka and Norman 2000: 11)

The purpose of this section is to clarify some of the key conceptual and normative issues on Indian rights and citizenship. My general question is: How can Indian demands for group rights and culture be accommodated in lieu of justice and citizenship, while respecting the rights of others? This discussion is based partly on a critical review of Will Kymlicka and Wayne Norman's recent general treatment of this subject (2000). The importance of these Canadian political theorists' work, particularly Kymlicka's (1995), resides in the fact that it has been influential in liberal and post-liberal academic circles throughout the Americas, as well as in Europe and elsewhere (Kymlicka and Opalski 2001). By juxtaposing their largely establishment-friendly perspective with the bottom-up theory of political-class formation, I hope to contribute to establishing better grounds for further dialogue between the state and Indian peasant movements in the negotiation of how to expand national borders within. I start with Mexican perspectives on what some post-liberal views of the nation look like.

The challenge for the liberal state is to move from a vision of its constituents as individuals only, to one that also acknowledges some notion of group or 'ethnic citizenship' (de la Peña 1997). Ethnic collectivities would have to be considered as subjects of public rights, with autonomy and self-determination being critical among them, as allowed for by the 1989 Convention 169 of the International Labour Organization (to which Mexico is a signatory state, Van Cott 2000). Rather than losing territory, the nation-state gains in its ability to be more inclusive of people that have long been marginalized from the benefits of national 'development'. For Luis Villoro, a Mexican philosopher, the point of acknowledging Indian peoples would not be to return to the ancestral, pre-modern, Indian community, which imposed its collective prejudices over all its individual members. A modern community would have to base itself on 'the unrestricted protection of fundamental personal liberties, which would not be violated by any communitarian decision' (Villoro 2001: 28).

EZLN's Comandante David expressed his idea about a post-liberal, multicultural democracy very eloquently in Tzotzil language in 1995: What Indians want, he said, is 'to live in a world where all the worlds fit'. In Mexico, a dramatic advance on Indian rights and culture was achieved on paper in the San Andrés Accords between government and the EZLN in February 1996 (Hernández Navarro and Vera Herrera

1998). But then a long impasse ensued, spurring considerable debate about Indian rights and the reform of the state (Franco Mendosa 2000; Díaz-Polanco and Sánchez 2003). While a 2001 constitutional change acknowledged Indian peoples, the most critical issues of autonomy and self-governance were left to be defined by state legislatures as to their nature and extent. Therefore, this legislation was rejected by most Indian organizations, including the EZLN. Failing federally to grant autonomy to Indian peoples, and to consider Indian communities as subjects of public rights, leaves their lands and territories open to capitalist development and exploitation without them having any say in the matter (Harvey 2002). The EZLN's spokesman, Subcomandante Insurgente Marcos, cites a study of the Fox administration's plans for local development by a human rights organization:

> The fact that the Indian rights and culture legal initiative was not approved [as proposed by COCOPA] made it very clear to indigenous organizations of Guerrero state that this is a well-planned job geared to have an indigenous law in line with the needs of transnational capital. The communities will not be capable of deciding within their own territories, nor will they be able to design their own plans that have to do with ethnodevelopment in which communities get to decide. (Marcos 2003).

After almost two years of silence as a protest against this spurious legislation, the EZLN support bases launched a massive demonstration, taking over the highlands city of San Cristóbal de las Casas, Chiapas, on 1 January 2003. More than 20,000 indigenous men, women and children, many with machetes in hand, filled the central plaza for more than three hours, during which time seven EZLN commanders spoke to the masses (Bellinghausen 2003).

So, how can the Mexican state and the Indian peoples move towards a resolution of their antagonisms and impasse? Although phrased in slightly different terms, the ideals of acceptance of cultural difference are contained in the notion of 'multicultural integration' proposed by Will Kymlicka and Wayne Norman (2000). Given that these authors have theorized this issue mostly in regard to more advanced liberal democracies, their conceptual and normative apparatus no doubt represents a considerable challenge for implementation in emerging democracies like those in Latin America.

The main challenge to resolve is twofold. First, there is the ideology of the ruling classes. Recent legislation reflects the refusal to grant significant Indian rights, or to move them beyond the constitution into enabling laws. The nineteenth-century idea of nation as being a culturally homogeneous entity (Hale 1996) is thus still alive and well. Even 'left' modernists advocate promoting capitalist development as the means to assimilate Indian peoples (Blanco 2001). The question, to be addressed shortly, is: to what extent can this ideology be transcended by the ruling classes, so as to accommodate cultural difference? The second challenge posited by post-liberal thinking has to do with the fact that redressing Indian demands includes going beyond recognition and granting of rights to Indian culture; it also requires, in many cases, the redistribution of land as a condition for its reproduction. In this section I will address only the first challenge, which has to do with the ideological and normative aspects of Indian rights and citizenship, while outlining the problems entailed by the second challenge.

Indian rights and citizenship have been central in two major debates in political theory of the 1990s, one about minority rights and multiculturalism (Díaz-Polanco and Sánchez 2003), and the other about citizenship and civic virtue. To a large extent, these have been separate debates, and yet advocates of minority rights and citizenship have shown some mutual suspicion (Kymlicka and Norman 2000). Defenders of minority rights suspect that appeals to some ideal of 'good citizenship' necessarily entail subordinating minority rights to majority rule (Samson 1999). Conversely, promoters of robust civic virtue and democratic citizenship suspect appeals to minority rights as reflecting the narrow self-interest that they seek to overcome (Assies 2000: 19). Despite suspicions, argue Kymlicka and Norman (2000), any attractive and plausible political theory must attend both claims. Here is a synthesis of these authors' attempt.

The debate on minority rights has seen two waves, the first of which was focused on 'justice' claims by minorities for accommodation of their cultural differences. The second, to be dealt with below, has to do with the articulation of justice for minorities on citizenship issues. According to prevailing liberal ideology, justice requires state institutions to be 'colour-blind', or 'difference-blind'. In this view, assigning rights or benefits on the basis of membership of an ascriptive or culturally different group is seen as morally arbitrary and inherently discriminatory. It will necessarily create first- and second-class citizens.

Hence the first task confronting any defender of minority rights was to 'show that deviations from "difference-blind" rules that are adopted in order to accommodate ethnocultural differences are not inherently unjust' (Kymlicka and Norman 2000: 3). The problem with 'difference-blind' institutions is that, while they purport to be neutral, they in fact are tilted towards the needs, interests and identities of the majority group. Therefore the adoption of minority rights is required to help remedy their disadvantages. In our case, if the Mexican state fails to recognize and respect Indian culture and identity, the result can be serious damage to their self-respect, and even to their sense of belonging to the larger, 'transcendent' national identity. The idea here is that, with recognition, Indians can both reproduce their cultures and better integrate into the Mexican nation.

There is at least one caveat with Kymlicka and Norman's discussion of minority rights: their tendency to speak from the point of view of the dominant culture. In doing so, rights would be 'given' to the minority groups. The implicit assumption is that only certain groups would have stronger rights by their association with the stronger language and culture, i.e. Spanish and mestizo in the case of Mexico. These groups would have a right to 'a' societal culture – that of the majority, says Richard Day (2000: 212) while critiquing Kymlicka (1995) about multiculturalism in Canada. The problem is that Kymlicka implicitly assumes that the dominant culture, the heirs of the colonizers, have a liberal-theoretical right to such societal culture (Day 2000: 212). In Kymlicka's work, says Day, 'there is a constant reference to a passively voiced "we" that will decide what gifts to give to "them"' (ibid.: 215).

From the point of view of the theory of political-class formation, however, it should be clear that as long as bourgeois hegemony prevails there will hardly be any concessions or gifts from the state, other than those which may be directed to coopting subordinate groups, communities and classes. Therefore, when it comes to Indian rights and culture, these will have to be extracted from the state with continued pressure from below. Such pressures raise further questions about the prospect for the legal and practical recognition of these rights by the ruling classes and about the possibility that such recognition will strengthen, not weaken, the Mexican nation-state.

In fact, another concern voiced by advocates of citizenship is that granting or recognizing minority rights may weaken larger citizenship rights, e.g. by seeking secession. This was Mexico's President Zedillo's excuse for reneging on the San Andrés Accords in November 1996. Kymlicka and Norman's main conclusion in this regard is that, in most cases, minority rights can be safely introduced while actually *strengthening* citizenship. But this is really an empirical question, they warn, which must be addressed on a case-by-case basis. The world problem on this matter is pointedly brought to light by the following figures: there are 5,000 to 8,000 ethnocultural groups and only about 200 states, 90 per cent of which are multiethnic (Kymlicka and Norman 2000: 13). Hence the need that states have for methods of 'managing' ethnic conflict.

These methods include now illegitimate ones that try to eliminate ethnic conflict, in some cases physically, such as genocide and forced mass population transfers, or via assimilation or hegemonic control. Even partition and/or secession are seen as problematic, to the extent that these methods merely transfer the ethnic conflict to the new entity. Therefore, multicultural integration is the most viable and just method to eliminate or reduce ethnic conflict. Both multicultural integration and assimilation involve the fashioning of a transcendent identity. Yet multicultural integration is preferable, because it does not require, as assimilation does, the elimination of subcultural groups' identities.

Now, how is cultural diversity to be respected in a pluralistic society, without also 'damaging or eroding the bonds and virtues of citizenship?' (Kymlicka and Norman 2000: 17). The peculiarity of indigenous peoples, say Kymlicka and Norman, is that they usually seek 'the ability to maintain certain traditional ways of life and beliefs while nevertheless participating on their own terms in the modern world' (ibid.: 20). This point rightly highlights the non-antagonistic nature of indigenous cultural rights claims within a liberal democracy. Kymlicka and Norman put this issue pointedly:

> [I]n so far as the historic conquest of indigenous peoples and the stripping of their self-government rights were grounded in racist and imperialist ideologies, then restoring rights of self-government can be seen as affirming the equal standing and worth of indigenous peoples. In these and other ways ... far from eroding equal citizenship status, 'the accommodation of differences is the essence of true equality'. (ibid.: 33)

The last phrase is a quotation from a judgment of the Canadian Supreme Court of 1986, interpreting Canadian constitutional provisions for equality.

While Kymlicka and Norman offer a convincing discussion of the non-antagonistic nature of Indian rights and culture, however, they neglect a critical issue: the fact that Indian struggles usually include the demand for land and territory, which are critical conditions for their cultural and material reproduction. This point may indeed become antagonistic, at least with some local or regional fractions of ruling classes. In these cases, the state can act for the larger good of society by engaging or completing a land reform process, even if it must compensate expropriated landowners. Only in this form can the original expropriation of native peoples be redressed, and the conditions established for their cultural reproduction.

In Latin America, the discussion about Indian rights, citizenship and democracy has also presented itself in the form of mutual distrust. Willem Assies (2000) sets out the conceptual and normative context of this discussion, with regard to Indian struggles over territory and self-governance. He offers a good synthesis of the discussion, while establishing connections with social movement theories and the debate about democratic transition and neoliberal reform. But in the end he seems to tilt more towards the citizenship camp, rather than towards that of the Indian or the minority-rights camp, as if the two had to be mutually incompatible. In fact, he says that the strength of the Indian movement may lie in going beyond formulating national proposals for indigenous peoples' problems; that they should instead move towards indigenous proposals in relation to national problems. This is how Assies puts it:

> considering their critique of present forms of economic organization and domination, indigenous peoples' movements are part of a 'popular movement', but at the same time their claims to particular rights on the grounds of being 'originary' at times constitute a source of friction with movements aiming for broadly defined citizen's rights in the context of a far-reaching revision in the political imaginary of contemporary democracy. (ibid.: 19)

In other words, Assies seems to suggest that Indians should subordinate their 'particular' interests and address the 'broader' (universal?) interests of other popular groups with a democratic imaginary. Similar arguments were heard by feminists struggling in socialist parties during the 1970s: that they had to subordinate their gender grievances to class issues.

The problem with this position is its underlying assumption that there is a mutually exclusive dichotomy between those who struggle for multicultural rights and citizenship rights advocates. As our discussion of Kymlicka and Norman has shown, most of the apprehensions expressed by citizenship advocates about minority rights are unfounded. Perhaps the main cultural and political contribution of the Indian movement is, precisely, to have fundamentally questioned the presumption that being Mexican must exclude other cultural identities. The multicultural and radical democratic view proposed by the Zapatistas goes well beyond the conception of a pre-constituted and transcendent 'national interest', and proposes that each group politically constitute itself to build a civil space. The EZLN does not want to become the vanguard of subordinate groups as former Leninist parties did. Rather, the newly constituted groups, communities and classes would strengthen civil society and contribute to building a 'world where all the worlds fit'. Moving in this direction entails a fundamental reform of the state, with an alternative, popular-democratic hegemony; one that admits the multicultural integration of all Mexicans.

Conclusions

From the preceding discussion, we can arrive at three conclusions: one theoretical, one substantive and one normative and policy-related. First, we need a synthetic theory such as PCF to understand and explain contemporary social movements whose demands involve both material and identity issues, and definitely for Indian peasant movements.

In terms of specific demands, the EZLN has thus far achieved only a paper triumph: the San Andrés Accords on Indian Rights and Culture of 1996. These accords have not been translated into satisfactory legislation to implement them, and the EZLN continues to be an oppositional organization. But in terms of organizational and civil-society growth, the EZLN has had a much more substantial success. In fact, I have argued elsewhere that the EZLN was a crucial factor in encouraging the 'thickening' of civil society that resulted in the PRI's electoral defeat in 2000 (Gilbreth and Otero 2001). Therefore, although the EZLN has not yet reached its 'subjective moment of struggle', it is clearly an oppositional and a popular democratic organization that has strengthened civil society.

The second, substantive, conclusion is that Indian peasant struggles represent a significant challenge to national borders from within, to the extent that they run directly counter to some key ideological elements of neoliberal globalism. Successfully to integrate Indian peasants into national development as equal citizens, in the terms posited by their own organizations, requires that nation-states go well beyond a merely liberal democratic regime to acknowledge their group differences. Nations must expand their borders within, in reconstituted states, in order to accommodate their Indian peoples and other subordinate groups, communities and classes.

Third, the policy conclusion from the conceptual and normative discussion presented here regards the present and future political dynamic, not only in Mexico but in all of the Latin American nations with significant indigenous populations; from a 'dialectic of opposites', of antagonism, confrontation and repression, it becomes possible to move in the direction of a 'dialectic of the diverse' in which differences may be resolved by discussion, negotiation and dialogue. The condition for such transition is that ruling classes must first understand that the ancestral dynamic of struggle between Indian peoples and Latin American states has involved a dialectic of opposites for half a millennium. It is always possible for the state to keep repressing these populations and/or to buy off their leadership or otherwise coopt their movements. But this approach merely displaces antagonism and conflict into the future. At least with regard to Indian peoples in contemporary capitalist societies, there is a clear prospect of resolving the main antagonisms by expanding currently hegemonic frameworks and, yes, by affecting the material interests of some fractions of the ruling classes. Once such antagonisms are resolved, however, it is conceivable that a new dynamic may ensue, one based on a 'dialectic of the diverse' rather than a dialectic of opposites. The pay-off for all will be that a larger proportion of citizens, social groups, communities and classes will live in a more integrated, participatory, cohesive, egalitarian, deliberative, democratic and just society.

Note

This chapter is based on parts of my contribution to Otero and Jugenitz (2003). I thank two anonymous reviewers for the *Canadian Review of Sociology and Anthropology* for their useful critiques to and suggestions for that article, Tatiana Schreiber for comments on this chapter, and Peter Singelmann for his critique of previous versions of this chapter.

About the contributors

Deborah Barndt teaches in the Faculty of Environmental Studies and is a fellow of the Centre for Research on Latin America and the Caribbean at York University, Toronto. She is the editor of *Women Working the NAFTA Food Chain: Women, Work, and Globalization* (1999), and the author of *Tangled Routes: Women, Work and Globalization on the Tomato Trail* (2002).

Armando Bartra is Director of Instituto de Estudios para el Desarrollo Rural Maya, AC. Originally trained in philosophy, he has authored or co-authored over thirty books in fields ranging from literary essays and poetry to history and social sciences. For the past thirty years his main focus has been the peasant question. His publications include: *The Seduction of the Innocents: The First Tumultuous Moments of Mass Literacy in Postrevolutionary Mexico* (1994); *Guerrero Bronco* (1996); and *Cosechas de ira* (2003).

Laura Carlsen is Director of the Interhemispheric Resource Center's Americas Program, based in Mexico, and a researcher with the Center for Studies on Rural Change in Mexico (Centro de Estudios para el Cambio en el Campo Mexicano), Mexico City. She most recently co-edited *Confronting Globalization: Economic Integration and Popular Resistance in Mexico* (2003).

Jeffrey H. Cohen is Professor of Anthropology and Demography at the Pennsylvania State University. His recent publications include *Cooperation and Community* (1999) and *Economic Development: An Anthropological Approach* (2001).

Enrique de la Garza Toledo is Professor in the PhD programme in Social Studies at Universidad Autónoma Metropolitana, Iztapalapa, where he edits the journal *Trabajo*. He is the editor of *Tratado Latinoamericano de Sociología del Trabajo* (2000) and author of *La Formación Socioeconómica Neoliberal* (2001).

Raúl Delgado Wise is Professor and Director of the doctoral programme in Development Studies at the Autonomous University of Zacatecas. His most recent books are *Oil in the World Economy: Transformation of the International Oil Industry* (1999) and *Minería, Estado y gran capital en México* (2002).

Enrique Dussel Peters is a Professor at the Graduate School of Economics, Universidad Nacional Autónoma de México (UNAM). His publications include *Polarizing Mexico: The Impact of Liberalization Strategy* (2000) and *Claroscuros: Integración exitosa de las pequeñas y medianas empresas en México* (2001).

Humberto González is Professor in Social Anthropology at the Centro de Investigaciones y Estudios Superiores en Antropología Social at Guadalajara. He is co-author of the *Return to Aztlán: The Social Process of International Migration from Western Mexico* (1987), and co-editor of *Agricultura de exportación en tiempos de globalización: El caso de las hortalizas, frutas y flores* (2001).

Horacio Mackinlay is Professor of Sociology at Universidad Autónoma Metropolitana, Iztapalapa. He is a contributor to Richard Snyder (ed.), *Institutional Adaptation and Innovation in Rural Mexico* (1999) and Kevin J. Middlebrook (ed.), *Dilemmas of Political Change in Mexico*.

María Elena Martínez-Torres completed a PhD at the Center for Latin American Studies of the University of California at Berkeley, and is co-director of the Center for the Study of the Americas, in Berkeley, CA. Her publications have appeared in, among others, the *Journal of Peace Studies* and *Peace Review*. She has been a visiting scholar at the Interdisciplinary Program for Mesoamerican Studies of UNAM and the Center for Social and Anthropological Research (CIESAS-Sureste).

Gerardo Otero is Professor of Sociology and Director of Latin American Program Studies at Simon Fraser University, Vancouver. He is the editor of *Neoliberalism Revisited: Economic Restructuring and Mexico's Political Future* (1996) and author of *Farewell to the Peasantry? Political Class Formation in Rural Mexico* (1999). His current research is on neoliberal globalism and agricultural biotechnology and on indigenous struggles over autonomy and control of natural resources. e-mail: <otero@sfu.ca>

Peter Singelmann is Professor of Sociology at the University of Missouri, Kansas City. His most recent articles have appeared in *Revista Mexicana de Sociología* (2002) and *Alianzas Productivas para la Seguridad Alimentaria y el Desarrollo Rural* (Food and Agriculture Organization <http://www.rlc.fao.org/prior/desrural/alianzas/casos.htm> 2002).

Lois Stanford is an Associate Professor of Anthropology at New Mexico State University. Her recent publications have appeared in Humberto González (ed.), *Articulaciones e interdependencias globales en la agricultura de México* (in press), *Agricultural and Human Values* (2003); and in José Eduardo Zárate (ed.), *Tierra Caliente de Michoacán* (2001).

Abbreviations

AALs	Local agricultural organizations (Asociaciones Agrícolas Locales)
AID	Agency for International Development
AMUCSS	Association of Social Sector Credit Unions (Asociacíon Mexicana de Uniones de Crédito del Sector Social)
ANEC	National Association of Marketing Agencies of Rural Products (Asociacíon Nacional de Empresas Comercializadoras de Productos Rurales)
APHIS	Animal and Plant Health Inspection Service
ARIC	Collective Interest Rural Associations (Asociaciones Rurales de Interés Colectivo)
ATOs	Alternative Trade Organizations
BANRURAL	Rural Development Bank
CAC	California Avocado Commission
CAP	Permanent Agrarian Congress (Congreso Agrario Permanente)
CAPA	Central American Protected Areas
CARTT	*Tosepan Titataniske* – 'We shall overcome'
CCAD	Central American Commission on Environment and Development
CCAP	Central American Council on Protected Areas
CCE	Entrepreneurial Coordinating Council (Consejo Coordinador Empresarial)
CEN	National Executive Committee (Comité Executivo Nacional)
CEPCO	State Coordinator of Coffee Producers of Oaxaca (Coordinadora Estatal de Productores de Café de Oaxaca)
CI	Conservation International
CIAOC	Independent Peasant and Agricultural Workers' Central (Central Independiente de Obreros Agrícolas Campesinos)
CICAFOC	Indigenous Peasant and Afro-American Coalition of Community Agro-Forestry
CNC	National Peasant Confederation (Confederación Nacional Campesina)
CNI	National Indigenous Congress (Congreso Nacional Indígena)

CNIAA	Chamber of the Sugar Industry (Cámara Nacional de la Industria Azucarera y Alcoholera)
CNOC	National Network of Coffee-growers' Organizations (Coordinadora Nacional de Organizaciones Cafetaleras)
CNOP	National Confederation of Popular Organizations (Confederación Nacional de Organizaciones Populares)
CNPA	National Network 'Plan de Ayala' (Coordinadora Nacional Plan de Ayala)
CNPP	National Confederation of Small Proprietors (Confederación Nacional de Pequeños Proprietarios)
CNPR	National Confederation of Rural Producers (Confederación Nacional de Productores Rurales)
CNTE	National Coalition of Education Workers (Coordinadora Nacional de Trabajadors de la Educación)
COPARMEX	Employers' Confederation of the Mexican Republic (Confederación Patronal de la República Mexicana)
COPRAVIC	Organismo de Promoción y Vigilancia Cañera
CROC	Revolutionary Confederation of the Workers and Peasants (Confederación Revolucionaria Obrera y Campesina)
CTM	Workers' Confederation of Mexico (Confederación de Trabajadores de México)
EOI	Export-oriented industrialization
EZLN	Zapatista National Liberation Army (Ejército Zapatista de Liberación Nacional)
FARMS	Foreign Agricultural Resource Management Services
FAT	Authentic Front of Workers (Frente Auténtico del Trabajo)
FDC	Democratic Peasants' Front of Chihuahua (Frente Democrático Campesino de Chihuahua)
FESEBES	Federation of Trade Unions in Goods and Services
FINASA	National Sugar Bank (Financiera Nacional Azucarera)
FNDCM	National Front in Defence of the Mexican Countryside (Frente Nacional de Defensa del Campo Mexicano)
FOBAPROA	Fondo Bancario de Protección al Ahorro
FTA	Free Trade Agreement
FTAA	Free Trade Area of the Americas
GCF	Gross-capital formation
GDP	Gross Domestic Product
GEF	Global Environment Fund
GNP	Gross National Product
HFCS	High Fructose Corn Syrup
ICA	International Coffee Agreement
IFOAM	International Federation of Organic Agriculture Movements

IMSS	Mexican Social Security Institute (Instituto Mexicano del Seguro Social)
INAH	National Institute of Anthropology and History (Instituto Nacional de Antropología e Historia)
INMECAFE	Mexican Institute of Coffee (Instituto Mexicano del Café)
INS	Immigration and Naturalization Service
ISI	Import-substitution industrialization
ISMAM	Indigenous People of the Motozintla Sierra (Indígenas de la Sierra Madre de Motozintla)
IUCN	World Conservation Union
MBC	Mesoamerican Biological Corridor
NAFTA	North American Free Trade Agreement
NCB	National Confederation of Bank Debtors
NGOs	Non-Government Organizations
NIA	New Institutional Arrangements
NPAs	Natural Protected Areas
NSM	New Social Movements
NUB	National Union of Agricultural Producers, Merchants, Industrialists and Service Providers, El Barzón
OCIA	Organic Crop Improvement Association
OECD	Organization for Economic Cooperation and Development
PAN	National Action Party (Partido de Acción Nacional)
PCF	political class formation (theory of)
PGR	Office of the Attorney General of the Republic
PIDER	Rural Development Investment Programme (Programa de Inversion para el Desarrollo Rural)
PPP	Plan Puebla-Panamá
PRD	Party of the Democratic Revolution (Partido de la Revolución Democrática)
PRI	Institutional Revolutionary Party (Partido Revolucionario Institucional)
PROFEPA	Federal Office of Environmental Protection
PSE	Economic Solidarity Pact (Pacto de Solidaridad Económica)
RAFI	Rural Advancement Foundation International
SAGAR	Ministry of Agriculture and Rural Development (Secretaría de Agricultura, Ganadería, y Desarrollo)
SARH	Ministry of Agricultural and Water Resources (Secretaría de Agricultura y Recursos Hidráulicos)
SEC	US Security and Exchange Commission
SME	Mexico Electricians' Union (Sindicato Mexicano de Electricistas)

SNTE	National Education Workers' Union (Sindicato Nacional de Trabajadores de la Educación)
SRA	Secretariat of Agrarian Reform (Secretaría de la Reforma Agraria)
STUNAM	Union of Workers of the National Autonomous University of Mexico (Sindicato de Trabajadores de la Universidad Nacional Autónoma de México)
TCO	Organized Common Labour (Trabajo Común Organizado)
UAEP	State Union of Agricultural Producers (Unión Agricola Estatal de Productores)
UAM	Autonomous Metropolitan University Union (Universidad Autónoma Metropolitana)
UCIRI	Union of Indigenous Communities of the Isthmus Region (Unión de Comunidades Indígenas de la Region del Istmo)
UCIZONI	Union of Indigenous Communities of the Northern Sierra of the Isthmus (Unión de Comunidades Indígenas de la Zona del Istmo)
UE	Union of *Ejidos* (Unión de Ejidos)
UNC	National Sugarcane Growers' Union (Unión Nacional de Cañeros)
UND	Democratic Sugarcane Growers' Union (Unión Cañera Democrática)
UNDP	United Nations Development Programme
UNOFC	National Union of Community Forestry Organizations (Unión Nacional de Organizaciones Forestales Comunitarias)
UNORCA	National Union of Autonomous Regional Peasant Organizations (Unión Nacional de Organizaciones Regionales Campesinas Autónomas)
UNPCA	National Union of Sugarcane Producers (Unión Nacional de Productores de Caña de Azúcar)
UNT	National Union of Workers (Unión Nacional de Trabajadores)
UPCV	Union of Coffee Producers of Veracruz (Unión de Productores de Café de Veracruz)
URAP	Regional Union of Agricultural Producers (Unión Regional Agrícola de Productores)
USDA	United States Department of Agriculture
UUE	Unión de Uniones de Ejidos
WTO	World Trade Organization
WWF	World Wildlife Fund

Bibliography

Agarwal, B. (1991) 'Engendering the Environmental Debate: Lessons Learnt from the Indian Subcontinent'. CASID Distinguished Speaker Series, Monograph 8. East Lansing: Michigan State University.

Alexander, J. M. and C. Mohanty (1997) *Feminist Genealogies, Colonial Legacies, Democratic Futures*. New York: Routledge.

Alonso, J. (1991) 'Apuntes sobre la convergencia', Paper presented at an Internal Seminar, CIESAS Occidente (typescript).

Alvarez, S., E. Dagnino and A. Escobar (1998) 'Introduction: The Cultural and the Political in Latin American Social Movements', in S. Alvarez, E. Dagnino and A. Escobar (eds), *Cultures of Politics – Politics of Culture: Re-visioning Latin American Social Movements*. Boulder, CO and Oxford: Westview Press.

Angus, I. (2001) 'Subsistence as a Social Right: A Political Ideal for Socialism?', *Studies in Political Economy*, 65 (Summer): 117–35.

Appendini, K. (2001) *De la milpa a los tortibonos: La restructuración de la política alimentaria en México*, Mexico City: El Colegio de Mexico, Instituto de Investigaciones de las Naciones Unidas para el Desarrollo Social.

— (1999) 'From Where Have All the Flowers Come? Women Workers in Mexico's Non-traditional Markets', pp. 127–140 in D. Barndt (ed.), *Women Working the NAFTA Food Chain: Women, Food, and Globalization*. Toronto: Sumach Press.

— (1995) 'Revisiting Women Wage Workers in Mexico's Agro-Industry: Changes in Rural Labor Markets', Working Paper 95, no. 2. Copenhagen: Centre for Development Research.

Archer, M. S. (1988) *Culture and Agency: The Place of Culture in Social Theory*. Cambridge: Cambridge University Press.

Arenas Melo, M. L. (1981) *Factores Que Afectan La Comercialización Del Café*. Colombia: ANIF Fondo Editorial.

Arteaga, A. and J. Carrillo (1990) 'Automóvil: hacia la flexibilidad productiva', *El Cotidiano*, 21.

Aspe Armella, P. (1993) *El camino mexicano de la transformación económica*. Mexico City: Fondo de Cultura Económica.

Assies, W. (2000) 'Indigenous Rights and Reform of the State in Latin America', pp. 3–22 in W. Assies et al. (eds), *The Challenge of Diversity*.

Assies, W., G. van der Haar and A. Hoekema (eds) (2000) *The Challenge of Diversity: Indigenous Peoples and Reform of the State in Latin America*. Amsterdam: Thela Thesis.

Ayala Aceves, A. (2000a) 'Editorial: Productores de aguacate unidos', *El Aguacatero*, 3(12).

— (2000b) 'Editorial: Promocionar el aguacate Hass', *El Aguacatero*, 3(13).

— (2000c) 'Editorial: Comisión para la promoción del aguacate en México', *El Aguacatero*, 3(14).

— (1999a) 'Invertir en nuestra huerta: mensaje editorial', *El Aguacatero*, 2(8): 2.

— (1999b) 'Editorial: mantener un alto precio en el aguacate michoacano', *El Aguacatero*, 2(9): 2.

Baker, G. (1995) 'Sector externo y recuperación económica en México', *Comercio Exterior*, 45(5): 398–408.

Bakker, I. (ed.) (1996) *Rethinking Restructuring: Gender and Change in Canada*. Toronto: University of Toronto Press.

Balassa, B. (1988) 'The Lessons of East Asian Development: An Overview', *Economic Development and Cultural Changes*, 36(3) (supplement).

Barndt, D. (2002) *Tangled Routes: Women, Work, and Globalization on the Tomato Trail*, Lanham, MD: Rowman and Littlefield; Aurora, Ontario: Garamond Press.

Barreda, A. (2001) 'Peligros del Plan Puebla Panamá', in A. Bartra (ed.), *Mesoamérica. Los ríos profundos* Mexico City: Instituto Maya.

— (2003) 'Cuatro casos de biopiratería en México', in L. Carlsen, H. Salazar and T. Wise (eds), *Enfrentando la globalización: Integración económica y resistencia social*. Mexico City: M.A. Porrua.

Barrón, M. A. (1999) 'Mexican Women on the Move: Migrant Workers in Mexico and Canada', pp. 113–126 in D. Barndt (ed.), *Women Working the NAFTA Food Chain: Women, Food, and Globalization*. Toronto: Sumach Press.

— (1993) 'Los mercados de trabajo rurales: el caso de las hortalizas en México', Tesis de doctorado en economia, Universidad Nacional Autonoma de Mexico, Facultad de Economía.

Barth, F. (1992) 'Towards Greater Naturalism in Conceptualizing Societies', in A. Kuper (ed.), *Conceptualizing Society*. New York: Routledge.

— (ed.) (1969) *Ethnic Groups and Boundaries: The Social Organization of Culture Difference*. London: Allen and Unwin.

Bartra, A. (2002) 'La invención de Mesoamérica', *La Jornada*, 11 May 2002.

— (1999) 'El aroma de la historia social del café', *La Jornada del Campo*, 28 July, p. 32.

— (ed.) (1993) *De haciendas, cañeros y paraestatales. Cien años de la historia de la agroindustria cañero-azucarera en México: 1880–1980*. Mexico City: UNAM.

— (1985) *Los herederos de Zapata*. Mexico: ERA.

Bartra, A., L. Paz Paredes and J. Manuél Arrecoechea (1993) 'La agricultura cañera-azucarera en los setenta. Redefinición del modelo en el contexto de una persistente crisis política, financiera y de producción', pp. 215–95 in A. Bartra (ed.), *De haciendas, cañeros y paraestatales*.

Bartra, R. (2002) *Blood, Ink, and Culture: Miseries and Splendors of the Post-Mexican Condition*. Durham, NC, and London: Duke University Press.

— (1993) *Agrarian Structure and Political Power in Mexico*. Baltimore, MD: Johns Hopkins University Press.

Bartra, R. and G. Otero (1987) 'Agrarian Crisis and Social Differentiation in Mexico', *Journal of Peasant Studies* (London), 14(3): 334–62.

Bartra, R. et al. (1978) *Caciquismo y poder político en México rural*. Mexico City: Siglo XXI Editores.

Basok, T. (1997) 'Forms of Control within the Split Labor Market: A Case of Mexican Seasonal Farm Workers in Ontario', Paper presented to the Rural Sociology Conference, Toronto, Ontario, August.

Beck, U. (1992) *The Risk Society. Towards a New Modernity*, Theory, Culture and Society Centre, London: Sage.

Bejarano, F. (2003) 'El conflicto del basurero tóxico de Metalclad en Guadalcázar', in L. Carlsen, H. Salazar and T. Wise (eds), *Enfrentando la globalización: Integración económica y resistencia social*. Mexico City: M.A. Porrua.

Bellinghausen, H. (2003) 'Más de 20 mil indígenas preguntan al presidente Vicente Fox dónde está la paz', *La Jornada*, 2 January. Available at:<http://www.jornada.unam.mx/003n1pol.php?origen=index.html> (accessed 2 January 2003).

Bellon, M. R. (1995) 'Farmers' Knowledge and Sustainable Agroecosystem Management: An Operational Definition and an Example from Chiapas, Mexico', *Human Organization*, 54(3): 263–72.

Bhagwati, J. (1991) 'Is Free Trade Passé After All?', pp. 31–44 in A. Koekkoek and L. B. M. Mennes (eds), *International Trade and Global Development*. London: Routledge.

Bizberg, I. (2003) 'Transition or Restructuring of Society?', pp. 143–75 in J. S. Tulchin and A. D. Selee (eds), *Mexico's Politics and Society in Transition*. Boulder, CO and London: Lynne Rienner.

— (1990) *Estado y sindicatos en México*. Mexico City: Colegio de México.

Bizberg, I. and L. Meyer (eds) (2002) *Cambio y resistencia: treinta años de política en México*. Mexico City: Océano.

Blanco, J. (2001) 'La autonomía de los riesgos', *La Jornada*, 3 April. Available at: <http://www.jornada.unam.mx/2001/abr01/010403/017a1pol.html> (accessed 3 April 2001).

Block, F. and M. Somers (1984) 'Beyond the Economistic Fallacy: The Holistic Social Science of Karl Polanyi', pp. 47–84 in T. Skocpol (ed.), *Vision and Method in Historical Sociology*. New York: Cambridge University Press.

Bonilla Macharro, C. (1975) *Caña amarga: Ingenio San Crisóbal 1972–73*. Mexico City: Publicidad Editora.

Boshier, D. H., C. E. Hughes and W. D. Hawthorne (1999) 'Biological Criteria for Corridor Selection and Design'. Global Environment Facility, Meso-american Biological Corridor Project, Mexico, and Department of Plant Sciences, Oxford.

Bourdieu, P. (1989) 'Social Space and Symbolic Power', *Sociological Theory*, 7(1): 14–25.

Boyer, R. (1990) *The Regulation School: A Critical Introduction*. New York: Columbia University Press.

Brachet-Márquez, V. (1996) *El pacto de dominación: Estado, clase y reforma social en México (1910–1995)*. Mexico City: Colegio de México.

Braidotti, R., E. Charkiewicz-Pluta, S. Hausler and S. Wieringa (eds) (1994)

Women, the Environment, and Sustainable Development: Toward a Theoretical Synthesis. London: Zed Books.

Brandes, S. (1988) *Power and Persuasion: Fiesta and Social Control in Rural Mexico.* Philadelphia, PA: University of Pennsylvania Press.

Bruhn, K. (1997) *Taking on the Goliath: The Emergence of a New Left Party and the Struggle for Democracy in Mexico.* University Park, PA: Pennsylvania State University Press.

Brysk, A. (2000) *From Tribal Village to Global Village: Indian Rights and International Relations in Latin America.* Stanford, CA: Stanford University Press.

Burguette Cal y Mayor, A. (ed.) (2000) *Indigenous Autonomy in Mexico.* Copenhagen: International Work Group for Indigenous Affairs.

Busch, L. and A. Juska (1997) 'Beyond Political Economy: Actor Networks and the Globalization of Agriculture', *Science, Technology, and Human Values,* 21(1): 3–27.

Calva, J. L. (2000) *México más allá del Neoliberalismo. Opciones dentro del cambio.* Mexico: Plaza y Janés.

— (1994) 'La reforma neoliberal del régimen agrario mexicano: implicaciones en el largo plazo', in E. Ochoa and D. Loren (eds), *Estado y agricultura en México. Antecedentes e implicaciones de las reformas salinistas.* Mexico City: Universidad Autónoma Metropolitana.

Camacho, M. (1988) *El futuro inmediato.* Mexico City: UNAM-Siglo XXI Editores.

Cancian, F. (1965) *Economics and Prestige in a Maya Community: The Religious Cargo System in Zinacantan.* Stanford, CA: Stanford University Press.

Cano Vega, R. (1995) 'Antecedentes, situación actual y perspectivas de la comercialización del aguacate en el estado de Michoacán', Thesis, Facultad de Agrobiología, Universidad Michoacana de San Nicolás de Hidalgo, Uruapan, Michoacán (unpublished).

CAPAs (Central American Protected Areas) (2000) *Hoja Informativa,* 10, January. Available at <www.capas.org/pdf/hoja/10.web.pdf> (accessed May 2002).

Carlsen, L. (2002) 'Self Determination and Indigenous Autonomy in Latin America: One Step Forward, Two Steps Back'. Available in Self Determination profiles at Foreign Policy in Focus website: <www.fpif.org>.

Carrillo, J. and M. E. de la O (2002) 'Condiciones y relaciones de trabajo en la maquila', in E. de la Garza and C. Solas (eds), *La situación del trabajo en México.* Mexico City: AFL-CIO.

Carruthers, D. V. (1995) 'Agroecology in Mexico: Linking Environmental and Indigenous Struggles', Paper presented at Conference on the Politics of Sustainable Agriculture, University of Oregon, Eugene, 7–8 October.

Castañeda, J. (2001) 'Los ejes de la política exterior de México', *Nexos,* 288: 66–74.

Castellanos Castellanos, J. A. (2000) 'Por una nueva cultura gremial', Paper presented at the Seminario Nacional: Estrategias para el Cambio en el Campo Mexicano, Chapingo, Universidad Autónoma de Chapingo.

Castles, S. and M. J. Miller (1998) *The Age of Migration. International Population Movements in the Modern World,* 2nd edn. London: Macmillan.

Castro Salazar, M. (2000) Speech made in Managua, Nicaragua, 11 April 2000, to inaugurate the project for a Mesoamerican Biological Corridor. Available at: <www.undp.org.ni/cbm/discurso_mauricio_castro.htm>. Translated by the author (accessed 28 January 2003).

CELADE (2001a) 'Urbanización y evolución de la población urbana de América Latina (1950–90)', *Boletín Demográfico* (Edición Especial) (LC/G.2140-P/E).

— (2001b) 'América Latina: población por años calendarios y edades simples 1950–2050', *Boletín Demográfico*, 66 (LC/G.2099-P/E).

Celis, F., G. Ejea and L. Hernandez Navarro (1991) *Cafetaleros la construcción de la autonomía*. Mexico City: Coordinadora Nacional de Organizaciones Cafetaleras.

CEPAL (2001) *México: evolución económica durante 2000* (LC/MEX/L.468). Mexico: CEPAL.

Chand, V. K. (2001) *Mexico's Political Awakening*. Notre Dame, IN: University of Notre Dame Press.

Charles, J. (1999) 'Searching for Gold in Guacamole: California Growers Market the Avocado, 1910–1914', Paper presented at the conference, Food and Drink in Consumer Societies, Wilmington, DE, 11 November.

Chauvet, M. (1994) 'El desafío de la modernización ganadera en México: del rancho familiar a la empresa ganadera', in E. Ochoa and D. Loren (eds), *Estado y agricultura en México. Antecedentes e implicaciones de las reformas salinistas*. Mexico City: Universidad Autónoma Metropolitana.

Chollett, D. (1996) 'Culture, Ideology, and Community. The Dynamics of Accommodation and Resistance to Restructuring of the Mexican Sugar Sector', *Culture & Agriculture*, 18(3): 98–109.

CICAFOC (1996) Letter to directors of MBC. Available at: <www.cicafoc.com> (accessed May 2002).

Clements, H. P. (1996) 'Hitting the Wall and Changing the Question: Studying Folk Art Production in Oaxaca', Paper presented at the annual meeting of the American Anthropological Association Meeting, San Francisco, November.

CMSD (1992) *Foleto del Mueso Shan-Dany. Santa Ana del Valle, Tlacolula, Oaxaca*. Comite del Museo Shan-Dany, Instituto Nacional de Antropología e Historia, y Gobierno Constitucional de Santa Ana del Valle, Tlacolula, Oaxaca. CNI (2000) <www.biodiversidadla.org/documentos/documentos124.htm>.

CNIAA (Cámara Nacional de la Agroindustria Azucarera y Alcoholera) (2001) 'Situatión y Problemática de la Industria Azucarera Mexicana', Mexico City, June (internal document).

Cockcroft, J. D. (1983) *Mexico: Class Formation, Capital Accumulation, and the State*. New York: Monthly Review Press.

Cohen, J. H. (2001a) 'The Shan-Dany Museum: Community, Economics and Cultural Traditions in a Rural Mexican Village', *Human Organization*, 60: 272–80.

— (2001b) 'Transnational Migration in Rural Oaxaca, Mexico: Dependency, Development and the Household', *American Anthropologist*, 103: 954–67.

— (1999) *Cooperation and Community: Economy and Society in Oaxaca*. Austin, TX: University of Texas Press.

— (1998) 'Craft Production and the Challenge of the Global Market: An Artisans' Cooperative in Oaxaca, Mexico', *Human Organization*, 57: 74–82.

Collier, G. A. (1999) *Basta! Land and the Zapatista Rebellion in Chiapas*, rev. edn. Oakland, CA: Food First.

— (1995) 'Structural Adjustment and New Regional Movements: The Zapatista Rebellion in Chiapas', *Ethnic Conflicts and Governance in Comparative Perspective*, Working Papers Series, 45. Washington, DC: Woodrow Wilson Center for Information, pp. 28–50.

Collins, P. H. (2000) *Black Feminist Thought: Knowledge, Consciousness, and the Politics of Empowerment*. New York: Routledge.

Comaroff, J. and J. Comaroff (1985) *Ethnography and the Historical Imagination*. Boulder, CO: Westview Press.

Commission for Environmental Cooperation (1999) 'Measuring Consumer Interest in Mexican Shade-grown Coffee: An Assessment of the Canadian, Mexican and US Markets', CEC Report, Montreal, Canada (37 pp.).

CONAPO (Consejo Nacional de Población) (1999) *Proyecciones de la población económicamente activa*. Mexico City: CONAPO. Available at: <http://www.conapo.gob.mx/m_en_cifras/5_1.htm>.

Cook, S. (1984) *Peasant Capitalist Industry: Piecework and Enterprise in Southern Mexican Brickyards*. Lanham, MA: University Press of America.

Cook, S. and L. Binford (1990) *Obliging Need: Rural Petty Industry in Mexican Capitalism*. Austin, TX: University of Texas Press.

Cordero Díaz, B. (1998) 'La política cotidiana de los cañeros y el estado en un ingenio de Michoacán 1975–1990', *Regiones* (Universidad de Guanajuato), 9 (February–June): 98–120.

Córdova, A. (1972) *La formación del poder político en México*. Mexico City: Ediciones Era.

— (1974) *La política de masas del cardenismo*. Mexico City: Ediciones Era.

— (1991) 'Diez lecciones de la reforma económica en México', *Nexos*, 158: 31–49.

Cornelius, W. (1996) *Mexican Politics in Transition: The Breakdown of a One-Party-Dominant Regime*. La Jolla, CA: Center for US–Mexican Studies, University of California, San Diego.

Cornelius, W. and D. Myhre (eds) (1998) *The Transformation of Rural Mexico: Reforming the Ejido Sector*. La Jolla, CA: Center for US–Mexican Studies, University of California, San Diego.

Corona, R. (2001) 'Monto y Uso de las Remesas en México', *El Mercado de Valores*, 61(8): 27–46.

Cortéz, W. W. (2001) 'What is Behind Increasing Wage Inequality in Mexico?' *World Development*, 29(11): 1,905–22.

Covarrubias, A. (1992) *La flexibilidad laboral en Sonora*. Hermosillo: Colegio de Sonora.

Craig, J. (1994) 'La teoría de la movilización de recursos y el estudio de los movimientos sociales', *Zona Abierta*, 69.

Craipeau, C. (1993) 'Actitudes Diferenciadas De Los Pequeños Productores En

Zonas Cafetaleras Marginales, Costa Rica', Paper presented at the Simposio Latinoamericano De Modernización Tecnológica, Costa Rica.

Cunningham, N. and M. Young (2001) 'Redesigning Environmental Regulation. The Case of Biodiversity Conservation'. Available at: <www.elaw.org/resources/text.asp?ID=705> (accessed May 2002).

Cypher, J. M. (2001) 'Developing Disarticulation within Mexican Economy', *Latin American Perspectives*, 28(3): 11–37.

— (2000) 'El modelo de desarrollo por la vía de exportaciones: el caso de México', Paper presented at the Segunda Conferencia Internacional: Los Retos Actuales de la Teoría del Desarrollo, Red Eurolatinoamericana de Estudios sobre el Desarrollo Económico Celso Furtado, Mexico, 17–20 October.

Dávila, E., G. Kessel and S. Levy (2000) 'El Sur también existe: Un ensayo sobre el desarrollo regional de México' [The South Also Exists: An Essay on Regional Development in Mexico]. Subsecretaría de Egresos, Secretaría de Hacienda y Crédito Público (photocopy).

Day, R. J. F. (2000) *Multiculturalism and the History of Canadian Diversity*. Toronto: University of Toronto Press.

de Grammont, H. C. (2001) 'El Barzón, un movimiento social inserto en la transición hacia la democracia política en México', in N. Giarracca (ed.), *¿Una nueva ruralidad en América Latina?* Buenos Aires: CLACSO, Colección Grupos de Trabajo.

— (2000) 'El Barzón ¿un movimiento social en contra de la crisis económica, o un movimiento social de nuevo cuño?' CD: *El ajuste estructural en el campo mexicano*. Mexico City: Asociación Mexicana de Estudios Rurales, SAGAR, UNAM and IICA.

— (1994) 'La organización gremial de los agricultores frente a los procesos de globalización', Paper presented in 'México al Mediodía', Seminar Series, Center for Latin American Studies, Austin, TX: University of Texas.

— (1979) 'Historia de las luchas sociales en la zona cañera de Atencingo', pp. 185–262 in L. Paré (ed.), *Ensayos sobre el problema cañero*. Mexico City: Universidad Nacional Autonóma de México.

de Grammont, H. C., M. Angel Gómez Cruz, H. González and R. Schwentesius Rindermann (eds) (1999) *Agricultura de exportación en tiempos de globalización: el caso de las hortalizas, frutas y flores*. Mexico City: Juan Pablo, Editores.

de la Garza, E. (2001) *La formación socioeconomica neoliberal*. Mexico City: Plaza y Valdés.

— (1998) *Modelos de industrialización en México*. Mexico City: UAM-I.

— (1994) 'El corporativismo: teoría y transformación', *Iztapalapa*, 34 (July–December): 11–28.

— (1993) *Reestructuración productiva y respuesta sindical en México*. Mexico City: UNAM.

— (1990a) 'La crisis del sindicalismo en México', in G. Bensusán (ed.), *Estado y Sindicatos en México*. Mexico City: UAM-Xochimilco-Fundación Ebert.

— (1990b) 'Reconversión industrial y cambio en el patrón de relaciones de trabajo en México', in A. Anguiano (ed.), *La modernización de México*. Mexico City: UAM-X.

de la Garza, E. and J. Melgoza (1994) 'Estrategias sindicales y productividad en México', Paper prepared for the seminar Inequalities and New Forms of Popular Representation in Latin America, Columbia University, New York.

de la Peña, G. (1997) 'Sobre la ciudadanía étnica', Paper presented at the 21st meeting of the Latin American Studies Association, Guadalajara, Mexico, April.

Delgado, R. and G. Carlo (2002) *La Amenaza Biológica. Mitos y falsas promesas de la biotecnología*. Mexico City: Plaza y Janés.

Delgado Wise, R. and O. Mañán (2000) 'México: the Dialectics of Export Growth', *Working Papers in International Development*, 2 October 2000, Halifax, Nova Scotia: Saint Mary's University.

Delgado Wise, R. and H. Rodríguez (2001) 'The Emergence of Collective Migrants and Their Role in Mexico's Local and Regional Development', *Canadian Journal of Development Studies*, 22(3): 747–64.

DeWalt, B. R. and M. W. Rees, with A. D. Murphy (1994) *The End of Agrarian Reform in Mexico: Past Lessons, Future Prospects*. Transformation of Rural Mexico Series, 3, *Ejido* Reform Research Project. La Jolla, CA: Center for US–Mexican Studies, University of California, San Diego.

Díaz-Polanco, H. and C. Sánchez (2003) *México diverso: El debate por la autonomía*. Mexico City: Siglo XXI Editores.

Dicum, G. and N. Luttinger (1999) *The Coffee Book Anatomy of an Industry from Crop to the Last Drop*. New York: New Press.

Doering, D., A. Casara, C. Layke, J. Ranganathan, C. Revenga, D. Tunstall and W. Vanasselt (2002) *Tomorrow's Markets: Global Trends and Their Implications for Business*. World Resources Institute, UN Environment Programme, World Business Council for Sustainable Development.

Dornbusch, R. and S. Fisher (1978) *Macroeconomics*. New York: McGraw-Hill.

Dunlop, J. T. (1958) *Industrial Relations System*. New York: Henry Holt.

Dussel Peters, E. (1997) *La economía de la polarización*. Mexico City: Ed. JUS.

— (ed.) (2001) *Claroscuros. Integración exitosa de las pequeñas y medianas empresas en México*. México: CEPAL, CANACINTRA and JUS.

— (2000) *Polarizing Mexico. The Impact of Liberalization Strategy*. Boulder, CO and London: Lynne Rienner.

— (1996) 'From Export-Oriented to Import-Oriented Industrialization: Changes in Mexico's Manufacturing Sector, 1984–1994', pp. 63–83 in G. Otero (ed.), *Neoliberalism Revisited*.

Dussel Peters, E., L. M. Galindo and E. Loría (2003) *Visión microeconómica de los impactos de la integración regional en la inversión inter e intrarregionales. El caso de la inversión extranjera directa en México*. Buenos Aires: UNAM-BID/INTAL, Segunda Convocatoria (mimeo).

The Economist (2002) 'Mexico's Farmers: Floundering in a Tariff-Free Landscape', *The Economist*, 30 November, pp. 31–2.

Edwards, S. and S. J. Burki (1995) *Latin America After Mexico: Quickening the Pace*. Washington, DC: World Bank.

El-Guindi, F. and H. A. Selby (1976) 'Dialectics in Zapotec Thinking', in K. H.

Basso and H. A. Selby (eds), *Meaning in Anthropology*. Albuquerque, NM: University of New Mexico Press.

Espinosa, G. (1999) 'Modelo infalible para armar una crisis. El caso de la agro-industria cañero-azucarera', *Nueva Epoca*, 17–18: 142–63.

— (1993) 'La reforma agraria y el nuevo modelo agroindustrial 1935–1947', pp. 125–58 in A. Bartra (ed.), *De haciendas, cañeros y paraestatales*.

Espinosa, G. and J. Manuel Aurrecoechea (1998) 'Privatización del ingenio Emiliano Zapata y sus efectos en en el empleo y el desarrollo regional', pp. 305–50 in L. Concheiro B. and M. Torrío G. (eds), *Privatización en el mundo rural. Las historias de un desencuentro*. Mexico City: UAM Xochimilco.

— (1993) 'La década de las sesenta. De la crisis de sobreexplotación a la expansión sostenida con exportaciones crecientes', pp. 187–213 in A. Bartra (ed.), *De haciendas, cañeros y paraestatales*.

Esteva, G. (1999) 'The Zapatistas and People's Power', *Capital & Class*, 68 (Summer): 153–83.

EZLN (1994) 'First Declaration from the Lacandón Jungle'. Available at: <http://www.ezln.org/documentos/1994/199312xx.en.htm> (accessed 1 January 2003).

Facultad de Agrobiología (1999) 'Control fitosanitario en la movilización de aguacate'. Memorias: Octavo evento de aprobación y quinto evento de actualización en el manejo fitosanitario del aguacatero (NOM-066-FITO-1995), 24–28 May.

Feder, E. (1978) *Capital Financiero y Descomposición del Campesinado*. Bogotá: Punta de Lanza.

Fentanes, C. (1995) *Los actos ilícitos de la banca y los jueces. Aspectos jurídicos del capitalismo salvaje mexicano* (privately published).

Flores Lúa, G. (1987) 'Historia de las organizaciones cañeras: 1940–1972', pp. 46–84 in L. Paré (ed.), *El estado*.

Foweraker, J. (1988) 'Movimientos populares y transformaciones del sistema político mexicano', *Revista Mexicana de Sociología*, 51(4).

Fox, J. (1997) 'The World Bank and Social Capital: Contesting the Concept', *Journal of International Development*, 9(7): 963–71.

— (1996) 'How Does Civil Society Thicken? The Political Construction of Social Capital in Rural Mexico', *World Development*, 24(6): 1,089–103.

— (1994) 'Political Change in Mexico's New Peasant Economy', in *The Politics of Economic Restructuring. State-Society Relations*. La Jolla, CA: Center for US–Mexican Studies, University of California, San Diego.

Fox, J. and J. Aranda (1996) *Decentralization and Rural Development in Mexico: Community Participation in Oaxaca's Municipal Funds Program*. La Jolla, CA: Center for US–Mexican Studies, University of California, San Diego.

Fox, J. and G. Gordillo (1991) 'Entre el Estado y el mercado: perspectivas para un desarrollo autónomo en el campo mexicano', pp. 47–100 in A. Bartra et al., *Los nuevos sujetos del desarrollo rural*, Cuadernos de desarrollo de base, 2. Mexico City: ADN Editores.

Fox, V. (2001) 'Anexo Estadístico del Primer Informe de Gobierno', Mexico: Oficina de la Presidencia de la República.

Franco Mendosa, M. (2000) 'The Debate Concerning Indigenous Rights in Mexico', pp. 57–76 in Assies et al. (eds), *The Challenge of Diversity*.

Friedland, W. (1994) 'The Global Fresh Fruit and Vegetable System: An Industrial Organization Analysis', in P. McMichael (ed.), *The Global Restructuring of Agro-Food Systems*.

Friedland, W., L. Busch, F. Buttel and A. Rudy (eds) (1991) *Towards a New Political Economy of Agriculture*. Boulder, CO: Westview Press.

Fujii, G. (2000) 'El comercio exterior manufacturero y los límites al crecimiento económico de México', *Comercio Exterior*, 50(11): 954–67.

García Canclini, N. (1993) *Transforming Modernity: Popular Culture in Mexico*, trans. L. Lozano, Austin, TX: University of Texas Press.

García Chávez, L. R. (1998) *La industria de la fructuosa: Su impacto en la agroindustria azucarera mexicana*. Chapingo: Universidad Autónoma de Chapingo – CIESTAAM.

— (1997) *La agroindustria azucarera de México frente a la apertura econónica*. Chapingo: Universidad Autónoma de Chapingo – CIESTAAM.

García Guzmán, M. (1999) 'Situación actual del barrenador pequeño del hueso (Conotrachelus aguacatae) en el Estado de Michoacán', *El Aguacatero*, 2(8).

— (1998) 'Norma Oficial Mexicana y Cartilla Fitosanitaria', *El Aguacatero*, 1(2).

— (1997) 'Exportación del aguacate hacia los Estados Unidos', *El Aguacatero*, 1(1).

García y Griego, M. (1988) 'Hacia una nueva visión del problema de los indocumentados en EU', pp. 139–53 in M. García y Griego and M. Verea (eds), *México y EU frente a la migración de los indocumentados*. Mexico City: UNAM and Miguel Ángel Porrúa.

García Zamora, R. and M. Moctezuma (2001) 'Trabajadores Temporales contratados por EU. Informe sobre el programa piloto del Gobierno de Zacatecas', Paper presented in Mesa Redonda Binacional, Programa de Trabajadores Temporales México-EU, Guadalajara, Mexico, 16 May.

Garrido, C. and C. Leriche (1998) 'Grandes grupos empresariales privados nacionales, crisis bancarias y Fobaproa', *El Cotidiano. Revista de la realidad mexicana actual* (Universidad Metropolitana), 15, November–December: 16–26.

Gilbreth, C. and G. Otero (2001) 'Democratization in Mexico: The Zapatista Uprising and Civil Society', *Latin American Perspectives*, 119, 28(4): 7–29.

Gilly, A. (1974) *La revolución interrumpida*, 4th edn. Mexico City: Editorial El Caballito.

Girón, A. (1994) 'La banca comercial de México frente al TLC', *Comercio Exterior* 44(12): 1,068–74.

Giugale, M. M., O. Lafourcade and V. H. Nguyen (eds) (2001) *Mexico: A Comprehensive Development Agenda for the New Era*. Washington, DC: World Bank.

Glyn, A., A. Hughes, A. Lipietz and A. Singh (1989) 'The Rise and Fall of the Golden Age', pp. 39–125 in S. A. Marglin and J. Schor (eds), *The Golden Age of Capitalism*. Oxford: Clarendon Press.

Gobierno del Estado de Michoacán (1997) 'Reglamento de la Ley de Organizaciones Agrícolas del Estado de Michoacán de Ocampo' (unpublished document).

Gómez Carpinteiro, F. (1998) *Tanto que costó. Clase, cultura y nueva ley agraria en un ejido*. Mexico City: Instituto Nacional de Antropología e Historia.

González, H. (1995) 'Movimiento "El Barzón": una contrapropuesta al neoliberalismo autoritario del Estado Mexicano', in J. Arroyo and D. Loren (eds), *Impactos regionales de la apertura comercial. Perspectivas del Tratado de Libre Comercio en Jalisco*. Mexico: University of Guadalajara Press.

— (1993) 'Liberalización económica y agricultura de exportación en la región costa de Jalisco', in J. Arroyo and D. Loren (eds), *Impactos regionales de la apertura comercial. Perspectivas del Tratado de Libre Comercio en Jalisco*. Mexico: University of Guadalajara Press.

Gordillo, G. (1988a) *Estado, mercado y movimiento campesino*. Mexico City: Plaza y Valdés.

— (1988b) *Campesinos asalto al cielo: una reforma agraria con autonomía*. Mexico City: Siglo XXI Editores.

GRAIN (1996) 'Investing in Destruction – The World Bank and Biodiversity'. Available at: <www.grain.org/publications/bio8-en-p.htm>.

Gramsci, A. (1971) *Selections from the Prison Notebooks*, ed. and trans. Q. Hoare and G. Nowell Smith. New York: International Publishers.

Greenfield, M. (1994) 'Alternative Trade: Giving Coffee a New Flavor', *Making Coffee Strong*, Boston, MA: Equal Exchange.

Grupo de Trabajo Colectivo del Istmo de Tehuantepec (T. Angel, L. Antonio, A. Román, W. Call, M. Godinez, L. Gómez, C. Beas) (2001) 'Un Territorio en Disputa: El Plan Puebla Panamá en el Istmo de Tehuantepec' (unpublished document).

Guillén, G. (2001) 'Erradicarán crimen de áreas naturales', *El Universal*, 25 December.

Guillén, H. (1997) *La contrarrevolución neoliberal*. Mexico City: Era.

Habermas, J. (1981) *Theorie des kommunikativen Handelns*, 2 vols. Frankfurt/Main: Suhrkamp.

Hale, C. A. (1996) 'Political Ideas and Ideologies in Latin America, 1870–1930', pp. 133–206 in L. Bethell (ed.), *Ideas and Ideologies in Twentieth Century Latin America*. New York: Cambridge University Press.

Haraway, D. (1991) *Simians, Cyborgs, and Women: The Reinvention of Nature*. New York: Routledge.

Hardner, J. and R. Rice (2002) 'Rethinking Green Consumerism', *Scientific American*, May.

Harvey, N. (2002) 'PPP y derechos indígenas', *La Jornada*, 28 December. Available at: <http://www.jornada.unam.mx/2002/dic02/021228/013a1pol.php?orige n=opinion.html> (accessed 28 December 2002).

— (1998) *The Chiapas Rebellion: The Struggle for Land and Democracy*. Durham, NC: Duke University Press.

— (1996) 'Rural Reforms and the Zapatista Rebellion: Chiapas 1988–95', pp. 187–208 in Otero (ed.), *Neoliberalism Revisited*.

— (1994) *Rebellion in Chiapas: Rural Reforms, Campesino Radicalism, and the Limits to Salinismo*. La Jolla, CA: Center for US–Mexican Studies, University of California, San Diego.

Hellman, J. A. (1983) *Mexico in Crisis*, 2nd edn. New York: Holmes and Meir.

Hernández, R. (1994) 'Inestabilidad política y presidencialismo en México', *Mexican Studies*, 10(1): 187–216.

Hernández Laos, E. (2000) *La competitividad industrial en México*. Mexico City: UAM/Plaza y Valdés Editores.

Hernández Navarro, L. and R. Vera Herrera (eds) (1998) *Acuerdos de San Andrés*. Mexico City: Ediciones Era.

Hewitt de Alcántara, C. (1984) *Anthropological Perspectives on Rural Mexico*. Boston, MA: Routledge and Kegan Paul.

— (1978) *Modernización de la agricultura mexicana*. Mexico City: Siglo XXI Editores.

Hidalgo Monroy, N. (1996) 'Organic Agriculture and Indigenous Communities in Chiapas, Mexico: An Alternative to Rural Development', Dissertation, Geography Department, University of California, Berkeley, CA.

Hulshof, M. (1991) *Zapotec Moves: Networks and Remittances of US Bound Migrants from Oaxaca, Mexico*. Amsterdam: University of Amsterdam.

IDB (2001) 'Puebla Panama Plan Finance Committee Analyses Outlook for Regional Integration and Development Projects', Press release, 7 August.

Iguarrúa, G. and F. Mestries (1987) 'El movimiento cañero de Veracruz a principios de los setenta', pp. 87–165 in Paré (ed.), *El estado*.

INEGI (Instituto Nacional de Estadística, Geografía e Informática) (2002) *Banco de Información Estadística*. Mexico City: INEGI. Available at <http://www.inegi.gob.mx>.

La Jornada (2002) 'Declaración del Presidente de la Comisión Nacional de Salarios Mínimos', 11 July.

— (2001) 'Quebrado, el modelo de subsistencia de los pueblos indios, dice Gálvez', 19 September.

Junguito, R. and D. Pizano (1993) *El Comercio Exterior y La Política Internacional Del Café*. Colombia: Fedesarrollo, Fondo Cultural Cafetalero.

Karl, T. L. (1990) 'Dilemmas of Democratization in Latin America', *Comparative Politics*, 23 (October): 1–21.

Katz, F. 1982. *La guerra secreta en México*, 2 vols. Mexico City: Ediciones Era.

Kearney, M. (2000) 'Transnational Oaxacan Indigenous Identity: The Case of Mixtecs and Zapotecs', *Identities*, 7: 173–95.

— (1996) *Reconceptualizing the Peasantry: Anthropology in Global Perspective*. Boulder, CO: Westview Press.

Kearney, M. and S. Varese (1995) 'Latin America's Indigenous Peoples: Changing Identities and Forms of Resistance', pp. 207–31 in R. L. Harris and S. Halebsky (eds), *Capital, Power, and Inequality in Latin America*. Boulder, CO, and Oxford: Westview Press.

Kerr, C. and P. D. Staudohar (eds) (1994) *Labor Economics and Industrial Relations. Markets and Institutions*. Cambridge, MA: Harvard University Press.

Kicza, J. E. (2000) 'Introduction', pp. xiii–xxviii in J. E. Kicza, *The Indian in Latin American History: Resistance, Resilience, and Acculturation*, rev. edn. Wilmington, DE: Scholarly Resources.

Kopinak, K. (1997) *Desert Capitalism: What are the Maquiladoras?* Montreal: Black Rose Books.

Krueger, A. (1983) *Trade and Employment in Developing Countries*. Oxford: Basil Blackwell.

— (1978) *Liberalization Attempts and Consequences*. Cambridge: Ballinger.

Kymlicka, W. (1995) *Multicultural Citizenship: A Liberal Theory of Minority Rights*. Oxford: Oxford University Press.

Kymlicka, W. and W. Norman (2000) 'Citizenship in Culturally Diverse Societies: Issues, Contexts, and Concepts', pp. 1–41 in W. Kymlicka and W. Norman (eds), *Citizenship in Diverse Societies*. Oxford: Oxford University Press.

Kymlicka, W. and M. Opalski (eds) (2001) *Can Liberal Pluralism be Exported? Western Political Theory and Ethnic Relations in Eastern Europe*. New York: Oxford University Press.

Laclau, E. and C. Mouffe (1985) *Hegemony and Socialist Strategy: Towards a Radical Democratic Politics*. London: Verso.

Lara, S. (1998a) 'Feminización de los Procesos de Trabajo del Sector Fruti hortícola en el Estado de Sinaloa', *Cuicuilco*, 21 (April–June): 29–36.

— (1998b) *Nuevas Experiencias Productivas y Nuevas Formas de Organizacion Flexible del Trabajo en la Agricultura Mexicana*. Mexico City: Juan Pablos.

— (1994) 'La Flexibilidad del Mercado del Trabajo Rural', *Revista Mexicana de Sociologia*, 54(1) (January–February): 41.

Lara Flores, S. and M. Chauvet (eds) (1996) *La inserción de la agricultura mexicana en la economía mundial*, Vol. I of *La sociedad rural mexicana frente al nuevo milenio*, H. C. de Grammont and H. Tejera Gaona (series eds). Mexico City: Plaza y Valdés.

Layard, R., S. Nickell and R. Jackman (1991) *Unemployment. Macroeconomic Performance and the Labour Market*. Oxford: Oxford University Press.

Léonard, E. and H. Mackinlay (2000) '¿Apropiación privada u organización colectiva? Vicisitudes y expresiones locales de la desincorporación del monopolio estatal Tabamex en el estado de Veracruz', *Alteridades* (Mexico City) 10(19): 123–41.

Levy, D. C. and K. Bruhn, with E. Zebadúa (2001) *Mexico: The Struggle for Democratic Development*. Berkeley, Los Angeles, CA, and London: University of California Press.

Littlefield, A. (1978) 'Exploitation and the Expansion of Capitalism: The Case of the Hammock Industry of Yucatan', *American Ethnologist*, 5: 495–508.

Llambí, L. (1994) 'Comparative Advantages and Disadvantages in Latin American Nontraditional Fruit and Vegetable Exports', pp. 190–213 in P. McMichael (ed.), *The Global Restructuring of Agro-Food Systems*.

Loaeza, S. (1999) *El Partido Acción Nacional: La larga marcha, 1939–1994: Oposición leal y partido de protesta*. Mexico City: Fondo de Cultura Económica.

Lombana Mejia, P. M. (1991) *Café Año 2000: Investigación Acerca de los Efectos del Rompimiento del Pacto de Cuotas del Convenio Internacional del Café*. Manizales, Colombia: Papiro.

López Luján, J. (1998) 'Mensaje editorial: fortalecer nuestra asociación', *El Aguacatero*, 1(3).

López Novo, J. P. (1998) 'Clientelismo', pp. 117–18 in S. Giner, E. Lamo de Espinosa and C. Torres (eds), *Diccionario de Sociología*. Madrid: Ciencias Sociales-Alianza Editorial.

Lozano, F. (2000) 'Experiencias internacionales en el envío y uso de las remesas', pp. 147–66 in R. Tuirán (ed.), *Migración México-Estado Unidos. Opciones de Política*. Mexico City: Secretaría de Gobernación, CONAPO and Secretaría de Relaciones Exteriores.

Luhmann, N. (1984) *Soziale Systeme: Grundriß einer allgemeinen Theorie*. Frankfurt/Main: Suhrkamp.

Luna, M. and R. Pozas (eds) (1992) *Relaciones corporativas en un período de transición*. México City: Instituto de Investigaciones Sociales, Universidad Nacional Autonoma de México (UNAM).

Mackinlay, H. (2002) 'Rural Producers' Organizations and the State in Mexico', in K. Middlebrook (ed.), *Dilemmas of Change in Mexican Politics*. Center for US–Mexican Studies, University of California, San Diego.

— (1999) 'Institutional Transformation in the Tobacco Sector: Collective or Individualized Bargaining?', pp. 9–50 in R. Snyder (ed.), *Institutional Adaptation and Innovation in Rural Mexico*. La Jolla, CA: Center for US–Mexican Studies, University of California, San Diego.

— (1996) 'La CNC y el Nuevo Movimiento Campesino (1989–1994)', pp. 165–238 in H. C. de Grammont (ed.), *Neoliberalismo y organización social en el campo mexicano*. Mexico City: IIS-UNAM, Plaza y Valdéz.

— (1991) 'La política de reparto agrario en México (1917–1990) y las reformas al artículo 27 constitucional', pp. 117–67 in A. Massolo et al. (eds), *Procesos Rurales y Urbanos en el México actual*. Mexico City: Departamento de Sociología, UAM-Iztapalapa.

McMichael, P. (ed.) (1994) *The Global Restructuring of Agro-Food Systems*. Ithaca, NY: Cornell University Press.

Makin, K. (2001) 'Workers' Right to Unionize Backed by Top Court', *Globe and Mail*, 21 December.

Mandel, M. (2002) 'Big Boom, Weak Profits', *Business Week*, 12 August, pp. 30–3.

Marcos (2003), Subcommandante Insurgente. 'Décima etapa/Guerro: La fiscalía especial, trampa del Ejecutivo y Legislativo', *La Jornada*, 19 February. Available at: <http://www.jornada.unam.mx/2003/feb03/030219/006nlpol.php?orige n=index.html> (accessed 19 February 2003).

Martínez, J. (1999) 'Los emigrados y la nación mexicana: la evolución de una relación', pp. 241–59 in M. Moctezuma and H. Rodríguez (eds), *Impacto de la Migración y las Remesas en Crecimiento Económico Regional*. Mexico City: Senado de la República.

Martinez-Salazar, E. (1999) 'The Poisoning of Indigenous Migrant Women Workers and Children: From Deadly Colonialism to Toxic Globalization', pp. 100–109 in D. Barndt (ed.), *Women Working the NAFTA Food Chain: Women, Food, and Globalization*. Toronto: Sumach Press.

Martínez-Torres, M. E. (2003) 'Sustainable Development, Campesino Organizations and Technological Change among Small Coffee Producers in Chiapas, Mexico'. PhD Dissertation, University of California-Berkeley.

Matos, D. (1993) 'Proceso de construcción de identidades transnacionales en América Latina en tiempos de globalización', in D. Matos (ed.), *Teoría y política de la construcción de identidades y diferencias en América Latina y el Caribe*. Caracas: UNESCO and Editorial Nueva Sociedad.

Meda, D. (1995) 'From Cultural Survival and Liberation Theology to Medflies and Political Assassinations: A Study of the ISMAM Cooperative of Chiapas, Mexico', Paper presented to the 'Politics of Sustainable Agriculture' Conference, University of Oregon at Eugene, 1–8 October.

Medea, B. (1993) *Directory of ATOs in the U.S. and Canada*. San Francisco, CA: Global Exchange.

Medin, T. (1972) *Ideología y praxis política de Lázaro Cárdenas*. Mexico City: Siglo XXI Editores.

Mestries, F. (2000a) 'Globalización, crisis azucarera y luchas cañeras en los años noventa', *Sociología* 15(44): 41–68.

— (2000b) 'El Brazón ¿Asociación ciudadana, organización de productores o movimiento político?', CD: *El ajuste estructural en el campo mexicano*. Mexico City: Asociación Mexicana de Estudios Rurales, SAGAR, UNAM and IICA.

Meyer, L. (1977) 'Historical Roots of the Authoritarian State in Mexico', pp. 19–22 in J. L. Reina and R. Winert (eds), *Authoritarianism in Mexico*. Philadelphia, PA: Institute for the Study of Human Issues.

Michl, T. R. (1988) 'The Two-Stage Decline in U.S. Nonfinancial Corporate Profitability, 1948–1986', *Review of Radical Political Economics*, 20(4).

Miller, S. and A. Seymour (2001) 'Third Binational Roundtable on Mexico–U.S. Migration: The New Bilatiralism', *Mexico-U.S. Advocates Network News*, 12. Available at: <http://www.enlacesamerica.org/news_esp/newsarchivespdf/Mexico_US_Adv_Ntwk_1101.pdf> (accessed 22 February 2002).

Mitter, S. (1986) *Common Fate, Common Bond*. London: Pluto Press.

Moctezuma, M. (2001) 'Clubes Zacatecanos en los EU. Un Capital Social en Proceso', Paper presented at Segundo Seminario sobre Migración Internacional, Remesas y Desarrollo Regional, Zacatecas, Mexico, 21–22 September.

Mohar, G. (2001) 'Historia Reciente y Debate en EU sobre Migración y Presencia de los Mexicanos', *El Mercado de Valores* 61(8): 47–55.

Mondragón, Y. (1994) 'Cambio en la relación corporativa entre Estado y sindicatos: el caso del STRM, 1987–1994', Thesis, Instituto Dr José María Luis Mora, Mexico City.

Montiel, Y. (1991) *Organización del trabajo y relaciones de trabajo en VW de México*. Mexico City: Cuadernos de la Casa Chata.

Mountz, A. and R. Wright (1996) 'Daily Life in the Transnational Migrant Community of San Agustín, Oaxaca and Poughkeepsie, New York', *Diaspora*, 5: 403–28.

Muir, J. (1901) *Our National Parks*. Cambridge, MA: Riverside Press.

Murray, D. L. and L. T. Raynolds (2000) 'Alternative Trade in Bananas: Obstacles and Opportunities for Progressive Social Change in the Global Economy', *Agriculture and Human Values*, 17: 65–74.

Myhre, D. (1998) 'The Achilles' Heel of the Reforms: The Rural Financial

System', pp. 39–65 in W. Cornelius and D. Myhre (eds), *The Transformation of Rural Mexico*.

Nader, L. (1990) *Harmony Ideology: Justice and Control in a Zapotec Mountain Village*. Stanford, CA: Stanford University Press.

Nash, M. (1989) *The Cauldron of Ethnicity in the Modern World*. Chicago, IL: University of Chicago Press.

Nigh, R. (1997) 'Organic Agriculture and Globalization: A Maya Associative Corporation in Chiapas, Mexico', *Human Organization*, 56(4): 427–36.

North American CEC (Commission for Environmental Cooperation) (1999) 'Measuring Consumer Interest in Mexican Shade-grown Coffee', 10 January. Available at: <www.cec.org/files/pdf/ECONOMY/shade-e_EN.pdf> (accessed May 2002).

Nuñez, Ma. C. (1995) '¿Nuevos Actores Sociales en el Campo Cañero Mexicano? Los Productores de Caña Frente a la Reestructuración de la Agroindustria Azucarera', pp. 55–62 in P. Singelmann (ed.), *Mexican Sugar Cane Growers: Economic Restructuring and Political Options*, Transformation of Rural Mexico No. 7. La Jolla, CA: Center for US–Mexican Studies, University of California, San Diego.

O'Donnell, G. and P. C. Schmitter (1986) *Tentative Conclusions about Uncertain Transitions*. Baltimore, MD: Johns Hopkins University Press.

Ortega Riquelme, J. M. (1997) 'Sobre el desarrollo de la teoría del neocorporativismo', *Revista Mexicana de Sociología*, 59(4): 31–45.

Otero, G. (2003) 'The Indian Question in Latin America: Class, State and Ethnic Identity Construction', *Latin American Research Review*, 38(1): 248–66.

— (1999) *Farewell to the Peasantry? Political Class Formation in Rural Mexico*. Boulder, CO, and Oxford: Westview Press.

— (1998) 'Atencingo Revisited: Political Class Formation And Economic Restructuring in Mexico's Sugar Industry', *Rural Sociology*, 63(2): 272–99.

— (1996a) 'Mexico's Economic and Political Futures', pp. 233–46 in G. Otero (ed.), *Neoliberalism Revisited*.

— (1996b) 'Neoliberal Reforms and Politics in Mexico: An Overview', pp. 1–26 in G. Otero (ed.), *Neoliberalism Revisited*.

— (ed.) (1996c) *Neoliberalism Revisited: Economic Restructuring and Mexico's Political Future*. Boulder, CO, and London: Westview Press.

— (1989) 'The New Agrarian Movement: Toward Self-Management and Democratic Production', *Latin American Perspectives*, 16(4): 29–59.

— 'Agrarian Reform in Mexico: Capitalism and the State', pp. 276–304 in W. Thiesenhusen (ed.), *Searching for Agrarian Reform in Latin America*. Boston, MA: Unwin Hyman.

Otero, G. and H. Jugenitz (2003) 'Challenging National Borders from Within: The Political-Class Formation of Indigenous Peasants in Latin America', *Canadian Review of Sociology and Anthropology*, 40(3): 503–24.

Panitch, L. (1992) 'El desarrollo del corporativismo en democracias liberales', in P. Schmitter and G. Lehmbruch (eds), *Neocorporativismo I*. Mexico City: Alianza Editorial.

Papail, J. (2001) 'Remesas e inversiones de los ex-migrantes internacionales radicados en áreas urbanas de Jalisco, Guanajuato y Zacatecas', Paper presented at Segundo Seminario sobre Migración Internacional, Remesas y Desarrollo Regional, Zacatecas, Mexico, 21–22 September.

Paré, L. (1987a) 'Insubordinacion de los líderes tradicionales: Las huelgas de la zafra 1974–75', pp. 166–84 in L. Paré (ed.), *El estado, los cañeros y la industria azucarera 1940–1980*. Mexico City: UNAM.

— (1987b) 'Estudio de caso: Aspectos políticos y organizativos de la subordinación del trabajo y de la tierra campesina en la agroindustria azucarera: El caso de la zona cañera del ingenio *La Margarita*, Oaxaca', pp. 247–79 in L. Paré (ed.), *El estado*.

— (1979) 'El análisis económico de las clases sociales de Atencingo', pp. 59–113 in L. Paré (ed.), *Ensayos sobre el problema cañero*. Mexico City: UNAM.

Paré, L. and J. Morett (1987) 'La unificación de las organizaciones cañeras', pp. 202–29 in L. Paré (ed.), *El estado*.

Parra Vazquez, M. R. and R. Moguel Viveros (1996) 'Emergencia de ONG's de cafeticultores indígenas en Chiapas. Estrategias frente a las políticas agrícolas'. San Cristóbal de Las Casas, Chiapas.

Partida Bush, V. (1999) *Proyecciones de la población económicamente activa de la matrícula educativa de los hogares y las viviendas y de la población por tamaño de hogar*. Mexico City: CONAPO.

Paulsen, L. (1999) 'Globalization and Survival of the Smallholder: The Role of Agricultural Restructuring in Land Use Change in Michoacán, Mexico'. MA thesis, University of Arizona.

Paulson, J. (1999) 'Chronological History of the Dialogue between the EZLN and the Mexican Government, 1994–1998'. Available at: <http://www.ezln.org/archivo/fzln/timeline.html> (accessed 1 January 2003).

Paz Vega, R. (1987) 'La organización de los aguacateros en otros paises, módelos para los Michoacanos?', *Fruticultura de Michoacán*, 2, I(12): 11–12, 15, 28.

PEF (Poder Ejecutivo Federal) (2001) *Primer Informe Presidencial. Anexo*. Mexico City: PEF.

Pemex (Petróleas Mexicanos) (2000) 'Boletín de prensa', no. 156/2000, 30 July.

Pérez Castañeda, J. C. (2002) *El nuevo sistema de propiedad agraria en Mexico*. Mexico City: Editorial Palabra al Vuelo.

Perezgrovas, V., E. Cervantes, L. Carlsen and J. Burstein (forthcoming) 'The Mexican Case', in L. Carlsen (ed.), *Coffee: A Sustainable Solution to the Crisis*. Silver City, NM: Inter-hemispheric Resource Center.

Perezgrovas, V. et al. (1997) *El cultivo del café orgánico en la Unión Majomut. Un proceso de rescate, sistematización, evaluación y divulgación de tecnología agrícola*. Mexico City: Red de Gestión de Recursos Naturales/Rockefeller Foundation.

Perkins, E. (1997) 'Introduction: Women, Ecology and Economics: New Models and Theories', Special Issue on Women, Ecology and Economics, *Ecological Economics* 20(2).

Petras, J. and H. Veltmeyer (2001a) 'Are Latin American Peasant Movements Still a Force for Change? Some New Paradigms Revisited', *Journal of Peasant Studies* 28(2): 83–118.

— (2001b) *Globalization Unmasked. Imperialism in the 21st Century.* London and New York: Zed Books.

Pichardo, N. A. (1997) 'New Social Movements: A Critical Review', *Annual Review of Sociology*, 23: 411–30.

Plaza Sanchez, J. L., E. Contreras Murphy and D. B. Barton (1998) 'A Basket of Benefits: Ecosystems, Economics and Organizations in the Production of Organic Coffee in Chiapas, Mexico', Paper presented at the XXI Congress of the Latin American Studies Association, Chicago, IL.

Polanyi, K. (1944) *The Great Transformation.* New York and Toronto: Rinehart and Co.

Posada, M. and I. Velarde (2000) 'Estrategias de desarrollo local a partir de productos alimenticios típicos: El caso del vino de la costa en Buenos Aires, Argentina', *Revista Problemas del Desarrollo*, 31(121): 63–85.

Poulantzas, N. (1987) [1968] *Political Power and Social Classes.* London: Verso.

Presidencia (2001) 'Plan Puebla Panamá'. Available at: <www.presidencia.gob.mx> (accessed May 2002).

Przeworski, A. (1989) 'Democracy as a Contingent Outcome of Conflict', Ch. 2 in R. Slagsted and J. Elster (eds), *Constitutionalism and Democracy.* New York: Cambridge University Press.

Raynolds, L. T. (2000) 'Re-embedding Global Agriculture: The International Organic and Fair Trade Movements', *Agriculture and Human Values*, 17: 297–309.

Recio, P. (1998) 'Trabajará la Unión Agrícola en mejorar los productos agrícolas', *Cambios de Michoacán*, 14 October, p. 8.

Reichert, J. (1982) 'A Town Divided: Economic Stratification and Social Relations in a Mexican Migrant Community', *Social Problems*, 29: 411–23.

Rello, F. (1986) *El Campo en la Encrucijada Nacional* (Foro 2000). Mexico City: Secretaría de Educación Pública.

Restrepo, J. C. (1990) *Ensayos de política económica cafetera.* Colombia: Editorial Presencia.

Rice, P. D. and J. McLean (1999) *Sustainable Coffee at the Crossroads.* Washington, DC: Consumer's Choice Council.

Rice, R. A. (1993) *New Technology in Coffee Production: Examining Landscape Transformation and International Aid in Northern Latin America.* Washington, DC: Smithsonian Migratory Bird Center.

Ritzer, G. (1993) *The McDonaldization of Society.* Thousand Oaks, CA: Pine Forge Press.

Rodríguez, G., M. G. and G. Torres (1994) 'El Barzón y COMAGRO: la resistencia de los agroproductores a la política neoliberal', *Espiral*, 1(1): 70–94.

Rodríguez Sosa, C. F. (2001) 'Por el respeto al derecho de libre asociación en el ramo cañero', Mexico City: UNPCA (unpublished document).

Roldán, G. (2001) 'Política migratoria y derechos humanos', *Diversa*, 2–3: 71–87.

Roldán, M. (1981) 'Trabajo asalariado y condición de la mujer rural en un cultivo de exportación: el caso de las trabajadoras del tomate en el estado de Sinaloa,

Mexico', Paper presented at Seminario Tripartito Regional para América Latina sobre el Desarrollo Rural y La Mujer, Pátzcuarco, Michoacán.

Ronfeldt, D. (1973) *Atencingo: The Politics of Agrarian Struggle in a Mexican Ejido*. Stanford, CA: Stanford University Press.

Rooner, L. (1981) 'Las mujeres asalariados en los cultivos de exportación: el caso del municipio de Ensenada, Baja California Norte, México', Paper presented at Seminario Tripartito Regional para América Latina sobre el Desarrollo Rural y La Mujer, Pátzcuaro, Michoacán.

Sachs, C. (1996) *Gendered Fields*. Boulder, CO: Westview Press.

SAGAR (Secretaría de Agricultura, Ganadería, y Desarrollo Rural) (1998) 'Cumplimiento del plan de trabajo para la exportación de aguacate Hass de México a los Estado Unidos de Norteamérica, 1997–1998' (unpublished reports), Morelia, Michoacán, February.

Salazar, G. (1986) 'Las obreras agricolas en el cultivo de hortalizas. Estudio de caso en el Valle de Culiacán, Sinaloa', Thesis de licenciatura en Antropología Social, Escuela Nacional de Antropología e Historia, México, December.

Salazar, L. (ed.) (1997) *Elecciones y transición a la democracia en México*. Mexico City: Cal y Arena.

Salinas de Gortari, C. (2001) *México. Un paso difícil a la modernidad*. Mexico: Plaza y Janés.

Samson, C. (1999) 'The Dispossession of the Innu and the Colonial Magic of Canadian Liberalism', *Citizenship Studies*, 3(1): 5–25.

Samstad, J. G. (2002) 'Corporatism and Democratic Transition: State and Labor During the Salinas and Zedillo Administrations', *Latin American Politics and Society*, 44(4): 1–28.

Sanchez Lopez, R. (1990) *Manual práctico del cultivo biológico del café orgánico*. Mexico City: ISMAM.

Sandilands, C. (1999) *The Good-Natured Feminist: Ecofeminism and the Quest for Democracy*. Minneapolis, MN: University of Minnesota Press.

Sandoval, J. M. (2001) 'El plan Puebla-Panamá como regulador de la migración laboral mesoamericana', pp. 215–67 in A. Bartra (ed.), *Mesoamérica. Los Ríos Profundos. Alternativas Plebeyas al Plan Puebla-Panamá*. Mexico: Instituto Maya, El Atajo Ediciones, Fomento Cultural y Educativo, RMALC, Equipo Pueblo, CASIFOP, ANEC, CCECAM, SEMAPE CEN, PRI.

Sandstrom, A. R. (2000) 'Ethnic Identity and Its Attributes in a Contemporary Mexican Indian Village', pp. 269–81 in J. E. Kicza (ed.), *The Indian in Latin American History*.

Saxe-Fernández, J. and O. Núñez (2001) 'Globalización e Imperialismo: la transferencia de excedentes de América Latina', in J. Saxe-Fernández and J. Petras (eds), *Globalización, Imperialismo y Clase Social*. Buenos Aires: Lumen-Humanitas.

Scherer-Warren, I. (1989) '¿Qué hay de "nuevo" en los movimientos sociales en el campo?' *Revista Paraguaya de Sociología*, 26(75): 22–33.

Schmitter, P. (1974) 'Still the Century of Corporatism?', *Review of Politics*, 38: 85–131.

Shiva, V. (1994) 'Development, Ecology, and Women', in C. Merchant (ed.), *Ecology: Key Concepts in Critical Theory*. Atlantic Highlands, NJ: Humanities.

Sieder, R. (2002) *Multiculturalism in Latin America: Indigenous Rights, Diversity and Democracy*. New York: Palgrave Macmillan.

Sierra Reyes, A. (1997) 'Muy limitada, exportación del aguacate mexicano a E.E.U.U.: Enrique Bautista', *Guía*, 22 June: 26–7.

Singelmann, P. (2003) 'La transformación política de México y los gremios cañeros del PRI', *Revista Mexicana de Sociología*, 65(1): 117–52.

— (2002) 'Liberalización de mercados, privatizaciones y nuevas reglas de articulación entre los productores de caña y la industria azucarera en México', *Alianzas Productivas para la Seguridad Alimentaria y el Desarrollo Rural*. Santiago, Chile: Food and Agriculture Organization. Available at: <http://www.rlc.fao.org/prior/desrural/alianzas/casos.htm>.

— (1998) '"Se gana poco, pero se queda algo": Liberalismo económico y los campesinos cañeros en Nayarit', pp. 31–56 in L. P. Ladrón de Guevara and E. Heredia Quevedo (eds), *Nayarit a fin del milenio*. Tepic: Universidad Autónoma de Nayarít.

— (1993) 'The Sugar Industry in Post-Revolutionary Mexico: State Intervention and Private Capital', *Latin American Research Review*, 27(1): 61–88.

— (1990) 'La reorganización de la industria azucarera en el México postrevolucionario: Cambios y continuidades', pp. 210–28 in P. Arias (ed.), *Industria y estado en la vida de Mexico*. Zamora, Michoacán: El Colegio de Michoacán.

Singelmann, P. and J. Tapia (1979) 'La empresa cooperativa como medio de dominación: El caso de un ingenio azucarero', pp. 121–49 in V. B. De Marquez (ed.), *Dinámica de la empresa mexicana: Perspectivas políticas, económicas y sociales*. Mexico City: Colegio México.

Singelmann, P., S. Quesada and J. Tapia (1982) 'Land without Liberty: The Contradictions of Peripheral Capitalist Development and Peasant Exploitation among the Cane Growers of Morelos, Mexico', *Latin American Perspectives* 9(3): 29–78.

Smith, D. (1987) *The Everyday World as Problematic: A Feminist Sociology*. Boston, MD: Northeastern University Press.

Smith, G. (2002) 'Farmers are Getting Plowed Under: With Tariffs Disappearing, U.S. Exports to Mexico May Soar', *BusinessWeek*, 18 November: 53.

Snyder, R. O. (2001) *Politics after Neoliberalism: Reregulation in Mexico*. New York: Cambridge University Press.

Spinoso Foglia, R. (2001) 'Contra la fragmentación excesiva de la representación gremial cañera y a favor del respeto a la libre asociación'. Mexico City: UNPCA (unpublished document).

SRA (Secretaría de la Reforma Agraria) (1998) *La transformación agraria: origen, evolución, retos y testimonios*. Mexico City: Secretaría de la Reforma Agraria.

Stanford, L. (2002) 'Constructing Quality: The Political Economy of Standards in Mexico's Avocado Industry', *Agriculture and Human Values*, 19: 293–310.

Stavenhagen, R. (2000) 'Towards the Right to Autonomy in Mexico', pp. 10–21 in Burguete Cal y Mayor (ed.), *Indigenous Autonomy in Mexico*.

Stephen, L. (1991) *Zapotec Women*. Austin, TX: University of Texas Press.

Stern, S. (1987) *Resistance, Rebellion, and Consciousness in the Andean Peasant World, 18th to 20th Centuries*. Madison, WI: University of Wisconsin Press.

Tello, C. (1996) 'La economía mexicana: Hacia el tercer milenio', *Nexos*, 223: 47–55.

Tilly, C. (1999) 'Wise Quacks', *Sociological Forum*, 11(2): 589–601.

Tinoco Rubí, Gobernador Victor Manuel (1997) 'Presentación: Comprometido con el campo', *Al Grano*, 1, May: 4–6.

Toledo, V. M. (2000) *La paz en Chiapas: Ecología, luchas indígenas y modernidad alternativa*. Mexico City: Ediciones Quinto Sol/UNAM.

Torres, F. (1998) 'Uso productivo de las remesas en El Salvador, Guatemala, Honduras y Nicaragua', CEPAL, LC/MEX/R.662.

Torres, G. (1997) 'El derecho de barzonear y sus efectos politicos', in J. Alonso and J. M. Ramírez (eds), *La democracia desde abajo*. Mexico: Universidad Nacional Autónoma de México.

Tuirán, R. (2000) 'Desarrollo, comercio y migración: el caso de México', Paper presented at the seminar Los Acuerdos de Libre Comercio y sus Impactos en la Migración, 15–16 November, Guatemala.

Tuirán, R., C. Fuentes and L. F. Ramos (2001) 'Dinámica Reciente de la Migración México–EU', *El Mercado de Valores*, 61(8): 3–26.

TVE Earth Report (2000) 'The Path of the Jaguar'. Available at: <www.tve.org/erathreport/archive/25Aug2000.html> (accessed May 2002).

Unger, K. (1990) *Las exportaciones mexicanas ante la reestructuración industrial internacional: la evidencia de las industrias química y automotriz*. Mexico City: Colegio de México–FCE.

Unión Nacional de Productores de Caña de Azúcar (UNPCA) (2001) *Agroiniustria de la Caña de Azúcar: Datos Básicos*. Mexico City: Unpublished.

University of California (1988) *Economic Trends in the California Avocado Industry*. Berkeley, CA: University of California, Cooperative Extension, Division of Agriculture and Natural Resources.

USDA (US Department of Agriculture) (1997) 'Avocado Import Guildeines, Mexico' (unpublished document).

USDA/SAGAR (US Department of Agriculture/Secretaría de Agricultura, Ganadería, y Desarrollo Rural) (1997) 'Work Plan for the Exportation of Hass Avocados from Mexico to the United States of America/Plan de Trabajo para la Exportación de Aguacate Hass de México a los Estados Unidos de Norte America' (unpublished report, June).

US State Department. (2000) 'Climate Change: Carbon Sinks and the US View in 2000'.

Valdéz Ugalde, F. (1996) 'The Private Sector and Political Regime Change in Mexico', pp. 127–48 in G. Otero (ed.), *Neoliberalism Revisited*.

Valenzuela Feijóo, J. (1996) *El Neoliberalismo en América Latina. Crisis y Alternativas*. La Paz: CIDES–UMSA.

Van Cott, D. (2000) *The Friendly Liquidation of the Past: The Politics of Diversity in Latin America*. Pittsburgh, PA: University of Pittsburgh Press.

van der Haar, G. (2001) *Gaining Ground. Land Reform and the Constitution of Community in the Tojolobal Highlands of Chiapas, Mexico.* Thela Latin American Series. Amsterdam: Wageningen Universitet and Rozenberg Publishers.

Veltmeyer, H. (2000) *El capital global y las perspectivas de un desarrollo alternativo.* Mexico City: UNESCO–UAZ–COBAEZ.

Veltmeyer, H. and A. O'Malley (2001) *Transcending Neoliberalism. Community-Based Development in Latin America.* Bloomfield, CT: Kumarian Press.

Villar, S. del (1976) 'Depresión de la industria azucarera', *Foro Internacional,* 64: 526–85.

Villarreal, R. (2000) *Industrialización, deuda y desequilibrio externo en México. Un enfoque macroindustrial y financiero (1929–2000).* Mexico City: Fondo de Cultura Económica.

Villaseñor B. and J. Morena (2002) 'Breve visión sobre las medidas de control migratorio en la frontera norte de México', pp. 11–24 in *Migración: México entre su dos fronteras.* Mexico City: Foro Migraciones.

Villoro, L. (2001) 'En busca de la comunidad perdida', *Proceso,* 1269, 25 February: 28–9.

Wall, E. (1992) 'Personal Labor Relations and Ethnicity in Ontario Agriculture', in V. Satzewich (ed.), *Deconstructing a Nation: Multiculturalism and Racism in 90s Canada.* Halifax: Fernwood.

Waller Meyers, D. (2000) 'Remesas de América latina: revisión de la literatura', *Comercio Exterior,* 50(4): 275–88.

Warman, A. (1980) *Ensayos sobre el campesinado en México.* Mexico City: Nueva Imagen.

Watanabe, J. (1992) *Maya Saints and Souls in a Changing World.* Austin, TX: University of Texas Press.

Wearne, P. (1996) *Return of the Indian: Conquest and Revival in the Americas,* Foreword by Rigoberta Menchú. London: Cassell and Latin America Bureau.

Weber, Max (1958) *From Max Weber: Essays in Sociology,* ed. and trans. H. H. Gerth and C. Wright Mills. New York: Oxford University Press.

Wihtol de Wenden, C. (1999) *Faut-il ouvrir les frontiers? La bibliotèque du citoyen.* Paris: Presses de Sciences.

Williams, H. (2001) *Social Movements and Economic Transition. Markets and Distributive Conflict in Mexico.* Cambridge: Cambridge University Press.

Williams, R. G. (1994) *States and Social Evolution. Coffee and the Rise of National Governments in Central America.* Chapel Hill, NC: University of North Carolina Press.

Wilson E. O. and E. O. Willis (1975) 'Applied Biogeography', pp. 522–34 in M. L. Cody and J. M. Diamond (eds), *Ecology and Evolution of Communities.* Cambridge, MA: Belknap Press.

Wilson, T. D. (2000) 'Anti-Immigrant Sentiment and the Problem of Reproduction/Maintenance in Mexican Immigration to the United States', *Critique of Anthropology,* 20: 191–213.

Wise, T., H. Salazar and L. Carlsen (eds) (2003) *Confronting Globalization.* Bloomfield, CT: Kumerian Press.

Wolf, E. R. (1999) *Envisioning Power: Ideologies of Dominance and Crisis*. Berkeley, CA: University of California Press.

— (1990) 'Distinguished Lecture: Facing Power – Old Insights, New Questions', *American Anthropologist*, 92: 586–96.

— (1966) *Peasants*, Englewood Cliffs, NJ: Prentice Hall.

Womack Jr, J. (1969) *Zapata and the Mexican Revolution*. New York: Vintage Books.

World Bank (2000) 'Project Appraisal Document on a Proposed Grant from the Global Environmental Facility Trust Fund in the Amount of sdr. 11.5 Million to Nacional Financiera'.

— (2000b) 'Mesoamerican Biological Corridor Project', Report 23132 ME, (November).

— (n.d.) 'Central American Web Page'. Available at: <www.worldbank.org/ca-env> (accessed May 2002).

Yashar, D. (1999) 'Democracy, Indigenous Movements, and the Postliberal Challenge in Latin America', *World Politics*, 52(1): 76–104.

— (1998) 'Contesting Citizenship: Indigenous Movements and Democracy in Latin America', *Comparative Politics*, 31: 23–42.

Zárate Hernandez, J. E. (2000) 'The Reconstruction of the Purhépecha Nation and the Process of Autonomy in Michoacán, Mexico', pp. 137–49 in Assies et al. (eds), *The Challenge of Diversity*.

Index

11 September attacks, 138

3×1 Programme, 152

Abascal, Carlos, 115, 118
Acerca insurance company, 26–7
Acteal, massacre at, 182
Adopt a Community programme, 152
AFL-CIO, 117
age and family status segmentations, 40
Agrarian Law (1992), 12, 80
agrarian reform, 7, 79, 85, 175, 209
agricultural production, 163–4; of indigenous populations, 162–3
agricultural shield, creation of, 28
agriculture sector, contribution to GDP, 22
agroexports, 38
Aguilar Reyna, Jorge, 179
Alemán Velasco, Miguél, 97
Alliance for Progress, 171
Alonso, Jorge, 205
Alternative Trade Organizations (ATO), 175, 176, 184
anatocismo, 215, 217
Animal and Plant Health Inspection Service (APHIS), 190–1, 194
Appendini, Kirsten, 41
Araujo, Hugo Andres, 96
Asociaciones Rurales de Interés Colectivo (ARIC), 172
Assies, William, 232–3
Association of Bank Customers, 213
Association of Organic Certifiers, 177
Authentic Front of Workers (FAT), 112, 116
authoritarianism, 83, 84
automobile industry, 134; industry, exports of, 141; labour flexibility in, 111
Avocado Commission of the State of Michoacán, 190

avocado industries: bi-national integration of, 186–203; in Mexico, 188–9; in California, 188–9; US ban on Mexican avocados, 190, 201
avocado seed weevil, 188
Aztec Harvest, 175, 178

Bachoco Group, 33
Banamex, 143
Banco Bilbao Vizcaya, 143
Bancomer, 143
bank debtors, social movement of, 204–20
Barbosa, Maximino, 211, 217
Barrón, Maria Antonieta, 41, 47
El Barzón movement, 5, 16, 206, 208, 210, 211; membership of, 214; rivalry between groups, 212
Barzonism, culture of, 213
basketball, 157–8, 161, 165–6, 167
Becafisa-Volcafé, 33
Belize, 151
Bentham, Jeremy, 3
Bimbo Group, 33
bio-geography of islands, theory of, 61
biodiversity, 13, 35, 52–71; and economic integration, 61–7; conservation of, 61, 69; disturbed by military presence, 70; hotspots, 60, 68; integrated into world market, 52; loss of, 60; management of, 54, 58, 67
biopiracy, 70
bioprospecting, 30, 63–4
biotechnology, 55
Blackaller Ayala, Carlos, 96
borderland security, 149, 151
Bracero Program, 150
Brazil: destruction of coffee harvest in, 170; frost affects coffee production in, 173
bureaucratic elite, 84–6

Bush, George W., 63

caciques, 78, 79–81
Café Museo, 178
Calavo company, 193, 195, 196, 201
California, avocado industry in, 188–9
California Avocado Commission
    (CAC), 188–9
Californian Avocado Growers'
    Exchange, 188
Canada, food retailing in, 38
Cane Growers' Decree, 91, 92–3, 94
carbon sequestration, 63
Cárdenas, Cuauhtémoc, 9, 11
Cárdenas, Lázaro, 7, 11, 79, 80, 85,
    112
Cargill, 27, 33
Caribbean Conservation, 60
Casa del Pueblo, 158–9, 166
Castañeda, Jorge G., 138, 149
Castro González, Francisco, 97, 99,
    101, 103
Catholic Church, 7, 120, 179, 185
Central American Commission on
    Environment and Development,
    (CCAD), 60
Central American Council on
    Protected Areas (CCAP), 60
CEPCO, 178
Chiapas, 11, 15, 68, 70; coffee
    production in, 169–85; movement
    of indigenous peoples of, 206
chicken parts, imports of, 26
Chihuahua, bank debtors'
    mobilization in, 208
children, work of, 163
Chile, avocado exports of, 193, 196
Chinchilla, Alberto, 65
Chiquita, 202
Citibank, 143
citizenship, 153, 221–35;
    strengthening of, 231
civil society, 6, 13; thickening of, 221,
    234
class, segmentations, 40, 50
class formation, political (PCF), 5–6,
    169, 222–4
class struggle, rhetoric of, 115
clubs, organization of, 152

coffee, 33; and international markets,
    170–2; labelling of, 176, 177;
    organic, 15, 67, 169–85; price
    slump, 175; production of, 25, 27,
    29; organic, 169–85; shade-grown,
    67, 176, 177
Coffee Institutes, establishment of,
    171
collective bargaining agreements, 114
Colombia, 173
Colosio, Donaldo, 180
commodity chain, as methodological
    model, 187
Confederation of Mexican Workers,
    137
conservation, 52–71 passim;
    contradiction with consumption,
    59; corporate, 53–9 (critique of,
    56–9)
Conservation Finance Alliance, 56
Conservation International (CI), 56,
    58, 59, 60, 62
convergence: concept of, 204–20;
    culture of, 205
cooperación, 160, 165
cooperation: indigenous, 160, 164;
    traditions of, 165–7
cooperatives, 169–85 passim
corn: growers, crisis of, 25; imports
    of, 26
Corona, Rodolfo, 146
corporatism, 8, 13; as mode of
    political participation, 76;
    authoritarian, 77–8; Christian, 118;
    concept of, 73–8; of the state, 74–5
    (and peasant organizations, 72–88);
    of trade unions, 14, 104–20;
    societal, 74–5; survival of, 120
corruption, 26
craft production, 162
credit unions, 82
'Cristeros', 118
cultural diversity, 232
cultural services, 34
Cypher, James, 141

dams, construction of, 57
dance, 166, 167
David, Comandante, 228

Dávila, Enrique, 30
Day of the Dead rituals, 166
debt, external, 30, 123; crisis of, 104;
    government responsibility for, 216;
    moratorium for, 9, 216;
    restructuring of, 91, 209, 216 *see
    also* bank debtors
Debtors' Association, 213
democracy, 6; lack of, in trade unions,
    106
democratic transition, 233
democratization, 9, 101, 103;
    institutional, 89–103
deregulation, 104; of labour, 111
devaluation, 136
dialectic of the diverse, 235
diversity, 18; cultural, 59, 68 *see also*
    biodiversity
division of labour, gendered, 42, 45
double movement, in Mexico, 1–17

Economic Agreement for
    Competitiveness and
    Employment, 113
economically active population,
    growth of, 126–7
ecotourism, 64
ejido commissariats, 80
ejido system, 12, 23, 73, 78–81, 83, 89,
    182, 183, 189; privatization of land,
    23
'El campo no aguanta más', 19, 20–2
Empaque Santa Rosa, 38, 41, 43, 44,
    47, 48, 50
Employers' Confederation of the
    Mexican Republic (COPARMEX),
    115, 137
Energy Law, 21
Entrepreneurial Coordinating Centre
    (CCE), 9
Environmental Defense Fund, 69
environmental goods and services, 19,
    34–6; payment for, 62–3
environmentalism of the poor, 70
ethnic conflict, elimination of, 231
ethnicity, segregations, 50
ethnoecology, 68
European Union (EU), 18, 19
Excelsior newspaper, attack on, 84

exchange rate, overvaluation of, 126
export growth, relation to migration,
    143–7
export sector, transformation of, 140–1
export-oriented industrialization
    (EOI), 122, 123, 136

Fair Trade movement, 176–7, 184
family, structures of, 44, 160–2
Family Heritage Defence Front, 213
family status, segmentations, 50
Fauna and Flora International, 62
Federation of Trade Unions in Goods
    and Services (FESEBES), 114
Federal Office of Environmental
    Protection (PROFEPA), 70
feminization of labour force, 13, 38,
    44
Fentanes, C., 215
Financiera Rural, 87
Fischer, Franz, 19
flexibility: of labour, 38, 122;
    primitive, 38–9
flexibilization, of collective
    bargaining, 110–12
Fondo Bancario de Protección al
    Ahorro (FOBAPROA), 26, 218
food: security of, re-establishment of,
    33; self-sufficiency, 18–36;
    sovereignty, crisis of, 27
Ford Motor Company, 56, 114
Fordist equation, 122
Foreign Agricultural Resource
    Management Services (FARMS),
    37, 47, 48
Foreign Trade Law, 21
forests, 155; illegal logging of, 70; loss
    of, 60; protection of, 69;
    reforestation programmes, 65
Fox, Jonathan, 221
Fox, Vicente, 10, 11, 14, 72, 118, 139,
    229
Fox administration, 3, 26, 106, 115,
    119, 138–53
Free Trade Area of the Americas
    (FTAA), 31, 61, 69
free-trade zones, 38
Front of Mexican Unions (FSM), 117
fructose sweetener, 26; from US, 99

fruit, growing of, 13

Garcia Canclini, Néstor, 166
GDP, growth of, 124–5
General Foods, 170
General Motors, 114
genetic engineering, 35, 55
genetically modified products (GM), 63
George Weston Ltd., 38
Global Environment Fund (GEF), 62
global warming, 54
globalization, 202–3, 234; alternatives to, 198; contesting of, 221–35; from below, 38; relation to nation-state, 16
González Barrera, Roberto, 32–3
GRAIN, 71
Gramm, Senator, 150
Gramsci, Antonio, 1, 5–6, 223
Green Revolution, 57
greenhouse production, of tomatoes, 43–5
gross-capital formation, 134
Grupo Escorpión, 99
Grupo Pulsar, 68
Guatemala, 151
guelaguetza, 160, 164

haciendas, dissolution of, 89
Haraway, Donna, 41
Hayek, Friedrich, 1

identity: and economy, 162–5; struggles over, 221
Illegal Immigration Reform and Immigrant Responsibility Act, 148
Immigration and Naturalization Service (INS) (US), 148, 150, 151
import-substitution industrialization, 7, 12, 104; crisis of, 119
Indian peoples, 34, 59; ethnicity of, 227; identity of, 228; participation of, 66–7; recognized in constitutional change, 229; resistance to assimilation, 224; rights of, 21, 221–35; struggles of, challenge national borders, 234; use of label, 222

Indigenas de la Sierra Madre de Motozintla (ISMAM), 174, 177, 179, 185
Indigenous and Campesina Corridor, 65
Indigenous Peasant and Afro-American Coalition of Community Agro-Forestry (CICAFOC), 65
indigenous peoples: constitutional rights of, 66; contribution to conservation, 68; identity dependent on land access, 226; mobilization of, 206; movement in Chiapas, 225; peculiarity of, 232; stewardship of, 67–71
industrial relations, 104–20; changes to system, 110
industrial restructuring, 14
Industrial Revolution, 3
industrialization, 104
inflation, 123, 124; growth of, 114–15; reduction of, 107
informal sector, 23
inheritance, 79, 81
Institutional Revolutionary Party (PRI), 8, 9, 10–11, 13, 20, 28, 72, 76, 77, 81, 84, 85, 88, 89–103, 106, 112, 208, 209, 211, 218; defeat of, 93, 99, 118–19, 234; social organizations of, 72
Instituto Nacional de Antropología e Historia (INAH), 155
Inter-American Development Bank, 30, 52, 62
Inter-American Foundation, 183
interest-on-interest, 215
International Coffee Agreement (ICA), 171, 172; collapse of, 169, 180, 183, 185
International Coffee Quotas Agreement, 171
International Federation of Organic Agriculture Movements (IFOAM), 177, 180
International Labour Organization (ILO), 228
International Monetary Fund (IMF), 1, 9, 16, 91

investment, direct foreign, 107, 143
Irena, a migrant worker, 37, 47–9

Jalisco, bank debtors' mobilization in, 208
Juana, a packer, 42
just-in-time production, 38

Kafee Harz, 170
Kearney, Michael, 154
Kennedy, John F., 171
Kessel, Georgina, 30
Keynesianism, crisis of, 123
Kwon Dong *maquiladora*, 120
Kymlicka, Will, 228, 229, 230, 231, 232
Kyoto protocol, 56, 63

labour: as export commodity, 142, 145; self-sufficiency in, 18–36
Labour Congress (CT), 116, 117, 119
labour market, 14, 121–5; segmentation of, 126–7
labour policies, under Vicente Fox, 138–53
labour relations in Mexico, 105
labour security, re-establishment of, 33
labour sovereignty: crisis of, 27; loss of, 20
Lacandon jungle, 68, 174
Ladinos, 224
land, privatization of, 64
land-use decisions, control of, 58
Lara, Sara, 41, 42
latifundia, 79
leadership-constituency relations, 81–6
Levy, Santiago, 30
Ley law of sugar industry, 99
liberalization, 1, 101, 121, 136, 137; strategy of, in Mexico, 123–5; sustainability of, 137
Loblaws supermarket, 38, 39
logging, illegal, 70

Maderas del Pueblo, 180
Majomut cooperative, 174, 181–3, 185
mano de obra production, 163
manufacturing industry, 108, 130;

decline of, 114; reconversion of, 112; wages in, 121–37
maquiladoras, 30, 31, 32, 38, 42, 43, 50, 107, 108, 109, 120, 141, 142, 147; for fruit, 195
Marcos, Subcomandante, 225, 229
marginalization, 152
market, self-regulating, 2, 3, 4
Marx, Karl, 1, 5
Marxism, 223, 226, 227
Maseca company, 32–3
Max Havelaar Fair Trade Association, 175, 177, 180
Maxwell House, 170
May First Inter-Trade Union Coordination, 115, 116–17, 119
McDonald's, 38, 39
Mesoamerican Biological Corridor (MBC), 13, 52–71; social component of, 66
Mesoamerican Peasant Conference, 69
mestizo culture, 34, 41, 43, 45, 224, 231
Mexican Coffee Council, 178
Mexican Constitution: Article 27, 7, 23; Article 123, 7
Mexican Institute of Coffee (INMECAFE), 172–3, 181; privatization of, 169, 180, 181, 183, 184
Mexican revolution, 7, 8, 32, 86, 161
Mexico, 56; 1917 Constitution, 7; crisis of financial sector in, 207; deficit of economy, 142; dependence on US economy, 7; imports of grain, 24; independence from Spain, 6
Michels, Robert, 83
Michoacán state, 15; avocado industry in, 186–203; Law of Agricultural Organizations, 198
migrants: education of, 147; human rights denied, 148; to US, undocumented, 139; workers, wages of, 47
migration, 23, 26, 28, 30, 31, 40; benefits of, 147; countered by death threat, 148; criminalization of, 148; deaths of migrants, 151; liberalization of, 149; Mexican

policies of, 14–15; organization of migrant communities, 152–3; policies regarding, 138–53 (subordination of, 147–52); racism against migrants, 46; relation to economic growth, 146–7; relation to export growth, 143–7; rise in, 161; strategic importance of, 146; temporary, 144, 154; temporary worker programme, 149; to cities, 22; to US, 138, 155, 163 (history of, 144; non-availability of visas, 139); transformation of, 144–5 *see also* United States, Mexican population in *and* United States, migration to

Millan, Juan S., 117

minifundistas, 91

Ministry of Agriculture and Rural Development (SAGAR), 192, 197

Mission Produce Inc., 193, 195, 196, 201, 202

Moctezuma, Miguel, 152

monoculture, of tree species, 65

Mosca, Gaetano, 83

multicultural integration, 229, 231, 232

Museo Shan Dany, 155

MutVitz organization, 183–4

My Community programme, 152

NASA, 62

National Accounting System (Mexico), 130

National Action Party (PAN), 9, 10–11, 95, 100, 101, 119, 120, 218

National Agreement to Increase Productivity and Quality, 113

National Cane Growers' Union (UNC), 90, 95, 96, 100

National Confederation of Popular Organizations (CNOP), 76, 84, 95

National Coordinator of Coffee-Growers' Organizations, 178

National Credit Card Holders' Association, 213

National Development Plans, 138

National Indigenous Council (CNI), 225

National Peasant Confederation (CNC), 76, 78, 81, 87, 90, 91, 95, 96, 98, 100, 103

National Sugar Bank (FINASA), 91

National Union of Agricultural Producers, Merchants, Industrialists and Service Providers, El Barzón (NUB), 211

National Union of Autonomous Regional Peasant Organizations (UNORCA), 175

National Union of Sugarcane Producers (UNPCA), 90, 95–101, 103

National Union of Workers (UNT), 5, 108, 114, 115, 117–18, 119

nationality, Mexican, cannot be lost, 148, 153

native population, identity of, 159–60

Natural Protected Areas (NPAs), 68, 69, 70

Nature Conservancy, 56, 62

Naturland, 180

neo-Cardenista approaches, 112

neoliberalism, 73, 140, 170–2, 206–8; transition to, 106–10

Nestlé, 33, 170, 178

New Federal Labour Law, 118

'new institutional arrangements' (NIA), 86, 88

New Labour Culture, 118, 137; Agreement for, 115, 120

new technology, of packing, 44–5

New World Order, 9

'nimble fingers' of women, 50

non-governmental organizations (NGOs), 120, 177, 179

Norman, Wayne, 228, 229, 230, 231, 232

North American Free Trade Agreement (NAFTA), 1, 10, 22, 24, 25, 26, 28, 31, 38, 47, 94, 109, 117, 121, 124, 130, 136, 137, 148, 188; death sentence for indigenous ethnicities, 225; negotiations, 189–90; proposed moratorium on agricultural chapter, 21

North–South asymmetries, 39, 50

Nurio Declaration of the National

Indigenous Congress of Mexico, 67

Oaxaca state, 15; social change in, 154–68
oil, exports of, 104
oil industry, 130; nationalization of, 7
Olympic Games, in Mexico City, 8
open borders, demand for, 153
Organic Crop Improvement Association (OCIA), 175
organic production, 71 *see also* coffee, organic
Organization for Economic Cooperation and Development (OECD), 122
Ortega, Manuel, 211
Ortíz Junguitud, Miguél, 95–6
Otero, Gerardo, 102, 154, 169

Pacto de Solidaridad Económica, 123
paper production, 65
Pareto, Vilfredo, 83
participation, 204–6
Party of the Democratic Revolution (PRD), 11, 20, 21, 93, 100, 101, 117, 211, 216, 218
Paseo Pantera project, 60
patents, on genetic materials, 63
patrimonialism, 77–8, 106
patron-client traits of corporatism, 77–8
Pérez Bonilla, Manuél, 96–7
peasant organizations, 169–85; and state corporatism, 72–8
peasants, 20, 40, 65, 154, 162; constitution into political class, 224; corn growers, 27; economy of, 33, 34; mobilization of, 89 (in 2002–3, 19); model of production, 34–5; organizations of, 20; polyphonic nature of, 33; poverty of, 23; seen as disposable, 36
Pemex petroleum company, 56
PepsiCo, 33
peso, devaluation of, 213
pesticides, 45, 47, 49; resistance to use of, 50
Peters, Enrique Dussel, 142

piecework, 46, 47
pineapple, canned, imports of, 26
Plan of Action for Cooperation on Border Safety, 151
Plan Puebla-Panamá, 29–30, 53, 64–5, 71, 151
Plaza of Tlaltelolco, protests of, 8
Polanyi, Karl, 2–5; *The Great Transformation*, 1
Polido Reyes, Isidro, 100
political action and political parties, 217–18
political class formation *see* class formation, political
political-party participation, 84–6
population growth, 22
post-peasant economy, 154
poverty, 23, 30, 36; reduction of, 152; rural, 26
presidential system, 77
pricing, politics of, 24
privatization, 9, 10, 53–71 *passim*; of banks, 214; of land, 64 (of *ejido* lands, 23; of Indian lands, 7); of Mexican agricultural sector, 203; of Mexican Institute of Coffee, 169, 180, 181, 183, 184; of nature, 13; resistance to, 68
producer alliances, 199–200
productivity, 109, 113, 125–30; bonus strategy, failure of, 114–16; growth of, benefits of, 121–37
protest, new forms of, 210–12
Proyecto de Ley de la Agroindustria Azucarera, 94
Purina, 33

race/ethnicity segmentations, 40
Ramirez, Alfonso, 211, 217
Regional Union of Agricultural Producers (URAP), 200
regulation school, 122
remittances of migrants, 32, 144, 145–6, 170
restructuring, 110, 111, 169, 184
Revolutionary Confederation of the Workers and Peasants (CROC), 114
Reyna, an indigenous farmworker, 46–7

Robinson Bours family, 33
Rockefeller Foundation, 183
Rooner, Lucila, 41
Royal Blue Organics, 175
rural collapse, 19
Rural Development Bank
    (BANRURAL), 180
Rural Development Investment
    Programme, 172
rural/urban segmentations, 40–1

Saavedra, Rolando, 95, 96
SAGARPA Agricultural Secretariat,
    27, 28
Salas, Quirino, 217
Salazar, Gilda, 41
Salinas administration, 113, 119, 207–
    8
Salinas de Gortari, Carlos, 28, 95, 120
San Andrés Accords, 66, 225, 228, 234;
    reneging on, 231
Sánchez, Sergio, 116
Sandstrom, A.R., 227
Santa Ana del Valle, 154–68
Schettino Pérez, Jorge, 97
Schmitter, Philippe, 74
Security and Exchange Commission
    (SEC), 197
self-managed democratic production,
    87
La Selva cooperative, 182, 185
servicio, 157, 160, 167
Servitje, Lorenzo, 33
Shell Foundation, Energy
    Programme, 59
Shell Oil, 56
Sierra Foranea, 179
Silos Miguel Alemán, 27
silver mines, 161
single mothers, in employment, 48
six proposals for the salvation and
    revaluation of the Mexican
    countryside, 21
small farmers, redundancy of, 23
Smith, Adam, 3
social liberalism, 28
social movements in Mexico, 204–20
social property, 79, 80
social services, 33–4

socialist education, 7
Socialist Union League, 116
Socialist Workers' Party, 116
Soledad, a greenhouse planter, 44
sovereignty, issue of, 58
soybeans, 24
Starbucks, 55
state, minimalist, 123, 124
statism, 106
stewardship, peasant, concept of,
    67–71
strikes, 105, 114
structural adjustment programmes, 9,
    140
student movement of 1968, 8, 84
subsidies, 19, 29, 141; agricultural, 12,
    24, 26, 27, 28
sugar industry, 26; crisis of, 90, 93, 95;
    import quotas to US, 92; mills,
    taken over by government, 93,
    98–9
Sugarcane Decree, 99, 100
sugarcane growers, unions of, 89–103
sujetos de crédito, 174
sustainable development, 35, 36, 69
sweatshops, 23

Tabacos Mexicanos (Tabamex), 86–8
tariffs, elimination of, 28
Taylorism-Fordism, 108, 110
technology, appropriate, 69
Tello, Carlos, 142
Telmex workers' union, 112
temporary workers see migration
tequio, 160, 164, 167, 179; participation
    in, 156–7
tobacco production, 72, 86–8
Tomasa, a fieldworker, 45–6
Tomasita Project, 37–9, 40–1, 47, 50
tomatoes: corporate, production cycle
    of, 38; export of, 13; greenhouse
    production of, 43–5; production
    cycle of, 37–51 (in Mexico, 41–7)
tourism, 155, 163, 166; industry, 30, 31
Toyotaism, 108, 110, 115
trade unionism, new, 113–14
trade unions, 120; at Telmex, 112;
    converted into state bodies, 105;
    corporatism of, 104–20; lack of

democracy in, 106; yellow, 111
tree plantations, 65

UN Development Fund, 62
UN Development Program (UNDP), 60
UN Economic Commission for Latin America and the Caribbean, 11
UN Environment Program, 54
undocumented workers, 32
unemployment, 11, 12, 31, 125–6, 127
Unión de Comunidades Indigenas de la Region del Istmo (UCIRI), 177, 179, 185
Unión de Ejidos y Comunidades Majomut, 182
Unión de Uniones de Ejidos (UUE), 172
Unión de Ejidos (UE), 172
Unión de Ejidos de la Selva, 178
Union of Agricultural Producers (Michoacán), 198
Union of Oaxacan Community Museums (UMCO), 155
unions, 14, 20, 21, 50; corporatist, 8; difficulties of unionization, 48–9; fees of, 82; of mill workers, 101; of sugarcane growers, 89–103; resistance to, 38
United Conference of Mexicans Abroad, 150
United Farmworkers of America, 48
United States of America (USA): agricultural imports from, 25, 186; as net debtor, 140; exports to, 44; food imperialism of, 19; labour relations with Mexico, 139; Mexican dependence on food imports from, 13; Mexican exports to, 11, 24; Mexican population in, 138, 143 (education of, 144; as illegals, 150); Mexican subordination to, 138–53; migration to, 11, 13, 14–15, 32, 45; number of Mexican inhabitants in, 32; plundering of surpluses, 143; recession in, effect on Mexico, 149; sugar import quotas, 92; trade relations with Mexico, 140–3

urbanization, 22
US Agency for International Development (AID), 60, 172
US Agricultural Security and Rural Investment Act (2002), 24–5
US Department of Agriculture (USDA), 188, 190–1, 194
US Farm Bill (2002), 28
Uruguay Round, agricultural negotiations, 18–36
Usabiaga, Javier, 26, 28–9
usos y costumbres, 155–6

Villoro, Luis, 228

wages, 14, 43, 49, 109, 114–15, 125–30, 157; growth of, 11–12, 108, 137; in manufacturing, 121–37; lowering of, 38; minimum, 150; policy, 107; reduction of, 124, 129, 135, 136, 147
Wall Street-Treasury Complex, 9
Washington Consensus, 9
water, drinking, scarcity of, 34–5
watersheds, protection of, 63
weaving, 163, 167
Weber, Max, 77
Wildlife Conservation Society, 56, 60
Wilson, Pete, 148
Wilson, Tamar, 154
Wolf, Eric, 187, 191
women, in post-NAFTA food system, 37–51
women workers: Mexican, in Canada, 47–9; Mexican, in Mexico, 41–7
Workers for Socialism League, 116
Workers' Confederation of Mexico (CTM), 76, 101, 111–12, 114, 115, 116, 117
World Bank, 1, 9, 16, 52, 57, 58, 62, 172; failure of biodiversity practices of, 71
World Business Council for Sustainable Development, 54
World Conservation Union (IUCN), 56, 62
World Resources Institute, 54, 56, 62
World Trade Organization (WTO), 16, 59

World Wildlife Fund, 56, 59, 62;
    Business Partners Progress, 55

Yolanda, a sorter, 42–3
Yvonne, a greenhouse packer, 44–5

Zapatista National Liberation Army
(EZLN), 11, 16, 66, 183, 185,
212–13, 221–35; as political-class
organization, 225–6; march to
Mexico City, 225–6; shaping of
demands of, 222; uprising, 25, 180
Zedillo, Ernesto, 231
Zedillo administration, 97, 107, 109